Claudette Colbert

Hollywood Legends Series
Ronald L. Davis, General Editor

Claudette Colbert

She Walked in Beauty

Bernard F. Dick

UNIVERSITY PRESS OF MISSISSIPPI • JACKSON

www.upress.state.ms.us

The University Press of Mississippi is a member of the Association
of American University Presses.

First printing 2008

Library of Congress Cataloging-in-Publication Data

Dick, Bernard F.
    Claudette Colbert : She walked in beauty / Bernard F. Dick.
        p. cm. — (Hollywood legends series)
    Includes bibliographical references and index.
    ISBN 978-1-60473-087-6 (cloth : alk. paper) 1. Colbert, Claudette.
2. Motion picture actors and actresses—United States—Biography.
I. Title.
PN2287.C659D53   2008
791.4302'8092—dc22
    [B]   2008003953

British Library Cataloging-in-Publication Data available

For Katherine

CONTENTS

ACKNOWLEDGMENTS

I have been fortunate in being able to correspond with a number of people who either knew Claudette personally and were eager to talk about her or were sufficiently knowledgeable about her career to offer valuable help. My deepest gratitude goes out to the following:

John E. Burke, who read this manuscript diligently and offered much useful criticism;

Ned Comstock, the University of Southern California's premier archivist (as well as one of the best in the country), for finding Claudette Colbert material in collections that I would never have thought of consulting;

Sharon Drum, Washington Irving High School librarian, who gave me access to the school's archives;

Marjorie Fox, wife of the eminent stage designer Frederick Fox, who designed the set for *Julia, Jake and Uncle Joe*, the play that both Claudette and the Foxes felt should never have been produced on Broadway;

George Gaynes, who came to my aid again and described the tryout tour of *A Community of Two*, in which he costarred with Claudette;

Father James Grear, who met Claudette in Barbados and became her confessor;

Anthony Greco, who supplied me with much needed tapes of Claudette's films;

Paul Gregory, who produced Claudette's most successful Broadway play, *The Marriage-Go-Round*, and recounted the enormous problems he had with her;

Barbara Hall, head of Special Collections at the Margaret Herrick Library, who arranged for me to hear the tapes of the Lux Radio Theatre programs in which Claudette starred;

Kitty Carlisle Hart, who confirmed what several of Claudette's early films reveal, namely, that she had a fine singing voice and hoped to succeed Katharine Hepburn in the Broadway musical, *Coco*;

Father Frederick D. Hoesli, OP, who recalled the times she attended mass at her parish church, St. Vincent Ferrer, and who was a co-celebrant at Claudette's memorial mass there;

Kristine Krueger, of the National Film Information Service (NFIS), who tracked down the article that included the "infamous" picture of Claudette and Marlene Dietrich, thus enabling me to remove what Claudette referred to throughout her life as the "stigma";

John Mainieri, who told me a wonderful story about the effect Claudette had on some young film stars who spotted her at a French restaurant where he was working;

Julie Newmar, Tony award winner for her performance in *The Marriage-Go-Round*, whose account of her experience working with Claudette is radically different from the producer's;

Lynn Redgrave, one of the stars in Claudette's last Broadway play, the revival of *Aren't We All?* who attested to Claudette's pursuit of perfection even at eighty-two;

MaryAnn Sena, who works in Periodicals, at Weiner Library, Fairleigh Dickinson University, for locating some hard-to-find articles;

Ken Starrett, North American director of the Noël Coward Society, who provided me with detailed information about Coward's *Island Fling* (*South Sea Bubble*), in which Claudette appeared in summer stock, and reminisced about meeting her when she was appearing in the tryout of *A Mighty Man Is He*;

Kathleen Stein-Smith, the stalwart of Fairleigh Dickinson University's Weiner Library, on whose reference skills and fluency in French I relied to track down details about Claudette's early life;

Janet Waldo, who only worked with Claudette in a radio play but found her warm and supportive.

I owe special thanks to Helen O'Hagan, Claudette's closest friend and companion during the last twenty years of her life. She knew Claudette, her family, and friends better than anyone and, in a series of unforgettable conversations, shared her memories with me. Without them, there would have been a void in this book that, I hope, no longer exists. If my portrait of Claudette is in any way lacking, it is the author's fault, not Helen O'Hagan's.

My greatest debt lies in the dedication. Katherine Restaino Dick is not only my wife, but also my co-researcher, colleague, best friend, and severest critic.

PREFACE

A film actor's life is a palimpsest; beneath the porous parchment of facts and dates arranged sequentially or causally—the stuff of obituaries and testimonials—lies another text, a visual one. This is the actor's true life, his or her creative life, which, finally, is the only life. The facts add up to a chronology; the films, to a legacy. And if the actor has been able to acquire a screen image or persona that is so striking or distinctive that audiences speak of an "Actor X film" or an "Actor X performance," the actor has achieved the status of icon.

Claudette Colbert is such an actor. She began in the theatre, making her Broadway debut in 1923 when she was twenty—a high school graduate with limited stage experience who felt no need to enroll in drama school or work in a stock company. By 1929, she had developed a theatrical style such that a *New York Times* drama critic described another actress as performing in "the Claudette Colbert manner," probably meaning that she displayed an irresistible zest for living and a natural ebullience that flowed across the footlights, gladdening hearts and making confirmed pessimists feel better about the world, if only temporarily. If Claudette had worked primarily on the stage, with a few forays into pictures, she would have vied with Broadway's leading exponent of sophisticated comedy, Ina Claire, who was, initially, her idol.

But Claudette left Broadway for Hollywood and returned a quarter of a century after making her talking picture debut in 1929. Her stage magic was intact, and if the plays were not exactly classics, she gave them the semblance of high art. And, for a few hours, you believed they were.

As one who saw Claudette in four New York productions, I can vouch for the effervescence and radiance that she exhibited on the stage, which found their way into her films, without losing much in transition. Certainly, there was no loss of spontaneity. Study her performance in a comedy classic like *Midnight* or *The Palm Beach Story*, and the action seems to be evolving with the same momentum that one finds on the stage. Even with the cuts, fades, and dissolves, her best films have always seemed like plays. Because she also did live television drama, visitors at the Paley Center for Media, formerly the Museum of Television and Radio, with locations in New York and Beverly Hills, can observe the way she approached stage acting, which, frankly, is not that different from the way she approached film. She could easily adapt to the small screen, scaling down what she did on the big screen, just as she modified her stage technique, and eventually her stage makeup, for the movies.

Claudette never seemed to be acting. If, as the philosopher Heraclitus believed, there is unity in diversity, the same principle applies to an actor's gallery of characters. Claudette's characters are emanations of her persona, so that they all seem different yet similar, in the way that members of a large family are all individuals but with similar characteristics and family resemblances.

I have seen all but two of Claudette's sixty-four (sixty-five, if one includes the French version of *Slightly Scarlet*, *L'enigmatique Monsieur Parkes* [1930]) films: her first and only silent, *For the Love of Mike* (1927) and *The Wiser Sex* (1932). Because so many of them are unfamiliar, I discuss their plots in greater detail than I would if they were better known. But they are important because they reveal the way Paramount, her home studio for fifteen years, perceived her. She ran the gamut from minx and voluptuary at one end to sufferer and sophisticate at the other; in between were the working professional, lady with a past, gold digger, and careerist. Each character was different, yet each was Claudette. When she played Cleopatra, the queen seemed to be residing either on New York's Upper East Side or in Beverly Hills. Always Claudette, but always the character. Yet when she had a chance to play against type, as she did in *Since You Went Away* and *Three Came Home*, she was strikingly real. There was no persona, just the person because the characters—a wife and mother struggling to manage while her husband is away at war, another wife and mother in a Japanese internment camp during World War II, respectively—bore no resemblance, except physically, to her screen image. One would have liked to see more of the other Claudette, but most audiences probably wouldn't; an occasional deviation, yes, but not a complete makeover. And Claudette knew that. She realized she had a range, but she also understood her public, whose Claudette Colbert was not a wife who has to take in a boarder or a woman brutalized by Japanese soldiers. Theirs was the lady with the lilt in her voice and mischief in her eyes.

Claudette's career began with a walk-on in a forgettable 1923 Broadway play; it ended sixty-four years later in a television miniseries, *The Two Mrs. Grenvilles*, for which she won a Golden Globe. She was then eighty-four. Hers was a career that spanned four media: stage, screen, radio, and television. She witnessed the radical changes that affected all four and always found a way of adapting to the new model.

In Sartre's *No Exit*, Ines tells Garçin, "You are your life and nothing else." That may be true if one is in hell, like Sartre's characters. But Claudette's life, like that of every actor, is concentric—the outer circle circumscribing the biography of a woman who was christened Emilie (Lily) Chauchoin in 1903 and died as Claudette Colbert in 1996 and the inner circle enclosing the art of Claudette Colbert as expressed in her work on stage, screen, radio, and television. Neither circle can exist without the other, even though the inner is the only one that reveals the actor's essence.

I recall seeing a fountain in Vienna where cascading jets of water formed graceful crystalline arcs. When I think of the labor, creativity, and aesthetics that produced that geometrically precise display, the result of both nature and science, I think of Claudette Colbert, who perfected her own natural gifts until they became an art. Unlike Katharine Hepburn and Bette Davis, she was not mannered. With Claudette, artifice was not all; with her, the labor that went into her art disappeared into that labyrinth where an art, once mastered, resides as a natural resource.

If you told Claudette she was an artist, she would agree. But she would interpret "artist" as "painter." She was a gifted painter, whose specialty was children. Although she once envisioned a career as a fashion designer, she never lost her sense of style or taste for color. She may not have understood "the beautiful and the good," but she did understand beauty.

Claudette probably read John Keats's "Ode on a Grecian Urn" at Washington Irving High School. If so, she must have been subjected to a discussion of the enigmatic line, "Beauty is truth, truth beauty," a favorite phrase for a full-period discussion, after which students knew no more than they did before they read the poem. For Claudette, there was nothing theoretical about beauty. Endowed with an aesthetic sense and a talent for both art and acting, she instinctively brought beauty with her, whether she was displaying it on a canvas or on the movie screen.

> She walks in beauty, like the night
> Of endless climes and starry skies;
> And all that's best of dark and bright
> Meet in her aspect and her eyes.
> —George Gordon Byron, aka Lord Byron, "She Walks in Beauty"

Claudette Colbert

CHAPTER 1

Lily of Saint-Mandé

On 13 September 1903 in Saint-Mandé, an eastern suburb of Paris named after a sixth-century saint and located a little more than three miles from the heart of the city, Jeanne Marie Chauchoin, age twenty-six, gave birth to a second child, a daughter. The child was born at home in the Chauchoins' apartment on 5 rue Armand Carrel (now l'avenue du Général de Gaulle), the same street where the Chauchoins had a pastry shop, La pâtisserie Chauchoin. The Chauchoins already had a son, Charles Auguste, born five years earlier on 21 September 1898.

Immediately after his daughter was born, Georges Claude Chauchoin headed over to the parish church, Eglise Catholique Notre-Dame de Saint-Mandé, to arrange for the infant's baptism. Jeanne and her mother, Marie Augustine Loew, wanted the girl to be christened "Lillie." It was not an arbitrary choice. Since Marie Augustine had adopted an orphan, Emilie, known as Emilie Loew, two Emilies in the family were one too many. Equally important was Marie Augustine's birthplace: the Island of Jersey, the largest of the Channel Islands, where the popular actress Lillie Langtry, "the Jersey Lily," was born in 1853. Langtry attracted numerous admirers, including President Theodore Roosevelt, the playwrights George Bernard Shaw and Oscar Wilde, the artist John Everett Millais, and King Edward VII, supposedly one of her lovers when he was Prince of Whales.

Even though Jersey was off the coast of Normandy, it was British-governed but, technically, not part of the United Kingdom. Since English was widely spoken there, Lillie Langtry, born Emilie Charlotte le Bréton, was bilingual, as was Marie Augustine, who made certain that her daughter and grandchildren were, too. Her daughter, however, balked at learning a language that she considered inferior to French. Eventually, Jeanne Chauchoin learned English, or at least enough of it to communicate her wishes or, more often, her demands. Otherwise, it was French; in fact, with her daughter it was *only* French.

Since girls were often named "Lillie" after Lillie Langtry, Mme. Chauchoin saw no reason why hers couldn't be, too. The spelling was a bit eccentric, and she would have settled for "Lilie." However, the priest who was to perform the baptism would settle for neither: It must be a saint's name, and there was no St. Lilie, much less one with two *l*'s. There were, however, an Emilia and two Emilies: the fourteenth-century Emilia of Vercelli and two nineteenth-century Emilies: Emilie de Rodat and Emilie de Vialar, both of whom had founded religious communities and achieved cult status among the pious even though they had only been beatified and would not be canonized until 1950 (Emilie de Rodat) and 1951 (Emilie de Vialar).

The Catholic Church had spoken, but the Chauchoins found a way of circumventing the decision. Their daughter's birth certificate would read "Emilie," which would also become her baptismal name—but only for the record. Otherwise, she was Lilie; by the time she was eight, the "*ie*" became "*y*." Emilie "Lilie" Chauchoin was now Lily Chauchoin, and Emilie Loew was "Tantine" ("Auntie"). Even after Lily changed her name to Claudette and took Colbert as her surname, Emilie Loew was always Tantine to her. Although Tantine never married and was not a blood relative, she was in many ways more of a mother to Lily Chauchoin/Claudette Colbert than her own. Throughout her life, Claudette always kept Tantine's picture on her night table.

Claudette Colbert rarely spoke of Saint-Mandé, where she lived for a mere eight years before coming to America. And except for local historians and archivists, few in Saint-Mandé speak of her or even know she was born there. Yet most seem to recall that the actress Martine Carol, who never achieved Claudette's popularity, was a Saint-Mandéenne. Yet Saint-Mandé played a significant role in Claudette's life.

Lily adored her father, who was thirty-six when she was born but had not yet settled into a profession. He had been a banker who, unfortunately, made some unwise investments. Although Marie Augustine was willing to help the Chauchoins financially, she knew that if Georges continued to remain in Saint Mandé, he would drift from one job to another. Thus she encouraged him to try his luck in America, specifically, New York, which offered more opportunities for employment than Saint-Mandé.

Eventually, Lily learned of her parents' frustrated ambitions. Her mother always believed she had married beneath herself; she was convinced she could have been an opera star if she had not become the wife of Georges Chauchoin, a well-intentioned dreamer who held a variety of jobs but none leading to a career. Mme. Chauchoin favored her son over her daughter, perhaps because he was the firstborn, but more likely because she envied her daughter's talent, which manifested itself first in art and then in acting. Even after Lily Chauchoin became Claudette Colbert, stage and screen star (in that order), her mother never gave Claudette the recognition she so desperately sought from her. Claudette Colbert may have had the adulation of the movie-going world, which was pretty much the world in general. But that world did not include Jeanne Chauchoin; to her mother, Claudette Colbert was *une actrice*. Her father felt differently; he was thrilled when his daughter became an actress. But George Chauchoin's untimely death in 1925, two years after Claudette made her New York stage debut, deprived him of witnessing her extraordinary rise to fame.

Fortunately, Claudette had her grandmother and Tantine. She adored them both, eulogizing Marie Augustine Loew in the pages of the *Saturday Evening Post*, in which she credited her grandmother for inspiring "a sort of *esprit de famille*; a weaving together of all we had been and were yet to be." If the young Claudette learned English so quickly, having a bilingual grandmother helped. When Georges Chauchoin died unexpectedly at the age of fifty-seven, it was Marie Augustine who held the family together once she realized that Jeanne could not cope with her husband's death. And it was Marie Augustine who saw Claudette off to Los Angeles, "her mission . . . accomplished, and all the years of drive and determination . . . put at rest."

In the same article, Claudette said little about her parents, hinting only at her father's lack of ambition and her grandmother's efforts to steer him in the right direction, which meant America.

On 18 September 1906, Georges Chauchoin sailed from Le Havre on the SS *La Savoie*, which reached New York on 25 September when the temperature was a pleasant 65 degrees. He gave as his profession "baker," declared $250, and claimed he was joining his brother-in-law, surname Vedel, who lived at 474 Sixth Avenue. Under "Condition of health, mental and physical"/"Deformed or Crippled, Nature and Cause" was written "lost right eye," followed by "blind in right eye." Georges was not lying; he had really lost the sight in his right eye, which may partially explain his spotty employment record.

Two months after George departed for America, his wife did likewise, but only to make sure that her husband could provide for his family before agreeing to something as radical as immigration, a subject that she and Marie Augustine had often discussed. Well aware of her husband's aimlessness, Jeanne was taking no chances. Since Marie Augustine had already been to America and Charles, then eight, was still in school, Jeanne decided to take her three-year-old daughter with her as well as Tantine, who traveled under the name of Emilie Loew. Jeanne booked passage for the three of them on the SS *La Provence*, which sailed from Le Havre on 17 November and arrived in New York on Saturday, 24 November, five days before Thanksgiving. For the end of November, the temperature was a comfortable 45 degrees. The ship manifest reveals that this was their first trip to the United States. Under "Calling or Occupation," "dressmaker" was recorded for Tantine; nothing for Jeanne. Jeanne declared $140; Tantine, $100. Asked if they were staying with a relative or friend and, if so, where, Jeanne gave the name of her husband, whose address was 31 West Twenty-ninth Street.

Claudette always claimed that she first came to America in 1906, a date that was frequently misinterpreted as her immigration year, which was actually 1911. But she was right: she first saw New York as a three-year-old in 1906. Jeanne, Lilie, and Tantine did not stay on but soon returned to Saint-Mandé. Jeanne's doubts were temporarily assuaged; with her husband's record of failed business ventures, a fresh start might be the best thing for the family. Georges seems to have remained until 1910. The 1910 U.S. Federal Census lists him as a New York resident. The accuracy of the information that Georges or a spokesperson provided, however, is problematic. It was not so much a question of the census taker's competency, which in 1910 was determined by a competitive examination, as it was the way the census was conducted: "The enumerator wrote down what the respondent told him. Enumerators did not have to see each family member to confirm what they had been told by a household member."

When the enumerator arrived in mid-April 1910, Georges or a respondent provided the names of his family and their ages: himself, forty-three; his wife, Jeanne, thirty-three; his son, Charles, eleven; his daughter, Leillie (*sic*), six; Emily Loew (Tantine), thirty-two; and Jeanne's mother, identified as Marie Loew, sixty-two. Since Jeanne was born in 1874, seven years after her husband, and shared her son's birthday, 21 September, she would have been thirty-five in April 1910. There was no street address. Written vertically along the left margin was "Third Avenue." Less specific was the ward number: nineteen. At least we know that Georges was now living on the East Side, since the Nineteenth Ward extended from around East Forty-eighth Street to East Eighty-sixth Street. Eventually, the Chauchoins would settle in an apartment on East Fifty-third Street between Third and Second avenues, but at the time of the census it seems unlikely that Georges was living there, but probably on East Sixty-eighth Street.

Georges described his profession as "cook for a private family" and his wife's and Tantine's as "dressmaker." Written next to the name of Marie Loew was "widow." The immigration year was given as 1907, which, of course, is incorrect. Some of the information, however, is accurate. In the column, "Whether able to speak English, or if not, give language spoken," "English" was recorded for Georges and Marie Loew. No such claim was made for "Leillie" (how could it be?) or her mother.

There are two possible explanations for the wrong immigration date. Since Claudette described her father as "a gentleman, a saint, really," it would have been in keeping with his character, whether or not he had an interpreter, simply to furnish the information about his family without suggesting that they were all living under the same roof. As far as Georges was concerned, his first trip to America was in 1906. Perhaps that is how he or the respondent understood the question; and if one of them was off by a year, so be it. The rest of the information was correct, except for Jeanne's age. A more cynical interpretation, of course, is possible, but it would have required the kind of cunning and duplicity of which Georges seemed incapable. And if 1906 or even 1907 were the immigration year, why would Georges have waited until 13 September 1912 to file for naturalization? But since 1911 was the correct date, filing within a year of arrival makes perfect sense.

Georges must have returned to Saint-Mandé after April 15, when the census evaluators began canvassing the country. On 30 September 1911, Georges, Jeanne, their two children, and Tantine departed from Le Havre on the SS *Chicago*, which reached New York on 9 October. The weather was ideal: 58 degrees by 4:00 p.m. According to the ship manifest, Georges was still a cook; Jeanne, a housewife; and Emily Loew (Tantine), a dressmaker.

Leillie was now Lily, and Charles's name remained the same, although he would later adopt "Wendling" as his surname.

Under the heading, "Whether going to join a relative or friend, and if so, what relative or friend, and his name and complete address," Georges informed the inspector that he was visiting a "friend," Maison Lucien, at 235 West Thirty-fifth Street. The inspector assumed Maison Lucien was a person; actually, it was the name of a leading wine importer and distributor. Georges apparently had a contact at Maison Lucien and may even have had a job waiting for him. But like most positions that he held, it did not last very long.

In the 1920 census report, 1907 was still the Chauchoins' immigration year. Georges's occupation was now "manager," the closest he could come to a description of the minor position he held at First National City Bank; Charles's was "secretary," although "C.P.A." would have been more specific. The 1930 census report finally got everything right, thanks to Claudette, who answered all the questions accurately. Her father had been dead for five years and she was now Claudette Colbert, a highly regarded stage actress and rising screen star who, by April 1930, had already played leading roles in several films. She, Tantine, her mother, and Marie Augustine (who had become bi-continental, alternating between New York and France) were living in an Art Deco apartment house on 55 Central Park West. Claudette acknowledged that she was head of a household consisting of herself, her mother, aunt (Tantine, identified as Emily), and grandmother. Claudette also gave the correct immigration year: 1911.

What her brother told the census taker in 1930 was not as accurate. Charles Auguste Chauchoin was now Charles August Wendling, the surname inspired by a distant relative's. At Saint-Mandé, "Chauchoin," although a bit unusual, did not provoke ridicule. It was different in New York, where his classmates dubbed him "Charlie Shoeshine." He also preferred a name that sounded less French, so much so that it could either be British or German, preferably the former. At least Claudette chose a distinctively French surname.

Charles repeated 1907 as the family's immigration year, describing himself as a manager who worked in the theatre, as did his wife at the time, Grace Thompson, Claudette's former secretary. In the *Saturday Evening Post* reminiscence, Claudette wrote that at one time her brother worked for the theatrical producer Florenz "Flo" Ziegfeld and was able to procure choice orchestra seats for their grandmother, who had become a regular playgoer. Charles would remain in show business, eventually becoming his sister's agent.

Charles also told the census evaluator that he was born in England. Although it might seem that he was fabricating his origins, he was actually telling the truth—within limits. When Charles applied for Social Security on 31 March 1937, he was, as his application states, Charles August Wendling, living in Beverly Hills and working for a talent agency. His place of birth, however, was not Saint-Mandé, like his sister's, but the "Isle of Jersey—England," like his grandmother's. Why Jeanne was in Jersey at the time of her son's birth is unknown. She could have been staying with her mother or a relative, or, given Georges's mercurial nature, the couple may have been living in Jersey in September 1898.

Regardless of his birthplace, in 1911, the future Charles Wendling was still Charles Auguste Chauchoin. The only name change that occurred was Claudette's, which was a minor one: Lily, instead of Lilie. Lily was sent off to Public School 59 at 228 East Fifty-seventh Street, now the Beekman Hill International School. The location couldn't have been more convenient; the school was a few blocks from the row house on 226 East Fifty-third Street, between Third and Second avenues, where the Chauchoins occupied a fifth-floor apartment, thanks to Marie Augustine, who found it for them. Each day when Lily came home from school, Jeanne gave her one piece of chocolate and sent her off to play in Central Park, which Jeanne considered the closest equivalent of the Bois de Vincennes in Saint-Mandé. Lily would enter the Park at Fifth Avenue. Her favorite part was Pilgrim Hill near the East Seventy-second Street entrance. One winter day when Lily and Charles were sleigh-riding on Pilgrim Hill, she looked up and saw a well-dressed boy watching them. It was George Cukor, who would later become one of Hollywood's most esteemed directors. Cukor was then living with his family on East Sixty-eighth Street near Third Avenue. Although *Zaza* (1939) was the only time Cukor and Claudette worked together, he remained devoted to her, always signing his letters, "Your friend from Pilgrim Hill in Central Park."

Lily's English improved rapidly. She learned quickly, thanks, in part, to her tutorials with Marie Augustine. Later when she became an actress, she rarely had trouble mastering the script. She always looked forward to her grandmother's return to New York; even after she became Claudette Colbert, a Broadway star with her own apartment, there was always room for Marie Augustine. By 1930, New York had become Marie Augustine's real home; it was there that her daughter, granddaughter, and Tantine resided. It was in Woodlawn Cemetery in the Bronx where Marie Augustine was buried near her son-in-law; this was a fitting location for the woman responsible for the Chauchoins' coming to America and the man who believed his family would fare better in the New World than they would in the old.

There would be no family plot—at least, not in New York. Destiny had other plans for Jeanne and her children: for Charles, a career on the fringes of show business; for Claudette, a high school education at one of New York's newest and most prestigious schools, where she discovered her creativity, realizing that she would either become an actress or an artist. The former turned out to be her profession; the latter, her avocation.

Since Washington Irving High School did not establish an archive until 1920, after Claudette had already graduated, it is impossible to determine her exact dates of attendance. Nor are yearbooks reliable; in fact, the early Washington Irving yearbooks did not list all the graduates. However, it seems to have been about five or six years after the school officially opened at 40 Irving Place, directly across from the home where Washington Irving once lived. Washington Irving High School, which originated as an all-girls institution, was an offshoot of the prestigious Wadleigh High School.

In 1902, Wadleigh was divided into two separate facilities: Wadleigh High School and the Commercial High School for Girls, whose name was shortly changed to Girls Technical High School. In 1906, Patrick McGowan, a true visionary, convinced a skeptical board of education, with the aid of some vocal students, not just to change the name of Girls Technical to the as-yet-unbuilt Washington Irving High School, but also to authorize a new home for it. Two years later ground was broken, and in February 1913 Washington Irving High School officially opened.

Although the school offered both technical (e.g., stenography, book-keeping, typing, dressmaking, home economics) and academic programs, McGowan believed in integrating, not segregating, the students in the two curricula, so that they could learn from each other; thus the academically motivated were exposed to technical disciplines, and vice versa.

Lily Chauchoin was about to finish grade school when Washington Irving admitted its first class. When she learned about the art program, she knew it was the place for her, even though it meant the end of walking to school. Instead, she would have to take the Third Avenue Elevated line, known to New Yorkers as "the Third Avenue El." It was at Washington Irving that the idea of a career began to take shape. The career itself was undefinable; Lily knew only that she was drawn to the creative arts. Inspired by Tantine, who was an excellent dressmaker, she began sketching women's fashions, as if she were a designer. For some reason, Lily believed her first and last names should begin with the same letter and include the same number of syllables. She was probably influenced more by euphony than convention (alliterative names in the arts were never de rigueur). "Lily" was fine for grade school, but not for high school. Her father must have been flattered when she chose the feminine of his middle name, Claude, and became Claudette Chauchoin.

Claudette attended Washington Irving at the height of the patriotic fervor that marked the beginning of World War I. McGowan supported America's involvement in the conflict; when President Wilson came before Congress to ask for a declaration of war in April 1917, McGowan mobilized the students, who responded by selling war bonds and rolling bandages. For Officers' Day, 1 November 1918, the students in the art program designed hand-painted commemorative cards with a patriotic motif. One card depicted a woman warrior with a red, white, and blue shield; another showed a young woman volunteering for the Red Cross with the American flag in the background alongside a white banner with "WI" embroidered on it, signifying that the volunteer was a Washington Irving student.

McGowan was committed to making the students responsible citizens. They marched for woman suffrage, and in 1918 denoted the proceeds from the school plays to the Red Cross. That same year, the most crucial of the war, assembly took place twice a week. The student flag-bearer would solemnly proceed to the stage. Once the flag was displayed, a selection from the Bible was read. The national anthem was then sung, followed by the pledge of allegiance. After the armistice was signed, McGowan succeeded in bringing General Ferdinand Foch to the school so the students could meet one of the heroes of the war. There is no way of knowing whether or not Claudette spoke to Marshal Foch, but it is hard to imagine McGowan bypassing the opportunity to introduce a native speaker of French to his distinguished guest.

In Claudette's time, Washington Irving High School fostered a creative environment that set it apart from most of New York's other public high schools. It was the kind of milieu in which someone with artistic aspirations, like Claudette, could thrive. Bizet's *Carmen* was performed by an all-student cast. Metropolitan Opera stars such as Madame Schumann-Heink and Louise Homer dropped in on voice classes, and it was not uncommon for a famous actor or actress, such as Billie Burke, the future Glinda of *The Wizard of Oz* (1939), to attend one of the plays. The introductory music course was conducted in the auditorium, a rotunda with a horseshoe balcony. The instructor stood on the stage alongside a reproduction of the musical staff, pointing to the notes as a student played them on the piano.

There was an active drama club, the Cynosure, that mounted productions of Shakespeare's *Twelfth Night, A Winter's Tale, Romeo and Juliet,*

The Taming of the Shrew, and *Much Ado about Nothing*, in addition to less-demanding fare, often written by faculty members. Claudette's only recorded appearance was in a play called *Launcelot George*, written by Alice Rostetter, one of the teachers with a budding but short-lived career as a playwright. Because the 1914–19 period is undocumented, the date of the play is unknown. Late in her career, Claudette told columnist Rex Reed about the first time she stepped on stage. The play was called *Grammar*: "A girl in the class play became ill. I was dragged into the production at the 11th hour because I was the only one in the school who really spoke fluent French." There is no record of *Grammar*, which seems to have been more of a class exercise than a Cynosure production. However, if Claudette is correct about the date of *Grammar*, December 1918, she probably was in her senior year. What Claudette told Rex Reed is at odds with what she herself said in her *Saturday Evening Post* reminiscence, in which she called *As You Like It* "my first play." Although there is no record of such a production, *As You Like It* would have been in keeping with Cynosure's predilection for Shakespeare.

Virginia Bird was a student at Washington Irving when she interviewed Claudette in her dressing room during the brief run of *The Mulberry Bush* in October 1927. In the interview, published in the *Washington Irving Sketch Book*, Bird wrote that "Claudette chose the Art Course in Washington Irving." Claudette made the right choice: Washington Irving was the first New York City high school to have an art gallery. In the art classes, each student had her own table at which to draw or paint. The school even offered courses in commercial art. In fact, many of the courses had a professional thrust. In the dressmaking classes, students not only learned to make clothes but also to tailor them, as they would if they were working in a dress shop, with the customer standing on a platform and the tailor pinning up the dress to create the right fit. The girls even sold the dresses they made in a room right off the library.

The emphasis on professional dressmaking increased Claudette's consciousness of fashion, which remained with her throughout her life.

Although she was generally collegial on the set, she was quite demanding when it came to her costumes, which did not so much have to fit the character, but Claudette's perception of the character; in short, Claudette as the character, not vice versa. Once she discovered that the left side of her face looked more sculpted than the right, she expected cinematographers to favor it. Her awareness of herself as an artist in whatever medium she was to enter began at Washington Irving.

The curriculum of Claudette's era is unthinkable in the twenty-first century. The goals were defined in the school's handbook, *Writs of Assistance*; the title had nothing to do with the historical Writs of Assistance, which authorized British soldiers to enter private homes in pre–Revolutionary War America. McGowan's *Writs* was the equivalent of a teachers' manual. The course of study called "Repertoire" required English instructors to devote the first and tenth weeks of each term exclusively to poetry. The students were required to read, among other works, such classics as Walt Whitman's "O Captain, My Captain," Thomas Gray's "Elegy Written in a Country Churchyard," Lord Byron's "She Walks in Beauty," William Wordsworth's "I Wandered Lonely as a Cloud" and "Composed on Westminster Bridge," Percy Bysshe Shelley's "To a Skylark," and Lorenzo's "How sweet the moonlight sleeps upon the bank," which opens the last act of *The Merchant of Venice*.

The Declamation Department expected the students to recite poetry was well as read it. The selections were different (one was Jaques's "All the world's a stage" speech from *As You Like It*, act 2, 7), and the emphasis was on delivery and interpretation. The goals, however, were the same: training the memory, enriching the imagination, and imbuing the students with a sense of cadence and rhythm.

Any school that called its course of study Repertoire and had, as its mission, preparing students to enter Shakespeare's metaphorical stage with its many entrances and exits and its myriad roles, more than justified its existence. But to Claudette, there was nothing metaphorical about the stage at Washington Irving High, where she discovered the magic of theatre.

The school was her training ground. She may have been born with a musical voice, but exercises in breath control, pitch, intonation, and inflection helped turn it into a musical instrument. Claudette was always grateful for the education she received there. Atop a shelf in the school library, next to a picture of President John F. Kennedy, stands one of Claudette that she autographed personally for her alma mater.

As she told Virginia Bird, "I know you think you work hard in school, but you'll work much harder outside. Success anywhere means just plain hard work. I know, because I thought I worked hard and then I found I had almost been lazy when I started on a stage career. But if you have work you like, it doesn't matter, for you will be having a good time which is half the battle. Whatever you do, find something you like, work in earnest, and have the patience of an angel for disappointment, and then you will be what they call successful."

"Having a good time" was her credo. Few actresses ever conveyed the sheer enjoyment they experienced practicing their art as did Claudette.

Bird understood: "Miss Colbert is an excellent example of her sentiments."

And this was only 1927, when Claudette had not even made her first talkie.

CHAPTER 2

Becoming Claudette Colbert

In 1919 Claudette had not yet begun to pursue a stage career, although one was beckoning from the wings. Alice Rostetter, who wrote *Launcelot George*, in which Claudette had appeared at Washington Irving High School, was elated when the Provincetown Playhouse accepted her new play, *The Widow's Veil*, for a February 1919 opening. The Provincetown Players had moved from Provincetown, Massachusetts, to New York in 1916; by 1919, the Playhouse, best known for presenting some of Eugene O'Neill's early works, was fulfilling its mission to give new voices in the theater a hearing. One such voice—but unfortunately, not one to be heard for long—was Alice Rostetter's, even though *The Widow's Veil* proved so popular that it was revived two months later and then transferred to Newark, New Jersey, for a week's engagement.

In the April revival, Rostetter herself appeared as Mrs. MacManus, a recently married woman convinced that her husband is dying. Her neighbor, the widowed Mrs. Phelan, tries to comfort her, and it is only after Mrs. MacManus discovers how attractive she looks in a black hat and veil that she resigns herself to widowhood. But Mr. MacManus quickly recovers, thus depriving his wife of the opportunity to don widow's weeds.

15

Claudette included *The Widow's Veil* among her early credits. Rostetter, who remembered Claudette from *Launcelot George*, either offered her a chance to appear in her new play or encouraged her to audition for it. Much later in her career, Claudette reminisced about *The Widow's Veil* during an interview: "We ran for a couple of weeks at the Provincetown Playhouse in Greenwich Village. . . . I played a young bride with a red wig and an Irish brogue." The role must have been Mrs. MacManus.

Without school records, it is impossible to verify whether Claudette was still at Washington Irving in February 1919 when she did *The Widow's Veil*. Although she told Rex Reed that she appeared in *Grammar* in December 1918, she could have graduated at the end of the fall term, in January 1919. Initially, Washington Irving, which opened its doors in February 1913, did not observe the traditional September–June school year. Then, too, there was the matter of Claudette's missing at least four months of school, and possibly more, in 1916, which would also have affected her graduation date.

By 1916, Claudette was undoubtedly a Washington Irving student. After class, she took swimming lessons at the local YWCA; in her eagerness to return home by 8:30 p.m., as her mother insisted, she failed to observe a traffic light, stepping off the curb at the corner of Fifty-third and Lexington and into the path of an oncoming truck. The accident left her with a broken ankle and knee, spinal injuries so severe that she had to remain immobile for four months, and back problems that plagued her throughout her life. "During the four months I was helpless in bed, and for the following five months when I walked on crutches, and then with a cane, I changed a lot." The change came from the attention she received from classmates and teachers who visited her during her convalescence. "Later on, I even dramatized my illness and clung to the cane long after I really needed it." The actress within was preparing to emerge; she would not have long to wait.

If, on the other hand, Claudette were still at Washington Irving in February 1919, Rostetter could have secured permission for her to appear in the play. It is hard to imagine Principal MacGowan objecting to one of his students performing in a piece written by one of his faculty, and for such a limited run. And if Rostetter assumed the role in the April revival, the reason might have been the graduating senior's perennial scramble to finish papers, complete projects, and prepare for finals.

By December 1919, there was no longer a conflict between school and stage. Claudette also claimed that she appeared in the Provincetown Playhouse's production of Edna St. Vincent Millay's *Aria da Capo*, which opened officially on 15 December after a few previews. The Provincetown Playhouse records for 1916 through 1919 are sadly incomplete. In the *Aria da Capo* program in the Billy Rose Collection of the New York Public Library for the Performing Arts, Columbine, the only role for an actress, was played by the author's sister, Norma Millay, who had a brief stage career. Whether Claudette assumed the role at some point during the three-week run, played it in previews, or was Norma Millay's understudy who went on for a few performances is unknown. Again, there is no reason to doubt her word. Claiming to have been in the forty-minute *Aria da Capo* would not have enhanced the career of an actress who, at the time of the interview, was sixty-seven and no longer making movies.

Claudette's selective memory of her stage career probably stemmed from her belief that it paled in comparison with her films, which alone would ensure her place in American popular culture. Yet one wishes she had spoken or written about the stage actors with whom she worked— e.g., Elliot Nugent, Walter Huston, Chester Morris, and Glenn Anders—as well as such playwrights as Elmer Rice, who also directed her in *See Naples and Die*, and Edna St. Vincent Millay, who staged *Aria da Capo*, which may have been just another Provincetown production to Claudette, but not to New York intellectuals. Claudette did not realize at the time that she was associated with a play that the formidable critic Alexander Woollcott called "one of the most beautiful and interesting plays in the English language now to be seen in New York." Although Woollcott attended a preview, he still could separate the text (which he admired) from the performance (which he did not, implying that it failed to do justice to the play).

Aria da Capo was Millay's response to the futility of World War I, never mentioned by name but suggested in the guise of a deadly dispute over water rights. The form was a mix of surrealism and allegory, anticipating the theatre of the absurd (especially Eugene Ionesco's *The Bald Soprano*) and the reality-versus-illusion dramas of Luigi Pirandello (e.g., *Six Characters in Search of an Author* and *Henry IV*) and Jean Anouilh (e.g., *The Rehearsal* and *Thieves' Carnival*).

Aria da Capo begins as a harlequinade or clown show, with Pierrot and Columbine trading the kind of non sequiturs that would have delighted the absurdists. Just when the play appears to be a farce, Cothurnus enters. The character's name (the *cothurnus* was the elevated shoe worn by the actors in Greek tragedy) signals a change of mood. The harlequinade ceases for the moment, and a two-character tragedy begins with the shepherds Thyrsis and Corydon, whose names derive from ancient pastoral poetry. In Virgil and Theocritus, Thyrsis and Corydon engage in singing contests; in Millay, they build a wall, which is completely at odds with the pastoral tradition in which the grazing land is held in common. The wall favors Thyrsis, who gains the water rights, refusing to share them with Corydon. When Corydon discovers precious stones on his side (rendered as colored confetti), Thyrsis agrees to share the water with him in return for the jewels. But Corydon is no longer concerned about his sheep now that he has struck it rich. Since wealth cannot slake thirst, Thyrsis offers Corydon a bowl of water which, unbeknownst to Corydon, has been poisoned. Corydon drinks the water while strangling Thyrsis at the same time (surrealism is logic-defying). Pierrot and Columbine, annoyed at the sight of the dead bodies, want them removed so the harlequinade can resume, illustrating Millay's point that what often seem petty and insignificant can escalate into war if the stakes are high enough, the nations powerful enough, and the enmities deep enough, and that to all but the victims, fighting over water (substitute land, minerals, natural resources, boundaries, and fuel lines for contemporary parallels) is an unpleasantness that, in the tradition of Greek tragedy, is best left off stage—narrated, rather than dramatized. Significantly, both Pierrot and Columbine are off stage during the violence, which is more shocking in idea than execution.

Although her work at the Provincetown Playhouse was the closest Claudette had come to professional acting, she was uncertain about a stage career. She found herself at the same crossroads that confronted the speaker in Robert Frost's "In a Yellow Wood." Two paths lay ahead of her: acting and art. She was drawn to both, not realizing that they would eventually coalesce and that she would become an outstanding actress as well as an accomplished painter. She only knew that she had grown as much as an artist as she had as an actress—possibly more as an artist, since she had studied art formally. Regardless, she was loath to subordinate one to the other.

After *Aria da Capo* closed, Claudette realized she needed more training in art (as opposed to acting, which is something one *does* rather than studies). She had heard about the Art Students League on West Fifty-seventh Street, where the tuition was affordable; the instructors, professionals; the scheduling flexible; and the curriculum diversified, ranging from printmaking and drawing to painting and sculpture. To pay for her courses, Claudette worked for a dressmaker and gave French lessons at three dollars an hour.

The years 1920–1922 were uneventful. Her acting career was on hold. Instead, Claudette continued giving French lessons (and perhaps working in a dress shop) and studying at the Art Students League, suggesting that she may have been inclining toward a career in art. Studying with professionals gave her an even greater sense of discipline. In whatever she did, she had to excel. In short, Claudette had become a perfectionist. Painting taught her that the human face is not uniform; one side is more distinctive than the other; it curves more gracefully and often has a sculptured look, while the other looks unshaped. Claudette knew she had a round face. However, her left side had a clearly defined line which the right did not. When she began applying makeup, she took special care to make her left side her best. In 1920, a career in the "flickers" was the furthest thing from her mind. But when she decided to enter the movie business and became an actress, she made certain that the director of photography favored her left side, rather than the one that soon became known throughout Hollywood as "the dark side of the moon."

Apart from her working and studying art, all that is known of that period is that Claudette, still with the surname Chauchoin, and her mother sailed to Paris in late summer 1922 and returned in early October.

Things changed in 1923. At a social event, alternately described as a tea or a cocktail party (more likely the latter, where stage star Katharine Cornell was one of the guests), one of Claudette's French students introduced her to actress-turned-playwright, Anne Morrison, later Anne Morrison Chapin, whose first play, *The Wild Westcotts*, was being cast. Their meeting seems to have been the "You ought to be on Broadway" kind, with Morrison, clearly taken by Claudette, suggesting that she audition for one of the roles. Claudette did and was cast as Sybil Blake, who only had a few lines, although supposedly more were added after the Stamford, Connecticut, tryout. Regardless, Claudette would not be appearing at the Provincetown Playhouse down on MacDougal Street, but on the Great White Way itself: the Frazee on Forty-second Street at fifty dollars a week—not bad for a walk-on.

Before her Broadway debut, Claudette believed she should do something about her last name. Her mother felt similarly. Jeanne Chauchoin, who looked down on her daughter's profession (but was not averse to enjoying the lifestyle it provided), knew that if Claudette succeeded as an actress, she would be drawing a higher salary than anyone in the family ever had. Jeanne suggested "Colbert." It was not a family name; Jeanne's inspiration was Jean Baptiste Colbert, Louis XIV's finance minister. Jeanne was already thinking big bucks; they would get bigger—much bigger— during the next decade.

Opening night was 24 December, which in 1923 was relatively mild for the third day of winter. In fact, the city had been going through a relative heat wave, which cooled down a bit by Christmas Eve. Still, it was evident that New Yorkers would not experience a white Christmas. The opening night curtain was set for 8:30 p.m. Claudette was a great walker; she might even have walked from East Fifty-third Street to the Frazee at 254 West Forty-second Street. The weather would not have been a problem: the temperature was in the forties. Otherwise, she could have taken the Fifth Avenue bus to Forty-second Street and walked a couple of blocks to the theater.

On Christmas Eve 1923, theatergoers had a choice of over forty shows. On the same street as the Frazee, *Abie's Irish Rose* was in its second year at the Republic; Madge Kennedy and W. C. Fields were costarring in *Poppy* at the Apollo; and the *Ziegfeld Follies* was drawing crowds to Forty-second Street's crown jewel, the New Amsterdam, Florenz Ziegfeld's creation, which was Disneyfied in the 1990s and played host to *The Lion King* from 1997 to 2006. Claudette probably knew little about the Frazee, where a few years earlier Eugene O'Neill's *Gold* (1920) closed after ten days. Seasoned performers like Elliot Nugent, the male lead in *The Wild Westcotts*, who later directed Claudette in *Three Cornered Moon* (1933), must have been aware of the Frazee's reputation as the home of flops. *The Wild Westcotts*, a comedy about two sisters and their romantic involvements, did not alter the theater's reputation. The *New York Times* (25 December 1923) grudgingly admitted that the play was entertaining, but that was it. Nugent came off well, but Claudette went unmentioned, as did another actress, who became a stage personality: Cornelia Otis Skinner. Each had to wait her turn.

Seven years later, the Frazee was converted into a movie theater. Claudette, Nugent, and Otis Skinner went on to perform in better plays and in theaters that bore no stigma. Anne Morrison was not discouraged by the short run of her first play. Her next, *Pigs*, which racked up 312 performances during the 1924–25 season, augured well; *Jonsey* (1929), less so, with 96 performances. When *No Questions Asked* (1934) lasted for 16, Morrison knew it was time to head for Hollywood, where the advent of sound proved a boon for New York playwrights able to dictate their own terms to an industry desperate for writers. Morrison and Claudette would meet again, but not for two more decades, when she was the coauthor of the screenplay of *The Secret Heart* (1946), one of Claudette's lesser films.

The *New York Times* may have taken no notice of Claudette, but producer A. H. Woods did. After she came to his office with a letter of introduction, he immediately put her under contract, notifying the press that Claudette was *his* discovery. She was also his protégée. A. H. Woods (1870–1951) was one of the most colorful stage producers of the early decades of the twentieth century. Born Aladár Herman in Budapest, Hungary, he adopted the name of A. H. Woods by using the initials of his first and last name and adding the surname of an actor he especially liked, N. S. Woods. As soon as he became aware of the infinite potential of show business, he narrowed his choices down to the art form he loved above all others: the stage. His producing career began in 1903 and ended in 1943; during that forty-year period he produced well over 150 plays, some of which were highly controversial: *The Green Hat* (1925) dealt with infidelity and suicide; *The Shanghai Gesture* (1926), with prostitution, illegitimacy, drug addiction, and a rare form of homicide: a mother's murder of her daughter; *The Trial of Mary Dugan* (1927), with a brother who defends the sister who sent him through law school with her murdered lover's money. Woods gave the public what it wanted—not high brow entertainment but melodramas and boudoir comedies with such titillating titles as *His Bridal Night* (1916), *Up in Mabel's Room* (1919), and *The Matrimonial Bed* (1927). He was totally unapologetic about his choice of plays: "I am not ashamed of my work. . . . I know that I have done a minimum of harm and a maximum of good in giving the entertainment that the masses of people want at a price they can afford."

About fifteen years after his producing career began, Woods thought that he could make even more money in exhibition. He began in Chicago, which in 1920 was a theater mecca, not on a par with New York, but fertile ground, nonetheless. He started with the Woods Theater on Randolph and Dearborn, and then opened another a year later, the Apollo, right across the street. Theater ownership proved less lucrative than he thought; the Apollo was sold to United Artists, which used it as a showcase for its films. He fared no better in New York; the Eltinge on West Forty-third Street was short lived, as was the Republic on Times Square, which became a movie theater renamed the Victory in the 1940s and is currently the New Victory, specializing in family-oriented stage productions.

Woods was a colorful figure, a cigar smoker with a fondness for silk shirts and whose signature piece of jewelry was a large jade ring. He knew how to endear himself to actors, gaining their trust by allaying their fears. Woods asked only that an actor entrust himself or herself to his care. Claudette did just that. Her contract with Woods initially turned out to be an apprenticeship in the theatre. Woods turned her into a working actress, which she remained for the rest of her career. For the next six years, Claudette worked steadily, both in New York and on tour, going from one play to the next, which was possible in the 1920s, when there were often as many as fifty shows on at the same time. Claudette never worked in a stock company, but she was gaining the same kind of experience. The pace may have been grueling, but she discovered, as she later told Virginia Bird, that she was willing to work much harder than she had at Washington Irving because she found something she loved. She had taken the right path; from now on, painting was her hobby. Perhaps her determination to succeed was influenced by her father's repeated failures, from which she learned one important fact: The correct idiom is not to "pursue" a career, but to "build" one.

Although Claudette did not appear on Broadway for two more years, she was by no means idle. In February 1924 Woods dispatched her to Chicago to join the company of *We've Got to Have Money*, a comedy about a playboy who proves to his guardian that he can succeed on his own by becoming a successful entrepreneur. A month later, she was in Washington, D.C., with the out-of-town tryout of *The Marionette Man* (retitled *Puppets* when it opened in New York in March 1925); the play was a melodrama about a puppeteer who befriends a southern woman (Miriam Hopkins in the Broadway production) and goes off to war, where he is erroneously reported as killed in action, but returns in time to save her from the clutches of white slavers. Claudette was not the lead; Woods never intended her to play leads in touring companies, only roles that enabled her to gain experience. In 1925, she spent May and June in Boston and then Chicago in the revival of the popular *Leah Kleshna*, in which the title character is a thief who mends her ways when she is rescued from a train wreck.

Still searching for the perfect vehicle for his discovery, Woods thought he had found one in the comedy *The Cat Came Back*; the critics disagreed, and the play closed after an unsuccessful tryout in Stamford, Connecticut, in January 1926. Then it was off again to Chicago, where she was a replacement in *High Stakes*, a drama with an unusual twist. This was the closest Claudette had come to a supporting part: a secretary in love with an aspiring dramatist, who envisions a play about two brothers, the younger of whom forces the older to realize that his wife is committing adultery with a houseguest. What the dramatist-brother has envisioned turns out to be the plot of *High Stakes*.

Finally Woods came up with a play that seemed a natural for Claudette: *A Kiss in a Taxi*, an adaptation of a French boulevard comedy, which opened on 25 August at the Ritz Theatre (now the Walter Kerr) on West Forty-eighth Street. Again, the *New York Times* was unimpressed; again, Claudette was ignored, even though she had the pivotal role of Genette, a would-be cabaret singer whom a middle-aged banker intends to make his mistress. His wife, mistaking Genette for an orphan, decides to adopt her, much to the dismay of the banker, who discovers that his would-be mistress is now his adopted daughter. The *New York Times*, however, was not the voice of theatergoers who were enchanted by Claudette—so much so that the play lasted for 103 performances. There was no one on Broadway whose eyes could flash innocence and experience at the same time and whose voice could range from demure to worldly without making a stop in between.

Aware of Claudette's audience appeal, Woods promoted her as his British discovery. The *New York Times'* "Who's Who on the Assorted Stages" column (8 November 1925) carried a story that Claudette and playwright Frederick Lonsdale, whose comedy, *The Fake*, Woods was producing, came from the same "town" in England. The only connection, and a tenuous one at that, is that Lonsdale hailed from the Isle of Jersey, the birthplace of Claudette's grandmother and brother. Claudette had also acquired a slight British accent from working with British actors on tour.

Lonsdale and Claudette must have met before casting began for *The Fake*, which premiered on 6 October 1924. The accent might have served her well if she had been cast as a politician's daughter whose father wants to marry her off to an alcoholic and drug-addicted peer, even though she is in love with her father's secretary. Since Lonsdale was not known for writing tragedies, a happy ending comes about with the peer's death, leaving the lovers free to marry. Just when it seemed that Claudette would be playing the female lead, "[Lonsdale] didn't like her interpretation and insisted she be replaced." Lonsdale was right. At this stage in her career, Claudette lacked the patrician bearing that the role required and that the more stately Frieda Inescort, who replaced her, possessed.

Woods had other plans for his "British discovery," who soon discarded the accent. The following year Claudette was back on Broadway in *The Ghost Train*, another Woods production that premiered in August 1926 at the Eltinge on West Forty-third Street. *The Ghost Train*, which survived for sixty-two performances, was the railway equivalent of the "old dark house" melodrama: the setting was a supposedly haunted train station where some travelers are forced to spend the night. The play did nothing for anyone's career, although three cast members—John Williams, Isobel Elsom, and Eric Blore—later did well for themselves in Hollywood. According to the *New York Post*, Claudette was *The Ghost Train*'s chief attraction; the *New York Sun* (26 August 1926) said as much: "Claudette Colbert, that little and lively brunette who made her debut last year in French farce, brings much zest to English melodrama." Claudette's appearances at benefits, dinner parties, and social events were duly noted by the press. When asked about actresses who avoid stage makeup in favor of a "natural" look, Claudette, who not only wore it but also applied it herself, replied, "I think those folks who talk about natural makeup are interesting, but I've never seen one who did not look like a ghost from the front."

After *The Ghost Train* closed, there was no rest for Claudette. She went right into *The Pearl of Great Price* that November. *Pearl*, an allegorical drama, produced by the Shuberts after Woods gave up his option on it, starred Claudette as the Pilgrim, making a journey through the various deadly sins, which were more than seven. The Pilgrim keeps her pearl (chastity) intact, kills Lust, is tried and vindicated, and finds her soul mate. *Pearl* was not panned, exactly, because no one knew what to make of it. The critics agreed that it was a great spectacle, but not much of a play. The *New York Times* commended Claudette, who "brings a good deal of feeling and sincerity to the difficult role." When *Pearl* closed after thirty-two performances, there was a much better vehicle in the offing—one that enhanced her reputation as a leading stage star and also brought her together with another actor, Norman Foster, who became her first husband.

The Barker, which opened on 18 January 1927 at the Biltmore, a theater that became Claudette's favorite, provided her with her longest run thus far: six months. The star was Walter Huston, as the manager of a tent show, who does not want his son (Norman Foster) to follow in his footsteps, preferring instead that he become a lawyer. To prevent his son from discovering that he has a mistress, the father plans to fire her from the show. When the mistress learns of his intentions, she bribes a snake charmer (Claudette) to seduce him. Instead, the snake charmer falls in love with the son, and vice versa. Indirectly, the father gets his wish. By the last act, the couple is married, the son is working in a law firm, and his wife has graduated from snake charmer to chanteuse.

After *The Barker* concluded its run in July 1927, Claudette had a brief respite before rehearsals began for *The Mulberry Bush*, a short-lived romantic comedy that opened in October 1927 and closed the following month. Claudette and James Rennie played a couple eager for a divorce, until the husband's would-be second wife discovers he is no longer in love with her.

The couple resolved their differences, and *The Mulberry Bush* succumbed after twenty-nine performances.

The predictable rhythm—a hiatus of a few weeks followed by another short-lived play—persisted for the next two years. First, there was *La Gringa*, with Claudette as a Mexican orphan involved in a hopeless love affair with an academic. *La Gringa* had an even shorter run: sixteen performances in February 1928. This time Brooks Atkinson found Claudette "a very promising young actress." Next came a revival of *Within the Law*, a crime melodrama, in which "Miss Colbert gave a very enjoyable performance." The *Daily Mirror* was even more laudatory, calling Claudette "one of our very best young stage actresses."

Within the Law had no sooner closed than Claudette and Foster boarded the SS *Aquitania* on 21 March to reprise their roles in the London production of *The Barker*, arriving in time for a few rehearsals and a brief tour prior to the 30 April opening. It was also during the London engagement that they were married, perhaps at the end of March. Claudette would only admit that they married in London under their real names.

To their fellow actors, Claudette and Norman Foster seemed like an odd combination. The Indiana-born Foster, né Hoeffer, was as American as Claudette was Continental. But what theatre people did not know is how desperately in love Claudette was with him. It was what Claudette would have called *grand amour*, a love so all-consuming that it can never recur—at least not in the same way. Even Claudette had to admit that while she loved her second husband, Dr. Joel "Joe" Pressman, it was never with the same ardor. But *grand amour*, rapturous as it is, is no substitute for independence or a career. Claudette wanted both. However, the independence she really sought was from her mother, which she never achieved. The closest Claudette came to her ideal was a husband whom she truly loved but who would not interfere with her career. Norman was easy, compared to Jeanne Cauchoin. Claudette only became independent of her mother when she died in 1970.

Foster made his stage debut three years after Claudette in *Just Life*, a comedy about marital infidelity that opened to poor reviews on

14 September 1926. Foster was the epitome of the male ingénue, handsome and unaffected—a type that made him easy to cast, even in melodramas about a decent young man gone astray. Like Claudette, he was in demand, going straight from *Just Life* to the comedy *Sure Fire* a month later. Foster was ignored by the critics until *The Barker*. Writing of his performance, Brooks Atkinson did not separate it from Claudette's: "Mr. Foster gives the part of Chris all the fresh charm of youth, and Miss Colbert expresses the earnestness under the tawdry existence of a midway slut."

Four months after *The Barker* closed in July 1927, Foster was appearing in *The Racket* with Edward G. Robinson, a drama about political corruption in which he played a cub reporter. Like Claudette, Foster discovered that Broadway in the 1920s was a revolving door: Exit one play, enter another. After *The Racket* closed, there was time for a few months' rest until rehearsals began for Phillip Dunning's *Night Hostess*, in which Foster came off with another good notice: "Mr. Foster does not let the part [of a hoofer] slip by him. . . . He goes through his paces in high spirits."

In November 1928, Claudette and Foster were reunited in *Tin Pan Alley*, which opened at the Biltmore, where they had appeared in *The Barker* and where Claudette would star much later in her career in *The Kingfisher* and *A Talent for Murder*. *Tin Pan Alley* depicted a sleazy New York filled with chorus girls, mobsters, hit men, and prostitutes. Foster received better reviews than Claudette, whom Brooks Atkinson described as "calefacient," although he felt she played the songwriter's wife "self-consciously." Foster, on the other hand, was "ingratiating" and acted the songwriter "delightfully." "Calefacient" must have sent *New York Times* readers scurrying to their dictionaries. Derived from the Latin *calefacere*, "to make warm," "calefacient" was a pedantic compliment, implying that Claudette radiated warmth. If "calefacient," she must have also been "ingratiating," which would have served for both herself and Foster. But the calefacient Claudette and the ingratiating Foster could not keep *Tin Pan Alley* from lasting for more than a month.

Carnival, a *Barker* spin-off, followed in April 1929 with Foster as another callow youth infatuated with a tent-show performer. It was clear that producers had relegated him to the "almost-but-not-quite-romantic lead" category, which would become a dead file when the bloom of youth disappeared. Fortunately, Foster had one more chance on Broadway, just as he was about to turn thirty, when he was cast in Ring Lardner and George S. Kaufman's satire on music publishing, *June Moon*, which provided him with his best role and the longest run of any play he had ever done: 9 October 1929 to 4 June 1930. The *New York Times* review, although favorable, called attention to Foster's youthful appearance, which did not do much to facilitate his transition from boy/man to leading man: "Mr. Foster played an aspiring song writer in the animated and boyish style that makes him so attractive in these parts."

Claudette and Norman called theirs a "modern marriage," which even the fan magazines, accustomed to the unconventional behavior of the stars, found odd, particularly their living arrangements. Claudette continued to live on Central Park West with her mother, grandmother, and Tantine; Foster, at the Lambs' Club on West Forty-fourth Street. Claudette admitted that their kind of marriage was "not practical for everybody," but "for professional people with individual incomes, separate establishments seem to be ideal."

Claudette also justified living apart as the ideal way—for her, at least—to deal with personal problems without involving her husband. Such a marriage, she argued, keeps romance alive. The example she gave—getting dressed up when Norman would be spending the evening, as opposed to the night, at her apartment—was strictly for the fans who still doubted that their modern marriage was, in fact, a real marriage and not one of convenience. Norman was never a frequent visitor at 55 Central Park West. Claudette's mother and brother hated Foster; in fact, once Foster so enraged Charles that he hauled off and socked him in the jaw. Since the fan magazines were aimed at women whose romantic illusions were nurtured by the movies, and who assimilated everything they learned about their favorite stars, Claudette's marriage was portrayed as if it was the latest trend in adult living, the sort of arrangement that civilized people who drank Veuve Cliquot and smoked gold-tipped cigarettes chose.

When Claudette and Foster moved to Los Angeles, the magazines were still curious about their living arrangements. Some of the articles bore titles that were intentionally mocking. In "Part-Time Wife," Claudette was quoted as saying: "Between a husband and a career, I'd choose a career"; "The most important requirements for a successful marriage are living apart and lack of jealousy"; and "Men will always have more freedom than women. There will always be a double standard." Foster was labeled a "bachelor husband," whose home was four blocks from Claudette's. "It was Norman's idea to live as they do and that they will continue to live that way," *Modern Screen* reported in the February 1934 issue, which reached the stands a year before Claudette announced that their marriage was over.

What Claudette could never tell interviewers was that they had to live apart because Jeanne Chauchoin would not allow Norman to become one of the family. It was bad enough that her daughter was *une actrice*; her son-in-law was *un acteur*. Claudette would continue to live with her mother and Tantine; Norman could live wherever he wanted. Jeanne had no intention of abdicating her matriarchy. To Jeanne, Norman was an intruder who should live by himself—which he did, telling the press that "it's better for their artistic careers." If Claudette and Foster ever had a conventional marriage, she never would have become Claudette Colbert, the movie icon; and Foster could never have discovered his true métier: directing.

At first, there was every reason to think the marriage would work. After *The Barker* finished a four-week engagement in London, Claudette and Foster hopped on a tramp steamer for their deferred honeymoon, taking a trip around the world that they recorded on eight reels of film. September found Claudette back in New York for *Fast Life*, her last A. H. Woods production, which opened in late September 1928. *Fast Life* was another melodrama in which Claudette's husband, wrongly accused of a murder, is saved from the electric chair when the real murderer confesses. It was also a quick flop, freeing Claudette to go into *Tin Pan Alley*.

Shortly after *Tin Pan Alley* closed, Claudette learned she would be playing the female lead in Eugene O'Neill's *Dynamo* (1929), which followed on the heels of *Strange Interlude*, his nine-act, five-hour (with dinner intermission) conflation of Greek tragedy, Nietzschean philosophy, and Freudianism. In 1929, O'Neill was a three-time Pulitzer prize winner for *Beyond the Horizon* (1920), *Anna Christie* (1922), and *Strange Interlude* (1928). How Claudette felt about *Dynamo* after the first run-through is another matter. *Dynamo* conformed to what the popular mind associated with high tragedy, which O'Neill supplied in excess, dredging up the neuroses lurking within Greek drama and embedding them in characters that only highly skilled actors could portray convincingly without turning them into Freudian stereotypes. *Strange Interlude* was a case study in neurosis: a daughter obsessed with her father, a son with his mother, the mother with her dead lover and the child she was denied, and the man willing to accommodate the mother by siring the son of her dreams. Everyone was trapped in a cycle of recurrence, as sons first pass into their mothers, then their mother's successors, and finally their fathers; daughters into their mothers-in-law, oedipal suitors into impotence, and potent lovers into oblivion. *Strange Interlude* was not so much melodramatic as operatic, with interior monologues complete with free association (really a combination of asides and abbreviated soliloquies) in lieu of arias. Despite the many demands *Strange Interlude* made on audiences, length being just one of them, the public embraced the play, which often played to standees.

 Dynamo used the same techniques, but in truncated form. Yet anyone seeking a compendium of O'Neill's obsessions has the equivalent of a reader's guide in *Dynamo*, which opened at the Martin Beck Theatre on West Forty-fifth Street on 11 February 1929 for a disappointing run of fifty-three performances. Claudette was cast as Ada Fife, the sexy daughter of Ramsay Fife, the superintendent of a hydroelectric plant, the dynamo of the title. Next door to the Fifes is a minister's family: the Reverend Light, his wife, and their son, Reuben. Unlike the minister, Ramsay is an atheist whose God is the electricity generated by the plant. Anyone who saw *Strange Interlude* might have recalled the final scene in which Nina Leeds describes life as a "strange dark interlude in the electrical display of God the Father."

Nina, who once worshiped Mother God, has now conceded power to God the Father, realizing that a woman is only a stopover on the male's journey to adulthood, which ends with his absorption into his father.

Reuben Light is torn between his father's Christian fundamentalism and Fife's atheism. He leaves home, renounces religion, and becomes an acolyte of the dynamo, personified as the feminine principle, "a great, dark mother." Convinced that he has betrayed the dark mother, as well as his own mother, by having sex with Ada, he shoots her and literally embraces the dynamo, electrocuting himself in the process as he cries, "Never let me go from you again! Please, Mother!"

Reading *Dynamo* is an exercise in disbelief that refuses suspension. The characters' inner thoughts are the verbal equivalent of the swirls in a Jackson Pollock drip painting–a tangle of colors splashed across the canvas and lines that curve in on themselves and then disappear within the grand design. On another level, *Dynamo* is a whodunit, where we discover at the end that while Reuben pulled the trigger, the dynamo is the villain—an idol worshiped as a deity that, like any force of nature, is both beneficent and destructive. Much of the writing is undeniably powerful when it is not overwrought; yet one has the feeling that O'Neill had descended so far into the labyrinth of the unconscious that no thread could guide him back to the more mundane concerns of motivation and verisimilitude that had been left behind in the cave of the heart.

Brooks Atkinson, still J. Brooks Atkinson, must have felt the same way when he reviewed *Dynamo* in the *New York Times*. Although he accepted O'Neill's rejection of realistic theatre, he isolated the play's faults ("lurid dialogue," "unreal fervor") while at the same time commending the playwright for tackling another controversial subject: the birth of a new religion with its own incarnation myth—the god of the machine replacing the god of the sky. Atkinson praised the cast, singling out Claudette for giving the "best performance in her career, vivid and descriptive, without a trace of self-consciousness"; but that was not enough to keep *Dynamo* running beyond a month and a half.

Claudette thought she might have better luck with Elmer Rice's new play, *See Naples and Die*, with the playwright himself directing. Rice had just won a Pulitzer prize for *Street Scene* (1929), which was still running at the Playhouse on West Forty-eighth Street, the same street where *Naples* was scheduled to open on 26 September 1929 at the Vanderbilt, one block west. On the strength of Rice's reputation, *Naples* had a large advance sale.

Before each performance, Claudette would say, sometimes audibly, "Mon Dieu, aide moi." Interestingly, she used the familiar form of the verb, rather than *aidez-moi*, as if she and the Deity were on intimate terms. The English translation, "My God, help me," sounds like a distress call or an afterthought following some grueling experience. To Claudette, it was her way asking for divine assistance.

No prayer could keep *See Naples and Die* from lasting more than two months. Billed as an "extravagant comedy in three acts," *Naples* was an uneasy mix of drawing-room repartee; political intrigue; topical references to the -isms (fascism, capitalism, expatriatism, communism); sprinklings of French, German, and Italian for the cognoscenti; and comic writing (never Rice's strong suit), often so unsubtle that the playwright seemed to be striking a bargain with the audience, asking them to laugh if they got the joke and, if not, laugh anyway.

There is a scene that illustrates Rice's habit of belaboring a joke that should have ended with a natural laugh line. When Claudette's character, Nanette, scrambles to get a carriage to Sorrento and hears it is *occupato*, she tries to ingratiate herself with the coachman by shouting, "Viva il Duce!" to which he replies "Viva Mussolini!" That obviously would have gotten a laugh. Instead of moving on, Rice has one of the characters ask incredulously if Nanette is really an admirer of Mussolini, to which she replies sheepishly, "Well, I do think something should be done about his face."

In 1929, that kind of line would have elicited not so much a laugh as a guffaw; by then—seven years after Benito Mussolini marched on Rome—audiences were familiar with his chest-pounding demagoguery. "Viva il Duce," followed by "Viva Mussolini!" is funny—and sufficient. "Well, I do think something should be done about his face" is not; it is an attempt to extract humor from someone's physical features, a technique used by comedians during World War II when donning a Hitlerian moustache or putting a finger under one's nose guaranteed a laugh.

The play, set in a pensione on the Gulf of Naples, has a host of potentially colorful characters, including a scatterbrain from Ohio, a voluptuous maid, the mistress of an Rumanian dictator, a jilted lover, a Russian prince and his faithful German attendant, and the prince's bride, played by Claudette "by special arrangement with A. H. Woods," as the playbill makes clear. There are also two chess players, who are on stage for all three acts and say nothing until the climax.

Claudette played Nanette Dodge Kossoff, who has reluctantly agreed to marry the Russian prince to save her sister's reputation. The prince, the ex-lover of Nanette's sister, has threatened to publish her sister's torrid love letters unless Nan marries him. Consequently, Nan jilts her fiancé, Charles Carroll, who, naturally, is at the pensione. At least Rice has found an ingenious way to resolve the plot. The chess players are Rumanian patriots who near the end of the third act jump up from their chairs and assassinate the Rumanian dictator and accidentally kill the prince, who happens to be talking with the dictator. But as one of the assassins explains, "We are the enemies of all hereditary aristocrats and so we cannot greatly regret having dispatched the Prince." Nan and Charles are free to marry, and the curtain falls as the sexy maid lures a fascist guard into the bedroom.

Atkinson's review was lukewarm and not at all complimentary to Claudette, who seemed "self-conscious" in delivering her lines. But the dialogue was not exactly the kind that would come trippingly off anyone's tongue.

During the week of 22 October 1929, there were signs that the stock market was behaving erratically. Then it happened: Monday, 29 October. The next day, the headline of the *New York Times* read: "STOCK COLLAPSES IN 16,410,030-SHARE DAY, BUT RALLY AT CLOSE CHEERS BROKERS." To those who read beyond the headlines, there was no reason to cheer: "From every point of view, in the extent of losses sustained, in total turnover in the number of speculators wiped out, the day was the most disastrous in Wall Street's history." If Claudette did not read the *Times* that day, she or someone in the *Naples* company would have caught *Variety*'s 30 October headline: "WALL ST. LAYS AN EGG." Would it be a case of Wall Street today, Broadway tomorrow?

Claudette always claimed that the Wall Street crash prompted her decision to relinquish the stage for film. Actually, she began making talkies a year before the crash and even did a silent film for Frank Capra in 1927. What the crash did was to convince her—and Norman, as well—that Broadway would no longer be what it was in the 1920s, when on some evenings a theatergoer had a choice of fifty stage attractions. Then, there was the disillusionment of appearing in two plays, one after the other, by Pulitzer prize winners, that were flops. Even if Claudette dismissed Atkinson's criticism of her self-conscious acting, she still might have questioned whether the next decade would bring her better roles or would be the usual round of short runs interspersed with tours, as it had been in the 1920s.

Claudette would return to Broadway, but that would not be for a quarter of a century. By then, A. H. Woods was dead. Unable to produce another play after 1943, he suffered the fate of the high and mighty when he fell out of favor. He was sent scripts, but none were producible, at least not by him. On 24 April 1951, A. H. Woods passed away in his room at the Beacon Hotel. Five years later, Claudette returned to Broadway. Meanwhile, Claudette's and Foster's medium of necessity—and then choice—was celluloid.

CHAPTER 3

Commuting to Work

"Claudette Colbert is about to go over to the talking films," the *New York Times* reported on 17 March 1929. Actually, Claudette already had; her first talkie, *The Hole in the Wall*, was scheduled to open the following month. In fact, Claudette made her screen debut in a silent: Frank Capra's *For the Love of Mike*, released in August 1927. During the 1926–27 season, it was impossible to work in the theatre without being aware of the impact movies were making on American popular culture and of the radical changes occurring within the film industry itself. A few weeks before *The Ghost Train* opened at the Eltinge, a far more significant event took place a few blocks away: the premiere of *Don Juan* at the Warner Theatre on 6 August 1926. *Don Juan* utilized the (then) revolutionary technology of the sound-on-disk Vitaphone system, in which the sound, recorded on shellac disks, was synchronized with the image. *Don Juan* began with an elaborate musical introduction that included the overture to Wagner's *Tannhaüser* and Canio's aria, "Vesti la giubba" from Leoncavallo's *Pagliacci*, sung by Metropolitan Opera tenor Giovanni Martinelli. Then the film began, thrilling the audience now able to hear the tolling bells and experience the sound of swordplay during the duels.

The following year, shortly before Claudette opened in *The Mulberry Bush*, another cinematic landmark occurred: the premiere of *The Jazz Singer*, also at the Warner Theatre, on 6 October 1927. *The Jazz Singer*, a more adventuresome Vitaphone release, included eight sound sequences, six with Al Jolson mesmerizing audiences with such popular hits as "Toot, Toot, Tootsie," "Blue Skies," and "My Mammy." It would take a few more years before the conversion to sound brought the silent era to a close—and with it, the careers of those who could not adapt to the talkies, such as actors with voices at odds with their physical appearance, writers who could not move from the scenario to the screenplay, and directors who felt their art was compromised by spoken dialogue.

Claudette, like so many stage stars, was at first leery of the movies. After seeing some silent films, she concluded that they required little of the actor. Certainly, there were no lines to memorize. But since the flickers were attracting audiences, why not give them a try if the price was right? The price was. Leland Hayward, at the time production manager at First National Pictures and soon to become a powerful agent and theatrical producer, was so taken with Claudette's work in *The Barker* that he recommended her for the female lead in Frank Capra's comedy, *For the Love of Mike* (1927), which First National would distribute. Capra was delighted to have a Broadway star in his movie, and Claudette saw no reason to decline, even though she then had no idea who Frank Capra was. Since *For the Love of Mike* would be filmed at the Cosmopolitan studio on East 125th Street, she could do the movie and perform in *The Barker* at the same time. What began as an adventure ended in disillusionment. Claudette hated the experience; she was convinced that she had no aptitude for screen acting. *New York Times* critic Mordaunt Hall disagreed; he ended his review by saying, "Claudette Colbert . . . lends her charm to this obstreperous piece of work. She seems quite at home before the camera." Hall's words were prophetic. She would even be more at home when she could speak her lines, not mouth them. She did not have long to wait.

By 1929 Claudette had appeared in enough plays to develop a stage technique that could, if modified, transfer to the screen, as was evident in

her first sound film, *The Hole in the Wall* (1929), the second movie version
of Frederick Jackson's melodrama, which had played for seventy-three
performances in 1920: a respectable run, particularly since 141 plays opened
that season, and 71 ran for fewer than seventy-three performances. A
silent movie version appeared the following year, generating enough rev-
enues to justify a sound remake. *The Hole in the Wall* had a corkscrew plot
with enough twists (and a guaranteed happy ending) to keep audiences
from feeling cheated. Jean Oliver, imprisoned for four years on a trumped-
up theft charge, avenges herself on the woman who framed her by kidnapping her grandchild. Jackson himself did the adaptation, with Claudette
as Jean and Edward G. Robinson as "the Fox," a jewel thief operating out
of a phony spiritualist's apartment. Robinson was also appearing in his first
talkie, but Claudette was touted as the bigger star, even though both of
their names appeared above the title, with hers preceding his: "See and
hear Claudette Colbert, famous dramatic star, in this overpowering role.
See and hear Edward G. Robinson and the superb cast of stage-trained
artists act this gripping drama."

When *The Hole in the Wall* began shooting on 3 December 1928,
Claudette was starring in *Tin Pan Alley*; Robinson had just closed in *A Man
with Red Hair* and was in rehearsal for his next show, *Kibitzer*, which he had
coauthored with Jo Swerling. The chief reason that each of them agreed to
do the film was, of course, money—in Robinson's case, $1,350 a week for
five weeks. Claudette probably received around the same. Then, too, the
shoot was convenient. *Hole* would be filmed at Paramount's Astoria Studio
in Queens, where there was one main sound stage and six smaller ones.
The studio was accessible either by car or subway. One could either drive
across the Queensboro Bridge or take the elevated to Astoria and walk a few
blocks to the studio. On matinee days, an actor in a play could leave at noon.

Acting in a sound movie for the first time was not easy. Robinson said,
"It was a nightmare, . . . a whole new technique, a revolutionary approach
for both Claudette and myself. We had to scale everything down." Then there
was the matter of the microphone, which could be placed anywhere: behind

a curtain, in a vase of flowers, even in an actress's décolletage. However, once Claudette and Robinson began to think of retakes as the movies' equivalent of reblocking scenes, adding new dialogue, and refining line readings, they adapted quickly to the new medium. Claudette discovered she liked the experience; in many ways, a sound movie was like a play, except that it was generally shot out of sequence. Even so, she was working at her craft— acting, not pantomime, which is how she regarded the silent movies.

Playing opposite Robinson was a challenge. He exuded that strange combination of menace and loneliness that made him the perfect Caesar Enrico Bandello in *Little Caesar* (1930), in which he sought Joe Massara's (Douglas Fairbanks) friendship with the same poignant urgency as he did Jean's love in *Hole*, believing they were two of a kind. Claudette held her own with Robinson and delivered a strikingly realistic performance, especially in the scenes with the grandchild, to whom she behaved so maternally that the girl began to think of Jean as her birth mother. Such mutual affection precluded the possibility of a tragic ending. Claudette, both of whose marriages were childless, was always a believable screen mother; the warmth she radiated when she bathed and fed the child made it seem as if Jean's incarceration was a tragic mistake; and her desire for revenge, a natural reaction to injustice.

To gain the Fox's cooperation in her kidnapping scheme, Jean agrees to impersonate the spiritualist, who has died in a subway derailment. Out of sight, the Fox would transmit encoded messages to the veiled spiritualist, seated on a specially wired chair, providing her with the information she needed to convince clients she was communicating with the dead. Meanwhile, the Fox entrusts the child to Goofy (the avuncular Donald Meek), who, unfortunately, decides to hide out at the waterfront, where he accidentally drowns. When the grandmother consults the spiritualist to learn about her granddaughter, Jean is so unnerved by her presence that one of the gang cuts the cord to the transmitter—but not before Jean has received word of the girl's whereabouts. Suddenly, Jean realizes that the information did not come from the Fox, but from the dead Goofy. The entire sequence, culminating in Jean's realization that she has made contact with the spirit world, was a tour de force for Claudette, who throws off her veil—her eyes registering shock and horror after discovering her newfound powers. The grandmother admits her guilt, the Fox is arrested (in the silent version he made a bid for immunity), and Jean is reunited with her old flame.

The Hole in the Wall was also director Robert Florey's first sound film. Since he had only worked in silents both in Europe and Hollywood, some of *Hole* was shot without sound. There are several scenes—for example, long shots involving three characters—where it is obvious the dialogue has been added in post-production. Florey took an expressionistic view of the material; thus, the apartment, the "hole in the wall," with its chiaroscuro lighting, asymmetrical walls, and flattened space, evoked the out-of-joint world of *The Cabinet of Dr. Caligari* (1919). He kept close-ups to a minimum, which was just as well, since it enabled Claudette and Robinson to draw on their stage technique, downsizing it a bit but not as much as they would have to do later, when reaction shots were needed. Eventually, both of them encountered directors who would shoot more than enough close-ups that could be edited into a scene if the action seemed to flag. In 1928, Florey was not that knowledgeable, although in time he evolved into a director with a keen sense of menace in such florid melodramas as *The Face behind the Mask* (1940), *Danger Signal* (1945), and, especially, *The Beast with Five Fingers* (1946).

Before *Hole* opened at New York's Paramount on 13 April, the studio arranged a preview. Robinson, convinced he would always be a stage actor, did not attend. Claudette did, and then wired Robinson: "We weren't too bad, baby. We weren't too bad. Love, Claudette." Actually, they were quite good and would get better. Within a year, Robinson's view of the movies had changed after Hal Wallis, Warner's production head, caught him in *Mr. Samuel* before it closed and persuaded him to come to Hollywood and make the classic *Little Caesar*. Robinson would return to Broadway—but not for two decades—in *Middle of the Night* (1956). Claudette would do one more play, *See Naples and Die*, before switching to film. Claudette discovered that, just as she had gone from show to show, she could now go from movie to movie, playing starring roles without having to worry about out-of-town tryouts, closing notices, and the frustration of finding the next job. Like Robinson, she would return to Broadway in 1956, and more than once.

Claudette knew she had more to learn about the movies, particularly when it came to makeup. Although she prided herself on doing her own makeup, her extravagantly applied eye shadow betrayed her theatrical roots. As soon as she learned that a movie actor's eyes did not have to be visible from the second balcony (which movie theaters lacked), she strove for a more natural look. But when it came to her voice, there was nothing to relearn, except perhaps to remove what Atkinson called "self-consciousness" by adopting a more conversational tone. Hers was an unusually versatile voice that lay somewhere between laughter and song, ranging from throaty worldliness to bubbly lyricism. Claudette never made a musical as such, yet her speech was so subtly cadenced that when she would breeze into a scene, she almost seemed to be singing, as if the film had became an operetta with silent music.

By 1929, her style of acting was known as the "Claudette Colbert manner." The anonymous *New York Times* critic in his review of Robinson and Swerling's *Kibitzer* observed that the ingénue gave a performance "in what has lately come to be known as the Claudette Colbert manner, but whatever it was, it more than sufficed." He probably meant that unlike other ingénues, whose ideas of characterization ranged from coy and spunky to fluttery and amorous, Claudette defied any kind of taxonomy. She could play the gamine and the sophisticate, the minx and the lady; she could turn a wisecrack into a bon mot, and vice versa. She had an effervescence that sprang from a dual source: a personality that was naturally vivacious and a highly polished persona that reflected her craft. The self-consciousness that Atkinson detected was the unresolved tension between her personality and her technique. Thus, what one critic might call craft, another would consider artifice. Eventually, Claudette learned to bring these two aspects of her art into harmony after being cast in run-of-the-mill films that required her to work doubly hard to convince audiences that what they were watching was worth their time; it was even more difficult when the passivity of her male costars threatened to undermine her efforts, forcing her into overdrive to achieve some semblance of truth. If she exhibited the same ease in both boilerplate movies and classics, it is because she had mastered the principle underlying every art: *ars artem celare* (it is an art to conceal an art).

While filming *The Hole in the Wall*, Claudette had not decided to "go Hollywood"; she was convinced that as long as movies were being shot in Astoria, she could enjoy the best of both worlds. Between stage plays she could make movies; in fact, she could even make them while starring in a play, thereby earning two salaries.

Claudette was free between the time *Dynamo* closed and rehearsals began for *See Naples and Die*. When Paramount beckoned with *The Lady Lies* (1929), with Walter Huston as the male lead, Claudette did not hesitate. She would draw the equivalent of a double salary, since she would reprise her role in the French version, *Une femme a menti*, which would be filmed simultaneously with a French-speaking cast. It is interesting that Monta Bell, Astoria's head of production, considered her a dramatic actress. Most of the films she made at Astoria between 1929 and 1932 were melodramas. That changed after she made *It Happened One Night* (1934), in which she emerged as a full-fledged comedienne. That was the Claudette Colbert the public preferred, and while she alternated between comedy and drama, the comedies were the ones that endeared her to audiences.

She did not have a chance to look glamorous in *Hole*, but in *The Lady Lies* she is a fashion statement as Joyce Roamer, a salesperson (or maybe even part owner) of a fashionable dress shop, who becomes the lover of Robert Rossiter (Walter Huston), a widower with two pre-adolescent children. The couple seems headed toward marriage until Rossiter's self-righteous children discover that their father has taken up with a woman who is not one of them (that is, Boston bluebloods). Apparently, they are not savvy enough to realize Joyce is their father's mistress. The son deceives Joyce into believing that his father has had a serious accident. When she comes to his house, the children accuse her of being socially unworthy of their Brahmin father. Joyce does not exactly tell them where to go, but she comes close. However, father knows best, the kids apologize, and the two legalize their union.

Except for an awkward close-up, in which she had to register concern that her face did not convey, Claudette seemed genuinely at home with the camera. Soon she would even be able to provide a close-up that was in character. Periodically, there were announcements in the press about a possible return to the stage:

> Providing she does not permit her stage activities to interfere with those of her screen contract, Claudette Colbert, who was last seen in "The Lady Lies" and who will appear shortly opposite Maurice Chevalier in "The Big Pond," may return to the footlights occasionally. (*New York Times*, 2 February 1930)

> [A. H.] Woods hopes to bring several of his former stars back to the stage from the talking pictures next season. Among them [are] . . . Lowell Sherman, Ann Harding, Claudette Colbert and Chester Morris. (*New York Times*, 29 May 1930)

But there would be no occasional returns to the footlights. Claudette would not be back on Broadway for a quarter of a century.

Claudette could never have become the star that she did if she had signed with any other studio. Paramount was the most Continental—as opposed to European—of the "Big Five," the others being MGM, Twentieth Century-Fox, RKO, and Warner Bros. In the 1930s, all the studios made some films with a European setting, but none of them could compete with Paramount in sophistication and urbanity. The reason lay primarily with Paramount's founder, Adolph Zukor, who traveled regularly to Europe, not just for pleasure but with an eye for recruiting new talent. Zukor was especially fond of Paris. While the other studios had a "New York" or "Chicago" street on their back lot, Paramount had a Paris street with quaint alleyways, bistros, and nightclubs. Whenever an interior was needed—a salon, a suite, and, especially, a bedroom—it was a vision in white, luminous and silvery, courtesy of art director Hans Dreier, who gave the studio its distinctive visual style, known as "the white look": "Decor in a Paramount production was seldom . . . merely a background; settings, draperies, gowns insinuated themselves into the action, guiding and occasionally dictating the feel of a film. . . . Paramount's was the cinema of high-light and suggestion; witty, intelligent and faintly corrupt."

There was Paris, France, and there was Paris-Paramount. Cole Porter's song from *Fifty Million Frenchmen*, "You Don't Know Paree," expressed the difference in a single verse: "You may know Paris, you don't know Paree." Paramount's Paris was the closest any studio ever came to Porter's Paree—the essence of the city distilled into a state of mind for those who knew it, and into a myth for those who didn't. It was a Paris that even moviegoers who had never visited the city could appreciate; for seasoned travelers, Paramount's Paree was the evocation of the city's soul, which can never be seen but only experienced, and its mysteries, which can never be solved but only encountered.

If there was any actor at Paramount in the 1930s who embodied Paree, it was Maurice Chevalier. In his autobiography, Zukor called Chevalier "one of the greatest showmen of his time." Zukor had known Chevalier long before he brought him to Paramount. What particularly impressed Zukor about Chevalier was his great rapport with audiences. When he winked at them or cast a knowing glance in their direction, he turned a generic look into a calling card. Zukor prized his friendship with Chevalier; theirs was "a tie of men who have spent half a century in show business, in addition to a long personal friendship."

When Zukor decided that Chevalier should star in *The Big Pond* (1930), it was obvious that his name would be above the title and Claudette's below.

Claudette was not at that stage in her career where she could object. Chevalier was an international star; she would be one, too, but not in 1930. Claudette was cast as Barbara Billings, the spoiled daughter of an American chewing-gum manufacturer. The role could have been played by any ingénue, except that in 1930 Paramount had a paucity of them. But since Claudette and Chevalier both hailed from France, Zukor thought Paramount had a romantic duo—short-lived, as it happened—who could also reprise their roles in the French-language version, *La grande mare*, which was filmed simultaneously. When *La grande mare* opened at the Fifty-fifth Street Playhouse in New York in mid August 1930, it drew large numbers of Francophiles and French-speaking moviegoers.

In the 1930s, any actress playing opposite Chevalier needed an operatic or operetta-trained voice to complement his boulevardier's style. With the seductive gleam in his eye and a beckoning voice that played with the lyrics, coating the most innocent words with a veneer of worldliness, Chevalier needed someone like Jeanette MacDonald, who would not settle for being a costar but expected to be a musical partner. A lyric soprano, MacDonald sang in a radically different but still complementary style, whose coquetry belied her innocence. Chevalier needed that musical tension between virginal warbling and heartfelt yearning to go into his "man-of-the-world" act, making it easy for MacDonald's character to shed her virginity as readily as she would a cumbersome garment. When MacDonald appeared opposite Chevalier in *The Love Parade* (1929), *One Hour with You* (1932), and *Love Me Tonight* (1932), she at least had her share of the songs; in *The Big Pond* Claudette was only given the opportunity to hum a few bars of "You Brought a New Kind of Love to Me" with Chevalier, who had appropriated the number.

The entire plot revolves upon Chevalier's character, Pierre, a jack-of-all-trades who emigrates to America, where he gets a crash course in capitalism by working in Billings's chewing-gum factory. A series of humiliations that would have sent any newcomer packing does not faze Pierre any more than it would have fazed the equally jovial Chevalier. Disillusioned with Pierre for not just embracing the American dream but living it as well, Barbara admits that she preferred the gigolo to the capitalist, sounding like a wealthy liberal who can afford to be critical of the American dream because she has the real thing.

Pierre discovers that the best way to market chewing gum during Prohibition is to flavor it with the essence of scotch, rye, and champagne, arguing that alcohol-enhanced gum would cut down on bootlegging. Since *The Big Pond* was both a satire on Prohibition and a tribute to capitalism, it raised no hackles. How could it with the debonair Chevalier wooing his public with "You Brought a New Kind of Love to Me" and "Living in the Sunlight?"

Whatever form *The Big Pond* had came from Preston Sturges, who later provided Claudette with one of her best roles in *The Palm Beach Story* (1942). Since Sturges had scored a huge success on Broadway with *Strictly Dishonorable* (1929), Paramount hired him at one thousand dollars a week to write a script for *The Big Pond*, which he completed in two weeks, although he was expected to take ten. Sturges had learned his lesson; the next time he took a full ten weeks.

Sturges expected sole credit for *The Big Pond*, not knowing that other writers had been assigned to the same project, each unaware of the other's identity—the goal being the best possible script to be gleaned from the efforts of the best possible writers. Thus, Sturges had no idea that Robert Presnell and Garrett Fort were also working on *The Big Pond*, or that Paramount would distinguish between scenario and dialogue, with Presnell and Fort receiving scenario credit; and Presnell and Sturges, dialogue credit.

James Ursini, who has analyzed Sturges's script of *The Big Pond*, credits him with "rewriting most of the dialogue," making "basic changes in structure, characterization, and plot," and fashioning the narrative along the lines of *Strictly Dishonorable*, in which an Italian opera star proves the right match for a southern belle, rather than her provincial fiancé from New Jersey. Similarly, in *The Big Pond* Pierre wins Barbara's affections, not the colorless Ronnie from America.

Claudette proved to be one of Paramount's most versatile stars, but not just because she could play a wide range of roles. She also embodied Paree, but in a different way. Claudette could invest films not even set in Paris with an aura of sophistication, making them seem wittier and more literate than they really were; or if they were melodramas, less contrived . She was also bilingual; and as long as Paramount was making films in French for the European market, she was willing to serve her studio—for a price, of course. Claudette's reasoning was simple: the more specialized the skill, the greater the compensation.

In February 1930, Paramount released *Slightly Scarlet*, with Clive Brooks and Evelyn Brent as a pair of jewel thieves. Believing that the film had potential abroad, the studio gave the French version a more provocative title, *L'Énigmatique Monsieur Parkes*, starring Claudette and Adolphe Menjou, who was born in Pittsburgh but spoke fluent French. Menjou played the title character; Claudette, an American masquerading as a countess but really in the employ of a Russian gangster who expects her to steal a pearl necklace, not knowing that Menjou has similar intentions. Naturally, the two thieves fall in love, and once Menjou succeeds in ridding the world of the Russian, much to the relief of the French police, the two apparently have enough money to retire from a life of crime.

Monsieur Parkes opened on 2 September 1930 at the Fifty-fifth Street Playhouse, two blocks from Carnegie Hall; the playhouse lacked a fancy marquee and a marble-columned lobby, but it played home for two decades to foreign-language films, many of them classics, and some, like *Monsieur Parkes*, that fell short of the mark but still deserved to be seen.

For Claudette, working at Paramount was like working for A. H. Woods, who sent her on tour to learn her craft. Claudette had a work ethic when she became Woods's client; by the time she was on her own, the ethic had become a philosophy. Claudette was a quick study; she learned film acting in the same way she learned stage acting: by doing it. Claudette had no sooner finished *The Hole in the Wall* than she was tagged for *The Lady Lies*, which was filmed simultaneously in French and premiered eight months later in December 1929. Then came *Young Man from Manhattan*, which reached the theaters in mid April 1930; *The Big Pond*, released the following month, was followed by *Manslaughter* in July and *Monsieur Parkes* four months later. In 1930, four Claudette Colbert films were in the theaters in both the United States and Europe; in 1931 it was the same.

Even before *The Big Pond* reached the screen, Paramount squeezed in *Young Man of Manhattan*, which paired Claudette with her then husband, Norman Foster. Although they performed creditably, they were handicapped by the direction of Monta Bell, whose pace was nonexistent. Only newsreel footage of a boxing match and baseball game provided some momentum. *Young Man* is a romantic melodrama, in which Ann Vaughn (Claudette), a successful columnist, and Toby McLean (Foster), a sports writer, are enjoying the first months of what seems to be an idyllic marriage until their careers diverge, with hers surpassing his. Jealous of her success, Toby takes up with Puff (Ginger Rogers in her feature film debut), whose signature line is "Cigarette me, big boy." The couple becomes reconciled only after Ann nearly goes blind from bathtub booze that Toby has brought home. Ann recovers, and Tony sells a story, regaining his self-esteem.

In real life it was different. Claudette and Foster divorced in 1935. She went on to become a screen icon; he made a few more films before turning to directing.

Manslaughter was one of Claudette's weaker films. However, it should not have been. The screenwriter-director was George Abbott, a recruit from Broadway, where he became so revered that he was addressed as "Mr. Abbott." Abbott received $42,000 for his work ($32,000 for direction and $10,000 for his contribution to the script). Claudette made $13,750; her costar, Fredric March, another stage personality, made $4,639. The total cost of the film was $295,000.

Abbott was a great stage director. He had an extraordinary sense of pace, as he revealed in such classic musicals as *Wonderful Town*, *The Pajama Game*, and *Damn Yankees*. Admittedly, these shows came later in his career. But even at the beginning he was known for his ability to keep the action from flagging. However, during the early part of *Manslaughter* the pace is languid. When it picks up, it is because of an avoidable tragedy that makes it extremely difficult to sympathize with the one who caused it—Lydia Thorne (Claudette), an heiress, so accustomed to exceeding speed limits that she inadvertently causes a traffic cop's death.

The district attorney, Dan O'Bannon (March), is infatuated with Lydia, even though he knows she cannot be acquitted. O'Bannon had a genuine affection for Lydia, as well as a sexual curiosity about her (as March did about Claudette). Lydia is also attracted to him, until she realizes that she would have to mend her ways if they married. Expecting O'Bannon to be compassionate, Lydia is so taken aback by his integrity, which she interprets as indifference, that she stoically accepts her sentence.

Of all the films that make up the women's prison genre, *Manslaughter* ranks as the most humane: there are no sadistic matrons or lowlifes, but rather a motherly figure who treats her wards as if she were a high school principal and they, truants. Lydia's humiliation consists of scrubbing floors and wearing prison garb that looks like a rain coat. Eventually, her lawyer manages to get enough signatures on a petition—including March's—to secure a pardon. Like Jean in *The Hole in the Wall*, Lydia seeks revenge, yet when she has a chance to have O'Bannon fired from his law firm, she refuses, for no reason other than *Manslaughter* was predestined for a happy ending, with Lydia lamenting what she had done as O'Bannon looks on sympathetically.

In his autobiography Abbott called *Manslaughter* "the best picture I made because it had the most believable story." Any credibility came from the performances, not from the script or the direction. Abbott's forte was the musical. To the movie versions of *The Pajama Game* (1957) and *Damn Yankees* (1958), he brought the same dynamism and the same fluidity that the shows had on Broadway. *Manslaughter* needed that kind of dynamism, but Abbott, a movie novice, could not supply it, at least not in 1930.

In 1930, Dorothy Arzner, often referred to by the press as a "woman picture director" because women rarely went behind the camera, had already made seven films for Paramount—eight, if one counts her contribution to the anthology movie, *Paramount on Parade*—when the studio dispatched her to Astoria for what was to have been called "Sex in Business" until the Production Code Administration, relatively lenient in 1931, intervened. The title became *Honor among Lovers* (1931), the next pairing of Claudette and March. Although Astoria's assembly-line approach to moviemaking was alien to Arzner, she did what she could with a script that expected the actors to reverse their characterization for the sake of a plot twist, on the assumption that if it could be done convincingly, the audience would accept the turnaround without asking "why?"

Paramount was banking on the growing popularity of Claudette and March. He played Jerry Stafford, a Wall Street executive; Claudette was Julia, his secretary, with whom he has a more than employer-employee relationship. Suspecting that Stafford is not the monogamous type, Julia marries Philip Craig (Monroe Owsley), the junior member of a brokerage firm, not realizing that he is emotionally unstable. After Stafford discovers Julia is married, he fires her; to prove he is not a complete cad, he offers Philip his account, which Philip uses to finance a get-rich-quick scheme. In a thoroughly ludicrous scene, Philip, convinced Stafford has slept with Julia, confronts him with a pistol, which accidentally discharges, wounding Stafford and revealing Philip as a craven neurotic. To absolve himself, Philip implicates Julia. Fortunately, the truth comes out, and Stafford and Julia leave for the south of France, without a marriage certificate, which would not have raised eyebrows in 1931. *Honor* is a pre-Code film, made before the enforcement of the Production Code in 1934; if it were made three years later, the Production Code Administration (PCA) would have insisted that their union be legalized, as if the inclusion of a marriage ceremony would have deterred anyone from engaging in pre-marital sex.

Arzner did what she could with the material, but her direction could not redeem a tabloid melodrama with so many plot twists that when the narrative cord was completely knotted, unraveling was impossible. Bring down the god from the machine, so true love can triumph. Claudette never made another picture with Arzner. Such was the fate of the "woman picture director," who also worked with Sylvia Sidney, Katharine Hepburn, Rosalind Russell, Joan Crawford, Maureen O'Hara, Lucille Ball, and Merle Oberon—but only once.

Nineteen thirty-one was another whirlwind year for Claudette. *Honor* was released in late February 1931, followed by *The Smiling Lieutenant* in July, *Secrets of a Secretary* in September, and *His Woman* in November. Taken together, the films trace Claudette's progress from woman-as-victim to woman-as-martyr, with a detour into woman with a checkered past.

In *His Woman* Claudette is an ex-hooker recruited by skipper Gary Cooper to look after an abandoned baby girl that he has taken on board. Claudette had another opportunity to manifest her maternalism in her scenes with the child. Eventually, Cooper discovers Claudette's past. He does not lash out at her as Joe did at Anna in Eugene O'Neill's *Anna Christie* when she divulges the truth about her sordid past. Instead, Cooper tosses her to his first mate, one of her former customers at a Caribbean brothel. Just as *Anna Christie* should have ended on a less optimistic note (if a man calls his intended a slut, maybe she should terminate the relationship), *My Woman* should have ended with Claudette's walking into the night. Yet despite her abuse at the hands of Cooper and the other males, the two of them end up together—and baby makes three. Cooper does not apologize for his ungentlemanly behavior; he merely shows Claudette a copy of a wire that he sent to a minister to arrange for a wedding. That Claudette has not consented is immaterial. What Hollywood proposes, man disposes.

Suffering for one's past is bad enough; worse is jeopardizing one's future for someone unworthy of it. Yet that is precisely what Helen Blake (Claudette) does in *Secrets of a Secretary*. Helen, a social secretary, agrees to take the rap for a murder she did not commit. Her employer's daughter, Sylvia (Betty Lawford), is betrothed to Lord Danforth (Herbert Marshall) but romantically involved with a gigolo, who happens to be Helen's estranged husband. When the gigolo is murdered, Helen comes to Sylvia's aid, although she has no reason to do so—except that she is secretly in love with Lord Danforth herself; and he, with her.

Secrets of a Secretary was Claudette's second film with George Abbott, who was now more familiar with the way stories are told on the screen. *Secrets* is rather tame for a pre-Code movie, yet it also illustrates Hollywood's distinction between the noble and ignoble male. The latter is a gigolo whom Helen marries on a whim; when her father's death leaves her penniless, her husband excoriates her, as if the loss of the inheritance was her fault. Forced to find work, her gigolo-husband winds up in a club where he is expected to fleece rich women.

Sylvia flaunts convention by resuming her affair with the gigolo despite her engagement to Lord Danforth. She also happens to be in her lover's room when he is murdered for failing to turn over stolen jewelry to his boss. The thoroughly implausible climax has Helen willing to risk imprisonment so that Sylvia will not be implicated. In the rushed denouement, Danforth discovers the truth, Sylvia goes on a trip with her parents, and Helen and Danforth are left to find whatever happiness there can be between a secretary and a titled Brit. No one can make a case for *His Woman* or *Secrets of a Secretary* as major woman's films, yet each, in its own way, illustrates how 1930s women were expected to view themselves and, more important, how men, convinced of their superiority, viewed women. When a man discovers his wife is not the heiress he thought she was, he dumps her and prostitutes himself to enjoy the life that he expected her fortune to provide. Lord Danforth is at least a gentleman, not to mention a good amateur sleuth. But Claudette was saddled with another role that placed her character in the debt of a man, whom she loved so much that she was willing to help his fiancée out of a tight spot, knowing full well that her magnanimity would never be reciprocated, much less acknowledged.

Claudette was on her way to becoming the other woman, either the one whom her lover chooses over a member of the privileged class, or the one who relinquishes her lover to a member of the privileged class. Usually, in operetta, the prince and the proletarian have nothing in common except their love for each other, like the barmaid and the heir apparent in Sigmund Romberg's *The Student Prince*, in which class distinctions that seemed on the verge of receding suddenly resurface, dispelling any hope of a happily-ever-after ending.

This should not have been the case in *The Smiling Lieutenant*, the first of two films Claudette made with the Berlin-born Ernst Lubitsch, known for "the Lubitsch touch," which is one of those phrases more easily described than defined. It was cinematic deftness, a graceful turn of the hand that banished orgasmic sighs and moans from the bedroom, driving them under the bed, where they would not be heard, and leaving in their place pure, sweat-less lovemaking that was even sexier in its transfigured state after receiving the Lubitsch imprint. Love was a game, whose rules were based solely on decorum: no rumpled sheets the night after, but only a perfectly made-up bed. Sex was a bedroom door that closed by itself or a camera slowly exiting a bedroom. For Lubitsch, double entendre was not the art of equivocation but the art of ambivalence with bifurcating dialogue: one level of meaning for those who understand innuendo, another for those who do not.

In Lubitsch's *One Night with You* (1932), Maurice Chevalier and Jeanette MacDonald are petting on a park bench when a gendarme strolls by and tells them they cannot make love in the park. Chevalier replies, "I can make love anywhere," to which MacDonald retorts, "And he can." In *Cluny Brown* (1946), Jennifer Jones, arriving at Reginald Gardiner's apartment to unclog a sink, asks enthusiastically, "Shall we have a go at it?" When Gardiner observes that she isn't dressed for plumbing, Charles Boyer replies, "What woman is?" There is nothing ear-burning about the dialogue, but what a wealth of innuendo in such deceptively simple sentences!

Even when Lubitsch was making a romantic comedy such as *The Shop around the Corner* (1940), in which a bedroom was just a place for sleeping, he was almost reverential in his handling of young love. In *Shop*, Lubitsch's least sexual film, the touch is a gentle push that guides his lovers—anonymous pen pals, unaware that they work in the same shop, where they are more antagonistic than collegial—along the path of mutual discovery. If eyes moisten at the end of *The Shop around the Corner*, it is because Lubitsch has restored an otherwise problematic relationship to wholeness, so that lovers at odds with each other can acknowledge their folly and embrace at the fade-out, which, in this case, happens to be on Christmas Eve.

The Smiling Lieutenant was the flip side of *The Student Prince* in terms of class consciousness, at least at the beginning. Why shouldn't Franzi (Claudette), a violinist in an all-female orchestra, and Niki (Maurice Chevalier), a Viennese lieutenant, find happiness together, since neither came from royalty? The reason they can't is that the visiting Princess Anna (Miriam Hopkins) assumed that Niki was smiling at her while he was really smiling at Franzi. Anna is shocked by what she thinks is familiarity until she meets Niki, whom she finds so irresistible that she has her father arrange for their marriage. Although Niki and Franzi are lovers, Niki is too weak to reject the princess and instead finds himself trapped in a marriage that he has no intention of consummating. Lubitsch applies his delicate touch to the wedding night ceremony, in which the servants debate the placement of the satin pillows, until one of them puts them on top of each other.

Will Niki reject Anna for Franzi or marry Anna and continue his affair with Franzi? When Anna summons Franzi to the palace, presumably to humiliate her, but really to learn why Niki seems so aloof, Franzi sizes her up and commands, "Show me your underwear." In the twenty-first century, such an order would send critics scurrying to find a lesbianic sub-text; in the 1930s, it may have raised a few eyebrows, but none from the Production Code commissars, who probably thought that women regularly compared their undergarments. Anna obliges, and Franzi contrasts her lacy lingerie with Anna's bland undies—the cue for the musical number (there are several) "Jazz Up Your Lingerie." Anna does, morphing into a flapper and becoming more desirable to Niki than she had been before. And Franzi returns to her orchestra.

Claudette was extremely touching, even magnanimous, in her scene with Hopkins when she turns Anna from a pouting princess into a desirable woman. But by this time, Claudette had learned the art of muted suffering, reflecting her loss in her eyes but never letting a lost love get her down. *The Smiling Lieutenant* was the closest Claudette ever came to a musical. Despite early publicity releases claiming that she wanted to be an opera singer (her mother's dream, not hers), her voice was not big enough: opera, no; operetta, perhaps, but only for a time; comedy, always.

Frank Capra seems to have originated the story that in the hitchhiking scene in *It Happened One Night*, Claudette refused to lift her skirt to stop a car, preferring to get by on talent, not anatomy; and when she saw a shot of her stand-in's leg, she insisted that hers was better, demanding to do the scene herself and thus revealing one of the shapeliest limbs in movies. In *The Smiling Lieutenant*, when Franzi realizes her relationship with Niki is about to end, she removes one of her garters, which she places on her "It was lovely until the end" farewell note. The camera not only records the removal of the garter but also provides a far-from-fleeting glimpse of a leg that most women would envy. It is difficult to imagine that three years later, when Claudette was making *It Happened One Night*, she could have turned so prudish. Claudette never verified Capra's version of the story; she only said that that may have been the way he remembered it, implying that it had receded into the mists of myth.

In "Jazz Up Your Lingerie" Claudette revealed such joyful abandon, as she pounded away at the piano, infecting the uptight princess with her refreshingly healthy approach to the fetishistic appeal of underwear, that for the first time we saw a quality in her that only the camera could reveal: her unapologetic joy in living, always restrained in the interests of decorum; but given the chance to cascade, it flowed across the screen in waves of giddy delight. The way Claudette and Hopkins launched into the number made it clear that the princess had shed her inhibitions and learned that the way to Niki's heart was through her knickers—but only if they were lace-trimmed.

The three principals repeated their roles in the French-language version, which, when it opened in Paris in winter 1932, was warmly received. The revelation was Miriam Hopkins, the Georgia-born actress who spoke elegant French.

The Smiling Lieutenant came close to being a classic; she would not appear in another classic until *The Sign of the Cross*. Her other 1932 films— *The Wiser Sex, The Misleading Lady, The Man from Yesterday, Make Me a Star* (in which she only made an appearance), and *The Phantom President*—were not embarrassments, but also did not enhance her reputation as an actress. Claudette had discovered that the rhythm of a movie career is as erratic as one in the theatre: a high followed by a low; a classic, by a potboiler, or worse, a mediocrity.

Since Claudette was one of Paramount's stage-trained actresses, she fitted in with the studio's policy of purchasing the rights to minor stage plays at minimal costs. *The Wiser Sex*, which was based on Clyde Fitch's 1905 melodrama, *The Woman in the Case*, finished production at Astoria in mid February and was released a month later. For an assembly-line product, *The Wiser Sex*, as the title implies, was at least not demeaning to women. When Margaret Hughes's (Claudette) fiancé, a crusading district attorney (Melvyn Douglas), is framed for murder by his ex-lover, Margaret poses as a woman of dubious virtue (not unlike the ex-lover) and manages to clear him, thus validating the film's title.

Less than a month after *The Wiser Sex* opened, *The Misleading Lady* (1932) had a dual premiere at Paramount's flagship theater in Times Square and the Brooklyn Paramount. *Lady* was not only a minor play, but also a forgettable film. However, within the context of pre-Code Hollywood, it offered such a graphic portrait of a woman's brutalization that one could almost understand if female audiences winced, or even gasped, at what they saw. Determined to snare the lead in a Broadway play, Helen Steele (Claudette) makes a deal with the producer: if she can get his friend, Jack Craigen (Edmund Loew), to propose marriage within three days, the part will be hers. Knowing that Craigen is infatuated with her, Helen records his proposal on a disk, which accidentally gets played in his presence. Rather than behave like Alfredo in *La Traviata* and denounce Helen in public, Craigen kidnaps her and brings her to a cabin, where he tells her to undress. The context is important; it is winter, and Helen is wearing an evening gown.

She assumes the worst when he starts removing her clothes forcibly, telling her to take off the rest, which she does in silhouette. Craigen begins to remove his jacket, and just as the scene seems to be heading toward rape, he throws her some clothes. So the kidnapper turns out to be a gentleman, who is only giving Helen her comeuppance. How a woman could have melted in the arms of a man who might have said that all he wanted to do was offer her warm clothes, but who behaved instead like a potential rapist, is even more incredible than the news that Helen has the lead in the show.

On 10 March 1932, the Astoria studio suspended production. Although the press erroneously reported that *The Misleading Lady* was the studio's last film, *The Big Broadcast* of 1932 was also filmed there, but only because some of the radio stars (Kate Smith, the Mills Brothers, Cab Calloway) could not travel to the West Coast. Later in the decade, *The Emperor Jones* (1933), *International House* (1933) and *Crime without Passion* (1934) were also shot there, as were army training films during World War II.

By the time *The Misleading Lady* opened, Claudette was in Los Angeles. No longer would she be commuting to work. Her studio was the Paramount on Melrose Avenue in Hollywood, not on Astoria Boulevard in Queens. Crossing the Atlantic at three, and emigrating at eight, Claudette was prepared for her next relocation. She was a movie star, and the stars were no longer shining across the Queensboro Bridge. She departed for Los Angeles, knowing that one phase of her life was over. But an even more glorious one was ahead.

CHAPTER 4

"Ready When You Are, C. B."

As soon as *The Misleading Lady* wound up production, Claudette started packing for Los Angeles. Since there was no more work for her at Astoria, the alternative was returning to the theatre. In 1932, however, she felt that she was no longer a stage actress, but rather an actress who could bring the essence of theatre to the screen. Besides, she was under contract to Paramount, which expected her to be on board for her next film, *The Man from Yesterday*, scheduled for a late June release. Marie Augustine was at Grand Central Station when Claudette and her mother boarded the Twentieth Century Limited for Los Angeles. It was an emotional departure; Marie Augustine was in her mid eighties, and while the Loews enjoyed length of years, Claudette wondered when, or if, she would ever see her grandmother again. She never did. Marie Augustine died a few years later. Claudette went through the normal course of grieving, but at least she knew that she had lived up to her grandmother's expectations. Now she had to prove herself in Hollywood, where the competition was fiercer than it had been at Astoria, where she reigned supreme. Claudette had little to fear; after acting for nine years on both stage and screen, she was secure in her craft. What Claudette really had to learn was the layout of the Paramount back lot and the geography of Los Angeles. She mastered both. The pace was no different than it had been at Astoria, except that this time she was at the home studio, not the annex. But it was the same inexorable rhythm: exit one film, enter another.

Foster did not travel with her, not because of their "modern marriage" (which was gradually turning postmodern), but because his first and only play, *Savage Rhythm*, was set to open at the Golden on 31 December 1931. Before he became an actor, Foster had been a reporter for the Richmond, Indiana, *Palladium* and never lost his love of the written word. When he came to New York in the early 1920s, there was a discernible African American presence on Broadway, offering an alternative form of theatre to audiences whose only knowledge of black entertainment came from the minstrel show. In the 1920s, black performers dispelled the racial stereotypes of the minstrel show by singing and dancing to music that reflected their own idiom, which Broadway audiences discovered in the *Blackbird* revues; Eubie Blake and Noble Sissle's *Shuffle Along* (1921), which ran for almost two years and featured the then unknown Paul Robeson and Josephine Baker; and *Running Wild* (1923), which introduced the Charleston. Jerome Kern and Oscar Hammerstein's *Show Boat* (1927), which dealt more openly with race than any other musical had, gave Jules Bledsoe, who created the role of Joe (which Paul Robeson played in the London production), the classic "Ol' Man River." In the same season as *Show Boat*, the Theatre Guild's production of Dubose Heyward's *Porgy*, which inspired George Gershwin's folk opera, *Porgy and Bess*, opened for a run of 367 performances.

Foster was not just another white liberal turned ethnographer-playwright, eager to capitalize on the latest craze. In between films, he and his collaborator Harry Hamilton traveled through the South, where they came upon communities in which Christian ritual was mingled with voodoo, black magic, and spirit worship, and where conjuring, rather than the law, determined guilt or innocence. Foster and Hamilton were eager to dramatize a world unknown to Broadway, using an all-black cast. Neither audiences nor critics appreciated their efforts, and *Savage Rhythm* closed after a disheartening twelve performances, marking the end of Foster's Broadway career. But he had an even better one awaiting him in Los Angeles.

Foster began in Astoria at the same time as Claudette and worked at the same pace. He was not hired on the strength of Claudette's name; he had his own set of favorable notices which, combined with his looks, made him readily employable. Like Claudette, Foster made his film debut in 1929; the film was *Gentlemen of the Press,* starring Walter Huston, who had played his father in *The Barker.* In his only movie with Claudette, *Young Man from Manhattan,* Foster came off better than she: "Norman Foster emerges . . . as an unaffected, genuine player whose naturalness before the cameras makes his an outstanding performance. Claudette Colbert, in comparison with Mr. Foster's easy playing, is given, sometimes, to overacting."

He later appeared with actresses on the threshold of major careers, such as Carole Lombard in *Up Pops the Devil* (1931), Loretta Young (whose sister, Sally Blane, he later married) in *Play-Girl* and *Week-End Marriage* (both 1932), Maureen O'Sullivan in *Skyscraper Souls* (1932) and *The Bishop Misbehaves* (1935), Sylvia Sidney in *Confessions of a Co-Ed* (1931), and Claire Trevor in *Elinor Norton* (1934).

Astoria prepared Foster for Hollywood, the chief difference being that the carousel had replaced the revolving door. It was a steady round of movies: ten releases in 1932 (a few of which were shot in Astoria); five in 1933, three in 1934, nine in 1935, and five in 1936. Then it was on to a new career, the one for which he will be remembered: movie director. Between 1929 and 1936, Foster appeared in forty-two films; Claudette, in twenty-nine. There was, however, a major difference; Foster was often cast in supporting roles that only required four or five days of shooting. Claudette played leads. Some of the films she made during that period became part of film history (e.g, *The Sign of the Cross, Cleopatra, It Happened One Night, Imitation of Life*); none of Foster's did, except perhaps *State Fair* (1933), in which he was eclipsed by Will Rogers and, especially, Janet Gaynor.

In Hollywood, Foster and Claudette soon realized that living apart brought them further apart. Their marriage had become an arrangement— a necessary one because Jeanne Chauchoin would never consent to Foster's living with them. And with Claudette's career in the ascendent and his earthbound, the arrangement continued until 1935, ending, as one might expect, in divorce.

Meanwhile, Claudette was looking for a suitable home for herself, her mother, and Tantine. Until she found one, the three of them stayed at the Alto Nido Apartments, a favorite residence for movie people (William Holden's character Joe Gillis, in *Sunset Boulevard*, lived there) on North Ivar, a little over three miles from the studio. Later, they moved to a house on North Rockingham Avenue in Brentwood. Marie Augustine's death at eighty-eight had reduced the quartet to a trio: Claudette was still *l'actrice* and bread winner; Jeanne was *Madame*; and Tantine was Claudette's friend, confidante, and surrogate mother—roles Tantine played until her death in 1954. Claudette had become so accustomed to her mother's imperiousness that she ignored it, even though at times she found her ingratitude and indifference to her success demoralizing. But there were more pressing matters: the quest for a role that would enshrine her in the film pantheon. That would happen when she caught the attention of Cecil B. DeMille.

Her first Hollywood film, *The Man from Yesterday* (1932), set during World War I, had some strikingly authentic battle scenes that almost made up for the soggy plot. Sylvia (Claudette) is pregnant when she receives news that her husband (Clive Brook) has been killed in action. René Gaudin (Charles Boyer), a surgeon, befriends her, and the inevitable occurs: they fall in love and take off for Switzerland, where Sylvia's husband, very much alive but terminally ill, spots them. Despite her attraction to Gaudin, Sylvia feels obliged to resume her role as wife. Her husband could care less, having grown so self-destructive (smoking and drinking despite doctor's orders) that his death wish is granted.

Claudette's scenes with fellow countryman Boyer had a real intimacy, unlike those with Brook, who played the character with such frigid aloofness that one wondered what Sylvia ever saw in him. Apparently, so did the screen writers, who had their marriage take place at the beginning of the film to avoid depicting their courtship. Claudette and Boyer would make two more films, the last in 1937, and two decades later costar on Broadway in *The Marriage Go-Round* (1959).

Jeanne Chauchoin was thoroughly taken with Boyer, but so were most of the women he encountered. With Boyer, who had the eyes of a clairvoyant and the smile of a seducer, it was never a question of his wanting to know a woman better, but vice versa. And Jeanne Chauchoin wanted to know the man better—the man she and Boyer's mother wanted Claudette to marry. Boyer was known to pinch an attractive derrière, as was Fredric March, whose hands had a libido of their own. But with Claudette, neither attempted any form of intimacy, unless the scene required it. It was not that Claudette discouraged familiarity; it was rather that she was in such control of her sexuality that she could channel it into her characters. Fredric March realized early in the *Manslaughter* shoot that Claudette had a rare combination of sensuality and propriety: "There was a tremendous, smouldering sensuality to her, and that kind of chemistry usually would make the average woman a wanton, . . . but Claudette had dignity and a sense of the fitness of things." "A sense of the fitness of things" is exactly what propriety is: behavior suited to the occasion.

But Claudette was not a prude. She did not mind an occasional prank. When she and Clark Gable were rehearsing a scene in *It Happened One Night*: "[Gable] put a hammer down the front of his pants and then pulled [Claudette] to him. When she let out a scream that brought everyone running, he took out the hammer and laughed so long that Capra had to call a second lunch break." If Gable signaled his availability, and Claudette was interested (and supposedly she was), she would indicate it. She may have played victimized women, but she was not one herself.

Although their mothers thought Claudette and Boyer would make a smashing couple, nothing came of their matchmaking efforts. Boyer had already found the right woman for himself: Pat Paterson, an English-born actress who enjoyed a brief career in Hollywood in the 1930s, receiving enough favorable reviews to impress any studio eager for new talent. But Paterson preferred to be the wife of Charles Boyer, whom she married in 1934. They remained together until she died of cancer in August 1978; two days later, Charles Boyer committed suicide.

Claudette's name did not appear in the credits for *Make Me a Star* (1932), Paramount's version of Marc Connelly and George S. Kaufman's *Merton of the Movies*; but then, neither did the names of Gary Cooper and Talullah Bankhead, who, along with Claudette, made fleeting appearances on the Paramount lot which doubled as Majestic Films in the movie. *Make Me a* Star takes a sympathetic view of a yokel's determination to become a movie star. Merton Gill (Stuart Erwin in an unusually touching performance) beats the odds, but at a price; imagining himself a dramatic actor, Merton is forced to confront the truth: his forte is comedy, and the westerns that he thought were serious were really parodies.

If Claudette had been able to pass on *The Phantom President* (1932), she would have. But as a contract player, she had no other choice but to be a member of the supporting cast in the film debut of George M. Cohan. The premise was promising: a political machine, planning to run a banker, Theodore K. Blair (Cohan), for president, discovers that he is completely uncharismatic. When they stumble upon a Blair look-alike, Peter Varney (Cohan again), a charlatan with his own traveling medicine show, they concoct a scheme to put Blair into the White House by using Varney to get the votes that Blair cannot. As the love interest courted by Blair/Varney, Claudette had little to do. She may have been the female lead, but there was really only one lead: Broadway showman George M. Cohan, whose enormous ego would not brook competition. Even Jimmy Durante, usually a scene stealer, found himself with nothing to steal. Varney wins Claudette, while Blair, who thought he could rid himself of Varney by having him shipped off to the North Pole, ends up there himself with a seal for a companion.

What the writers, Walter De Leon and Harlan Thompson, had hoped to create was a musical satire on the order of George Gershwin's *Of Thee I*

Sing, not so much in terms of plot but in topicality. But the pedestrian score by Richard Rodgers and Larry Hart, who may have thought the script was unworthy of their best efforts, was not in Gershwin's league. Cohan, a great performer as well as a megalomaniac, was never meant for the movies, nor was Claudette meant to languish in the shadows while another hogged the limelight.

Claudette's last 1932 film, *The Sign of the Cross*, brought her the kind of press that turns movie stars into icons, even though she did not have the leading role and, in fact, was third billed, receiving only fifteen thousand dollars, ten thousand dollars less than her usual salary. But she was in a Cecil B. DeMille production that more people saw than any of her other films that year.

The name of Cecil B. DeMille evokes a mixed reaction from those who know his work. To cynics, he was a purveyor of sex, who sanctified his fascination with the erotic by cloaking it under the trappings of religion and history. But it was not so much DeMille's fascination with the erotic as the public's, which his films only reflected. It may be hard to convince the skeptics, but DeMille was a religious man who believed that if sex sells religion, then the end justifies the means.

Religion was very much a part of his life, as it was his family's. One of his ancestors was a fifteenth-century abbot. The DeMilles eventually became Episcopalians after first having been Mennonites and then members of the Dutch Reformed Church. DeMille himself was a devout Episcopalian who happened to be a moviemaker and saw no contradiction between his religion and his profession. He did not consider himself part of the movie *industry*, a term reserved for scholars; he was in the movie *business*, which made him a businessman. But he was also a showman whose best—and least dated—film was *The Greatest Show on Earth* (1952), his tribute to circus life, which won a Best Picture Oscar. DeMille's philosophy was simple: "My profession is making motion pictures for popular entertainment." If the public wanted bedroom comedies, like *Old Wives for New* or *Don't Change Your Husband* (both 1918), so be it. They could no more be accused of encouraging promiscuity than Shakespeare's *Macbeth* of inspiring mass murder; or *Twelfth Night*, cross dressing. But when DeMille turned to religion, it was a different matter.

DeMille was raised in a family in which there was no conflict between the theatre and the Episcopal faith. His father, Henry Churchill DeMille, originally planned to become a priest but chose the stage instead, where he achieved a modicum of success as a playwright and itinerant actor. His brother, William, was also a playwright; his mother, Beatrice, opened her own talent agency, which soon became the DeMille Play Company, with Cecil as general manager. DeMille grew up in a theatrical environment where he was constantly in the presence of actors and producers; he toured cross country in plays and even did a bit of light opera. Show business was as natural to DeMille as it was to his parents and brother.

Around 1909, Jesse Lasky, a vaudevillian planning a career change and eager to find a librettist for *California*, a musical he was contemplating, sought out William DeMille, who declined. Sensing an opportunity for Cecil, Beatrice recommended her other son, who reluctantly agreed. DeMille and Lasky soon became great friends as well as associates when they decided to try the fledgling movie business. His friendship with Lasky led to his becoming part of the film company that became the forerunner of Paramount Pictures: the Jesse L. Lasky Feature Play Company, in which DeMille was director-general. The company would undergo other name changes—Famous Players-Lasky, Paramount-Famous-Lasky, Paramount-Publix—until it became Paramount Pictures and then, in 1950, Paramount Pictures Corporation.

At Paramount-Famous-Lasky, DeMille, no longer a general director, was simply the company's premier director, who by 1920 had his own production company, Cecil B. DeMille Productions—his bargaining chip if he ever had to leave the studio. That happened in 1924 when relations with Paramount's president, Adolph Zukor, became so strained, and the financial imbroglio over *The King of Kings* so exasperating, that he had no other choice but to leave. When MGM beckoned in 1929, DeMille made three films for the studio, including his first talkie, *Dynamite*.

DeMille felt very strongly about *The Sign of the Cross*, which he had seen as a stage play, and knew Paramount was the only studio where he could make the movie version his way. But he had to eat humble pie to return to Zukor's good graces, which meant bringing the film in on budget and adhering to an eight-week shooting schedule. He agreed; at least he was back at his home studio, where he remained for the rest of his career.

The Sign of the Cross, like *The Ten Commandments* and *The King of Kings*, had great personal meaning for DeMille. Set in first century Rome, during the reign of Nero, the film told the story of Marcus Superbus, a Roman prefect (Fredric March) who embraces Christianity when he realizes that his beloved Mercia (Elissa Landi) is so steadfast in her faith that she is willing to die for it, even if it means being torn apart by lions in the arena. Her faith inspires him to join her, and the film ends as the two mount the prison steps, a shaft of light illuminating their way and angelic music escorting them to their fate. The double doors of the prison close, revealing a luminous cross—a reminder of the film's title and all it represents.

The casting was almost complete. March and Landi would play the leads, with Charles Laughton as a delightfully epicene Nero. But DeMille lacked a Poppaea, the empress-wife of Nero. He was aware of Claudette, a regular on the Paramount lot; she intrigued him with her banked-down sensuality that could flare up, enkindling a scene of intimacy and leaving a residue of embers when passion was spent. Poppaea was really a supporting role (Claudette had a total of five scenes), but DeMille was determined to give her enough screen time to leave an impression. In his autobiography, DeMille described how he got her to play the part: " 'Claudette, how would you like to play the wickedest woman in the world?' " According to DeMille, Claudette did not hesitate: " 'I'd love it.' "

What Claudette did not love was the way her name was to appear in the credits. Although she knew she would have third billing after March and Landi, she insisted that "no other feminine player shall precede or appear in type larger than hers." But there was also a fourth name, Laughton's, which came after Claudette's. He wanted the same; thus, the main title read, "Cecil B. DeMille's *The Sign of the Cross* with Fredric March, Elissa Landi, Claudette Colbert, and Charles Laughton," with all the names in the same size lettering.

The Sign of the Cross was DeMille's most controversial film. Even before it went into production, B'nai B'rith wanted the script vetted by a rabbi, a request that DeMille politely ignored. However, he had one sent to a minister, Rev. Christian F. Reisner, who found it "cheap and disgusting," "suggestive and unclean," and was personally offended that Paramount had "such a cheap notion of him" that it assumed the film would receive his endorsement. There was no doubt that *The Sign of the Cross* could, and did, shock the bourgeoisie and that its excesses contributed to the enforcement of the Production Code and the creation of the Legion of Decency in 1934. DeMille made certain that his return to Paramount would generate the kind of buzz that would attract audiences, which Paramount needed to reduce its $15 million deficit. Although the film was a huge financial success, it could not banish the specter of bankruptcy that haunted Paramount throughout 1932. To avert such a catastrophe, a new board of directors with Wall Street connections was installed; and Zukor, relieved of the presidency, was relegated to board chairman.

The Sign of the Cross is an extraordinary example of an economically produced spectacle. Filming began on 24 July 1932 and ended eight weeks later; DeMille stayed within his $650,000 budget, and the film was ready for release on 30 November. DeMille was true to his word; he achieved decadence by seducing viewers with images of sumptuousness (bowls of burning incense, garlanded archways, imposing statuary, burnished pillars, curtained banquet rooms, orgy-friendly couches) and a world that looked vaster than the one recreated on Paramount's cramped soundstages. But clutter worked to the film's advantage. By filling the frame with all sorts of faux classic artifacts—or, as some might say, kitsch—DeMille gave audiences a Neronian Rome that conformed to their image of an age of surfeit without causing him to exceed his budget. To provide a respite from the surfeit, he carefully deployed his extras in the crowd scenes to evoke a more populous Rome than the one on Paramount's back lot.

The Sign of the Cross was shown uncut in New York, Pennsylvania, and, interestingly enough, Catholic Quebec, where the censors must have detected a core of spirituality beneath all the licentiousness, validating Claudette's claim that DeMille "really believed in what he was doing." Massachusetts wanted certain cuts for Sunday showings. What was deleted was minor compared to what was retained: Massachusetts preferred that Sunday moviegoers not see navels, cleavage, and Christians mangled by lions. In Mississippi, Poppaea's milk bath went by the boards. Initially, Ohio approved the film without cuts, until there was a hue and cry about the milk bath and an erotic dance. However, what bothered the Ohioans was not so much the dance, which is intrinsic to the plot, as its interruption by a chorus of Christians on their way to the arena. Ohioans considered the juxtaposition of the profane and the sacred sacrilegious. Actually, the scene was one of the film's few subtle moments and an excellent example of dramatic counterpoint. After Mercia has been dragged off to prison with the other Christians, Poppaea, who considers Mercia her rival, has her brought to the palace while an orgy is in progress. Learning of her whereabouts, Marcus tries to persuade Mercia to renounce her God, but to no avail. Frustrated, he turns Mercia over to the voluptuary Ancaria (Joyzelle), hoping that she will initiate Mercia into the pleasures of the flesh. Ancaria performs the "Naked Moon," singing and dancing suggestively around Mercia, fondling her but getting no response. Suddenly the singing of the Christians threatens to upstage Ancaria, forcing her to realize that she cannot compete with the sound of true believers. The juxtaposition of faith and debauchery, with the one drowning out the other, reinforces what was stated in the prologue: "The faith born then is still available."

Claudette enjoyed playing the oversexed Poppaea. The first time she appears on screen, she is luxuriating in a sunken pool of black marble supposedly filled with asses' milk, the empress's favorite form of bathing. DeMille achieved the same effect with powdered milk. However, shooting delays kept Claudette in the bath for so long that the milk curdled, leaving Claudette looking as if she had acquired a second layer of skin. Exactly what Claudette was wearing was left to the imagination. In 1979, she told the *New York Times* that she was "circumspectly attired in a white bathing suit." If so, the top part may have been flesh colored.

Although the milk bath sequence might have seemed an erotic diversion, it had a purpose. Poppaea is anxious to know why Marcus has neglected her. Her friend and source of gossip, Dacia (Vivian Tobin), drops by while Poppaea is treading water. "Take off your clothes," Poppaea orders, "and get in here and tell me all about it." Dacia complies; all one sees is a dress falling to the floor and a hand carefully removing each sandal. Anyone expecting more was disappointed.

The Sign of the Cross was reissued in 1944. Those who had never seen the original witnessed a slightly edited version with a contemporary prologue, in which two chaplains, one Catholic (Arthur Shields) and the other Protestant (Stanley Ridges), are flying over Rome near the end of World War II, eager for a look at the eternal city before the bombs start falling. The Catholic chaplain compares the men and women sacrificing their lives in the struggle against fascism with the early Christian martyrs. In the 1944 reissue, several of the controversial scenes were deleted, especially those in the overlong games sequence near the end, which may have been accurate but not always in the best of taste: for example, crocodiles slithering over to a girl suspended between two posts; a particularly gruesome combat with pygmies; and an ape lumbering over to a terrified young woman tied to a pillar, as the camera pans the spectators' reactions that range from glee to horror.

What mattered to Claudette was not that DeMille had a hit, his first since *The King of Kings*, but that she had a role that moviegoers would remember. Although Mordaunt Hall devoted most of his *New York Times* review to DeMille's impressive production and Laughton's performance, he had high praise for Claudette: "Miss Colbert is capital as the seductive empress." Claudette would work with DeMille again, but in the meantime it was a return to the standard repertoire.

Playing the empress made Claudette even more eager to become Paramount's reigning diva. Her only competition was Marlene Dietrich, who lacked both Claudette's range and popularity. Dietrich got by on her mystique; she belonged to a class of actresses that Parker Tyler called "somnambules," "ladies with sleep in their eyes." She was like an exotic bird, admired more for its plumage than its ability to fly. To Molly Haskell, Dietrich was a "creature of myth—and not, in any sociological sense, a 'real woman.' " Since the public preferred real women, Claudette had no competition. Also, no actress at Paramount was as versatile as she.

By 1933, Claudette had developed four specialties: the combination street girl/shop girl with her personal survival kit; the sultry gamine with an ambiguous past; the enchantress whose gowns streamed down her body, caressing her hips so lovingly that she seemed more sculpted than human; and the generic heroine, who, like the players in *Hamlet*, was not limited to any particular genre.

Claudette returned to the world of operetta sans music in *Tonight Is Ours* (1933), based on Noël Coward's *The Queen Was in the Parlour* (1926), a better play than the film version would suggest. Claudette was Nadya, the princess of the mythical Krayia, who flees her country, deserting her husband and taking up residence in Paris, where she pursues a life of pleasure. At a costume ball, Nadya encounters Sabien (Fredric March), and once they doff their masks, it is love at first sight. Claudette's scenes with March had an understated but palpable sensuousness; Claudette was responding not so much to March's character as to March himself, and one suspects, he to her. At any rate, they made a convincing pair of lovers.

When Nadya's husband dies, her patriotism is rekindled; reluctantly, she leaves Sabien and returns to Krayia as its new queen, only to confront insurrectionists, one of whom tries to assassinate her. Fortunately, Sabien is in the crowd and thwarts the attempt. Nadya and Sabien resume their affair, making proper use of the royal bedroom. Either the director, Stuart Walker, or, more likely, the associate director, the brilliant Mitchell Leisen, knew his Lubitsch. The camera pans left from the bedroom window to a hand turning off the light and then moves toward the bedroom door, which discreetly closes by itself.

Just when it seems that Nadya and Sabien will be caught *flagrante delicto*, the insurrectionists barge in, insisting that they only want a share in the government, which must have been greeted with cheers from Depression audiences, who wouldn't have minded having the same. Nadya not only complies but also shows that she is a proletarian at heart and presents them with her royal consort, Sabien. In Depression America, anything is possible, as 1930s screwball comedy insisted. And while *Tonight Is Ours* is not screwball, the ending certainly is. In screwball, social barriers collapse; heiresses marry newspaper reporters (as Claudette discovered the following year in *It Happened One Night*) and rich boys marry poor girls (Ray Milland and Jean Arthur in Leisen's *Easy Living*, 1937). Within the context of the founding fathers' rejection of monarchy in favor of democracy, where "all men are created equal," *Tonight Is Ours* had a strange relevance in 1933; if a queen can wed a commoner, anything is possible, even an economic recovery. And while subsequent screwball comedies did not promise such a miracle, they offered reasonable alternatives.

The Queen Was in the Parlour ends quite differently, with Nadya delivering an impassioned speech to the anarchists, who back off. However, Sabien, who has been hiding in her bedroom, is mistaken for one of them and shot. Fate has resolved Nadya's dilemma, leaving her no other choice but to share the throne with former Prince Keri of Zalgar and now co-regent—the only kind of royal couple the people would accept even in their newly democratized monarchy.

Coward was so unimpressed with *Tonight Is Ours* that he forgot the title: "I saw it once by accident . . . and left the cinema exhausted from the strain of trying to disentangle my own dialogue from the matted mediocrity that the Paramount screenwriters had added to it. It was performed doggedly by Claudette Colbert and Fredric March who were so obviously bogged down by the script that I felt nothing but an embarrassed sympathy for them."

Three Cornered Moon (1933) may have had a far greater effect on Claudette's career than she thought at the time. It was not so much a "soak the rich" movie as a genial satire of the idle rich forced to join the working class when a frivolous mother (Mary Boland) loses her fortune in the Great Depression. There is only one reference to the "Three Cornered Moon," and a passing one at that: it was the name of a worthless mine in which the mother had invested. It was also the title of the play on which the film was based. Although the play was not a hit, Paramount decided to retain the title, believing it was whimsical enough to peak an audience's interest. Initially, Claudette's character, Elizabeth Rimplegear, is as indifferent to the Depression as her three brothers are until they realize they must find jobs. Although Claudette would never rival Sylvia Sidney as Hollywood's proletarian princess, she was nonetheless believable as a shoe factory employee fired for rebuffing the advances of her sleazy boss. At the time, Claudette had no idea that she would be playing a runaway heiress in *It Happened One Night,* who had to convince her father's detectives that she was a plumber's daughter—with some help from Clark Gable. But the premise was the same: throw the rich into the refining fire of Depression America and see if they emerge transfigured or singed. In *Moon,* the Rimplegears emerged as neither. Two of the brothers find jobs, the third passes his law boards, and Claudette gets a doctor husband (stolidly played by Richard Arlen).

Eliot Nugent was not the ideal director for *Moon;* the theatre was his forte, and several of his long shots had a stage-bound look. Frank Capra would have been the right fit, except that his Columbia contract would have prevented his venturing over to nearby Paramount. *Moon* was incipient screwball, which Capra could have elevated to at least proto-screwball; it could never become pure screwball, for the same reason that Capra's *You Can't Take It with You* (1938) never could: Each revolved around a family of eccentrics whose antics overshadowed the male-female relationship that lies at the heart of screwball. Elizabeth's courtship by a pretentious novelist and a boringly earnest doctor recedes into the background when Mary Boland is dithering around, the Polish cook is fracturing the English language, and Elizabeth's brother, a would-be actor, is rehearsing his one line in *Monsieur Beaucaire*. However, in 1933, audiences responded to its egalitarian message: Work is the great leveler; and if Claudette Colbert can make shoes, anything is possible.

When Columbia's Harry Cohn was having a difficult time casting the female lead in *It Happened One Night*, he turned to Claudette—a strange choice (or was it?), since she had hardly done any romantic comedies, much less screwball. It may well have been because he saw *Three Cornered Moon* and sensed the similarity between them; in both, a child of privilege learns how the other half lives and is all the better for it. Claudette may have sensed it as well; supposedly, she signed on because she would get twice her Paramount salary. But she also had the opportunity to appear in a real screwball comedy with a dream lover of a leading man.

Cohn obviously did not seek Claudette out because of her other 1933 film, *Torch Song*, a woman's film that narrowly escaped becoming a three-hankie movie because Claudette negotiated the tricky curves of the melo-dramatic script with surprising agility. This, in itself, was amazing, since her character had to run the gamut from unwed mother to torch singer, who also doubles as the benign Aunt Jenny on a children's radio show. Seduced and abandoned by a Boston blueblood who left her pregnant and took off for China (but who, in the tradition of the seducer-impregnator, makes a return appearance), Sally Trent (Claudette) turns her suffering into art and becomes Mimi Benton, belting out songs of unrequited love ("Give Me Liberty or Give Me Love," "I'm Waiting for You," "Don't Be a Cry Baby") in posh nightclubs. When asked to undergo another metamorphosis and host the *Pure Foods Hour* as Aunt Jenny, Mimi agrees, only if she can broadcast from her apartment with a drink in her hand and her semi-inebriated guests as the audience. Aunt Jenny becomes an instant success, and Mimi uses her fame to locate the daughter she was forced to give up for adoption. Eventually, she succeeds in finding not only her daughter but also her former lover.

Coincidences piled up so quickly that there was hardly time to question their plausibility. But it did not matter because Claudette harmonized the dissonance within Sally/Mimi, refusing to play the *mater dolorosa*. Sally turned a social stigma into hard cash and, as Mimi, became as synthetic as her costume jewelry. Film scholar Jeanine Basinger caught the irony of Sally's transformation when she observed that "as a torch singer, [Sally] turns pain and enslavement into something defiant, and thus she acts out a form of anger and independence that men can accept, since she is, in fact, still serving them by performing."

Claudette looked exceedingly svelte, her shimmering gowns flowing gracefully down her slim-hipped body. She also did her own singing, affecting an earthy mezzo with a slight quaver that revealed Sally/Mimi's vulnerability, suggesting that while music may be the food of love, it cannot assuage its loss. Never one for high notes, Claudette could ease into an attenuated soprano and then drop down to her natural range for the coda. Again, Claudette was the perfect mother; again one marveled at her naturalness. Children, however, were never part of her life, only part of the script. Being a mother in real life would have altered her image, as she undoubtedly realized.

A year after *The Sign of the Cross*, Claudette made her second film for DeMille, *Four Frightened People* (1934). Again, she was not the star, but neither were the others who made up the quartet: Mary Boland, the scatterbrained champion of Planned Parenthood, eager to reduce the birth rate of the overpopulated Third World; William Gargan, a scoop-hungry journalist; and Herbert Marshall, a Brit in the rubber trade with an acute inferiority complex. Claudette was the fourth: a prim, bespectacled hair-in-a-bun grade school teacher from Chicago, secretly longing for adventure and finding more than she bargained for. The main title identified the star: "The Cecil B. DeMille Production of *Four Frightened People*." Claudette's name may have preceded the others, but it was still under the title.

The four are passengers on a tramp steamer traveling around the Malayan coast. An outbreak of bubonic plague among the crew forces the four to head for the nearest island, which turns out to be inhabited by a less-than-hospitable tribe. At this point, the plot bifurcates into a comic diversion, in which Mary Boland introduces the women of the island to family planning and is so successful that they refuse to be breeding machines; and the main action, in which the other three must forage for food, face the unknown, and cope with the sexual tension that automatically results when two men and one woman are thrown together on an island as lushly beautiful as it is dangerous. While the men are ambivalent about the island, Claudette luxuriates in it, even bathing (suggestively unclothed) under a waterfall. Gone are the spinsterish glasses and hairdo. Claudette goes native, literally letting her hair down, disappearing into the brush, and emerging in a sexy outfit made of fronds—a tribute to the character's ingenuity or DeMille's decision to give her a change of costume.

Just as the natives are about to execute Marshall and Claudette, Gargan comes to the rescue. The four return to civilization and their respective careers, except for Marshall, who leaves his wife and seeks out Claudette, now the prim schoolteacher, teaching geography and concentrating on the Malay peninsula. Even though her hair is back in a bun when Marshall shows up at her classroom, one knows that it will soon cascade down her back.

Four Frightened People was not one of Claudette's happier experiences; the other members of the cast, all of whom endured bouts of dysentery, felt similarly, although one would never know it from the way they threw themselves into their parts. In his quest for authenticity, DeMille chose Hawaii for the exteriors. Claudette was game, thinking that the shoot would be a lark. But on 25 August 1933, on the eve of her departure, she suffered an attack of acute appendicitis. Since DeMille had no idea when she would be available, he immediately contacted Elissa Landi and Gloria Swanson, with whom he had worked before. Either would have bailed him out, except that they had other commitments. To DeMille, Claudette was expendable. All that mattered was the film. As it happened, by 10 September, Claudette was able to join the company; although not in the greatest of health, she did what was expected of her.

Four Frightened People was a pedestrian film. Ironically, except for *Torch Song*, Claudette's best roles between 1933 and 1937 came from loan-outs: *I Cover the Waterfront* (1933, United Artists), *It Happened One Night* (1934, Columbia), *Imitation of Life* (1934, Universal), and *Tovarich* (1937, Warner Bros.).

In *Waterfront*, released in mid May, Claudette looked and sounded like her character, Julie Kirk, the daughter of a West Coast fisherman. Claudette shed all traces of glamour, taking on a voice that was her most American to date, complete with "yeah," "doin'," and "gettin'." The film was basically an exposé, involving an investigative reporter (Ben Lyon) hunting for evidence to convict Eli Kirk (Ernest Torrence), Julie's father, of smuggling Chinese immigrants into the United States. The relationship between father and daughter is genuinely poignant, with Julie always calling him "Eli," as if they were old friends. Torrence had the most difficult role in the film; it was one thing to traffic in illegal aliens, but something else to take their money, chain them, and toss them overboard. When a body ends up in the belly of a shark, Eli is exposed; he may be a loving father, but he has degenerated into a remorseless killer. The denouement is so quick that one almost forgets that the reporter's story would have sent Eli to jail, had Eli not died from a gunshot wound. Julie's bitterness over her father's death disappears in the last scene, as she and the reporter take up housekeeping in their waterfront home, which Julie in a gesture of goodwill has redecorated.

Waterfront is a morally ambiguous film; an affectionate father-daughter relationship is undermined by the father's blatant disregard for human life. Although Torrence in his final movie role (he died in 1933) tried to unify Eli Kirk's polarized character, the script worked against him. It is difficult to sympathize with a man who frequents Mother Morgan's Boarding House, a combination speakeasy-brothel, when he is not dumping immigrants into the Pacific.

As 1934 drew near, so did the year in which she would win her first and only Oscar for a movie that she would have preferred not to make.

CHAPTER 5

That Wonderful Year

In 1933, *Cosmopolitan* published *Night Bus*, reprinted the following year as a Dell 10-cent "vestpocket" in a series that already included Mary Roberts Rinehart's *Locked Doors*, W. Somerset Maugham's *Rain*, and Pearl Buck's *Journey for Life*. The author was Samuel Hopkins Adams, an investigative reporter who later became a successful writer of fiction. Adams's dialogue was realistically pithy, but when he had to rely on narration and especially description, the man of letters took over and the spindly language became quaintly literary—the kind that pulp writers use when they want to remind themselves and their readers that they are, first and foremost, writers and, second, writers for hire. Take, for example, the opening sentence of *Night Bus*: "Through the resonant cave of the terminal, a perfunctory voice boomed out something about Jacksonville, points north, and New York." Translation: the Miami—New York bus was ready for boarding.

On board are a man and a woman whose chance meeting sets the plot in motion. The man, Peter Warne, is far from handsome ("his physiognomy was blunt, rough, and smudgy with bristles"). His occupation is even less attractive: manufacturing pine tar, which obviously would have to be changed, along with Warne's physiognomy, if *Night Bus* were to become a movie. The woman's name is not revealed immediately; she is unaccustomed to bus travel, much less to someone like Peter, who, when he finds bundles of newspapers occupying the only available seat, heaves them out the window. Eventually, she reveals her first name, Elspeth, but claims she is the wife of the fabulously wealthy Corcoran Andrews. It was not a total lie: Corcoran was her brother's name; Andrews, their surname; and both are the spoiled children of a Park Avenue millionaire. It turns out to be a small world: Corcoran and Warne were in college together.

Elspeth's inattentiveness results in the theft of her suitcase, causing her to become increasingly dependent on Warne, who becomes increasingly interested in her—so much so that when Elspeth uses the rest stop to bathe and discovers that the bus has left without her, she finds that Warne, in a gesture of sheer gallantry, has remained behind. A bridge washout forces them to spend the night in a tourist camp, where they register as a married couple. Ever the gentleman, Warne strings a blanket between their twin beds, declaring it the walls of Jericho. Almost imperceptibly, Adams turns the trip into one of mutual discovery, until the walls of class, like those of Jericho, collapse.

Adams's thirty-page narrative is so economically written that it could serve as the template for a movie version. Just when the action seems to be winding down, Adams extends the plot, adding further complications. Although we assume that Elspeth and Warne will surmount whatever obstacles are thrown in their way, it is the nature of those obstacles that sustains our interest. First, there is the news that Elspeth's father has offered $10,000 for information leading to her whereabouts. When Warne hears that one of the passengers, the smarmy Horace Shapley, has figured out who Elspeth is and plans to collect the reward, the two have no other choice but to leave the bus and proceed on foot and by boat, until they are reduced to hitchhiking. A seemingly benign driver picks them up and then takes off with Warne's suitcase. But the resourceful Warne not only retrieves the suitcase but commandeers the car as well, so that, after a few more narrative detours, he can deposit Elspeth at her Park Avenue home.

When Warne contacts Mr. Andrews, Elspeth and her father assume it is to collect the reward. But all he wants is to be reimbursed for what he had spent on Elspeth: $18.56. Differences resolved and marriage implied, the two spend their honeymoon at the tourist camp where Warne had erected the walls of Jericho. This time Warne blows a toy trumpet, and the walls come tumbling down, a disarmingly innocent ending, and one that would—and did—make a memorable fadeout: toot of trumpet, falling blanket, THE END.

The same year that the *Night Bus* vestpocket came out, Columbia Pictures released the movie version, Frank Capra's *It Happened One Night*, which went on to become one of the world's most beloved films, confounding the skeptics, one of whom was Claudette, who thought that nothing good could come out of Columbia, the Poverty Row studio that geographically was not that far from Paramount but artistically on another planet. The *It Happened One Night* story has been told so many times that a paraphrase should suffice. Capra needed another film to follow *Lady for a Day* (1933), which made a $600,000 profit for Columbia. Capra and Robert Riskin—who had written the screenplays of Capra's *Platinum Blonde* (1931), *American Madness* (1932), and *Lady for a Day*—had become "a duo . . . looking for stories to put on screen." After Capra read *Night Bus* in a Palm Springs barber shop, he was intrigued by its possibilities. That *Cosmopolitan* published it augured well; it had also published Damon Runyon's "Madame La Gimp," which Riskin turned into *Lady for a Day*. Although Columbia's president, Harry Cohn, had strong reservations about *It Happened One Night*, he also knew that it would not bankrupt the studio; the rights were only $5,000, and the budget was set at $325,000, including the performers' salaries. Besides, Cohn reasoned, how many costume changes would the principals need if they were traveling by bus, hitchhiking, and driving from Florida to New York?

The biggest problem was the casting. No actress was interested in playing Elspeth (now Ellie) Andrews. Supposedly, Constance Bennett, Miriam Hopkins, Carole Lombard, and Margaret Sullavan passed on the role.

Although in 1933 Clark Gable had not yet become one of MGM's leading men, he was Capra's second choice for Peter Warne after Louis Mayer refused to loan out Robert Montgomery. Gable's darkly masculine looks forced Riskin to ignore Adams's description of Peter as someone who "by no stretch of charity could . . . be called an ornament to the human species." If any actor in Hollywood was "an ornament to the human species," it was Gable.

"Casting Colbert was Cohn's idea," which may well have come from seeing her in *Three Cornered Moon*. When it came to casting, Cohn's instincts were generally sound. He sensed that Rosalind Russell, even though she was an MGM contract player, was the ideal Harriet Craig for Columbia's *Craig's Wife* (1936); that Paul Muni would make a better resistance fighter in *Counter-Attack* (1945) than Alexander Knox; and that spending $1 million for the rights to Garson Kanin's *Born Yesterday* would—and did—pay off when Judy Holliday walked off with a Best Actress Oscar in 1951.

Claudette had already planned a vacation in Sun Valley when Cohn contacted her. Despite her reservations about the script, she agreed to play Ellie with the understanding that the shoot would be over in four weeks and that she would be paid twice her Paramount salary ($25,000 per picture), thus earning five times more than Gable, who received a mere $10,000. Production began in late November 1933, and the film opened at Radio City Music Hall on 22 February 1934. And Claudette had her vacation.

Although auteurists think of *It Happened One Night* as "a Frank Capra film," it would not have been one without Riskin, who wrote the scripts for Capra's best movies, except for *It's a Wonderful Life* (1946). Their collaboration resulted in a new Hollywood coinage "Capriskin." Riskin and Capra understood each other—Riskin writing a Frank Capra screenplay and Capra converting into a Frank Capra film. Riskin treated Adams's short story as if it were a series of ellipses that had to be filled in. He began with Adams's depiction of Elspeth's relationship with her father, Alexander Andrews, whom she affectionately calls "Scotty" (he's a Scot). If father and daughter were so chummy, why does the daughter suddenly decide to leave home with all its creature comforts and resort to mass transportation? In the story, Elspeth explains, "It was about King Westley. . . . He and I have been playing around together." Riskin found his hook: Westley, a playboy-aviator, was Ellie's deliverer from a world of governesses and tutors who denied her the adventuresome life for which she longed. And, Riskin concluded, if she were so infatuated with Westley, they would have eloped—which is precisely what they did. Finally, how would Alexander Andrews have reacted to his daughter's elopement? Answer: he would have her kidnapped and confined to his yacht in Miami.

The plot was now starting to jell. Ellie must be more resourceful than Elspeth, who seemed incapable of fending for herself. Ellie obviously needs Peter, but, if necessary, she can function on her own. In the film, she is first seen on her father's yacht, staging a hunger strike. In anger, she knocks over a tray of food, causing her father to strike her. Hurt, Ellie dives off the yacht and, in the next scene, shows up in a Miami bus station. How she changed from a swimsuit to a dress is partly inferred, partly explained: She returned home, packed her bag, and pawned her watch for bus fare. Clearly, Ellie is not helpless. Riskin has fashioned an exemplary script, motivating whatever seemed implausible (a change from a swimsuit to a dress) and infusing the action with the spirit of humanity to which Capra, with the aid of Claudette and Gable, added the missing ingredient: warmth.

It Happened One Night is a film of summer, or at least spring. No autumnal winds, no wintry frosts, and no overcoats. We are in the green world, where love, even with the over-twenty set, can thrive. Ellie and Peter meet on a night bus, as they did in the story, but not quite in the same way. Clark Gable hardly conformed to a moviegoer's image of a pine-tar processor. Knowing he had to change Peter Warne's occupation, Riskin decided on "reporter." He took his cue from the proliferation of newspaper films that, in 1931 seemed to be giving birth to a new genre—or at least a subdivision of urban melodrama and screwball comedy.

The paradigm was *The Front Page*, followed by the "Capriskin" *Platinum Blonde* (both 1931). Not to be ignored were *Five-Star Final* and *Scandal for Sale* (also 1931). Thus, Riskin made Warne a journalist, eager for a scoop. And what better copy than the day-by-day experiences of a runaway heiress who dived off her father's yacht and hopped on a bus to New York to be reunited with her celebrity husband?

Night Bus is too brief for romance to flourish; it can only bloom, with the flowering left to the imagination. Riskin made it blossom, so that the opportunistic Warne and the aristocratic Ellie cease being single-minded as they discover qualities in each other that they never knew existed. We expect Warne to handle a crisis; the revelation, however, is that Ellie can, too— but in her own way. When drivers ignore Warne with his turned-out thumb, which he insists is a foolproof way to hitch a ride, Ellie proves the limb is mightier than the thumb by exposing a leg and bringing a car to a screeching halt. When Andrews's detectives show up at the auto court, Warne and Ellie pretend to be a bickering couple and are so convincing that the detectives apologize for intruding.

In *Henry V* (act 5, scene 2) the king tells Katherine that she has witchcraft in her lips. Claudette's witchcraft lay elsewhere—in her voice and eyes. The same was true of Gable, who had deviltry in his. The first time we see Gable in *Gone with the Wind* (1939), he is standing at the foot of a staircase studying Scarlett O'Hara so intently that he makes her uncomfortable; it is as if "he knows what I look like without my shimmy," she confides to her friend. With Claudette, it was different. Gable did not have to undress her mentally as much as bring her down from her bower of privilege to the good earth. After discovering Ellie's identity, he admonishes her: "You'll never get away with it, Miss Andrews." When Gable delivers the line, he sounds smug and censorious, his eyes probing but teasing, as if he were daring her to try to proceed without him, but at the same time not volunteering his services. And Ellie, realizing she is in a real predicament (suitcase stolen and little money) responds by offering to pay him handsomely when she gets to New York. He wants a story; she wants anonymity. The battle of the sexes is on and will end in a tie.

Claudette was not popular with the crew, who characterized her as "bitchy," "snooty," and "standoffish." She may well have been. Despite the rapport she felt with Gable, she wondered how audiences—particularly those who had seen *The Sign of the Cross*—would react to a film that was totally devoid of glamour. She even looked sexier in her jungle wear in *Four Frightened People*. But in *It Happened One Night*, sex took the form of undercurrents of desire that kept circulating in her scenes with Gable. Clothes made neither the man nor the woman. What mattered was the humanization of Ellie Andrews, which Warne initiated and the passengers finished. A couple of musicians try to alleviate the boredom of the long bus trip by breaking into "The Daring Young Man on the Flying Trapeze," which grows into a sing-along with Ellie and Warne joining in. That scene represents Capra at his most egalitarian. The passengers become a chorus, experiencing the camaraderie that comes when, just for a few minutes, individuals meld into a group, so that for the duration of the song all distinctions vanish. Claudette threw herself into the number, as did Gable; the years fell away (Claudette was thirty, Gable thirty-two) as the two of them behaved like high school seniors returning from a class trip. From that point on, Warne and Ellie will have their differences, but they overcome them with the same ease as the young man on the flying trapeze. Later, when a female passenger faints from hunger, Ellie becomes unusually compassionate, taking money from Warne to give to the woman's son. Ellie is now a card-carrying member of the human race.

Claudette may not have felt at home at Columbia, but she did with Gable, enjoying his phallic pranks without sanctioning them. To Claudette, Gable was naughty, not obscene. Since he frightened her when he put a hammer in his pants, he tried a different approach, this time lying on one of the twin beds with a potato masher in an upright position under the blanket. Capra, pretending that he was having a problem with the "walls of Jericho" scene, called Claudette over. She took one look at the priapic Gable and burst out laughing: "Awww! . . . *You guys*!" One could almost hear her musically earthy laugh, as if she took the prank as the equivalent of a sight gag, lacking in propriety but nonetheless damn funny. It was also the kind of prank that makes someone want to know the prankster better.

And Claudette did, realizing that what transpired between them was not even a short-term romance, but the casual kind that often occurs during a shoot, when two people are thrown into close contact with each other. The camera can lie, but there are times when it doesn't—for example, the scene in which Ellie and Warne, after leaving the bus, ford a stream and find themselves in a hay field, where Warne makes a bed of hay for Ellie. She lies on her back as Warne bends over her. Ellie is willing, as Claudette's eyes indicate. But Warne hesitates, even though everything seems right for a literal roll in the hay. For all her sophistication, Ellie is a novice when it comes to sex on the run. And Warne, for all his experience, is a true gentleman. He suddenly realizes that what Ellie longs for is a real lover instead of a social climber. Gable's reaction to Claudette's inviting body, brief as it is, is a study in restraint in the presence of temptation, making the hay-field sequence one of the most erotic unconsummated love scenes in film. Yet one has the impression that Claudette and Gable wished it were otherwise.

From their performances, it was evident that Gable and Claudette found a good deal of themselves in their characters. Gable finally had a chance to do romantic comedy, in which he could bewitch with his eyes, using them to activate a woman's conscience that had been dormant for years. Claudette discovered that she and Ellie were not that different. Although Claudette did not come from Park Avenue, she did come from the avenue below it, Lexington, and knew the difference between them. She could also play the residents of either equally well. She may not have had a gilded childhood, but she also did not have a deprived one. The Chauchoins, unlike many immigrants, managed to avoid ending up on New York's lower East Side.

Night Bus, with all of its detours and stopovers on the road to true love, ends abruptly. It was the sort of ending that readers would accept, but moviegoers would not. The falling blanket provokes a smile, but what has preceded it? Riskin wanted to preserve Adams's ending, but he couldn't until he connected some more dots. He found his connections in one of the oldest conventions of comedy: misunderstanding. One lover, assuming the other is attracted to someone else, takes up with his or her second choice or sulks in silence until the situation is resolved; or one misinterprets the actions of the other and is on the verge of breaking off the relationship until an explanation is offered. When Peter and Ellie are just a few hours from New York, they stay at an auto court again, where Ellie practically gives herself to Peter after he describes a tropical island he longs to revisit. "Take me with you, Peter. Take me to your island," Ellie begs. Again, Peter resists temptation. "Better go back to your bed," he orders. Ellie no sooner does than Peter asks across the blanket partition if she would really accompany him. Ellie is now asleep, and THE SCENE that some moviegoers may have been hoping for fades out.

The final complication occurs when Peter leaves the sleeping Ellie to drive to New York, where he types out his story for his editor. Meanwhile, Ellie awakens to the sight of the outraged owners of the auto court, who evict her when she cannot pay the bill. Rescued by her father and convinced she was just a scoop for Warne, she agrees to a formal wedding to King Westley. Once Andrews discovers that Warne is a man of integrity, he informs Ellie as he escorts her down the aisle, adding that there is a car waiting if she wants to take off before saying "I do," which she does. The image of Ellie rushing toward the car, her veil trailing behind her, which she pulls in so it doesn't get caught in the door, signals "the end of the extravagant, wasteful, snobbish life of the upper classes of the twenties." One of the great joys of teaching film is to show *It Happened One Night* to college students, many of whom are ill-disposed toward black-and-white movies, and hear some of the young women shout, "Go, girl!" as Ellie bolts from the altar and races across the lawn to the car. They understood exactly what Riskin and Capra were getting at.

Riskin cleverly avoided turning the battle of the sexes into a one-sided victory. It was more of a case of win some, lose some. But he has staged an unusual battle because there is a third player: Alexander Andrews, without whose prescience the film would have ended with a mirthless wedding and a disaffected audience. Ellie would have gone through with the ceremony if her father hadn't told her the truth about Warne and devised an escape scenario for her. Father knew best, and daughter profited from his wisdom. If Depression audiences left *It Happened One Night* feeling good about the human race, it is because the trio traveled the ignorance-to-knowledge route, arriving with a deeper understanding of the vagaries of the human heart.

It may be hard to believe that *It Happened One Night* encountered censorship problems. Although Joe Breen commended Harry Cohn for making such a popular film, he still objected to Gable's thumbing his nose in the hitchhiking scene, but soon relented. Yet some of the states were less tolerant. Ohio insisted upon the deletion of the final image of the trumpet blast and the falling blanket; Ontario and Alberta, on the nose-thumbing; Australia, Peter's line when he notices Ellie's slip and stockings dangling over the blanket partition: "I wish you'd take those things off the walls of Jericho." What also disturbed the Ontario censors was the brief scene in which a passenger whispers something to an African American at the rest stop and is directed to the men's room. Fortunately, most of the world sympathized with a man who did not want to be tempted by the sight of a woman's lingerie or one who had to relieve himself and paid little attention to details that now would never be noticed.

The vast appeal of the film became evident a year after its release. In March 1935, it returned for a three-week engagement at two New York theaters: the Astor on Broadway and, surprisingly, the Little Carnegie Playhouse, a few doors down from Carnegie Hall. A booking at the Little Carnegie presaged a future classic, which is exactly what *It Happened One Night* became.

Three months after *It Happened One Night* premiered, the following notice appeared in the *New York Times*: "Claudette Colbert has been engaged by Universal Pictures to play the lead in Fannie Hurst's 'Imitation of Life.'" Nineteen thirty-four was Claudette's banner year, with three outstanding films: one, a masterpiece, *It Happened One Night*, released in February; another, an epic extravaganza (or camp classic to some), DeMille's *Cleopatra*, in October; and the third, an exemplary woman's film, *Imitation of Life*, in

November. All were nominated for Best Picture, the honor going to *Night*, which also won for best actor, actress, screenplay, and director. *Cleopatra* won for set decoration, and *Imitation* went unacknowledged. Claudette was at her best in *Night* and *Imitation*, both at other studios. In *Cleopatra*, Claudette had to be alternately coy, seductive, authoritative, and tragic; but because the script did not allow her time to unify those facets of her character, much less explore their gradations, her performance is one of moods and poses— grand, yes, and often moving, but ultimately marmoreal, like the opening credits. Her Bea Pullman in *Imitation of Life* is another matter. In Bea, Claudette had a real character arc to trace, resolving Bea's conflicting and often contradictory emotions so that the audience is able to understand, if not necessarily accept, her decision to put aside marriage to a man she loves for fear of losing her daughter.

By 1930, Universal was about to go big time. Founded as the Universal Film Manufacturing Company under the supervision of "Uncle" Carl Laemmle, the studio was never taken seriously, except for a few classics such as Eric von Stroheim's *Blind Husbands* (1919) and *Foolish Wives* (1922), which were viewed as aberrations: masterpieces from a studio that was not noted for them.

In 1929, when Carl Laemmle Jr. took over as production head, he was determined to bring Universal into the forefront. He was convinced he had succeeded when *All Quiet on the Western Front* (1930) received the Best Film Oscar. For the first half of the 1930s, Universal released some impressive films, all of which cost the studio more than it could afford. As a result, the Laemmle era ended in 1936.

Until then, the studio was riding high, but so were the budgets. The studio's premier director was not James Whale, despite the popularity of *Frankenstein*, *The Old Dark House*, and *Bride of Frankenstein*, but John Stahl, who probably looked with disdain upon Whale's films. Stahl had the ability to transform popular fiction such as Lloyd Douglas's *Magnificent Obsession* into class-act "woman's films," handsomely produced, with sentiment kept within the bounds of good taste, even at the expense of the budget.

Not only was a "John Stahl Production" expensive; so was John Stahl, who received $60,000 for *Imitation of Life* and $85,000 for *Obsession*. When it came time to cast *Imitation of Life*, Stahl knew that there was only one actress who could play Bea Pullman. Claudette took advantage of the clause in her seven-picture Paramount contract that allowed her to do three films elsewhere and headed over to Universal in the San Fernando Valley, where she was treated—and paid—royally, making almost twice what she received for *It Happened One Night* ($90,000 for eight weeks of work) and looking far more soigné than she did in her austerity-budget wardrobe in *Night*. Her *Imitation* costumes cost $5,841; even the two house dresses she wore were not bargain basement. Universal paid $600 for them because Claudette was dissatisfied with the ones that had been designed for her.

To Carl Laemmle Jr., prestige was all that mattered; a high-gloss production was something that Stahl could deliver, even if it meant exceeding his budget, which he did to the tune of $99,000, bringing the total cost to around $665,000. Such extravagance could not last much longer, especially during the Great Depression, when Universal's grosses were declining so rapidly that by 1936 either a declaration of bankruptcy or a takeover was inevitable. As it happened, it was the latter. But until then, Carl Jr. hoped that quality films would refurbish the studio's image as well as turn a profit. For the most part, they only accomplished the former.

The opening credits of *Imitation of Life* read: "The New Universal presents a John Stahl Production." John Stahl's *Imitation of Life* is quite different from Fannie Hurst's. The movie version bears only the slightest resemblance to the 1933 novel. For one thing, William Hurlbut's screenplay bypasses the first fourteen chapters, which, if dramatized, would have provided a context for Bea's determination to succeed in male-dominated corporate America, despite a series of tragedies that would have discouraged a less resilient woman: a mother's prolonged death, a father's debilitating stroke, and a train wreck that killed her husband and left her a single parent with an invalid father and an infant daughter to support. The film begins with Bea, a widow, taking over her husband's maple syrup franchise and her chance meeting with an African American woman, Delilah Johnson, and her light-skinned daughter, Peola. Delilah's secret pancake recipe and unswerving loyalty make it possible for Bea to become a multimillionaire and for Delilah to achieve a level of financial security she had never known before. But prosperity brings happiness to neither woman.

In the novel, the product is not pancakes but waffles. Furthermore, Hurst's Bea takes advantage of Delilah's Midas-like ability to turn maple syrup into heart-shaped lozenges. Once the candy line was underway, Bea moved on to waffles, which, when doused with maple syrup, became the main attraction in her diner, the shape of which was inspired by her surname: a Pullman, where Delilah, wearing a chef's hat, presided over the griddle. Eager to conceal her gender, Bea hid behind initials that, in the early decades of the twentieth century, would have automatically suggested a male. The Atlantic City B. Pullman became the first of a chain that would eventually encircle the globe. And as if that were not enough, Bea began dabbling in real estate.

If Hurst's novel had been filmed as written, it would have been the first time on the screen that a female entrepreneur appeared who worked—rather than slept—her way up the corporate ladder, whose rungs were not made for high heels, and reached not just one executive suite but a host of them scattered throughout the world. It would also have been the first film in which an African American woman enabled a white to found such an empire that, without her, would have been a purely local or regional phenomenon. But, as the title implies, Bea's life is a pale reflection of the real thing; although she is obscenely wealthy, one source of happiness eludes her: love. The man she had hoped to marry—Frank Flake, her business manager—finds her daughter, Jessie, not only more desirable but also younger. At the end of the novel, one is to assume that Bea will go on launching B. Pullmans, transforming tenements into luxury buildings, and leading a loveless life. Delilah did not fare much better. Although she profited from Bea's entrepreneurial genius, she also lost a daughter, not to a man, but to a practice that she had always deplored: passing for white. The last thrust of the knife comes when Peola visits her mother, informing her that she has now broken with the past and is about to marry a man whose job requires relocation in Bolivia, where she intends to live as a white woman married to a white man—a white woman who has succeeded in convincing her future husband that she is incapable of bearing children, so that her interracial background will remain secret.

Hurst's novel depicts life as a "walking shadow," to use Macbeth's metaphor; the film version treats life as a kind of shadow dance performed by Bea and Jessie, Delilah and Peola, and the two male characters created exclusively for the film: Elmer (Ned Sparks), Bea's granite-faced business manager, who is a far cry from Frank Flake, and Stephen Archer (Warren William), an ichthyologist to whom both Bea and Jessie are attracted. The women never move out of the shadows into the sobering glare of reality. Bea is absorbed in her business; Delilah agonizes over Peola's rejection of her racial heritage. Peola is obsessed with "passing"; and Jessie, with acquiring airs. Accountants and scientists, on the other hand, have no other choice but to live in the real world. By the end of the film, the sextet has been reduced to a trio: Bea, Jessie, and Peola.

The film, then, is a condensed and reworked version of the novel, beginning almost immediately with Delilah's arrival at Bea's home, which apparently she has mistaken for someone else's. But the way the extraordinary Louise Beavers plays Delilah, one suspects that she knew exactly what she was doing. Delilah was only interested in finding a home where she could offer her services in exchange for room and board for herself and Peola. What single mother would pass up the chance of having a combination nanny-housekeeper who only wanted a place to stay?

In the film, Delilah is the equivalent of a deus—or rather, dea—ex machina. The same is true in the novel, in which their meeting is better motivated. Bea needs someone to care for her father while she is working. Unsuccessful in her attempts to hire a live-in housekeeper, she approaches an African American woman on the street, who happens to be Delilah. Her choice of race is not surprising, given the setting, Atlantic City, with its sizeable black population. Bea assumes that only a black woman would be interested in such a position. Delilah replies in wonderfully colorful (but by the standards of political correctness, racially demeaning) black English: "I sho does, miss, and dat's me." But it is a package arrangement: mother and daughter. Delilah refers to Peola as "the purfectest white nigger dat God ever dropped down in de lap of a black woman from Virginie." Like the late African American playwright August Wilson, Delilah uses the racial obscenity freely, even referring to her late husband as a "white nigger."

Delilah's ebonics make some of Mark Twain's language in *The Adventures of Huckleberry Finn* seem innocuously quaint. While Delilah uses the "n-word" regularly, she explains that she can use it with impunity. To her, the n-word is ambivalent. Blacks can use it about their own (as they do in August Wilson) or, as in Delilah's case, even about themselves. When whites use it, it is the supreme racial insult: "a tame-cat word when we use it ourselves ag'in' ourselves, and a wild-cat word when it comes jumpin' at us from the outside."

Delilah is the most complex character in the novel. She expects her daughter to "be proud" of being black, since God intended the races to be separate. To Delilah, the ultimate sin is passing, which Peola does—a decision that hastens her mother's death.

Hurst makes enormous demands on her readers, asking them to empathize with a black woman who accepts racism as God's will and rhapsodizes about the funeral she has arranged for herself. Delilah's form of religion—a mélange of superstition, Pentecostal ardor, and biblical lore—is alien to Peola, who has had enough of an education to realize the economic disparity between the races and wants to be part of the dominant class. From Delilah's standpoint, rejecting one's race is a deterrent to salvation; from Peola's, it is the only way to succeed in white America. Hurst's Peola even tells her mother that she had tried to come to terms with her racial heritage by reading black authors, but to no avail. "Let me go," Peola begs. Finally, Delilah acquiesces, dying shortly thereafter.

Although the film purports to be liberal, it still has undercurrents of racism, admittedly subtle, that did not exist in the novel. In the film, once Bea learns about Delilah's secret pancake recipe, the two parlay it into Aunt Delilah's Pancake Shop, and then Aunt Delilah's Pancake Flour, obviously inspired by the popular Aunt Jemima's Pancake Mix, also made from a secret recipe and packaged with the same image of a black woman in a bandanna.

When Bea and her accountant decide to go corporate and form Delilah, Inc., Bea offers Delilah a 20 percent interest in the company—a strange gesture in a film that implicitly condemns racism and also makes it clear that it was Delilah's recipe that made Bea a millionaire with a New York townhouse. (Given the size of her role, Beavers's compensation was also disproportionate: $2,900, compared to Claudette's $90,000 and Warren Williams's $25,000.) But even if Delilah reflects on the inequity, she is too trusting a soul to negotiate. All she wants is a home for herself and Peola, who reveals her rebellious streak when Delilah arrives at her classroom one rainy day to bring her an umbrella, only to discover that Peola has been passing for white and is humiliated by her mother's appearance.

The older Peola was played by Fredi Washington, who was born in the same year as Claudette, although neither looked thirty-one in the film. Washington was a gifted light-skinned African American who fared better in theatre. Unfortunately, her political activism and association with the radical left minimized her chances for stage work during the McCarthy era. When Washington appears on screen for the first time, her body is so taut that it seems as if her emotions are not so much knotted as coiled, ready to spring apart at any moment, as they eventually do when Delilah tracks her down at a restaurant, where she is a cashier.

In her own way, Washington gave a performance as impressive as Claudette's and Beavers's; the only difference is that Peola's character has already been formed by the time Washington appears. Claudette, on the other hand, had to build her characterization, progressing in graduated stages as she undergoes the transition from working mom to CEO and New York hostess with a throng of admirers, to a woman in love, and finally to a mother who sacrifices that love for her daughter. She is uncommonly subtle in the scene when Delilah appears at her back door. Bea does not react to Delilah's color; she is only concerned about being late and will do anything to get Delilah to leave, even offering her carfare. But Beavers (who would have had to be nominated for Best Supporting Actress if such a category existed in 1934) responds by adopting a tone of gentle persuasiveness, reminding Bea that she is offering her services in exchange for a place to stay. Delilah doesn't appeal to Bea's maternalism as much as her sense of expediency, and Beavers plays the scene with the right combination of sincerity and shrewdness, knowing she is making Bea an offer she cannot refuse. The two actresses tapped into their characters' seemingly dissimilar natures, yet at the same time making it evident that they had much in common. In a sense, Bea and Delilah are mirror images, each reflecting motherhood from a different angle; one is an adroit salesperson; the other, a woman with no product to sell except a work ethic and radiant benevolence.

The film steers clear of melodrama until the daughters grow up. The turn that the Delilah-Peola subplot takes has the familiar air of tragic inevitability. Once Peola decides to sever all relations with her mother and enter the white world, Delilah's health declines, resulting in a restrained but wrenching death scene. And since daughters who renounce their mothers deserve to suffer guilt, Peola reappears at the funeral, weeping over the casket and embracing it lovingly.

Imitation of Life, however, does not end with the funeral. Peola joins Bea and Jessie in the limousine. Peola and Jessie are in the front seat, photographed from Bea's point of view. The similarity between the daughters is striking; their hair styles and clothes could be interchangeable. From the look on Bea's face, it is evident that she has no intention of ending up a mother bereft of her daughter. In fact, she now has two daughters—one natural, one surrogate. A matriarchal household is in the making. That one shot anticipates the film's ending, in which Bea resolves the dilemma caused by her engagement to Stephen Archer, with whom her daughter is infatuated.

After Delilah's funeral, Bea grows protective of Jessie, fearing the same estrangement that Delilah suffered, if she should marry Stephen. Forget that the spoiled Jessie is returning to school (a school that offers a choice between majoring in English Composition and Drama!) and would eventually have gotten over her crush. Claudette has to play the scene in such a way as to reveal her love of both Stephen and Jessie, making it evident that the latter takes precedence. After kissing him passionately, she tells him that she cannot jeopardize her relationship with Jessie by marrying a man her daughter also loves—but not as a potential stepfather. "When she forgets you, I'll come to you, no matter where you are," she says consolingly. Claudette's delivery of the line is so emotionally honest that moviegoers hoping for a happy, or at least tentatively happy, ending were not entirely disappointed.

Fans of the novel might have been, though. In the novel, when Bea virtually proposes marriage to Flake, dismissing the age difference between them, he cannot bear hearing any more. At that point, unaware of what has transpired between Flake and her mother, Jesse barges into the parlor to announce what Flake could not: that they are in love. Had the film followed the novel, the climactic scene would have been a challenge to Claudette or any actress, who must react as if she had sustained a body blow until she sees the couple together. Then the face that looked stunned relaxes into resignation. The novel's last line, in which Bea accepts a match that is far more appropriate than the one she envisioned for herself, would have to be delivered as voiceover, with a close-up of a pensive Claudette flashing her trademark smile, this time slightly tinged with ruefulness as the audience hears her thoughts: "They were so young standing there . . . so right."

In the movie version, Claudette gets a close-up at the end, but in a far different context. *Imitation of Life*, which opened with a shot of a rubber duck in the bathtub where Bea was bathing young Jessie, ends with mother and daughter, sans any male interloper, walking into the frame, as Bea, a film of tears coating her eyes, reminds Jessie of the time she kept saying, "I want my quack quack." It is as if nothing had happened since Bea was peddling maple syrup and Jessie was a toddler. But that is precisely what Bea wants: a return to the past. She has learned too much about the dark side of mother love to end up like Delilah. If she must cater to Jessie, it is better than ending up on a deathbed, reviewing the details of her funeral.

When Universal announced that it had bought the rights to *Imitation of Life*, the Hays Office reacted as if the studio had thrown down the gauntlet. After reading the script, Joe Breen did not mince words: A film in which miscegenation is an integral part of the plot "not only violates the Production Code but is very dangerous from the standpoint both of the industry and public policy." Translation: How will the film play in the South—or will any southern exhibitor even book it? Carl Jr. was undaunted. But to be on the safe side, he made a note to himself requesting the screenwriter to consider attributing Peola's skin color to some genetic disorder. Fortunately, Carl Jr. recovered his courage and let production proceed without any further compromises. The novel had been sufficiently disemboweled.

On the eve of the film's release, Breen finally gave it his imprimatur: "This picture satisfactorily meets the Code requirements; and contains nothing which could be considered reasonably censorable." It could not have been otherwise; Hurst's novel had been surgically altered and resectioned so that all that remained were the parallel stories of two mothers and their daughters with their triumphs and travails. Actually, there was little opposition; there was none in the North, and in a few states the censor boards requested some dialogue deletions. Naturally, it was banned in South Africa.

One major source of criticism, however, came from Robert Gaylord, Standard Bearer of the Grand Encampment of Knights Templar (i.e., a Masonic order), who wrote to Breen, addressing him as "Moving Picture Censor" and expressing his dismay at the funeral service of the "negro mammy." In the film, Delilah is given an elaborate funeral with the members from her lodge dressed in full regalia, which Gaylord thought closely resembled that of the Masons. Breen, not knowing how to handle such a complaint, admitted to Gaylord that he too "regretted the scene" but assured him that a black minister had been brought in as a consultant to make sure that it was "an accurate reproduction of a full negro ceremony never before seen on the screen." To assure Gaylord that he was sympathetic to his concerns, Breen made an admission that was probably true: "I do not think of Masonry and negroes in the same thought"; and since there was "no negro masonry," Masons need not be offended. While Gaylord's language revealed his racism, so did Breen's, although less blatantly. Still, writing "Negro" in lowercase and capitalizing "Mason" was saying, in effect, to use the familiar cliché, "I feel your pain."

Gaylord did not stop with Breen. He wrote to Carl Laemmle Jr., again inveighing against the attire of the lodge members that tended to "cheapen the Order" and arguing that blacks should not "ape the attire of an Order by which they are not recognized." He even contacted Will Hays, who replied that none of his Masonic friends were offended by the sequence. If the script had followed the novel, there would not have been a problem, since Hurst never included a funeral procession. But there would not have been the kind of resolution to which 1934 audiences were accustomed.

Cleopatra, which Claudette made right after *It Happened One Night*, completed her 1934 trio of films; it was also her last partnership with Cecil B. DeMille, whose dark side she finally had to acknowledge. DeMille had become unsympathetic to Claudette's health problems, real as they were. Anything other than robust health, on which he prided himself, was a sign of weakness. Until DeMille was forced to confront his mortality, he behaved as if he were immortal and expected others to do likewise. Claudette failed to live up to his expectations. When he was casting the female lead in *The Crusades*, he made it clear that he would use Claudette "only if we are absolutely stuck for someone to play the part." The part went to Loretta Young.

In 1933, when *Cleopatra* went into production, neither Claudette nor DeMille knew how their relationship would end. To DeMille, all that mattered was that she was the only star on the Paramount lot who could play the Queen of the Nile his way. Travis Banton designed costumes for her that were provocative but never tasteless. Since *Cleopatra* was filmed just before the enforcement of the Production Code, Claudette could wear a halter with straps that crisscrossed over her breasts, revealing a hint of each, so that no one could accuse the far-from-voluptuous star of being padded. The bottom part of her costume had a V-slit that stopped short of exposing her backside.

The script followed the traditional Caesar-Cleopatra-Antony version, embellished with a bit of anecdotal history (Cleopatra's unorthodox introduction to Caesar wrapped up in a rug from which she materializes when it is unrolled) and legitimized by borrowings from Shakespeare's *Antony and Cleopatra* (the double suicide, in which Antony stabs himself and Cleopatra holds an asp to her breast) and Plutarch's *Life of Antony*, in which Cleopatra is described as an expert poisoner who experiments with convicts. DeMille's Cleopatra is also an amateur pharmacist, who only dabbles in poison because she has been urged to kill Antony before Rome conquers Egypt. Although Cleopatra never lets Antony drink the poisoned wine, she obviously values her empire as much as her lover.

The main title was pure DeMille; the cast, headed by Claudette, appeared at the end of the main title as if carved on stone. Although the actors, for the most part, were relegated to artifact status, they managed to raise DeMille's faux epic several notches above kitsch—no easy feat considering that they had to contend with a production that threatened to turn them into set decorations. As Antony, Henry Wilcoxon was so unaffectedly virile that Claudette was forced to play an ambivalent Cleopatra, who is physically attracted to him but at the same time knows that he is more powerful than she. Aware of his fondness for wine and exotic fare, Cleopatra does not so much ply him with food as tempt him with it, making it readily available as if he were at a banquet. The seduction takes place on the royal barge; after the entertainment, consisting of, among other attractions, women in leopard skins leaping through flaming hoops, there is an elaborate backward-tracking shot that is a model of restrained sensuality. Twin curtains intersect, shielding the recumbent lovers from view. A dancer moves sinuously, and petals rain down from above. The same musical theme is repeated, each time with greater urgency, as if it were accompanying the lovemaking that has been decorously concealed from view. No one needed to see what was transpiring behind the curtains; the music said it all. The camera tracks back at a deliberately slow pace, until the full length of the barge is revealed, with galley slaves rowing to the measured beat of a drum, as if they too were affected by the languorous mood that took hold of the barge as soon as Antony came on board and saw Cleopatra reclining on a white divan in a low-cut, beaded gown.

Historians may take DeMille to task for his recreation of the Battle of Actium, a naval encounter (and not much of one) that he dramatized as a land and sea campaign. Visually, it is the most exciting sequence in the film, especially the shots of the fire-hurling catapults. DeMille, however, does not take liberties with Cleopatra's death; as in *Antony and Cleopatra*, she dies on her throne, robed and crowned. But since much of the film is stylized, so is Cleopatra's death. Although stylization has nothing to do with character portrayal, it has everything to do with DeMille's vision of a world that looked better on a Paramount sound stage than it ever did in real life.

Claudette never worked with DeMille again. When he was having trouble casting the female lead in *Union Pacific*, he thought of Claudette, only because he had seen her in *Under Two Flags* as the feisty Cigarette and felt she could be a credible western heroine. After DeMille approached Claudette about *Union Pacific*, she replied that she and DeMille were too much alike. In his usual patrician style, DeMille responded, saying, in effect, that she was right: "The blow was somewhat assuaged by the charming way in which you put it and by your acknowledging of the fact that we have something in common as director and star." What they had in common was perfectionism, a quality DeMille admired, but only when it coincided with his own. The role in *Union Pacific* went to Barbara Stanwyck, who truly impressed DeMille, although he never sought her services again.

Cleopatra was not Claudette's last encounter with DeMille. They met again when DeMille was host of *Lux Radio Theatre*, an enormously popular program that remained on the air for almost two decades (1936–55) and featured one-hour radio versions of movies, often with the original stars. Claudette appeared frequently on *Lux Radio Theatre*; during the intermission of *Skylark* on 2 February 1942, DeMille encouraged an aspiring actress to "see every picture Claudette Colbert made." When Claudette returned to the microphone for *Once upon a Honeymoon* on 21 April 1943 in the role created by Ginger Rogers, DeMille was effusive in his praise: "She has that priceless something called glamour." He then added, "Counting both pictures and radio, I believe I've starred Claudette Colbert in more plays than any other artist in Hollywood." He was right. DeMille never created a stock company like John Ford's with "John Ford actors" such as John Wayne, Maureen O'Hara, Harry Carey Jr., and Ben Johnson. The closest DeMille came to a director-actor collaboration was with Gloria Swanson and Geraldine Farrar in his silent movies. But in his sound films, Claudette and Gary Cooper, who made three and four films for him, respectively, came the closest to being DeMille regulars.

Actually, there was only one star in a Cecil B. DeMille production: himself. No matter how many times an actor worked for DeMille, he or she was just a member of the cast—star or otherwise. Although DeMille gave Claudette two memorable roles, she was never his creation. Claudette Colbert was partly a product of Paramount Pictures, partly a product of her own invention.

CHAPTER 6

A Night to Remember

When the Academy of Motion Picture Arts and Sciences announced its nominations for 1934, Claudette was flattered to see her name in the Best Actress category. She might also have been pleased that her three films of that year—*Cleopatra*, *Imitation of Life*, and *It Happened One Night*—were up for Best Picture. If she gave the matter any thought, she would have concluded that, of the three, *Imitation* could be the dark horse in a race dominated by MGM (*The Barretts of Wimpole Street*, *The Thin Man*, and *Viva Villa*), Fox (*The House of Rothschild*, *The White Parade*), and Warner Bros. (*Flirtation Walk*, *Here Comes the Navy*). Hollywood insiders would have considered *Cleopatra's* nomination a sop to De Mille, whose *Sign of the Cross* had been excluded from every category except cinematography, and the five nominations for *It Happened One Night* (picture, actor, actress, director, writer) as the Academy's way of giving Columbia hope, as if the studio were a C student in need of encouragement.

Originally, Claudette's competition consisted of Norma Shearer (*The Barretts of Wimpole Street*) and Grace Moore (Columbia's *One Night of Love*). Bette Davis's name was finally added for RKO's *Of Human Bondage*, after the omission—the result of Warner Bros. lack of support for its star because she had defected to RKO to appear in the film version of W. Somerset Maugham's novel—became such a cause celebre that the Academy was forced to agree to a write-in ballot, with Davis becoming "the most promising write-in candidate." Davis's searing portrayal of the doomed Cockney waitress ranks as one of her finest. Many Academy members agreed, but there were not enough votes to bring Davis the recognition she desperately sought. That would come the following year in the form of a consolation prize for the vastly inferior *Dangerous* (1935). However, until the evening of 27 February 1935, Davis seemed to be a shoe-in.

Claudette thought so, too, and had no intentions of changing her vacation plans to attend the awards banquet. In 1935, the Academy Awards ceremony was not the media event into which it has devolved; there were no paparazzi, red carpet, screaming fans, stars in designer gowns and borrowed jewelry, or reporters desperate for sound bites. On 27 February 1935, the Oscars were awarded at a banquet at the Biltmore Hotel in downtown Los Angeles. Claudette had booked a compartment on the Super Chief, scheduled to leave the city that evening, arriving in New York on 3 March.

Claudette had gone straight from *Imitation of Life* into *The Gilded Lily* (1935), which opened two weeks before the awards ceremony, and *Private Worlds*, which premiered a month later. She had experienced some health problems, including a bout of influenza, and looked forward to a vacation once the films were completed.

The popularity of *It Happened One Night* did not escape Paramount's attention. The studio promptly commissioned screenwriter Claude Binyon to create the proletarian rejoinder. Ellie became Marilyn David, a member of the working class, wooed by a Peter Warne type, journalist Peter Dawes (Fred MacMurray) and a British peer in lieu of King Westley, Charles Gray (Ray Milland). When Dawes discovers his rival's identity, he creates a media blitz, known only in the movies of the 1930s when a romance between a British lord and an American stenographer could drive the Great Depression off the front page. Dawes's campaign is so successful that Marilyn becomes an instant celebrity, lionized in the press as the "No Girl" because of her indifference to the privileges of class. Dawes even arranges a nightclub engagement for Marilyn, despite her limited singing and dancing abilities. Marilyn's debut was a tour de force for Claudette. Visibly nervous and insecure, she misses her introduction and asks the conductor to take it from the top, much to the delight of the audience, whom she wins over by her unpretentiousness and vulnerability. She works the circular room, moving from table to table; when she forgets the lyrics, she makes up her own, noting that at least they rhyme.

Despite her newly acquired fame, Marilyn still pines for Gray, until he suggests they spend a week at a country inn. A close-up of Claudette indicates that she has grasped his intentions: "A week? Some little inn?" she asks, skeptically. Having no wish to be either a mistress or a sideshow attraction, she heads back to New York—and Peter Dawes.

Claudette and MacMurray were a natural fit. The warmth the two of them generated as they sat on a stone bench at the New York Public Library, eating popcorn, filtered into the audience, who thought of them as the ideal couple, until Gray arrived on the scene. Milland's Prince Charming was so at odds with MacMurray's common man that audiences hoped Marilyn would make the right choice.

In 1935, audiences were conditioned to fairy-tale endings (and, in fact, relished them). Even *It Happened One Night* made it seem that the only deterrent to the marriage of an heiress and a newspaper reporter was the blanket that separated their beds; and once that fell, so would social barriers. In *The Gilded Lily*, there was no line of demarcation because Marilyn and Dawes came from the same class. Peter Dawes and Peter Warne, however, had one trait in common: a sense of decency that, despite their machinations, endeared them to audiences as well as to Ellie and Marilyn, who found a humanity behind the facade. The ending, in which Marilyn and Dawes are reunited—sitting coatless on the library's stone bench in the midst of a snowfall—returns the film to the realm of fairy tale, where weather has no effect on true love, and only ordinary mortals catch pneumonia.

After finishing *The Gilded Lily*, which was well received, Claudette was even more in need of a rest and vowed she would take one after completing *Private Worlds* (1935), scheduled to open at Paramount's Times Square showcase on 27 March. *Private Worlds*, a Walter Wanger production directed by Gregory LaCava, is set in a mental institution in which Jane Everest (Claudette) and Alex MacGregor (Joel McCrea) are a psychiatric team. Their close working relationship is threatened by the arrival of the new superintendent, Charles Monet (Charles Boyer), who announces immediately that he does not believe psychiatry is a woman's profession and relegates Jane to outpatient care. Aware of her second-class status as a "woman doctor," she accepts her demotion "like a man," leaving the audience to wonder whether Jane will (1) cry sexism and radicalize the staff (an impossibility in view of the overwhelmingly male presence); (2) make a play for MacGregor, whose wife (Joan Bennett) behaves like one of the inmates and is due for a crack-up (which would be unprofessional); or (3) win over Monet after he is injured by a homicidal inmate whom she manages to pacify (most likely scenario). The paucity of female reviewers in 1935 might have accounted for the critics' indifference to the chauvinism pervading the film; in an age of equal opportunity and affirmative action, feminists would boo through most of *Private Worlds*, only to groan at the end when Jane admits that she is in love with Monet; and he, with her. Since Monet has now learned to respect female doctors, he may even allow Jane to continue practicing psychiatry.

Claudette played Jane as if she really believed women were (or were perceived to be) inferior to men, making it necessary for them to work doubly hard to prove their worth. It may have been part of her education in the entertainment business, first in the theatre, then film. And a woman's worth, if she is an actress, can best be expressed in two ways: salary and roles—ideally, both. But if it is a mediocre role, salary will suffice. Thus, if Claudette was known to be a hard bargainer in salary negotiations, it was primarily because she was aware of the industry's ambivalence toward women: as a woman in a male-dominated business, she was an inferior; as an actress, she was royalty. Her ability to exude sophistication or homespun naturalness, depending on the script, paid off. By 1935 she could command a salary of five thousand dollars a week, which placed her in the stars' pantheon, according to *Motion Picture Herald*, which voted her one of the top ten moneymakers of the year. Claudette was great copy for the fan magazines; she had an appeal that transcended gender: men found her sexy, and women envied her sense of style.

Knowing she was a desirable commodity, Claudette priced herself accordingly. The commodity's terms were nonnegotiable: her work day ended at 5:00 p.m. sharp (no exceptions), and if the director of photography by some chance had never heard about her obsession with the left side of her face, he soon learned. From the theatre, Claudette knew that the script was sacrosanct; you played the part, even though you didn't believe in it. In *Private Worlds*, Claudette's name appeared in massive print above the title, with Boyer's name below it. That may have said nothing about her character, but it certainly did about her worth to Paramount Pictures. And in the absence of a script in which she believed, compensation and star billing would suffice.

Thus, Claudette did not think twice about missing the awards banquet, at which either Bette Davis or Norma Shearer would go home with the gold. For her, 27 February was not just her departure date; it was part of an itinerary that she had no intention of changing. She would travel to New York by train, where she hoped to relax for three weeks, see some plays, and shop. But she would not be returning by train. Claudette decided on a leisurely return to the West Coast on the SS *Virginia*, scheduled to leave New York on 25 March, making its way to Havana and Panama before arriving in San Francisco around April 8.

According to Frank Capra's biographer Joseph McBride, "in those days, the winners were informed of their awards about an hour before the ceremony and were paraded before the newsreel cameras to make acceptance speeches." Gable was present that evening and expressed his thanks to both Capra and Claudette. Capra was there also, looking haggard from his recent hospitalization, but Claudette was nowhere in sight. She was about to board the Super Chief when an Academy publicist arrived just in time to cajole her into at least making an appearance. Claudette was unmoved; she could not alter her plans, and, equally important, she was not properly attired. But once she realized that an Oscar could enhance her negotiating power at contract time, she agreed to stop by, accept the award, and then return to the station, where the train was being held for her. Shirley Temple, who received a special award that evening for her "outstanding contribution to screen entertainment," stood on a chair to hand Claudette her Oscar. Claudette was moved, now realizing that the statuette meant more than bargaining power; it was a bona fide tribute from her peers, who were rarely known to honor screwball comedy. And if *It Happened One Night* won the Oscar for Best Picture, it might not have with any other Peter Warne and Ellie Andrews. For the next five days en route to New York, Claudette was able to ponder the personal implications of the movie's title.

Claudette did not appreciate the effect the Oscar had on the public until she arrived in New York, where she could not attend a matinee without being besieged with requests for autographs during the intermission. Claudette obliged, sometimes causing the next act to be delayed for as long as ten minutes. " 'I could just hear the people backstage calling me a certain forceful five-letter word, but what could I do?' " When the *New York Times* reporter asked the inevitable question about the unexpected five Oscars for *It Happened One Night*, she admitted that she thought of it only as "a cute picture that would probably make money because Gable was in it," but at the same time credited Capra for its extraordinary appeal. Ironically, Gable in his acceptance speech thanked the absent Claudette, "who was gracious enough to costar with me." In short, the three of them—and the invaluable Robert Riskin—made it the critical and popular success it became.

When Claudette returned to Los Angeles the second week of April 1935, she expected her next film would be Columbia's *If You Could Only Cook*, only to learn that it had been cast with Jean Arthur and Herbert Marshall. Instead, she would be starring in *She Married Her Boss* with Melvyn Douglas.

The success of *It Happened One Night* inspired Columbia to come up with another vehicle for Claudette, this time with her name above the title and Douglas's below. *Boss*, however, bears no resemblance to Capra's classic, even though the studio was bent on forging one. However, it is hard to imagine all but the most perceptive moviegoers making the connection. All the two films have in common is Claudette, this time as Julia Scott, executive secretary to department store owner Richard Barclay (Melvyn Douglas), whose administrative skills are vastly inferior to hers. This time, there is no prescient father to rescue Julia from an ill-conceived wedding or a scoop-minded reporter to humanize her. In *Boss*, it is Julia's employer who needs humanizing. Although Julia has a playboy admirer, a King Westley clone, there is less likelihood of her running off with him than there was of Ellie's marrying Westley. In each case, a male solves the heroine's dilemma: a father in *Night* and a husband in *Boss*.

She Married Her Boss is a curious film; it was written by Sidney Buchman, who became a Communist in 1938 and remained a party member until 1945. When he wrote the screenplay, he was still a progressive, about to move over to the radical left. Naturally, capitalism comes in for a drubbing, the affluent are portrayed as shallow, and only Julia, who is really middle class before she marries her boss, is granted some measure of integrity. Marriage to Barclay means taking over the household of a divorced man with a brattish child and an overprotective sister. Julia doesn't even try to negotiate a truce with the sister, but she does succeed with the daughter (Edith Fellows)—another instance of Claudette's ability to endear herself to a child by neither catering nor condescending to her.

When Barclay realizes the effect that marriage has had on Julia, who now looks like a woman rather than an executive, he berates her for abandoning the corporate dress code. Julia grudgingly resurrects her executive look, but she cannot conceal her disappointment with her husband. In the only subtle attempt at social criticism in the film, Julia and the playboy sneak into the display window of one of Barclay's stores, where they address the mannequins as if they were members of Barclay's family circle and then proceed to get drunk on champagne. Their antics create a minor scandal, which sends Barclay into a rage; Julia starts packing for a trip to Panama with a man who at least does not criticize her wardrobe. But since *Boss* revolves around the premise that husband knows best, Barclay and Julia end up sailing to Panama, but not before they evidence their contempt for capitalism. In a thoroughly mindless and offensive attempt to prove he loves Julia more than his department store, Barclay, slightly tipsy, starts hurling bricks through the store windows. Yielding to the frenzy of the moment, Julia throws a brick herself, finding the experience thoroughly liberating. But from what has she been liberated? With another actress, the window-breaking scene would have left a sour taste. With Claudette, it almost seemed as if Julia were a kid throwing rocks through the windows of an abandoned house and then scurrying into the night when the police arrive.

Buchman went on to write some outstanding scripts (*Mr. Smith Goes to Washington*, the Oscar-winning *Here Comes Mr. Jordan*, *The Talk of the Town*, etc.), but in *Boss*, he could not weave the various plot threads together (social criticism, male chauvinism, female empowerment), so what might have been a blend of screwball, romantic comedy, and feminism became another movie in which a supremely talented woman and a man whose only talent seems to be making money solve their problems by taking a cruise, leaving the audience to wonder what happens when the vacation is over—and what will be left of the Barclay Department Store once the looters have had their fill.

Like *It Happened One Night*, *She Married Her Boss* opened at Radio City Music Hall. The reviews, while not ecstatic, were laudatory. But the yardstick was *It Happened One Night*, to which *She Married Her Boss* did not measure up.

Neither did Paramount's *The Bride Comes Home*, which was closer to the spirit of Capra's film than *The Gilded Lily*. Paramount had still not given up trying to distill the essence of *It Happened One Night* into a formula for a hit screenplay. Again Claude Binyon was brought in as screenwriter; he fashioned a plot revolving around a quartet of characters consisting of a (once) rich father, his pampered daughter, her wealthy beau, and her middle-class rival. Imagine Ellie Andrews forced to find a job because her father was on the verge of bankruptcy. That was the point of departure for *The Bride Comes Home*, in which Jeanette (Claudette), Ellie redivivus and speaking in the vernacular, ingratiates herself with her childhood sweetheart-turned-millionaire, Jack Bristow (Robert Young), to get a job on the magazine that he and his ex-bodyguard Cyrus Anderson (Fred MacMurray) have started. Since Anderson considers Jeanette a creature of privilege (cf. Peter Warne in *Night*), it is only a matter of time before the triangle collapses, leaving a base occupied by Claudette and MacMurray, as audiences would expect, having already seen them as a potential couple in *The Gilded Lily*.

Looking for a way to end the film with an interrupted wedding ceremony, Binyon imitated his model and added a scene of misunderstanding, which, comparatively, is quite weak: Anderson goes into a snit when Jeanette tidies up his bachelor apartment to make it more livable, convinced that she is attempting to make him over into her image of a respectable mate. His tirade sends her rushing back to Bristow, who proposes marriage. Once Anderson comes to his senses, he and Jeanette's father take off on a motorcycle to stop the ceremony, arriving just before the exchange of vows. However, nothing could compete with the aborted wedding in *Night*, so that all moviegoers got in *The Bride Comes Home* was a wedding they knew would never materialize and a happy ending that they knew would.

Claudette and MacMurray had become a marketable team. They would costar in four more films—two for Paramount and two for Universal—that would draw on their ability to project a naturalness, purged of the phony wholesomeness to which some actors resort when they have to play real people, a species with which they seem to be unfamiliar. Claudette and MacMurray had to fake it in *Maid of Salem*, but otherwise they were always an endearing couple, with Claudette's sophistication complementing MacMurray's homespun ingenuousness.

A Fred MacMurray type, however, was not what Claudette sought in real life when her marriage to Norman Foster ended.

CHAPTER 7

The End of a Modern Marriage

Claudette's Oscar paid off—literally. In July 1935, Paramount rewarded her with a seven-picture contract that raised her salary to $150,000 a picture and permitted her to make at least three more at other studios. The year 1935 proved memorable for another reason: her relationship with Dr. Joel "Joe" Pressman, whom she first met in August 1933, when he performed her appendectomy, changed dramatically. Plagued by periodic attacks of sinusitis, Claudette learned that Pressman was also an otolaryngologist and arranged for a consultation. Soon they were no longer doctor and patient. Claudette discovered a man who, unlike the actors she had known, shunned the spotlight and was interested only in achieving prominence in a profession that had nothing to do with show business, about which he cared little. Actors suffer from insecurity, which they conceal behind a meticulously crafted persona. Pressman, however, did not need a persona; he was secure in the knowledge that he was one of the best practitioners in his field. And yet, Pressman had to admit he never had a patient like Claudette, who could enchant with a smile and seduce with a look. In Claudette's case, it was not the same kind of passion that she experienced with Foster; it was the kind of love that two people discover when the heyday in the blood is subsiding, as companionship and compatibility take on greater importance than sex. Claudette had now found a man who respected her both as a woman and an artist, but was interested in her only as the former; Pressman found a woman who had a life totally different from his—a life that would consume as much time on sound stages, location shooting, and publicity junkets as his did in consultation, surgery, and research. To use the movie cliché, they were made for each other.

By 1934, Claudette had become so involved with Pressman that she had no other choice but to initiate divorce proceedings against Foster. Their marriage was no longer modern; in fact, it had become so ultra modern that it was not even a marriage. She and Foster not only lived apart, but worked apart, even though they were in the same business. While Claudette had a home studio, Foster did not; he freelanced. In 1936, he made a startling—but, in retrospect, understandable—transition to directing. But before he turned director, Foster thought he had reached his nadir, personally and professionally. Around Academy Award time, rumors began circulating that Claudette was seeking a divorce; in fact, on 2 March, en route to New York after winning her Oscar, Claudette admitted it when she had to transfer at Chicago's LaSalle Street station for the Twentieth Century Limited.

That August, the marriage formally ended when Claudette filed for divorce in Juarez, Mexico. According to the press, the divorce was amicable, with Foster announcing his intention to marry Sally Blane, Loretta Young's older sister. But there was still a residue of regret, even though each had found someone who eventually proved to be the perfect mate. Claudette at least acknowledged that her modern marriage was a failure, as she told *Photoplay*: " 'I believe that one of the troubles with a 'modern marriage' is that it does away with the small intimacies of daily living.' " Although Claudette's modern marriage scenario was a flop, she at least came out of it unscarred. Foster's scars were not just emotional; they were visible. Around the time of the divorce, he was reportedly attacked by an unidentified as sailant and badly beaten, but not disfigured. In the documentary *Directed by Norman*

Foster, film scholar Scott MacIsaac placed the attack in context: "[Foster's] marriage to Claudette Colbert was breaking up and there was a terrible incident that seems related to the breakup." "Related to the breakup" is the crucial phrase. The attacker boasted, "You're never going to work again." Since Foster was not an A-list actor, it was hardly a case of professional rivalry. Claudette's niece, Claudette "Coco" Lewis, recalled a story that her father (Claudette's brother, Charles Wendling) told about an incident that took place at a family dinner, at which Wendling "ended up hauling Foster off, flattening him out, and breaking his nose. Aunt Claudette took him to the best surgeon in town to have his nose fixed—and that turned out to be Jack Pressman." Whether that was the "terrible incident" to which MacIsaac alluded or whether Foster was assaulted on another occasion is unknown. But if MacIssaac is correct, there seems to have been some connection between the marital breakup and the attack.

Regardless, it turned out to be a blessing in disguise: Norman Foster went on to a far more rewarding and lucrative career, which he might not have done, or not as soon, if the incident had not occurred. His attacker, however, was wrong; Foster *did* work, but for the most part behind the camera, acquiring a reputation as an accomplished director, albeit of B movies—a director with whom actors enjoyed working because, as one of them, he was sensitive to their needs.

Foster's 1937 publicity photos showed no sign of a battered face; actually, he looked handsomer and more rugged than before. Still, he was leery about returning to acting, perhaps because he remembered his assailant's words. From then on, Norman Foster was primarily a director and often a writer-director.

Foster had spent a year at Carnegie Tech (now Carnegie Mellon), which sparked his interest in art, not from an aesthetic standpoint, but from a practical one. As a film actor, he was more aware of lighting and scenic design than most of his colleagues, to whom a set was simply an acting area; and lighting, a means of creating depth, casting shadows, and removing age lines. Foster was also intrigued by East Asia, particularly China and Japan, which he and Claudette visited for the first time on their round-the-world honeymoon. Twentieth Century-Fox believed that Foster's sensitivity to the "mysterious East," as East Asia was popularly known, could work to the studio's advantage. In the early 1930s, Fox embarked on a series inspired by Earl Derr Biggers's Chinese detective, Charlie Chan, whose expert sleuthing was already familiar to moviegoers from several silent films. Although Foster would later direct a few Charlie Chan movies, Fox wanted him primarily for its new series about Mr. Moto, Chan's Japanese counterpart.

Kentaro Moto, the creation of novelist John P. Marquand, never achieved the celebrity of Dashiell Hammett's Sam Spade or Raymond Chandler's Philip Marlowe: he was not a private eye but an amateur sleuth—a Japanese Nick Charles, without a Nora and a tumbler of martinis. Foster was the ideal director to introduce Mr. Moto. What Foster saw on his honeymoon made him curious about a culture so different from his own that he wanted to strip away, or at least peer through, the curtain that Hollywood had pulled across it. Foster's aim was to combine exoticism, which audiences expected, with a certain degree of realism by at least reducing the stereotypy that such films invite (and to which audiences were accustomed). What Foster did not want were extras that looked as if they came from Central Casting. Foster's intentions were honorable, but they could not be fully realized in a low-budget series, each of whose films averaged around seventy minutes.

If Foster could not change preconceived ideas, he could at least undermine them. Foster was very much a champion of the marginalized; his understanding of minorities was never more apparent than in his Oscar-nominated documentary, *Navajo* (1952), which dramatized the plight of a Native American boy in an all-white school. His compassion for victims of discrimination may well have stemmed from his marriage to Claudette, which prompted gossip-mongers to label it a sham, a subterfuge that allowed the two of them to pursue same-sex relationships, which have never been verified and exist only in rumors circulated among industry insiders who equate inference with fact.

In the late 1930s, and especially during the 1940s, no Hollywood director could eradicate the image that audiences had of Asians, even Asian protagonists. Thus, Foster could not alter Moto's appearance, but he could, and did, change that of the actor portraying him, the Hungarian-born Peter Lorre. Lorre was given a complete makeover: "With hair blackening, eyeliner, a blending of grease paints, and steel-rimmed glasses (the teeth were his own), the makeup department attuned cosmetic detail to current stereotypes." Lorre may have conformed to the audience's image of a Japanese male (soft-spoken, slight of build, and uncommonly polite), but at least Foster humanized Moto by endowing him with physical prowess, awesome powers of deduction, and a vocabulary that far exceeded the fortune-cookie aphorisms of Charlie Chan.

In *Think Fast, Mr. Moto* (1937), the first of the series, Mr. Moto is an importer as well as a master of disguise, who works secretly with federal agents to unmask a smuggling ring. Moto is no stranger to violence; en route to Shanghai, he thinks nothing of tossing a steward overboard after discovering that he is in league with the smugglers.

The intricate plot—a model citizen is revealed as the arch villain, and the woman of dubious allegiance is a white Russian forced to work for the syndicate—is resolved with far more intelligence than many B movies of the era. Thoroughly dissatisfied with the script, Foster rewrote it, sharing authorship with Howard Ellis Smith. Of the eight films in the series, Foster directed and coauthored six: *Think Fast, Mr. Moto; Thank You, Mr. Moto* (both 1937); *Mr. Moto Takes a Chance; Mysterious Mr. Moto* (both 1938); *Mr. Moto's Last Warning;* and *Mr. Moto Takes a Vacation* (both 1939).

To achieve an air of authenticity, Foster raided the Fox library for stock footage of the cities where the main action is set (e.g., San Francisco and Shanghai in *Thank You,* Port Said in *Last Warning,* London in *Mysterious Mr. Moto*). For the judo scenes, he used a double, since Moto, unlike Lorre, was a judo expert. The judo scenes, framed in long shot, were done so realistically that it scarcely mattered. What mattered was that Moto was a pro. When a disguise was needed, he adopted one (a street peddler in *Think Fast,* a Japanese valet in *Mysterious*); when he had to confront a killer, he knew how to point a gun—and fire it.

Mysterious Mr. Moto is the best of the series. Moto, now a member of the international police, has infiltrated the penal colony at Devil's Island, masquerading as an inmate so he can become friendly with another prisoner, Paul Brissac (Leon Ames), a key member of the League of Assassins, a murky organization involved in smuggling contraband material and obtaining secret formulas. Exactly what the league planned to do with the formulas is never specified, but easily inferred. The film was released in 1938, when the world was a year away from war; two league members have German-sounding names. Obviously, the formulas are for manufacturing armaments that were not destined for Britain and its allies.

Moto engineers an escape from Devil's Island so he and Brissac can make their way to London, where Moto poses as Brissac's valet. The London sequences gave Foster a chance to indulge his passion for atmosphere, even if it had to be recreated on a soundstage. Fog swirls around the dockside pubs, where the only light comes from street lamps. Menacing faces and enigmatic types abound, so that one is never sure who is on which side of the law.

Foster also took advantage of the London setting to take a few swipes at British snobbery, which is tinged with racism. Until Mr. Moto is recognized as an agent in league with Scotland Yard, he is treated as an inferior. In a pub he is deliberately overcharged; one of the patrons even trips him as he is bringing a drink back to the table. When he asks for another, he is charged even more. Then one of the patrons growls, "We don't want your sort around here."

And yet it is Mr. Moto who saves the day by exposing the real head of the league (the least likely suspect). The climax of the film was inspired by *The Phantom of the Opera* and is just as effective. The chandelier that was supposed to fall on a Czech industrialist comes crashing down on his friend, who is really the mastermind of the League of Assassins.

The renewal of interest in the Mr. Moto series, which resulted in a deeper appreciation of Foster's work as a director, debunks the myth that his major achievement was RKO's *Journey into Fear* (1942), based on Eric Ambler's popular espionage novel. Before Orson Welles made his legendary film debut in *Citizen Kane* (1941), he screened a number of movies (not just John Ford's *Stagecoach*) to familiarize himself with the language of cinema. He was particularly interested in those that were shot in chiaroscuro and seemed to be taking place in a kind of half light; that was the visual style he was seeking for *Kane*. Among the films Welles viewed were Foster's Mr. Moto films. He was impressed by Foster's manipulation of light and shadow, but also by his skill in skirting the pitfalls of caricature.

When Welles realized he would not be able to direct *Journey into Fear* because he was too involved in editing *The Magnificent Ambersons* (1942), which RKO later recut, he put Foster in charge of the film—or rather entrusted the direction to Foster under *his* supervision. First, Foster had to be recalled from Mexico, where he was shooting *My Friend Bonito,* which he had written with John Fante. *Bonito* was to have been part of another Welles film—one about which the director was passionate—called *It's All True*, a three-part Latin American documentary in support of President Roosevelt's Good Neighbor Policy. What exists of *My Friend Bonito* and the other segments of *It's All True* became available in 1993. One can understand why Welles sought out Foster for *It's All True*; if Welles had been able to complete it, the film would have been more of an ethnographic study than a documentary. Foster did not shy away from ethnicity; in fact, he embraced it. *My Friend Bonito* revealed Foster's compassion for a Mexican boy whose pet bull is conscripted for the bull ring. The spectators are so moved by the boy's devotion to the bull that they insist that the animal's life be spared.

After completing *Journey into Fear*, Foster returned to Mexico to make a few more pictures in a country that he had grown to love. By 1948, he was back in Hollywood, working nonstop, much as he did as a movie actor in the 1930s. He directed his sister-in-law, Loretta Young, in *Rachel and the Stranger* (1948) and other actresses of a certain age who were no longer at the peak of their fame: Joan Fontaine (*Kiss the Blood off My Hands*, 1948),

Rosalind Russell (*Tell it to the Judge*, 1949), and Ann Sheridan (*Woman on the Run*, 1950). Foster was extraordinarily adaptable. Since he did not think television was beneath him, he went on to a third career, beginning in the 1950s, as a TV writer-director, notably of Disney's *Davy Crockett* series with Fess Parker. He worked steadily until 1974, when he was diagnosed with colon cancer, from which he died two years later.

Claudette told her close friend Helen O'Hagan that Foster was the first man with whom she fell in love and that what she experienced with him could never be duplicated. But Claudette and Foster were in their twenties when they married, and it was the 1920s as well, when everything went because "anything goes," as Cole Porter summarized the era. Then Claudette looked and dressed like a flapper, a jazz baby, the kind who would end up at one of Jay Gatsby's parties and dance till dawn. But that was another world; this was Depression America, 1935.

As early as 1934, Claudette and Dr. Joel Pressman had become what the columnists called an "item"; by November 1935, they were a couple lacking a marriage certificate. Pressman, a graduate of the Harvard School of Medicine, had been practicing in Los Angeles since 1928 and, at the time, was a recognized otolaryngologist and co-chief of head and neck surgery at the City of Hope Medical Center. On the morning of 29 November 1935, a couple identified as "Dr. and Mrs. J. M. Pressman" left Los Angeles by plane for San Francisco, where Pressman was scheduled to deliver a paper entitled "The Larynx" at UCLA. When they arrived, they were mobbed by newspaper reporters with flashbulb cameras. Pressman knew that he was not the center of attraction. He had a reputation to maintain and had no intention of being photographed with Claudette until it was time to announce their wedding plans. A few days earlier, Pressman went into a rage when a photographer surprised the two of them in Hollywood and snapped their picture. He demanded the negative, which he promptly destroyed.

In San Francisco, the situation turned ugly: "Waiting newspapermen and cameramen were shunned by the medico as he rushed toward a waiting limousine. When they succeeded in ferreting him out for pictures, the physician lost his temper, flew toward flashbulbs and cameras, and mixed with one photographer. Airport attaches separated them as his colleagues snapped shots of the melee." Another account described how "Pressman smashed the flashlight bulbs held by a photographer and threw the camera to the ground after taking out a plate and smashing it. The cameraman's hand was cut in the melee." The incident showed that Claudette's future husband had much to learn about endearing himself to the media. It was Claudette who had to restore some semblance of civility, even though she was visibly disturbed by Pressman's behavior. Claudette insisted that she and Pressman were only engaged and that the ticket issued to "Dr. and Mrs. J. M. Pressman" was the fault of the agent, who assumed they were married. When asked why she was on the flight, Claudette turned on the charm: "It is customary to accompany one's friends, isn't it?" Attempting to explain Pressman's irrational behavior, Claudette became coyly diplomatic: "I do not mind being photographed . . . but men seem to resent it and especially Dr. Pressman, because he is not an actor." Once they married, whenever they went to the theatre, Claudette entered first, so that just before the curtain went up, the publicity-shy Pressman could quickly come down the aisle and take the vacant seat next to hers.

Now that the press was aware of their relationship, they had no other choice but to marry as quickly as possible. Pressman originally told the *Los Angeles Times* (30 November 1935) that it would be in early 1936. But once he regained his composure and agreed to pose for pictures upon their return to Los Angeles, Pressman knew Claudette's public (which would, in part, become his) expected something sooner. It would not be a rushed marriage, the kind to which couples resort to avert scandal. On the other hand, Claudette's explanation for the names on the ticket was not entirely plausible, even though she insisted that she discovered the error in mid flight and had it corrected; how, she never explained.

If they were having an affair, the press did not play it up. Still, it would be professionally advantageous for them to marry before the new year. On 23 December, Claudette informed the influential gossip columnist Louella

Parsons that she and Pressman would leave Los Angeles early the next morning for Yuma, Arizona, where they planned to be married before a justice of the peace. Certain dates have an undeniable cachet, Christmas Eve being one of them. For someone as media-savvy as Claudette, a Christmas Eve wedding makes for good copy and happy fans, especially those who wax sentimental around Yuletide. Pressman, Claudette, and her brother Charles drove to Yuma, where the ceremony was performed by Justice of the Peace Earl A. Freeman, who was overjoyed: "She's my favorite actress, and I never had met her." Claudette was simply but tastefully dressed in a gray tailored suit with a yellow motif and matching hat and coat. After the ceremony, they traveled to Yosemite for a five-day honeymoon.

For her new life, Claudette wanted a new home. She had seen a house on 615 North Faring Road, directly across from actress Irene Dunne's, in exclusive Holmby Hills. What first attracted her was the two-acre property with its tennis court, vegetable and flower gardens, four-car garage, and servants' quarters. It lacked a swimming pool, but that could be easily remedied. What Claudette did not like was the house itself, which she had razed and rebuilt according to her taste. She wanted a house in the Georgian style, with an impressive but inviting exterior and a circular driveway. The interior also conformed to her specifications. Lyle Wheeler, the Twentieth Century-Fox art director, extolled her gift for interior design in a 1952 *Photoplay* article, describing the way she combined symmetry (a round coffee table balanced by a rectangular one; a color scheme of gray, green, and beige) and whimsy (a powder room with red-lacquered walls with white monkeys). Her bedroom was a study in pink and white: a pink bed and sofa, white carpeting, and a white bedspread with an aquatic motif that she had designed herself. Pressman's was green and white: white ceiling, walls, and woodwork; green carpeting and lounge chair; and drapes in green, yellow, and white. But from the way Wheeler described the entrance hall, it was apparent that if Claudette had never become an actress, she could have been an interior decorator for those who wanted not just a home but one that reflected the owners at their best, even if they might not have known what that was, but were willing to trust someone who could divine it:

> The entrance hall gives the indication of the graciousness of the rest of the house, for it uses the same colors as the drawing room—beige and apricot—and has the same beige rug on its floors. Walls have been painted a rich apricot color with the woodwork white for contrast. The staircase is at the right, traveling up and around so that the upper half seems to be a balcony around the wall of the entrance hall. The same apricot walls and white trim continue down the hall at the left which leads to the living room.

As an actress, Claudette not only understood how lighting could sculpt the face, but also appreciated the way an art director, such as Paramount's Hans Dreier, could design a room worthy of a museum. Claudette's knowledge of art—combined with her appreciation of the subtleties of decor that probably eluded most movie actors, and a natural appreciation of beauty—formed her aesthetic sense. Even though Claudette had never read the major treatises on aesthetics, she would have understood the nature of beauty as the harmonization of disparate elements (light, color, balance, etc.) that in lesser hands would have produced a patchwork quilt; but in those of an artist, an expertly woven coat of many colors.

The fan magazines gave the impression that Jeanne Chauchoin lived with her daughter and son-in-law. Edie Goetz, the wife of producer William Goetz, told Claudette in no uncertain terms that if she wanted her second marriage to succeed, her mother must live by herself. The situation was complicated by the fact that Jeanne liked her son-in-law; she even overlooked his being Jewish because he had a real profession, as opposed to her daughter, who was only an actress. Claudette found a house for her mother far enough away from her own to discourage frequent visits. Claudette's one concession to family harmony was the Friday night ritual. Unless Claudette had a pressing engagement, Jeanne would be chauffeured over to Faring Drive, where she would join her daughter and son-in-law for dinner.

Sometimes Claudette's brother Charles would also attend. Claudette must have drawn on hidden reserves of patience on those occasions when Pressman was absent. One can only imagine what the dinner conversation—in French, of course—was like between a famous daughter and a mother whose idea of a famous woman was not a movie star but an opera diva, which she had once hoped to be.

CHAPTER 8

Life after Oscar

Oscars often prove to be a mixed blessing. They are prestigious, of course, but they do not necessarily advance a career or recharge one that has been dormant. When Louise Fletcher won hers for *One Flew over the Cuckoo's Nest* (1975), there were more roles, but none as memorable as Nurse Ratched. The Oscar did more for her costar, Jack Nicholson, who won for Best Actor, and again for *Terms of Endearment* (1983) and *As Good as It Gets* (1997). Nicholson never lacked for parts tailored to his persona; Fletcher, lacking a persona, simply had to take what was offered her. Even winning two Oscars in a row, as Luise Rainer did for *The Great Ziegfeld* (1936) and *The Good Earth* (1937) did not guarantee longevity. Rainer's Hollywood career ended—perhaps with an assist from MGM's Louis Mayer, who balked at her independence—with the powerful but virtually forgotten World War II film, Paramount's *Hostages* (1943). On the other hand, after Spencer Tracy won two consecutive Oscars (*Captains Courageous*, 1937; *Boys Town*, 1938); the roles kept coming in: some great, others less so, but none unworthy of him.

In Hollywood, it is always hit or miss.

What Claudette's Oscar meant, apart from a new contract, was another spate of films that showcased her flair for romantic comedy, which she infused with warmth, wit, and, above all, charm; and she gave her personal take on the suffering/misunderstood heroine, who was always a woman of courage. It was not until 1939—the same year of *Gone with the Wind*, Clark Gable's best film since *It Happened One Night*—that Claudette starred in another classic; or at least a film now acknowledged as one: Mitchell Leisen's *Midnight*. Until then, there were leading roles, but no memorable ones.

When Fox decided to remake *Under Two Flags* (1936), which had already been filmed twice, first in 1916, and again six years later, the role of Cigarette, the vampish café owner (first played by Theda Bara) in love with Sergeant Victor (Ronald Colman), a French legionnaire, was originally intended as Simon Simone's American film debut. Since Fox's would be the first sound version of *Under Two Flags*, an authentically French Cigarette was what production head Darryl F. Zanuck wanted. And Simone Simon was the genuine article.

Simon, however, was thoroughly uncooperative, perhaps because she felt that American movie stars are expected to be temperamental, but, more likely, because she was insecure about her English. She managed well enough a year later in the remake of *Seventh Heaven* (1937), but even then there was something halting about the way she delivered her lines. In her best remembered film, *Cat People* (1942), one sensed that Simon understood the complex nature of her character, Irena, who can turn into a panther when she senses a rival or feels sexually threatened. Simon got to the core of the character by working through the subtext rather than the dialogue itself. Her troubled look and taut body indicated that the ancestral curse left Irena frigid, jealous, guilt-ridden, and murderous. The dialogue was only an entrée into Irena's psyche. By 1944, her English had improved, but by then World War II was winding down, and once it was over, Simon returned to France.

Initially, Hollywood seemed totally alien to Simon. She was habitually late on the set, claiming illness. Sensing that the crew had become exasperated with her, "she appeared one day with a thermometer in her mouth. When she was not before the camera, she reclined, taking her temperature. Whenever things occurred that were unpleasant for her she took the register out and showed a temperature of 105 degrees." Director Frank Lloyd could take no more of her antics and demanded her dismissal. The press was informed that Simon had been taken ill and would be replaced by Claudette, who was eager to make a film at the relatively new Twentieth Century-Fox.

Claudette was not the star; Colman was. But she liked the idea of making Cigarette a cocotte, not a camp follower. She also had an opportunity to sing in French and eloquently express the pain of unrequited love when Sergeant Victor (Colman) shows a greater interest in Lady Venetia (Rosalind Russell, on loan from MGM) than he does in her. And she had a truly operatic death scene. When Victor's battalion is surrounded by Arab tribesmen, Cigarette leads the rescue brigade, saving Victor for Lady Venetia but losing her life in the process. At least she dies in Victor's arms and is awarded the Medal of Honor posthumously. Claudette gave the best performance in the film. Only the climax, with Cigarette riding alongside the legionnaires, upstaged her, as it did the entire cast. The climax was the work of second-unit director Otto Brower, who staged it brilliantly with extras drawn from the local ranches in Yuma, Arizona, where the exteriors were filmed. Arab horsemen streamed down the dunes and fell from their horses on cue, giving the sequence a terrible beauty.

After *Under Two Flags*, Claudette returned to Paramount for *I Met Him in Paris* (1937). The (by now) familiar triangular scenario (female torn between two males) was augmented by a third male, who, fortunately, was not important enough to turn the script into a quadrangle. *Paris* was the last collaboration between Claudette and director Wesley Ruggles. The screenwriter Claude Binyon had become so familiar with the Claudette Colbert type of film that he turned one out that seemed different from the rest, partly because the on-location shooting in Sun Valley, Idaho (which doubled as Switzerland), gave Claudette the opportunity to demonstrate her skills as a champion skier and expert ice skater. Claudette was a natural athlete. When she was making *Manslaughter* for George Abbott, she refused a double for a water-skiing sequence and asked that it not be filmed until she learned how to water ski. She was a quick study, and there was no double.

In *I Met Him in Paris*, Kay Denham (Claudette) is on a dream vacation in Paris, where she meets playwright George Potter (Douglas) and novelist Gene Anders (Robert Young), who vie for her affection. To complicate matters, the persistent Berk Sutter (Lee Bowman) follows her to Paris, where he discovers that he has competition. Casting Young as a married playboy-writer, whose chief concern is scoring with Kay before Potter does, was a mistake. In his scenes with Claudette, the actor's youthful appearance (he was four years her junior but looked even younger) was more apparent than it was in *The Bride Comes Home*. In *Paris*, there is a love scene shot in profile, in which Claudette's half-moon eyebrows and provocative eye shadow suggest an older woman. Claudette was then thirty-four, and in that unflatteringly lighted scene, looked it. By comparison, Young could have passed for a college senior.

When the trio takes off for Switzerland, the pace accelerates, thanks to the skiing and tobogganing scenes; what the performers could not accomplish, brilliant process photography did. Until she hit the slopes, Claudette was a fashion statement in Travis Banton's gowns. But once she donned a pair of ski pants, she ceased being Kay Denham, a New Yorker to whom snow was slush, and morphed into a winter sports enthusiast, as Claudette was in real life. Claudette was not the only one to demonstrate a skill other than acting, Douglas did, too; he was a natural on the ice. There is an extended sequence in which Douglas and Claudette skate together, as he subtly woos her in what, in a musical, would have been a mating dance. At that point, there was no doubt as to who would win Kay's heart.

Paris was the last time Claudette worked with Douglas, with whom she evidenced such rapport. A decade later, Young was reunited with Claudette in the forgettable *Bride for Sale*, in which he still looked too young for her, even though the script called for her to choose him over George Brent. Meanwhile, Young found more age-compatible stars such as Laraine Day and Dorothy McGuire. Douglas, who could play urbane or tough, with gradations of each, went on to star opposite Hollywood royalty: Greta Garbo (twice), Merle Oberon, Joan Crawford, Loretta Young, Katharine Hepburn, Rosalind Russell, Maureen O'Hara, and Ava Gardner.

As for Claudette, it was back to work. At least she would be reunited with old friends Fred MacMurray and Charles Boyer: MacMurray at Paramount for *Maid of Salem* and Boyer at Warners for *Tovarich* (both 1937).

The Big Role still eluded her. It was certainly not the title character in *Maid of Salem*, set in 1692, the year of the Salem witchcraft trials. Some of the historical figures from the trials, such as Tituba, Rebecca Nurse, and Reverend Samuel Paris, appear as minor characters. However, they are better known, along with the more prominent Reverend John Hale and Deputy Governor Danforth, from Arthur Miller's play, *The Crucible*. Just as *The Crucible* evoked the miasma of McCarthyism when it opened on Broadway in 1953, *Maid of Salem* was an undisguised plea for tolerance, which, at the time of its release in March 1937, could not be voiced strongly enough. Mussolini had conquered Ethiopia, the Spanish Civil War was in its second year, Hitler had remilitarized the Rhineland, and racial laws had been enacted in Germany, forbidding intermarriage between Christians and Jews.

Although the film itself is unexceptional, it might have fared better with a different male lead and more subtle acting from the supporting cast. When a droopy-eyed alcoholic claims that the cows have been bewitched, one is tempted to smirk. But in 1692 Salem, the slightest reference to witchcraft could bring anyone before a tribunal of self-righteous judges, willing to indulge neighbors eager to air festering grievances and settle old scores.

Claudette's character, Barbara Clarke, is a nonconformist who wears a fancy bonnet to Sunday service, knowing it is inappropriate; nor is she embarrassed when Reverend Paris glowers at her from the pulpit. When Ann Good of the ironic surname (Bonita Granville, who had played another monstrous child the year before in *These Three*) discovers a book on witchcraft in her father's library, she and her friends read it; when confronted, Ann becomes hysterical, implicating others, including the black slave Tituba, thus causing further polarization between the community's freethinkers and hardliners and bringing Salem to the brink of extremism.

Initially, Barbara is oblivious to the darkening mood in the village, behaving like the "dizzy dame" of screwball, which was probably what the writers intended. When Barbara falls in love with the rebel Roger Coverman (Fred MacMurray, who periodically attempts an Irish brogue, sometimes succeeding but more often not), she feels a heightened sense of liberation. He teaches her to dance; when her aunt's impressionable son sees her, to protect Coverman, Barbara tells him she was dancing "with no man," which the tribunal interprets as meaning that her partner was no "man" because he was Satan.

Just when it seems that Barbara will die on the gallows, the eleventh-hour rescue comes in the person of Coverman, who convinces the boy to admit that he was the "man." Happy ending, nice and tidy, except that there was no reprieve for Rebecca Nurse, Giles Corey, and the other innocent victims of hysteria and intolerance. As if to herald the dawn of a new era, the villagers set fire to the hanging tree. The final image, striking as it is, could not compensate for the innocent lives that had been lost. Viewed within the context of pre–World War II Europe, *Maid of Salem* seems more prophetic than it actually was. Historically, the timing was right, but the film was a financial failure. Although Travis Banton designed Claudette's costumes, elegant finery was out of the question in theocratic Salem; audiences were not eager to see Claudette in regulation attire.

Tovarich (1937) was more of a Claudette Colbert film, although it was never intended as such. Claudette longed to play Joan of Arc, and Warners was interested. A Joan of Arc film, starring Claudette and directed by Russian-born Anatole Litvak, a recent Hollywood arrival, was announced in mid May 1936; seven months later, the press reported that the studio had abandoned the project. Instead, Litvak would direct Claudette in the movie version of *Tovarich*, which would satisfy her one-film commitment to Warners.

Set in Paris, *Tovarich* should have been a natural for Paramount, where Francophilia reigned since the 1920s. The Hungarian-born Adolph Zukor adopted a Continental approach to moviemaking, with Paris and Vienna as the cultural beacons for Americans looking for models of civilized behavior, particularly in terms of relationships between the sexes. Paramount entrusted the Continental touch to a variety of hands, including Gloria Swanson, whose looks were hardly American and could easily pass for Parisian, and, of course, Maurice Chevalier, whose accent matched the twinkle in his eye.

Paramount was also fortunate in having directors such as Ernst Lubitsch, Rouben Mamoulian, Mitchell Leisen, and, later, Billy Wilder, and the extraordinary set designer Hans Dreier, who gave Paramount films the white look, where sets shone with a luminescence no other studio could rival. If a French native were to wander onto the Paramount's famous Paris street, he or she would have experienced the charm of recognition. Paramount's back lot was an all-purpose Paris: "There was the Bohemian Paris of the painters; the champagne Paris of the ubiquitous rich; the artistic Paris of the Louvre; the fashionable Paris of Balmain and Chanel; the romantic Paris of Montmartre; the literary Paris of the sidewalk cafes; the dangerous Paris of the Apache."

Just as the ideal studio for *Tovarich* would have been Paramount, the ideal director would have been Ernst Lubitsch, whose proverbial touch would have given an operetta-like quality to a film about Russian royalty reduced to refugee status in Paris after the Bolshevik Revolution. However, it was not Paramount but Warners that acquired the rights to Robert E. Sherwood's 1936 translation of Jacques Deval's play. In his autobiography, *Starmaker*, Hal Wallis, Warners' head of production, lists it among the films he produced, although his name does not appear in the credits, nor does that of the associate producer, then called "supervisor," Robert Lord. The reason was simple: it was "An Anatole Litvak production." In fact, it was such an Anatole Litvak production that the usual credit, "Directed by," did not appear on the screen.

It was probably Wallis's idea to make the movie; as an avid theatergoer, Wallis was always looking for plays with film potential. In fact, *Tovarich*

arrived on the screen relatively intact. The film was also Wallis's first exposure to the Litvak school of directing, in which the director was not just an
auteur but a dictator as well, with the cast as his subjects. Wallis's memos
reflect his impatience with Litvak, who insisted on far more rehearsals than
Wallis thought necessary. Wallis's argument was simple: the more rehearsals,
the less spontaneous the performance. Litvak had no intention of changing
his ways; he knew that Warners wanted him, even though he was, in Bette
Davis's words, "a very stubborn director."

Tovarich was, in every respect, an Anatole Litvak production. Although
Robert Lord, a highly regarded producer at Warners, had been assigned to
the film, he had no idea who would star in it until he saw an announce-
ment in the trades. Lord immediately wrote to Wallis, questioning the suit-
ability of both Charles Boyer as Mikhail ("a sad, meek little man . . . adored
by women") and Basil Rathbone as Gorotchenko (who would throw the
film "completely off balance") and proposing Fredric March or Brian Aherne
as Mikhail and Edward G. Robinson as Gorotchenko. Apparently, Lord
thought Claudette was well cast.

If Lord was unaware of the casting, it was because Litvak did not consider him worth consulting. Litvak must have consulted with Warner and
Wallis, since Claudette was not a Warner Bros. contract player and, in fact,
had never worked at the studio; she was taking advantage of the clause in
her Paramount contract that allowed her to make a few films elsewhere.
Boyer was not under contract to any studio, preferring two- or three-picture
deals. Since Boyer had worked with Litvak in the French film *Mayerling*
(1936) and had played opposite Claudette in *Private Worlds*, the director
knew they would make a perfect Prince and Grand Duchess. As far as Litvak
was concerned, Lord was merely a supervisor, which at Warners meant keeping the film on schedule.

Tovarich was the first of nine films that Litvak made at Warners between
1937 and 1942. At first Jack Warner indulged him; Litvak was, after all, a
cultivated European who could inject a bit of sophistication into a studio
known primarily for melodramas and crime movies. And so Litvak made

his Warner debut in a movie about two white Russian émigrés, Prince Mikail (Boyer) and his wife, Grand Duchess Tatiana Petrovna (Claudette), who fled the Bolshevik Revolution, along with the equivalent of 40 billion French francs entrusted to them by the Czar. Rather than use the Czar's money for themselves, they prefer to live as refugees and work as servants in the Dupont household.

The moment of truth arrives when Dupont hosts a dinner party for the members of an oil cartel. Everyone is awaiting the arrival of the guest of honor, Commissar Gorotchenko (Basil Rathbone), hoping he will sign over the Baku oil fields to the cartel. Although Mikail and Tatiana have been forewarned of his presence, they do not blanch, even though Gorotchenko had tortured Mikail when he and Tatiana were being held in Lubyanka prison.

The dinner party is an extraordinary set piece, a model of civility even when the conversation turns to torture. As the guests are sipping cocktails, one of them recognizes Tatiana and kneels to her, addressing her as Grand Duchess. The Duponts, sticklers for protocol, must now treat the couple as servants as well as royalty. True to their station, Mikail and Tatiana serve the guests, even though they must stand by listening to Gorotchenko's justification of bloodshed and his torturing of Mikail, whom he now recognizes.

Soon, they have had enough. But servants to the end, they wash the dishes before leaving the Duponts. Since the kitchen is their domain, they are unprepared for a visit from Gorotchenko, who no longer speaks with icy dispassion. His face looks less bloodless, as if it had been suffused with a trickle of humanity. Gorotchenko cannot conceal his admiration for the couple, even though politically they are poles apart. Their Mother Russia is now his Soviet Union, but what they have in common are the interests of the Russian people. Gorotchenko informs them that unless they give him the 40 billion francs so he can buy tractors to keep the peasants from starving, he will be forced to sell the Baku oil fields to the cartel. Since Baku is Russia's main source of oil, they understand his dilemma. Thus, there is nothing sacrificial about their signing over the money. As long as Mikail and Tatiana are together, they know they will somehow survive.

On New Year's Eve, the Duponts realize they will never get better servants, and Mikail and Tatiana agree to stay on until replacements are found, which even the most literal-minded moviegoer would doubt. Meanwhile, they are off to celebrate New Year's Eve. Still, in character, Tatiana first puts out the milk bottles; and Mikail, the garbage.

"Ingrid, it's only a movie," Alfred Hitchcock explained to Ingrid Bergman when she fretted about having to deliver her monologue in *Under Capricorn* (1949) in a ten-minute-long take. *Tovarich* should be approached in the same way—as a movie, not a historical document. With the industrialization of the Baku oil reserves, Gorotchenko could not have been authorized to sell them. And the peasants starved anyway, once Stalin enforced collectivization, which led to widespread famine in Ukraine and the extermination of the Kulaks. Baku would become an issue in 1943 after Hitler set his sights on the oil fields, never realizing that the Russians would fight as heroically as they did at the battle of Stalingrad. Thus, it is best to think of *Tovarich* as only a movie, a charming and often poignant fable about a couple's ability to maintain their dignity under circumstances that would have caused most of us to lose ours.

Tovarich is such a delight that one would never suspect that it was an ordeal for Claudette. Ever conscious of her appearance, Claudette insisted on Charles Lang as cinematographer. She knew him only from his films, particularly *A Farewell to Arms* (1932), for which he won an Oscar. What she admired about it was the soft lighting, which she felt could work to her advantage. (Lang photographed seven more of her films: *Midnight; Zaza; Arise, My Love; Skylark; So Proudly We Hail; No Time for Love;* and *Practically Yours.*) Claudette thought she had succeeded until she arrived on the set and discovered Lang had been replaced: "After several pointed remarks she left the stage but was prevailed upon to return. When the new man's rushes were viewed the next day . . . Miss Colbert again withdrew and this time was appeased only by the rehiring of Lang." One could understand her insistence upon a particular cinematographer in a romantic comedy with high-key lighting, but not in *Tovarich*, in which Claudette was neither glamorously costumed nor ethereally lit. But if Claudette had been unhappy with Litvak—as she indeed was when she rushed to Lang's defense after hearing that he had been blamed for the production delays—it never showed in her performance.

For someone with Claudette's track record (three films each in 1935, 1936, and 1937), a single entry for 1938, Ernst Lubitsch's *Bluebeard's Eighth Wife*, seemed ominous: A career crisis? Lack of suitable roles? Neither was the case. Although Lubitsch, who left Paramount immediately after making *Bluebeard's Eighth Wife*, was a meticulous craftsman, he would never spend an inordinate amount of time on a film that ended up running eighty-six minutes and was a remake of an earlier Gloria Swanson movie. The reason was simple: Claudette was scheduled to make *Zaza* as soon as the Lubitsch film was finished. And as if to make up for her one 1938 release, there would be four the following year.

Lubitsch so enjoyed working with Claudette in *The Smiling Lieutenant* that he chose her for *Bluebeard's Eighth Wife*. Within the Lubitsch canon, the film occupies a minor role; but as a screwball comedy with a high quotient of innuendo and a battle of the sexes script in which woman trumps man, the film suggests that by 1938 a Claudette Colbert heroine could not only hold her own with any male but also beat him at his own game.

The film was also the second collaboration between Billy Wilder and Charles Brackett, who became known for their unusual "meet cute" openings. In *Bluebeard's Eighth Wife*, Michael Brandon (Gary Cooper), an American financier, enters a men's store on the French Riviera, determined to buy only a pajama top, but not the bottoms, insisting that 90 percent of men sleep only in tops. The salesman is adamant about selling him the pair, until a voice is heard saying, "I'll buy the trousers," followed by a shot of the purchaser, who, naturally, is Claudette as Nicole, the daughter of an impoverished marquis, who is purchasing them for her father. The marquis needs them because he cannot leave his hotel bed for fear of being evicted. "Pants" becomes a running gag as well as a source of double entendre ("I only have to look at your pants to know anything," Brandon informs the befuddled marquis). Brandon is intrigued by Nicole, who is seductively coy, and the "meet cute" turns into a conversation about sleeping habits. When Brandon confesses that he has difficulty falling asleep, Nicole suggests that he try spelling "Czechoslovakia" backwards. When Brandon asks when he should start the sleep-inducer, Nicole's reply causes the salesman's eyes to widen: "You turn off the light, and then you start."

Brandon becomes infatuated with Nicole, who, once she learns that he has been married seven times, insists upon a pre-nuptial agreement that would give her one hundred thousand dollars in the event of a divorce—twice the settlement that his other wives received. The lovesick Brandon agrees, but the marriage is not what either of them expected.

Nicole is much too liberated for Brandon. After reading *The Taming of the Shrew*, he marches into Nicole's room and slaps her on the face; he reads some more and then spanks her. Slapped and spanked, Nicole is still determined to win the battle of the sexes. On what was to have been a night of bliss, Nicole deliberately eats scallions. When Brandon hires a detective to spy on Nicole, she hires the same man to spy on him. Before Brandon can even admit defeat, he suffers a nervous breakdown. In the final scene, Nicole does all but seduce the straight jacketed Brandon, who extricates himself from the restraints, but not from Nicole, whose beckoning body and wickedly knowledgeable eyes signal that his eighth marriage will be his last.

The chief problem with *Bluebeard's Eighth Wife* was a miscast Cooper, who came alive only when he sat down at the piano and sang "Here Comes Cookie," grinning like a boy on the verge of manhood and eager to announce his glandular change. Surrendering to the moment with a rakish grin, Cooper looked more at ease than he did at any other time in the film. He could do comedy with such actresses as Jean Arthur (*Mr. Deeds Goes to Town*, 1936), Teresa Wright (*Casanova Brown*, 1944), and Ann Sheridan (*Good Sam*, 1948), who, sexually, were nonthreatening. But when the script moved into high gear, the drink of choice was champagne, and his costar was the essence of chic, he was thrown into a milieu that was alien to him, but not to Claudette, who knew that a clever hostess must rely on her conversational skills when the champagne loses its fizz. And if the conversation is scintillating enough, no one will notice that the champagne has gone flat.

Those who thought Claudette's career was in trouble in 1938 were proved wrong a year later when four of her films were released; for two of them, *Zaza* and *It's a Wonderful World*, she was not even the first choice.

In early 1938, Paramount decided to remake *Zaza* for the third time. It had been filmed first in 1915, then in 1923 with Gloria Swanson as the title character, a French music hall entertainer who falls in love with a married aristocrat. The remake was to have marked the American film debut of the excellent Italian actress Isa Miranda, which would have been in keeping with the studio's penchant for European talent. The reason given for Claudette's replacing her was Miranda's heavily accented English, which seems implausible, since that year she was cast opposite Ray Milland in another Paramount film, *Hotel Imperial*. Ironically, Miranda, back in Italy for the duration of World War II, starred in the Italian version of *Zaza*. Paramount needed a replacement, and quickly, since filming was scheduled to begin 6 June 1938. Claudette was the logical choice. By the time *Zaza* went into production, Claudette had played her share of suffering heroines. But she never had a role that allowed her to display such aggressive sexuality. *Zaza* marked the second time in three years (the first was *Under Two Flags*) that Claudette was able to bring an authentic Gallic sensibility to a character who behaved like a woman of affairs, but whose sequins and feathers could not conceal the greatness of soul within her.

Paramount encountered major censorship problems with the film, even though Zaza, like Violetta in Verdi's *La Traviata*, gives up her lover, Dufrense (Herbert Marshall), rather than bring scandal to his family. Still Joseph Ignatius Breen, who headed the Production Code Administration (PCA), rejected the script outright because the "adulterous affair . . . is not treated with the proper compensating moral values." He demanded that "alley cat" (slang for a promiscuous male) be deleted, along with "only one lover a time" from one of the lyrics. And that was just for starters. Unfortunately, another song by composer Frederick Hollander and lyricist Frank

Loesser (but soon to be a composer also), "The Stupidest Girl in the Class," went by the boards. It would have been a great number for Claudette, who would have winked at the suggestiveness and luxuriated in the double entendre:

> My botany teacher remains after hours
> To coach me regarding the bees and the flowers.
> Now why should a man waste his time and his powers
> On someone as green as the grass?

Naturally, it was cut, along with a scene in which the composer Bussy powders Zaza's back; however, a similar scene in which Zaza asks Dufrense to perfume her back, which he does, remained intact, suggesting that powder may be more erotic than perfume. The following exchange between Simone and Zaza was also eliminated:

> SIMONE: Were you ever in love?
> ZAZA: Me? Practically all of the time with somebody.
> SIMONE: Then it wasn't love.
> ZAZA: Maybe not. But it was always more exciting than anything else I could find to do. That's the way I'm made.

Only the prurient-minded would object to such dialogue. The cuts, absurd as they were, did not affect Claudette's characterization. In Paris, Zaza would have been a demimondaine. In the provinces, where she and Cascart (Bert Lahr) tour with their act, she is a fun-loving flirt with eyes that seem to have been widened by the sheer joy of living, as if she inhabited a world without pain. Zaza's world, however, is the theatre; off stage she is still a star, sprinkling sequined dust on men who confuse it with manna, when it is merely the residue of passion. But for Zaza, passion is ambivalent: she feels both a passion for life as well as a passion for *grand amour*, which she experiences for the first time with Dufrense.

Zaza has just stepped off a train with Cascart and her semi-inebriated stepmother, who stumbles and falls against a gentleman who turns out to be Dufrense. He is immediately attracted to Zaza, who seductively runs her hand across her right breast, complaining to Dufrense, whose name she does not even know, about the discomfort she experienced during the train ride. What discomfort had to do with her breast is left to the imagination.

And thus begins what Zaza considers *grand amour*, and what Dufrense regards as a welcome diversion from his straightlaced wife. When Zaza learns that Dufrense is married, she becomes vindictive. Determined to confront Mme. Dufrense, Zaza only finds their daughter at home. The daughter is so trustful that she shows Zaza a locket with her father's picture. Claudette, who often looked beatific in the presence of children, is so heartbreakingly maternal that it is obvious she cannot destroy the girl's illusions. In the film's most poignant scene, the daughter asks Zaza, "Have you any children, Madame?" When Zaza replies in the negative, she says, "If you did, you would love them very much." Concealing her grief, Zaza embraces the child as if she were her own. When Mme. Dufrense returns unexpectedly, Zaza quickly replies that she had been given the wrong address and leaves, taking one last, longing look at the child responsible for her decision.

Although Zaza becomes the toast of Paris, Dufrense still thinks of her as a mistress. Learning that he is in the audience, Zaza asks the conductor to change her opening song to "Hello, My Darling." Resplendent in white, with a costume hat decorated with a spray of ostrich feathers, she turns the song into a farewell, the lyrics expressing the kind of relationship she wants with Dufrense should they ever meet: "Just say hello, my darling/if we should meet again" and, finally, "Go, my love/though it is a bitter pill/I know, my love."

In *Zaza* Claudette gave one of her best performances, partly because Zoë Akins's screenplay allowed her to run the gamut from tease to trage-dienne, stopping midway so the two could coalesce in the final image of a woman able to forgive a lover's deception because she realized that the world of the music hall prepared her only for happy endings, not heartbreak, and partly because her director, George Cukor, refused to condescend to the material, which in less sensitive hands would have resulted in the worse kind of woman's film, the much derided "weepie." Although *Zaza* could not compete in popularity with Cukor's other 1939 film, *The Women*, it showed that Claudette could still generate pathos with her plangent mezzo, as she does in the last scene; but more important, she brought a true stage personality to the music hall numbers. If someone had created a Broadway musical for her, as Leonard Bernstein, Adolph Green, and Betty Comden did for Rosalind Russell in *Wonderful Town*, Claudette's career might have taken a different turn. In little more than a decade, Claudette would return to the stage, but never in a musical.

Zaza wound up shooting on 2 September 1938. When Breen saw a cut a month later, he was furious; the film still reeked of "adultery and illicit sex." Breen threatened to appeal to Will Hays; if he did, the changes that had already been negotiated were apparently enough. Breen did not have a case. Of course, there was adultery; it was obvious that Zaza and Dufrense were lovers. And even if the wages of sin were not death, they were the same as they had been in *Camille* (1937), another Cukor film, in which a woman makes the supreme sacrifice because of someone's daughter. In *Camille*, Marguerite gives up Armand after his father tells her that her notoriety will jeopardize his daughter's forthcoming marriage into a respectable family. After *Camille*, Cukor knew exactly how much pathos he could extract from *Zaza's* final scene. And what he did was in perfect taste.

Claudette had no idea in January 1939 that she would be making her MGM debut in a film with James Stewart. Originally, Myrna Loy had been set for the female lead in *It's a Wonderful World* (1939) as a "poetess" who becomes romantically involved with an escaped murder suspect (James Stewart). Then MGM decided that Loy's talents could be better utilized in the third Thin Man film, *Another Thin Man* (1939). If audiences were to see Myrna Loy in a screwball mystery, it ought to be with William Powell, not with Stewart, who, except for *After the Thin Man* (1938), in which he played a murderer, never appeared in another movie in the series.

After *It Happened One Night*, *The Bride Goes Home*, and *The Gilded Lily*, Claudette had joined the ranks of the screwball heroines, a category that Loy managed to avoid because the Thin Man films were a blend of whodunit and high comedy set in a milieu where martinis were the drink of choice; and witty banter, the mode of expression. And so, when MGM needed a madcap heroine (which Loy never was), Claudette came to the rescue and exercised her contractual right to make a movie at a studio other than Paramount.

It was a more physical part than she had been used to. Stewart had to pick her up and carry her under his arm, when he wasn't dragging her around the woods and, in one scene, socking her in the jaw. But Claudette was a good sport; it was, after all, in the script, which, surprisingly, was written by Ben Hecht, who realized that its success depended more on the stars' chemistry (which never even approximated the kind that Claudette and Gable had in *It Happened One Night*) than plausibility. But the action moved so swiftly (the film is not even ninety minutes) that no one ever thought to ask some basic questions such as: What is the well-known poet Edwina Corday (Claudette) doing in a deserted section of New York's Westchester County when she encounters Guy Johnson (Stewart), who jumps from a moving train while handcuffed to a police officer and miraculously swims to shore? Hecht, who understood the conventions of screwball (having written two of the best, *Twentieth Century* and *Nothing Sacred*), knew he needed an unconventional meeting of the two, which he accomplished by having Johnson come upon Edwina, who has seen him unshackle himself.

Johnson is a private detective who, by harboring a client wrongly accused of murder, has became a suspect himself. Hecht was obviously familiar with *It Happened One Night*; in high-concept language, *Wonderful World* is *It Happened One Night* meets *The Thin Man*, with Claudette as an amateur sleuth and Stewart as the man on the run. Accordingly, *Wonderful World* takes on the features of a road movie, but the trip is much shorter than the Miami–New York route in *Night*; it is only from Westchester County to upstate New York. Although the film is about sixteen minutes shorter than *Night*, the complications pile up so quickly that it is easy to get caught up in the action without questioning the logic. Hecht and MGM were counting on audiences' memories of *Night* and their familiarity with the *Thin Man* series. In *Night*, when Gable starts undressing in front of Claudette, she flees behind the walls of Jericho. When Stewart does the same in *Wonderful World*, Claudette reacts similarly.

While Claudette had only one opportunity to play act in *Night*, when she pretended to be a plumber's daughter, she must do more role-playing in *Wonderful World* once Edwina is convinced Johnson is innocent. When he tackles a Boy Scout and steals his clothes, looking like a near-sighted scoutmaster in an ill-fitting uniform, Edwina passes him off as a Brit; and later as an English actor, once they discover that the murderer is involved in a summer stock production of *What Price Glory*.

Unlike the typical battle-of-the-sexes comedy, there is only one combatant in *Wonderful World*, Edwina, whose quick thinking saves Johnson from the police. The plot may be as porous as a wedge of Swiss cheese, and Stewart and Claudette may have experienced too many close calls for romance to blossom. Still, the script called for Claudette at the fadeout to perform the ultimate screwball gesture: evidence her love for a man who had kidnapped, deserted, manhandled, and punched her. That she convinced the audience of something that Stewart could not is a testimonial to her ingenuity as an actress. But *Wonderful World* (the title comes from one of the poems that Edwina has written) never had a chance of gaining an audience in that *annus mirabilis*, 1939, when the screen was graced with more classic films in one year than ever before: *The Wizard of Oz, Dark Victory, The Women, Stagecoach, Destry Rides Again* (with Stewart, and a real classic), *Mr. Smith Goes to Washington* (ditto), *Ninotchka, Wuthering Heights, Young Abe Lincoln, Goodbye, Mr. Chips*, and, of course, *Gone with the Wind*.

Wonderful World was Claudette's film, not just because of the billing with her name above the title, and Stewart's below, but because Hecht discarded the premise of the *Thin Man* series, in which Nick and Nora Charles function as a team and instead made Edwina the real sleuth, whose powers of deduction, while not Sherlockian, come pretty close. Although neither star would consider *Wonderful World* a career highlight (Stewart's 1939 achievement was winning an Oscar nomination for *Mr. Smith*), the film was a bauble with Claudette providing whatever sheen it had.

It is difficult to figure out why Claudette agreed to return to Twentieth Century-Fox for John Ford's *Drums along the Mohawk*. One can only assume that she either enjoyed working at Fox in *Under Two Flags* or was attracted to the prospect of costarring with Henry Fonda in a film directed by Oscar-winning director John Ford. The film turned out to be Claudette's ordeal by fire. She was cast as the well-bred Lana, married to frontiersman Gil Martin (Henry Fonda) in the watershed year 1776. Marriage threw Lana, the Albany blue blood, into the role of frontier woman, a transformation that Claudette was expected to replicate, little knowing that she would be exposed to Ford's gruffness and the absence of amenities during the location shooting in Cedar Breaks, Utah.

Claudette was used to more sophisticated directors, such as Woody Van Dyke, who let her breeze through *It's a Wonderful World*. John Ford was cut from a rougher cloth. Kay Linaker, who played a haughty captain's wife in *Drums along the Mohawk*, recalled how Claudette behaved when she was on location and was staying at a nearby cottage without a bathtub. Ford accommodated the fastidious Claudette with a tub that he paraded around the set, with a sign that read, "See Miss Colbert's bathtub. $.25 without Miss Colbert. $.10 with."

It was bad enough that she had to rough it; worse was enduring Ford's way of bullying actors into giving him the performance that he wanted (and that he knew they could give). During the shoot, Claudette had developed a reputation for lateness, which was unusual for her. One day, when Claudette finally arrived in her limo, Ford went over to greet her, after which the two took a brief walk. Later, Linaker came upon a distraught Claudette, eyes swollen from weeping, who admitted that no one had ever spoken to her so sternly since she was four. Ford had taught her a lesson: "But I'll never do that again as long as I live. I realize how absolutely selfish I was."

Although Nancy Kelly was originally slated for Lana, it would not have mattered. The credits may have identified *Drums* as a Darryl Zanuck production, but it was in every way a John Ford film. Ford's playfully sadistic sense of humor comes through when Blue Back (Chief Big Tree), an Indian ally, gives Gil a walking stick so he can beat Lana if she gets out of line. Ford was a purist when it came to creating a mythology out of the shards of history, as he did in his westerns, or recreating one, such as the Ireland he fashioned out of stories and anecdotes in *The Quiet Man*, which may not be the most politically correct of films, especially when Maureen O'Hara, sensing she may have been too headstrong, provides John Wayne with a switch that he can use on her if she deserves it. Spousal abuse, by contemporary standards, was culturally acceptable by Ford's. In 1939 the scene with the walking stick undoubtedly garnered some laughs, as indeed did Blue Back, who had been baptized and departs by intoning "Alleluia, Alleluia."

The colonial militia does not leave the fort with the same rhythmic precision as the Seventh Cavalry did in Ford's later films, but there are some stunning long shots—one in particular of Lana when she sees the departing soldiers from a hill and then sinks down on the grass, as the shot assumes the look of a painting. And if the script called for Joe Boleo (played by Ford's brother Francis) to be captured by the Indians and tied to a hay wagon which is then ignited, the decision to arrange Joe's arms in cruciform position came from Ford, who used a similar composition at the end of *The Informer* (1935). To conclude the harrowing sequence on a note of ambivalence, a minister fires a bullet at the Christ figure to hasten his death.

Ford's biographer Andrew Sinclair claimed Claudette was "miscast" as Lana. Actually, Claudette was typecast; just as Lana had to relinquish her comfortable existence in Albany, Claudette had to abandon her Holmby Hills home for the wilds of Utah, where she had to rough it with the rest of the company, except that, as the star, she had the luxury of a cottage. Yet, as the filming progressed, so did her character. Gradually, Lana is exposed to the realities of frontier life; first she must endure the sight of their cabin torched by Indians; then she suffers a miscarriage. By the end of the film,

Lana had evolved into a pioneer wife; and Claudette, into a team player. She realized Ford was right in deflating her ego, which, left unpricked, would have derailed the film. Although they never worked together again, Claudette always respected him.

However, she never became totally selfless. No one could in a business where ego is a prerequisite for survival; and narcissism, a defense against the onslaught of time. She would continue to demand that cinematographers favor the left side of her face and that directors honor her policy of no filming after 5:00 p.m. But at least Claudette realized that, in *Drums*, she was part of a company that was working under a master who was one of the cinema's original mythmakers. She may also have sensed, in her scenes with Edna May Oliver as a feisty widow, that, if anyone's performance would be remembered, it would be Oliver's, particularly her beautifully restrained death scene. The Academy felt similarly and nominated Oliver for Best Supporting Actress. But that year, another greater film became part of American popular culture, *Gone with the Wind*; and Hattie McDaniell, whose red petticoat is as much of a cinematic artifact as Stanley Kowalski's torn T-shirt in *A Streetcar Named Desire*, won in that category. McDaniell was the first African American to be so honored.

A month after *Zaza* was completed, Claudette went into Mitchell Leisen's *Midnight*, one of the great screwball comedies of the 1930s (and one that has finally received the recognition it deserves). *Zaza* reached the theaters in January 1939. That May, another Claudette film went into release that bore no resemblance to it at all.

"What were you going to do? Gold dig him for a meal?" That was Peter Warne's stunned reaction in *It Happened One Night* when Ellie tries to wangle a meal from the vulgarian who gave them a lift. Looking slightly abashed but far from repentant, Ellie retorts, "Why not? I'm hungry." The way Claudette read the line suggested that Ellie not only would, if Peter had not prevented her, but that she also knew what a gold digger was. Like "geisha," "gold digger" has taken on a sexual connotation, although it originally referred to a woman who accepts expensive gifts from men: sometimes for services rendered; at other times, for services withheld until the price was right; and at still other times, for nothing other than companionship. Perhaps because she was French, Claudette was cast in parts that often brought out the gamine in her—the sly, impish flirt with enchantress eyes. And yet the primary meaning of "gamine" is equally applicable to Claudette: a kid schooled on the streets with the street smarts to prove it. Claudette was far from an urchin, but she could affect a toughness and a look that suggested a hard-knock life, which worked to her advantage in such films as *The Hole in the Wall, I Cover the Waterfront*, and *Torch Song*. When she darkened her naturally musical voice, one no longer thought of champagne bubbles but of brandy. In *Midnight*, when cabbie Tibor Czerny (Don Ameche) offers to drive her around Paris as she hunts for a job in a gold lamé gown, he innocently asks what kind of work she is looking for. Lowering her voice to a cynical throatiness, she replies dryly, "At this time of night, and in these clothes, I am not looking for needlework." Although there is no double entendre in the line, Claudette made it sound as if there were.

The way Claudette played gold diggers was all her own. Never brassy or tawdry, Claudette was always the high-maintenance type, who offered men a run for their money: a duel of wits, sparkling repartee, a round of double entendres, and, if they were fortunate, a good-night kiss. She was always the gold digger with class; her home studio was, after all, Paramount, not Warner Bros., which had its own *Gold Diggers* series. Those gold diggers were tough broads; Claudette was a classy dame.

When Claudette was cast as a woman out for a good time (as opposed to a woman "on the town"), she played the role with the worldly innocence of someone who had no intention of compromising herself but also knew that the way to a man's wallet was through his libido, which was only to be teased, not activated—or at least not until the relationship turned serious. Claudette used her theatrical alchemy to distill the essence of "gold digger/woman on the town" into a strain that was all her own: a woman of the world, a Colbert creation who was sexy but not promiscuous, a skilled trader of quips with a specialty in double entendre and subtext, and the

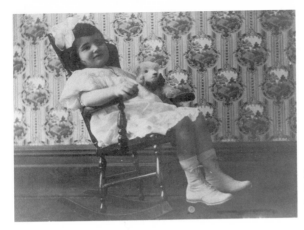

Emile (Lily) Chauchoin at three, twenty years before she became Claudette Colbert. Photofest.

Claudette and her mother, the formidable Jeanne Chauchoin, in the 1930s. Photofest.

Claudette met by her husband,
actor Norman Foster, in February
1933 after undergoing sinus surgery
in New York. Photofest.

Claudette and Edward G. Robinson in their first talkie, *The Hole in the Wall* (1929). Photofest.

Claudette as Poppaea, "the wickedest woman in the world," in Cecil B. DeMille's *The Sign of the Cross* (1932). Photofest.

Claudette as the Queen of the Nile in DeMille's *Cleopatra* (1934). Photofest.

Louise Beavers and Claudette as single mothers with daughters in *Imitation of Life* (1934). Photofest.

Shirley Temple presenting Claudette with her Oscar for Frank Capra's *It Happened One Night* (1934). Photofest.

Clark Gable and Claudette in the famous undressing scene in *It Happened One Night*. Photofest.

Claudette and Charles Boyer as aristocratic domestics in *Tovarich* (1937). Private collection.

Claudette as a pioneer bride in John Ford's *Drums along the Mohawk* (1939). Private collection.

Claudette as the title character of *Maid of Salem* (1937). Private collection.

Claudette in a music hall number
in *Zaza*. Private collection.

Claudette as the title character in George Cukor's *Zaza* (1939), singing farewell to
her lover. Private collection.

Claudette as a poet turned sleuth in the screwball mystery *It's a Wonderful World* (1940). Private collection.

Claudette playing cards with GIs at the Hollywood Canteen, May 1943. Photofest.

Claudette and her husband, Dr. Joel "Joe" Pressman, on his return to civilian life in 1945. Photofest.

Claudette as a mother in wartime with daughters Shirley Temple (left) and Jennifer Jones in David O. Selznick's production, *Since You Went Away* (1944). Photofest.

Offbeat casting: Claudette and John Wayne in *Without Reservations* (1946). Photofest.

Director Mitchell Leisen on the set of *Arise, My Love* (1940) with Claudette and Ray Milland. Photofest.

Claudette as Sister Mary Bonaventure in Douglas Sirk's suspense thriller, *Thunder on the Hill* (1951). Photofest.

Claudette and Troy Donahue in her last feature film, *Parrish* (1961). Private collection.

The notorious shot of Claudette and Marlene Dietrich sliding down the chute at the Venice Pier Fun House, June 1935. Photofest.

Clockwise from top: Mildred Natwick, Lauren Bacall, Claudette, and Noël Coward, starring in a live telecast of Coward's *Blithe Spirit*, on 14 January 1956. Photofest.

Claudette back on Broadway in *Janus* (Spring 1956), with Claude Dauphin as her summertime lover. Photofest.

Claudette and Charles Boyer backstage after a performance of *The Marriage-Go-Round* (1958). Photofest.

Claudette and Rex Harrison in the New York production of *The Kingfisher* (1978). Photofest.

Claudette with her co-star Jean Pierre Aumont, on the first day of rehearsal for *A Talent for Murder*, 14 August 1981. Photofest.

Claudette receiving the 1983 Lord and Taylor Rose Award for her artistry, grace, style, and glamour. Photofest.

Claudette and Rex Harrison in the New York production of the revival of Frederick Lonsdale's *Aren't We All?* (1985), her last stage appearance. Photofest.

Claudette as Alice Grenville in the television version of Dominick Dunne's *The Two Mrs. Grenvilles* (1987), for which she won a Golden Globe. Photofest.

Claudette, officially declared a legend by being featured in the *What Becomes a Legend Most?* ad campaign created by Peter Rogers for Blackglama mink. Courtesy of Peter Rogers and Helen O'Hagan.

perfect date for an unattached male eager to be seen with a woman who would make other men envy his good fortune.

Midnight was Claudette's second film for Mitchell Leisen; although Leisen shared credit for *Tonight Is Ours* with Stuart Walker, the film was more Leisen's than Walker's. The film also marked Claudette's return to pure screwball; *Wonderful World* was a divertissement or, better, a distraction. But the Billy Wilder–Charles Brackett script allowed her to resolve the myriad contradictions in the character of Eve Peabody, an American, first seen asleep in a third-class compartment after her train has pulled into Paris's Gare de l'est. She is wearing an evening gown but has no luggage and virtually no money. Instead of breaking the bank at Monte Carlo, she lost whatever the mother of an amorous suitor gave her to terminate the relationship with her son. It would have made sense if, upon arriving in Paris, Eve turned to the world's oldest profession. Claudette as a hooker? No. As a courtesan? Yes. And as a woman in financial distress who still maintains her standards, even after Tibor, the accommodating taxi driver, offers her his flat? No again, not even if there was no sex involved, of which there was little possibility since Ameche played the cabbie with a virginal self-righteousness that was the opposite of Gable's libido-on-hold in *It Happened One Night*. Having seen her share of men who insisted there were no strings attached and then expected compensation, Eve rushes off and wanders into a soirée, where, thanks to the brilliantly constructed script, she comes in contact with most of the characters that constitute the rest of the cast. Knowing that Eve has not been invited (and has used her pawn ticket for admittance), George Flammarion (John Barrymore, looking like an oracular owl with eyes to match and relishing one of his last roles before his death in 1942) plays fairy godfather to Eve's Cinderella, not out of benevolence but to keep his wife, Helene (Mary Astor), from succumbing to the oily charm of Jacques Picot (Francis Lederer).

Eve becomes Cinderella, ensconced at the Ritz and outfitted with a designer wardrobe. Having taken the taxi driver's surname, she passes herself off as the Baroness Czerny. The deception is successful until Tibor learns of her whereabouts and shows up. "Every Cinderella has her midnight," Eve ruefully remarks to Flammarion. But the clock has not yet struck. There is still time for the battle of the sexes to move into the combat zone, as each tries to outdo the other. Eve convinces everyone that there is a strain of insanity in the Czerny family, which seems the case when Tibor changes into a cabbie's uniform and claims he is really a taxi driver.

Since everyone believes Eve and Tibor are married, a divorce is necessary so Tibor can go back to driving his taxi; and Eve, to gold digging. In one of the few moments when the fluff lands on the hard soil of reality, the judge (played with unusual humanity by Monty Woolley) dismisses the charge of mental cruelty in view of the "vast world unrest" that makes marital squabbles insignificant. And when Tibor feigns madness, the judge invokes a statute that forbids a wife to divorce her insane husband. Wilder and Brackett were shrewd enough to admit one contemporary reference—and a vague one, at that—into the curtained world of screwball. When *Midnight* was released in March 1939, the world was seven months away from war. "Vast world unrest" was a euphemism.

As the film ends, everyone leaves the courtroom: Jacques to his swinging bachelorhood and the Flammarions to a marriage that is temporarily untroubled. With a minute of screen time left, Eve and Tibor have to act as if the past never happened, so that, like all the tarring and sparring movie couples, they can eventually resolve their differences and restore order and balance to the topsy-turvy world of screwball comedy.

Despite the low-grade chemistry between Claudette and Ameche, the pairing worked, chiefly because each brought a certain innocence to the role that, in Claudette's case, kept the gold digger from turning into a mercenary vamp. There is a moment in *Midnight* when Eve speaks of her loveless parents, presumably the reason for her obsession with money. But Claudette must have sensed that an unhappy childhood was not the only reason for Eve's love of the good life. Eve would have wanted it regardless. In a way, Claudette vindicated the character, who, like herself, wanted it all and generally got it; in Claudette's case, it was in life and often in film as well.

In its way, *Midnight* is a vindication of marriage, even though some marriages have to be restored the way paintings are and some just require giving up a stretch limo for a taxi. Eve did not have to worry about spending the rest of her life as a cab driver's wife. In a throwaway line, Tibor admits to being a distant relative of a Baron Czerny. And if Eve knows her apples, she can still wear gold lamé and have a chauffeur to boot.

CHAPTER 9

Blaze of Noon

These were Claudette's golden days, which would lose their luster by the end of the 1940s. Meanwhile, her fan base increased. According to the *New York Times* (7 January 1937), the *Motion Picture Herald* ranked her eighth among Hollywood's moneymaking stars of 1936; more important, the year before she came in sixth in terms of popularity, after Shirley Temple, Will Rogers, Clark Gable, Fred Astaire and Ginger Rogers, and Joan Crawford. The *New York Times* (21 March 1937) also reported that seniors at the New York University School of Commerce voted Robert Taylor and Claudette their favorite movie stars. Even young girls liked Claudette; the same paper (14 January 1938) summarized the results of a survey conducted by the Boys Athletic League, in which boys failed to single out any favorite female star, only males. The girls, however, came up with a balanced ten-best list: Shirley Temple, Jane Withers, Tyrone Power, Sonja Henie, Robert Taylor, Loretta Young, Ginger Rogers, Errol Flynn, Claudette, and Clark Gable. When one realizes that 22,416 children between the ages of six and sixteen were polled, the girls evidenced an unusually high level of taste.

Even Communists were fond of Claudette: "Putting aside their dialectical materialism . . . the Communists, in completely American fashion, selected Gary Cooper and Claudette Colbert as their favorite movie stars." Perhaps the reason was that they interpreted *It Happened One Night* as an attack on capitalism, with Claudette as an unwitting victim or knew that *She Married Her Boss* was written by one of their own, Sidney Buchman.

By 1936, Paramount was aware of Claudette's extraordinary appeal; in June the studio rewarded her with an amended contract that called for seven films between 6 June 1936 and 25 April 1939. In October 1937, the number was reduced to five, at $100,000 per picture: *Maid of Salem* (10 August 1936–17 October 1936), *I Met Him in Paris* (4 January 1937–13 March 1937), *Bluebeard's Eighth Wife* (26 October 1937–3 January 1938), *Zaza* (25 June 1938–2 September 1938), and *Midnight* (24 October 1938–31 December 1938). She was also allowed to make one film for Warners, which turned out to be *Tovarich*. In 1938 she became Hollywood's highest-paid star. The *New York Times* (23 January 1939) disclosed the salaries of corporation employees, including actors; Claudette's salary for the 1938 calendar year was $301,944.

Her Paramount contract underwent periodic revision, always to her advantage and always including outside productions, a condition of which she availed herself (*Drums along the Mohawk, It's a Wonderful World, Boom Town*). If travel was involved, she was guaranteed first-class transportation, including a drawing room. As her popularity increased, so did her salary; by 1943, the year before she left the studio, she was making $150,000 a film.

Early in 1940, MGM offered her the female lead in *Boom Town* with Clark Gable and Spencer Tracy as costars. She knew that she would not be top billed, but it was still an opportunity to team up again with Gable. She now appreciated the art of *It Happened One Night*, even though in 1934 she would never have predicted its inclusion in the pantheon of film comedy. The proof came in August 1940 when the Museum of Modern Art opened its retrospective "Forty Years of American Film Comedy" with *It Happened One Night*.

Although Claudette was third billed after Gable and Tracy, and the director was the "aggressively heterosexual" Jack Conway, it was amazing that she could neutralize the high testosterone level that threatened to overwhelm the film, especially since her character, an English teacher tired of teaching poetry to hormonal adolescents, was only a plot point. *Boom Town* is the story of two oil prospectors or "wildcatters," Gable and Tracy, as "Big John" Macmasters and Jonathan Sand, respectively, whose relationship runs the gamut from male bonding to schadenfreude, as their fortunes wax and wane—one succeeding at the other's expense—until at the end they are back where they started, but obviously about to strike it rich again.

Claudette's character, Betsy, is originally Jonathan's great love, until she gets a look at Macmasters; then it is *It Happened One Night* all over again. A few hours is all it takes for Betsy and Macmasters—or, to moviegoers, Claudette and Gable—to fall in love, get married, and explain to Jonathan that Betsy is no longer his fiancée. But the film is all about loss counterbalanced by gain in both drilling for oil and falling in love.

Gable's character is established early in the film: he can size up a woman at first sight. With Betsy, he behaves similarly; she warms to his sexy gaze, humanizing him by her feminine charm, yet knowing all the time that he was born under a wandering star and with a roving eye. With Gable, Claudette was relaxed, fitting smoothly in his embrace, as if she were folding herself in his arms. When their eyes interlocked, it was sexy but not erotic. One scene in particular recalls *Gone with the Wind*. Betsy reaches the top of a staircase when Macmasters shouts, "Come down here." What follows is a shot of Gable at the foot of the stairs, staring up at Claudette, making the same kind of piercingly sensuous eye contact that he did with Vivien Leigh in *Gone with the Wind*. It is no wonder that Betsy no sooner arrives in town and meets Macmasters than she agrees to marry him.

Boom Town is a two-hour film with melodramatic intervals that require the subtlest form of acting to be convincing. Although Betsy knows about Macmasters's reputation with women, she is not prepared for Karen

(Hedy Lamarr), the femme fatale, who arrives midway in the film and tries to snare Macmasters for herself. The one false note in *Boom Town* is Betsy's suicide attempt, which is inconsistent with her character. Claudette played women who could easily have gone over the edge, e.g., in *Sleep, My Love* and *The Secret Fury*. But Betsy was not one of them.

The ending of *Boom Town* should be of particular interest to Democrats wary of the corporatization of America. When Macmasters is on trial for violating the Sherman Anti-Trust Act by forming an oil cartel, Jonathan testifies on his behalf, arguing that his friend was really conserving oil reserves to prevent a shortage. Apparently, no one thought of applying the same specious reasoning to the Justice Department's 1947 decision that the Big Five (MGM, Fox, RKO, Warner Bros., and Paramount) constituted a monopoly and must therefore divest themselves of their theater chains. Then, the studios could have used someone like Jonathan to argue that they were not a monopoly but a confederation committed to ensuring a steady supply of quality films by preventing others from flooding the market with inferior product.

Jonathan's sophistry sways the jury; Macmasters, chastened, returns to Betsy; and Claudette heads back to Paramount for *Arise, My Love* (1940), the most political—and in many ways the most propagandistic—film Claudette ever made. Only *So Proudly We Hail* (1943) could compete with its unequivocal distinction between "us" (America and the Western democracies) and "them" (fascists).

The Wilder and Brackett screenplay was prophetic in 1940, arguing that it was only a matter of time before America would be involved in the Second World War and that the Spanish Civil War (never mentioned by name, but clearly implied) was the prelude to a global conflict that had already begun by the time the film was released in October 1940.

Arise, My Love opens with an unusual "meet cute." The setting is a Spanish prison in 1939, the year the Spanish Civil War ended, where Tom Martin (Ray Milland) is about to be executed as a "soldier of fortune" and enemy of Franco's Spain. The war, referred to in the film as the "palooka preliminaries . . . just before Hitler and Chamberlain warm up for the main event," was clearly the Spanish Civil War. However, to mention it and suggest that Martin was probably one of the thirty-three hundred idealists who joined the Abraham Lincoln Battalion of the Fifteenth International Brigade to defend the Spanish republic against Franco's Nationalists would have suggested that Wilder and Bracket supported the Loyalists, who were planning to establish a Socialist republic. The Abraham Lincoln Battalion was made up of volunteers who were so far to the left that they were Communists, or at least Socialists. In 1940s America, Communism was the flip side of Nazism and equally dangerous.

Martin's execution never takes place. News arrives that a pardon has been granted, thanks to the intercession of Martin's "wife." Martin, however, is unmarried. His supposed wife is Augusta "Gusto" Nash (Claudette), a journalist who devised the ruse because she wanted an exclusive. Once Martin and Gusto reach Paris, melodrama is about to give way to romantic comedy, until world events (the annexation of the Sudetenland, Anschluss, and finally the invasion of Poland) intensify Gusto's desire to be a war correspondent and Martin's to aid beleaguered Poland.

After their ship is torpedoed by a German submarine, they go their separate ways, Martin to Poland and Gusto eventually to Paris to cover the signing of the armistice at Compiègne. When a Nazi officer informs Gusto that because of the gravity of the occasion she must dispense with lip rouge, she looks at him coldly and replies in a voice matching her expression, "My lips will be as white as chalk."

Learning that Gusto is in Compiègne, Martin seeks her out. An injured arm precludes his flying any longer. To revive his spirits, Gusto reminds him of his takeoff prayer, "Arise, my love," from the *Song of Solomon*. She now turns the prayer into an anti-isolationist—or, as isolationist senators would have said, a premature antifascist—message, with America as Martin's new love: "This time we have to say it to America: 'Arise, my love. Arise, be strong, so you can stand up straight and say to anyone under God's heaven: All right, whose way of life shall it be—yours or ours?'" Being French,

Claudette felt deeply about the fall of France and the Nazi occupation of her beloved Paris. She delivered the final speech with such heartfelt sincerity that, for the moment, it seemed as if she had stopped acting and was rallying support for the French, who did not see the film in 1940. On 17 August 1940, two days after *Arise, My Love* finished shooting, the Nazis issued a ban on all American films. And although a few managed to slip through until early 1941, *Arise, My Love* would not have been one of them.

When Wilder and Brackett first began writing *Arise, My Love*, they did not have an ending. The fall of France in June 1940 supplied them with one. Significantly, production began on 24 June and concluded in mid August. The film was released on 17 October, fourteen months before Pearl Harbor brought America into the "big event."

Claudette would make another World War II film in 1943, but in the meantime, it was back to romantic comedy. Samson Raphaelson's *Skylark* (1939) was a great stage vehicle for Gertrude Lawrence, who charmed her way through this wise comedy of marital misunderstanding, deception, and reconciliation that should have transferred to the screen without loss of sophistication. The 1941 film, however, retained the play's buoyancy but not the wisdom of Raphaelson's portrait of a tenth wedding anniversary that almost turned out to be the last. On what should have been a celebratory occasion, Lydia Kenyon (Claudette) finds herself unable to tolerate the way her husband, Tony (Ray Milland), accedes to the whims of his employer, Harley Valentine, who is ruled by his proudly unfaithful wife, Myrtle (Binnie Barnes). When Myrtle throws enough far-from-subtle hints about wanting the Kenyons' cook, Tony concedes, interpreting it as an order if he wants to keep his job. Out of frustration, Lydia starts flirting with playboy-lawyer Bill Blake (Brian Aherne), whom Myrtle has earmarked for herself. To keep Lydia, Tony vows to quit his job although he has no intention of doing so. When Lydia insults Myrtle, Tony really gets fired, and Lydia seeks a divorce. Although there is little likelihood that the Kenyons will divorce (or if they do, they will remarry before the fadeout), the film misses the point of the play: that Lydia in her wisdom offers Tony the choice between adopting a simpler lifestyle or remaining in perpetual thralldom to a boss who humors his cheating wife. When a better job comes around, she does not stand in Tony's way; she simply wants him to make his own decision.

There is some awkward physical comedy in the film that did not occur in the play, which is set entirely in the Kenyons' living room. At one point, Lydia is on a sailboat with Blake during a squall; in a formless slicker and dumpy hat, she goes below to make coffee, losing her footing and sliding around the floor. Later, Tony also takes a fall and has to be carried by Blake, who finds the experience an affront to his masculinity (which was in character); from the look on Aherne's face, it was also an irksome bit of business.

The abrupt ending—with Tony en route to South America to help Latin Americans in their defense preparations (the film was released when World War II had already erupted in Europe) and Lydia arriving in Havana to join him—might have worked if there had been a reconciliation scene. But there was none. Allan Scott could write some exemplary scripts, but *Skylark* was not one of them. It was a far better play than it was a film.

Claudette had one triumphant moment when she ushered Binnie Barnes out of her home with a "Goodbye, you tramp." In the play, Lydia said "bitch" and even called Myrtle a "slut." In 1939, conservative theatre-goers were probably shocked to hear such language coming from Gertrude Lawrence. Barnes, who looked as if her features were forged of metal, exuded a trashiness that made "slut" *le mot juste*.

Claudette so enjoyed making *Under Two Flags* at Fox that she agreed to return to the studio for *Remember the Day* (1941), particularly since John Ford would not be behind the camera; the director was Henry King, who specialized in Americana, rendering small-town life with the pictorial quaintness of Norman Rockwell and Currier and Ives. If any film proves that Claudette was never intended to be a character actress, it is *Remember the Day*, which opens in 1940 with Nora Trinell (Claudette), a fiftyish school teacher, entering the lobby of a Washington, D.C., hotel, hoping to meet one of her favorite pupils, now a presidential candidate. Although she affects the walk and appearance of a woman who had been in the same profession for a quarter of a century, anyone who assumed that the dowdy clothes and granny glasses would soon be discarded was right. The film is a flashback with a frame narrative, beginning and ending in the same hotel. As Nora hears a familiar tune, nostalgia takes over, and 1940 dissolves into 1916, with a rejuvenated Nora in her classroom in Auburn, Indiana.

Grade school teachers today might go into shock when Nora reminds her class that they will be reading Shakespeare's *A Midsummer Night's Dream*; they might also be dismayed by the principal's insistence that Dan Hopkins (John Payne, who was nine years younger than Claudette and looked it), the shop teacher, tender his resignation because he and Nora had vacationed together. On the other hand, the principal's reaction may not have been all that unusual in 1916, particularly in a small Midwestern town, where teachers, especially bachelors and "maiden ladies," were supposed to be above reproach.

Believing he is destined for something higher than teaching shop, Hopkins takes off for Chicago, and soon he and Nora marry. World War I intervenes, Hopkins is killed in action, and Nora relocates in Washington. If events unfold at an unusually rapid pace, the reason is the film itself, which covers twenty-five years in eighty-five minutes. Eventually, Nora and the presidential candidate connect, even though at first he does not remember her. But what does it matter? He will obviously win the election, and Nora will be a frequent visitor at 1600 Pennsylvania Avenue.

It is difficult to believe that *Remember the Day* was originally intended to be a politically controversial film. Zanuck scribbled in pencil on the first draft continuity: "great—overwritten—but it has sock sentimental value." Zanuck wanted to forge a connection between Nora and the teacher whom presidential candidate Wendell Willkie embraced when he arrived in Elwood, Indiana, for his first radio broadcast. Zanuck also envisioned a climactic scene in which the presidential candidate was about to endorse isolationism as the only reasonable course for America until he caught sight of his former teacher and realized he could not espouse what he did not believe. Audiences would have immediately thought of the 1940 presidential campaign in which Willkie advocated aid to America's European allies, while Franklin D. Roosevelt vowed he would never involve the country in a foreign war. The isolationist speech never made it to the screen, although, ironically, the film was released on Christmas Day 1941, two-and-a-half weeks after Pearl Harbor. Had the scene remained, *Remember the Day* would have been hailed as prophetic.

There is one scene in *Remember the Day* that does not so much advance the plot as attest to Claudette's artistic ability. Nora has developed a close rapport with the student who will grow up to run for president. Since the boy is obsessed with sailing, Nora demonstrates her knowledge of ships (she hails from New Bedford) by illustrating on the chalkboard the differences between a barque and a brig. With another actress, King might have had to cut from Nora at the chalkboard to the shot of a hand—sketching the ships with a piece of chalk—that would be added in post production. With Claudette, King did not have to cut. The camera stayed on Claudette, who handles the chalk as if she were a trained artist (which she was), sketching each ship as she describes its features, timing her comparison so that it ends with the last stroke of the chalk. Moviegoers who knew that Claudette once considered a career as a commercial artist would not have been surprised at her expertise. Regardless, one is grateful that she chose acting over art, especially since *Remember the Day* is not especially memorable.

Claudette's 1942 film was supposed to have been Mitchell Leisen's *Take a Letter, Darling*, in which she would play "boss lady" to the title's "darling," her male secretary (Fred MacMurray). Claudette and MacMurray would work together the following year in *No Time for Love*, not so much a "boss lady" as a "career woman" movie. When Claudette had the chance to appear in Preston Sturges's *The Palm Beach Story*, she informed Paramount that she would pass on *Letter*. It was a wise decision. Leisen managed to replace her with Rosalind Russell, Hollywood's quintessential female careerist.

Unlike Claudette, Russell could play a woman at the controls, pushing the plot points as if they were buttons.

The Palm Beach Story, on the other hand, is a variation on the Cinderella myth, bearing a strong resemblance to *Midnight* with even more fairy god-fathers; it is also an acknowledged but unclassifiable classic: a mélange of screwball, romance, and slapstick. But it is not a Claudette Colbert film; it is a Preston Sturges film, to use the auteurist designation—in this case, deserved. In addition to writing and directing the film, Sturges elicited a flawless ensemble performance from his quartet of actors: Claudette, Joel McCrea, Mary Astor, and Rudy Vallee, whose styles mesh so perfectly that neither usurps the spotlight, even though Mary Astor comes close to requisition-ing a baby spot for herself.

Sturges was one of Hollywood's true anomalies. His privileged back-ground—an affluent stepfather and an eccentric mother who insisted that her son spend six months a year in Paris, where he was exposed to ballet, opera, and modern dance—should have prepared him for a career in the arts. Sturges seemed to be heading in that direction after the great success of his play, *Strictly Dishonorable* (1929), whose premiere coincided with the growing popularity of the talkies. Hollywood was wooing writers, and Sturges, who was ambivalent about his gilded youth, believed film was a more egalitarian medium than the stage. It was also more lucrative. Once he found a berth at Paramount and advanced from writer to writer-director, he knew he had found his niche.

Sturges was incapable of creating pure comedy on the order of *Holiday* or *The Philadelphia Story*. He knew he had a sophistication that was rare in Hollywood. (How many directors had mothers who consorted with Isadora Duncan, exposed their sons to the cultural life of Paris, and enrolled them in exclusive schools?) Yet Sturges always felt guilty about his charmed life, trying to compensate for it by adding scenes of low comedy and slapstick that he thought would appeal to a mass audience that might miss the wit. Those scenes (e.g., the free-for-all in the Automat in *Easy Living* [1937] and the trashing of the train in *The Palm Beach Story*) may have garnered laughs, but they also left some moviegoers with a sense of uneasiness. Imagine a club car filled with trigger-happy, inebriated men who use the windows for target practice. Funny? Only if you're not the bartender who has to dodge the bullets. Or people fighting for a free meal at the Automat in *Easy Living*, while Jean Arthur sits by herself, swathed in sable, calmly eating a beef pie. Funny? Perhaps under ordinary circumstances, but not during the Great Depression.

In Sturges's most autobiographical film, *Sullivan's Travels* (1941), a Hollywood director (Joel McCrea), determined to make the definitive movie about poverty, embarks on a journey to experience it firsthand. He finds the squalor for which he was looking; but he also suffers betrayal when his largesse results in his imprisonment, where he learns what it is like to be confined in a sweat box and work on a chain gang. Once his odyssey is over, Sullivan, like Sturges, realizes that comedy, not social realism, is his forte. Glowing with self-knowledge, Sullivan speaks the film's last lines: "There's a lot to be said for making people laugh. . . . It isn't much but it's better than nothing in this cockeyed caravan."

Claudette was so impressed with *Sullivan's Travels* that she expressed her desire to make a picture with Sturges, who obliged with *The Palm Beach Story*. The film was obviously written with Claudette in mind. Gerry Jeffers (Claudette) is not exactly the gold digger she was in *Midnight*, but a wife, who after five years of marriage to Tom (Joel McCrea), an idealistic architect, realizes that he cannot provide her with the luxuries without which marriage is meaningless. Sturges had a problem with the character; on the one hand, Gerry wants to be free so she can snare a wealthy husband, which makes her a kin to *Midnight*'s Eve Peabody; on the other, she plans to use her considerable sex appeal to get the ninety-nine thousand dollars needed to finance Tom's bizarre plan to build an airborne airport. Claudette had to convince audiences that Gerry's decision to leave her husband is based on an unconventional form of altruism: it is her way of furthering his career, something she can accomplish if she can entice a Palm Beach millionaire into providing the funding.

Sturges cannot have it both ways: Gerry is either a gold digger or a faithful wife, but not both. Yet Claudette plays the role so well that while she insists Tom would be better off without her, she also wants him to realize his dream, even if it means becoming a gold digger or, in her case, a gold digger/supportive wife/potential divorcée.

If anyone needs a fairy godfather, it is Gerry. Actually, she gets three of them. First, a sausage manufacturer, known as the "Wienie King," is so captivated by her that he doles out enough money to pay the rent and the grocery bills. But that is only a stopgap measure. Then it is on to Palm Beach. Standing at the gate at Penn Station as the Ale and Quail Club, a party of drinking and hunting buddies, board the train to Palm Beach, Gerry is so convincingly helpless that they make her their mascot, get her a compartment, and even serenade her. When they create so much havoc that their private car has to be uncoupled, Gerry takes refuge in the Pullman, where she encounters her third fairy godfather, John D. Hackensacker III (Vallee), as she tries to climb to the upper berth, accidentally stepping on his face and crushing his glasses. In record time, she has a magnificent wardrobe and a doting Hackensacker, willing to finance Tom's airport.

But Tom has his fairy godfather, too: the "Wienie King," who gives him plane fare so he can reclaim Gerry. When he arrives in Palm Beach, Gerry passes him off as her brother, which delights Hackensacker's sister, the much-married Princess Centimillia (delightfully played by Mary Astor, who speaks her lines so rapidly yet with such crystalline clarity that she invests the film with the air of drawing-room comedy).

The Palm Beach Story might have been a drawing-room comedy if it were not for the Ale and Quail Club sequence that many still find hilarious. In fact, *The Palm Beach Story* could have been the companion film to *The Philadelphia Story* if Sturges had reduced the Ale and Quail Club to deus ex machina status and eliminated the mindless havoc they wrought. But Sturges had no intention of making a "pure" comedy. The sequence was his way of satirizing a club that can afford to travel with hunting dogs and reserve a private railway car. As the title suggests, *The Palm Beach Story* is clearly a reply to *The Philadelphia Story*, if not a criticism of its over refinement, as if to suggest that perhaps a bit of farce or slapstick might have made Philip Barry's Main Line Philadelphians less elitist.

Yet when Sturges waxed romantic, he went far beyond anything in *The Philadelphia Story*. There is one extraordinary moment of sheer romance in *The Palm Beach Story* that is not marred by Sturges's customary hijinks. Hackensacker hires a band to play beneath Gerry's window while he croons "Goodnight, Sweetheart" so wistfully that the song becomes a nostalgic reminder of a time when life was simpler and love was in the air. Gerry is wearing a black strapless gown, as low cut as the Breen Office allowed. When she asks Tom to unhook it for her, the combination of her allure, the touch of his hands, the form-revealing gown (the sexiest Claudette ever wore), and the soothing strains of the music are too strong for either of them to resist, leaving the audience free to imagine what transpired after their passionate embrace. At that moment, we know their marriage is no longer in jeopardy.

When the moment of truth arrives, both brother and sister are disappointed, since Hackensacker had hoped to marry Gerry; and the Countess, Tom. When Hackensacker asks Gerry if she has a sister, Gerry replies that she has a twin. Hackensacker is intrigued. Gerry also informs him that she and Tom are both twins, to which Tom replies, "That's another plot entirely." "Plot" is correct. If anyone remembered the frenzied credits sequence, the pieces of the puzzle start interlocking.

The credits sequence is totally without dialogue; in fact, it looks like a silent movie, accompanied by cliffhanger music, including a bit of the *William Tell Overture*. A hysterical maid, engaged in a frantic telephone conversation, spots *something* and promptly faints. Next, an anxious minister is seen waiting for the bride and groom. A taxi pulls up to the wedding site and out steps a man in a tuxedo. Another man in a tuxedo (Joel McCrea) rushes over to him, points to *something* inside, and is hustled into the waiting cab. The bride or *a* bride (Claudette) is desperately trying to leave her apartment, while another Claudette, tied up in the closet and wearing a lace-trimmed satin slip, is struggling to break free. The bride hails a cab; the groom or *a* groom is in another cab, in which another man (presumably his best man) is helping him into a tuxedo jacket. Finally, groom and best man arrive and rush toward the altar, followed by the bride, and the relieved minister performs the ceremony. Then a title appears on the screen: "And they lived happily ever after. Or did they?"

The final scene, a double wedding, clarifies the credits sequence to some extent. It only makes sense if both Gerry and her twin were in some way involved with Tom, who cannot distinguish one from the other. Since only one of them can have him, one ties up the other so that she can be the bride. But was she the right bride? Since the twin Toms must have been rivals for Gerry's affection, which Tom was bundled into the cab? And why? Because he was the wrong groom? At to what was he pointing? Obviously, the interior of the building where the ceremony is to take place and where apparently he does not belong. And which Tom struggled to get into the tuxedo jacket? All one can say is that he was the Tom who arrived with his best man and married Gerry.

In the final scene, Tom and Gerry stand alongside Hackensacker and Gerry's twin, next to whom are the princess and Tom's twin. Since Gerry and Tom are still married, they are bridesmaid and best man; but the twins, from the looks on their faces, seem to have no idea of what is happening. But that, as Tom said, is "another plot."

Sturges knew Shakespeare's comedies, to which *The Palm Beach Story* owes a great deal. In *A Midsummer Night's Dream* (act 5, scene 1), Theseus compares the lover, the madman, and the poet: "Lovers and madmen have such seething brains, / Such shaping fantasies, that apprehend / More than cool reason ever comprehends." The poet, blessed with "a fine frenzy," "gives to airy nothing / A local habitation and a name." Sturges had that "fine frenzy" and could take something as "airy" as *The Palm Beach Story* and give it a pedigree. His lovers defy reason in pursuit of their fantasies: an airport in the air, a millionaire that will bankroll it, mirror images that find their reflections in a world governed by fancy and chance.

Shakespeare sent his lovers into the woods (*A Midsummer Night's Dream*) or into a topsy-turvy world where women disguised as boys attract other women, and men find themselves strangely taken with boys who are really women in drag (*Twelfth Night, As You Like It*). He restores order through marriage: a double wedding in *A Midsummer Night's Dream* and *Twelfth Night* and a quadruple one in *As You Like It*. Sturges resolves his plot by sending one pair of twins into a world where fortune's wheel revolves in their favor; the other pair, kept in reserve, also emerge as recipients of fortune's favors, even though they might not quite understand how it happened.

Exactly what Sturges wants the audience to take away from the film is unclear. Has Gerry changed her ways? And what will happen with Tom's modernist airport? The same title that appeared after the credits sequence returns at the end: "And they lived happily ever after. Or did they?"

The answer may lie in Mozart's opera, *Così Fan Tutte*, with which Sturges was familiar. In the opera, two sisters, Fiordiligi and Dorabella, are engaged to Guglielmo and Fernando, respectively. When the cynic Don Alfonso challenges the men to test their fiancées' fidelity, they go along with his plan. Claiming they must report for military duty, the men return disguised as Albanians, each seducing the other's fiancée. As a result, each sister becomes enamored of the other's disguised intended, unwittingly proving Don Alfonso's theory that women are fickle: "*Così fan tutte*" (So are they all). But when the disguises are discarded, and each sister is paired with her former fiancé, there is still an element of doubt. Many stage directors have felt similarly, choosing to end the opera on an ambivalent note with a tableau of the sisters and their would-be husbands in no particular order, leaving the pairing-off to the audience.

"Or did they?" Sturges asks. So did Mozart. And with whom? Which Gerry was Tom supposed to marry? The one in the wedding gown or the one tied up in the closet? And if he married the wrong one, did Hackensacker get the right one? And which Tom was Gerry supposed to marry? The one who fled the wedding scene or the one who finally arrived with the best man? Or were they both the same—the Tom in the tuxedo getting a case of cold feet? If they were not, which Tom did the princess marry? Or does it matter?

"Lord, what fools these mortals be!" Puck exclaims in *A Midsummer Night's Dream* (act 3, scene 2). *The Palm Beach Story* is Sturges's *A Midsummer Night's Dream*; the real and the illusory and chance and fate have become so intertwined that the end of the film seems like the end of a dream— pleasurable but hard to interpret. At the end of Shakespeare's play, Puck reminds the audience that they "have only slumbered here/While these visions did appear." Earlier, Puck (act 3, scene 2) predicted that "Jack shall have Jill/Nought shall go ill." Everything did work out, but which Jack got which Jill? There's the rub.

Claudette enjoyed working with Sturges, and he felt similarly, but not about her 5:00 p.m. rule. At the dot of five, Claudette waved good-bye and left the set. Sturges, unaccustomed to such behavior, said in front of the entire company, including Claudette, that her close-ups would have to be done early because "by five o'clock you're beginning to sag."

Claudette never worked with Sturges again, not because he mocked her working habits, but because his Hollywood career was in a downward spiral and would end seven years later, and not even at Paramount. But that was Claudette's fate. She worked with several of Hollywood's legendary directors, but only once: Frank Capra, John Ford, Anatole Litvak, George Cukor, Jean Negulesco, and Mervyn LeRoy. She was lucky with Ernst Lubitsch and Douglas Sirk (two films) and Cecil B. DeMille (three). However, her longest association was with Mitch Leisen, who may have been her favorite: "I adored Mitch as a person and admired his talent as an artist."

Claudette would have been miscast in *Darling*; she could easily play a careerist, but not boss lady, a type that would have clashed with her genial, life-loving image. It always seemed as if Claudette had channeled her natural vivacity into rivulets of *joie de vivre* to keep it from flooding the screen with cherry good-naturedness. What otherwise would have been just another peppy personality became the embodiment of the good life and what it can confer on those who pursue it in moderation: a sophistication that stops short of worldliness, a sense of humor that can never be confused with a sense of the absurd, a face suffused with a tranquility that no amount of front lighting can create, and a laugh that sounded like notes played on an instrument yet to be invented. Claudette was the only star of Hollywood's Golden Age who made it seem that the good life lay within everybody's reach.

Claudette looked forward to working again with MacMurray, with whom she made six films between 1935 and 1948. Moviegoers thought of them as a team, like Jeanette MacDonald and Nelson Eddy, or Greer Garson and Walter Pidgeon. MacMurray came on to women with a cocky self-assurance that was part male ego, part male chauvinism. He exuded charm that could be slick, smarmy, or both, depending on the circumstances. In *Double Indemnity* (1944) he no sooner meets Barbara Stanwyck than the two of them start trading double entendres. Russell could not handle such a type; thus *Take a Letter, Darling* ends with MacMurray turning into an alpha male, with Russell as his conquest.

Just as Claudette could never have been convincing in *Take a Letter, Darling*, Russell would have foundered badly in *No Time for Love*. However, what both films had in common was the screenwriter, Claude Binyon, who saw *Love* as the companion piece to *Darling*. Just as Russell hired the out-of-work MacMurray as her secretary, Claudette hires him after she inadvertently caused him to be suspended from his job. And just as MacMurray dragged Russell into his car in the finale, he throws Claudette over his shoulder and frees her from her insufferable circle.

In *No Time for Love*, Claudette was Katherine Grant, a photographer whose profession is cleverly revealed in the opening credits as her character is developing a series of pictures that turn out to be the credits. Grant may be a career woman, but Claudette invests her with such a down-to-earth warmth that one could easily imagine her falling for Jim Ryan (MacMurray), who earns his living as a sandhog. Assigned to photograph the men who are blasting away under the East River, Katherine accepts the challenge, only to polarize the crew, who believe that a woman's presence is bad luck, which, in this case, turns out to be true. Katherine gets her pictures, never expecting she would precipitate a brawl, which she then photographs. When the pictures are published, Ryan is suspended for four months.

When Ryan calls on Katherine to return her tripod, he senses that she longs to extricate herself from the web that her meddlesome sister, her stuffy fiancé, a gay playwright, and an asexual pianist (the only likeable one in the lot, endearingly played by Richard Haydn) have spun around her. To show that he is aware of her predicament and has the means to set her free, Ryan uses the appropriate body language, at which MacMurray was a master, giving her an unwanted (but not undesired) kiss.

No Time for Love was more intricately plotted than *Darling* and demanded much more of the actors, particularly in the cave-in sequence when the construction crew and Katherine (still eager for pictures) are literally up to their necks in mud. To see Claudette wading through what looked like cement that was just poured out of a mixer is to see a pro whose face was so begrimed that it was impossible to tell which her good side was.

When Ryan's invention for preventing cave-ins is dismissed as a failure, Katherine's photos prove it was not. However, by now it is *It Happened One Night* again. Believing there was no future for herself and Ryan, she agrees to an engagement party. This time there is no benign father to steer her into Mr. Right's arms, so Ryan takes it upon himself to be her liberator, which he does by tossing her over his shoulder, much to the consternation of the guests but not to Katherine, who expresses her delight with a bell-like laugh.

It is obvious that Katherine is looking for someone to release her from the tower in which, like Rapunzel, she is imprisoned. The night after she met Ryan she has a wish-fulfillment dream woven out of the day's events. Earlier she had told Ryan, whose primitivism disturbed her, that a chair in her bedroom had more character than he. Demanding to see his competition, he sits on the chair, which immediately falls apart. When some of Katherine's friends see her photos, one of the women swoons over the shot of Ryan, as if she had never seen a shirtless male before, and dubs him Superman. In the dream sequence, the chair spins through space; on the seat is a cliff, where a miniature Katherine is menaced by a figure in top hat and tails (presumably her editor-fiancé). Rather than yield to him, she jumps into the void, gliding through the air with her veils billowing like wings. Like a plane in a tailspin, Ryan, in a white Superman outfit, flies to her rescue and returns her to the cliff, from which he promptly ejects his rival.

The dream, apart from leaving Katherine looking radiant the next morning, predates the famous Salvador Dali dream sequence in Hitchcock's *Spellbound* (1945), which is considerably more surreal. But the dream also makes it clear that Ryan will come to her rescue when she is about to marry the wrong man.

Practically Yours (1944) was Claudette's last film for Leisen, but not with Fred MacMurray, who was again her costar and would continue to be for two more films, before their partnership ended in 1948 with *Family Honeymoon*. Although *Practically Yours* was never one of Leisen's favorites, it seemed to be his way of making up to Claudette for *No Time for Love*. This time, her character, Peggy Martin, is at the helm, steering the narrative to a conclusion in which the female gets the upper hand. Although by no means a satire on patriotism like Preston Sturges's *Hail the Conquering Hero* (1944), *Practically Yours* pokes genial fun at the nation's obsession with heroes, which the press encouraged whenever there was an opportunity for a real scoop, as there was when an Air Force pilot, Daniel Bellamy (MacMurray), deliberately flew his plane into a Japanese aircraft carrier in what was obviously a suicide mission. While the carrier was destroyed, the impact of the attack hurled the plane, or what was left of it, into the sea along with the pilot—or so Norman Krasna's script expects us to believe.

Before the attack, Bellamy spoke glowingly of someone (or something) whose name sounds like "Peggy," the tip of whose nose he longs to kiss as they roam through Central Park. The press assumes that "Peggy" is Peggy Martin, a former coworker at a typewriter company where Bellamy had been employed before entering the service. Although Peggy hardly knew him, the press accords her celebrity status, and she becomes the symbol of all women who lost their boyfriends in the war. But when the news arrives that Bellamy is alive, his reunion with Peggy, who has grown to believe that he really cared for her, is too good an opportunity for the media to pass up. The public will not be satisfied until the two marry. When Peggy learns that Bellamy was referring to "Piggy," his affectionate terrier, she realizes that they must continue the deception for the next two weeks—just enough time for Krasna to have them fall in love. Love, however, is not the issue; marriage is. Peggy wants to marry before Bellamy returns to active duty; Bellamy, only after the war has ended.

Peggy gets her way by using the occasion of a battleship christening to announce their impending nuptials on nationwide radio, rendering her alleged fiancé speechless but not reluctant to kiss her before the cameras. How Bellamy reacted afterwards we will never know; the film fades out with their embrace, followed by THE END.

MacMurray gave one of his least convincing performances because the script prevented him from playing the charmer, using his smug smile, delivering a smart rejoinder, or casting a sexy glance, all of which were part of his familiar persona. As Lieutenant Bellamy, MacMurray could not flaunt his virility, size up women as if they were potential lovers, or project an air of casual indifference. He was given a few quips, some of which were moderately clever, but nothing comparable to the kind of dialogue that Binyon wrote for him in *No Time for Love*, or even *Take a Letter, Darling*. He was clearly uncomfortable with the character. "Claudette, the trouble with this picture is that we're both too damned old for it," he complained. He was right. Peggy and Bellamy should have been their twenties. Claudette was forty-one; and MacMurray, thirty-six. Claudette could have passed for thirty, but not MacMurray, who always looked older than his years. The chemistry that once made them a team now needed a catalyst, which *Practically Yours* could not provide.

Practically Yours not only marked the end of Claudette's association with Leisen, but also with Paramount. It was unfortunate that her Paramount period came to a close with a film in which she was upstaged by a dog. Although Jean Arthur was only two years younger than Claudette, she could have added some quirky charm to Peggy, bringing a touch of screwball to a film that kept veering off in too many directions, as if to deflect our attention from its dubious premise—a suicide mission that achieves its purpose without the loss of life.

After the last day of shooting in mid April 1944, Claudette was a free agent. At the critical age of forty, there would be more films, but except for *Since You Went Away* (1944) and the unheralded *Three Came Home* (1950), nothing prestigious.

CHAPTER 10

Claudette and the "Good War"

The picture that should have marked the end of Claudette's Paramount period was *So Proudly We Hail* (1943); at least she would have played a woman closer to her age, and not one who should have been in her twenties. Once America entered World War II, the studios rallied around the flag, unleashing a barrage of films ranging from sensationalism (breeding camps in *Hitler's Children* [RKO, 1943] and the bayoneting of Chinese babies and the insertion of bamboo shoots under fingernails in *Behind the Rising Sun* [RKO, 1943]) to burlesque (Nazis as bumbling clowns in *Desperate Journey* [Warners, 1942]). Paramount had no problem packaging some of its films in Old Glory as if it were the latest form of gift wrap. The studio's contribution to the war effort was modest, yet a few (e.g., *Five Graves to Cairo, Hostages, So Proudly We Hail, Till We Meet Again*) resisted the temptation to demonize the enemy by placing human drama in the foreground. Paramount made one of the first creditable movies about the war, *Wake Island* (1942), which balanced male camaraderie with the pain of loss. There is a scene of unusual restraint in *Wake Island* when a major, himself a widower, attempts to console a lieutenant whose wife was killed at

Pearl Harbor by reminding him that now they are both men with memories.

Claudette must have assumed that, with America's involvement in the conflict, she would be cast in a war movie, or several of them. From the way she delivered the fadeout speech in *Arise, My Love*, it seemed as if she knew it was only a matter of time, which was the case. Six months before Pearl Harbor, Claudette joined the entertainment caravan that director Mark Sandrich spearheaded to tour army bases. Other stars included Jack Benny (with whom Claudette performed a skit), Marlene Dietrich, Carole Landis, Dick Powell, and Joan Blondell. After Pearl Harbor, Claudette, like so many Hollywood stars, participated in bond drives. In early 1942, during a Chicago bond rally, Claudette, playwright-screenwriter Allan Scott, and Sandrich overheard people inquiring about the fate of the nurses stationed at Corregidor, which fell to the Japanese the previous May. Sandrich had an inspiration; for the duration, the combat film would be celebrating the achievements of the various branches of the armed services, but who would ever think of dramatizing the contributions of the American Red Cross? Sandrich and Scott had to work fast.

The film that became *So Proudly We Hail* was an unusual undertaking for director-producer Sandrich, who was primarily identified with Fred Astaire and Ginger Rogers musicals (*The Gay Divorcée, Top Hat, Follow the Fleet, Shall We Dance?* and *Carefree*); Scott was also known for both musicals (*Carefree, Swing Time, Follow the Fleet, Roberta, Shall We Dance?*) and romantic comedies (*Skylark, Sun Valley Serenade*). Neither of them seemed the right match for a movie that covered the period from Pearl Harbor to the fall of Corregidor. Yet they embraced the project as if it were their special mission, with Sandrich even bringing in Eunice Hatchitt, a nurse who had been at Bataan and Corregidor, as technical advisor. He also had Scott do an enormous amount of research, much of which found its way into the film through voice-over. Scott plotted *So Proudly We Hail* as a flashback with a frame narrative, beginning and ending with the nurses' return voyage to the States. Lt. Janet Davidson (Claudette) is in a state of trauma because she believes her husband is dead. Until the end, which suggests that he is probably alive by the climactic image of a sunburst; some of the nurses function as narrators, providing historical as well narrative background.

The war scenes, frequent and bloody, were harrowing. Explosions ripped through the operating room during surgery, killing both a doctor and a nurse; the shelling did not even spare the makeshift outdoor hospital. Although the nurses worked under the specter of death or the possibility of being captured by the Japanese and sent to the brothels, they resolved to stay on until they were ordered to evacuate. The nurses were not motivated by patriotism but by a sense of duty that could not mask the frustration they felt, especially when they learned that General Douglas MacArthur had been sent to Australia—in effect abandoning them to the enemy. Sandrich committed himself so thoroughly to *So Proudly We Hail* that it hastened his death, which came two years after its release. He was only forty-five.

Sensing that propaganda would dominate the American World War II film, Sandrich urged Scott to minimize the flag-waving, which, admittedly, could not be completely avoided. Production head Buddy DeSylva found Scott's first draft a "bit too full of propaganda" and "preachy." Lt. Janet Davidson would have been about Claudette's age, forty. Since Scott had invented a love interest for her, he felt he should at least explain that she was still a virgin. Amused, Sandrich inquired why he went to such lengths: "Isn't that pressing it a bit when the lady is forty?" The propaganda was muted, and Claudette became a wife, whose marriage was consummated off screen.

Claudette had star billing, followed by Paulette Goddard as Lt. Joan O'Doul, who would not part with her black negligee, her only piece of feminine apparel; and Veronica Lake, in the problematic role of another nurse, Olivia D'Arcy, whose hostility to the others is eventually explained. However, the plot did not revolve around Claudette's character. There are three interrelated stories set against the background of the first year of the Pacific campaign: Janet's romance with, and eventual marriage to, Lt. John Summers (a miscast George Reeves, who went on to minor celebrity as television's *Superman* in the 1950s); Joan's with "Kansas," an ex-fullback, winningly played by the boyish Sonny Tufts; and Olivia's obsession with her dead fiancé, who was killed at Pearl Harbor.

The character of Olivia created major problems for Scott. Olivia holds the Japanese responsible for her fiancé's death and vows revenge. The Breen Office kept rejecting Olivia's rants against the Japanese, until Scott had her shout, "I know what I'm going to do. I'm going to kill Japs. Every bloody one I can get my hands on." Strangely enough, the Breen Office approved of Olivia's blood lust, insisting only on the removal of "bloody." Thus, Olivia ends up saying, "I'm going to kill Japs, every blood-stained one I can get my hands on." Olivia is so determined to do so that she asks to be assigned to the ward where she can tend to the Japanese wounded, but, once there, she cannot carry out her vendetta and undergoes a 180-degree change of character.

The most memorable scene in the film does not involve Janet but Olivia. An abortive evacuation attempt leaves the nurses stranded in a storage facility, with only hand grenades for protection. Hoping to gain time so she can start up the jeep, Janet hurls a grenade into the darkness, which results in gunfire, indicating that the Japanese are nearby. As if inspired, Olivia unpins her hair, letting it frame her face seductively, and places a grenade in her shirt. She walks out into the open, arms raised in a gesture of surrender; when the Japanese surround her, she pulls the pin, killing them and herself, so that the others can rush into the jeep and escape.

Scott did not minimize the bitterness the nurses felt because of medical supplies that never arrived and promises that were never kept. The abandoned of Bataan referred to themselves as "the battling bastards of Bataan; / No mama, no papa, no Uncle Sam; / No aunts, no uncles, no nephews, no nieces; / No pills, no planes, no artillery pieces. / . . . and nobody gives a damn!" "Bastard" was unacceptable, so in the film the "battling bastards" became the "battling orphans," which, although a euphemism, was more accurate. They had indeed been orphaned. Janet has a scene near the end in which she expresses her disillusionment, mockingly referring to their situation as a "holding action," but knowing full well that it was abandonment.

Although *So Proudly We Hail* won no Oscars, it was nominated in four categories: supporting actress (Goddard), original screenplay (Scott), cinematography (Charles Lang), and special effects. It is also one of the few World War II films that, except for the peroration ("This is our war, and this time it will be our peace"), holds up remarkably well.

Since You Went Away (1944) does also. In May 1943, producer David O. Selznick received a telegram from the eminent stage actress Katharine Cornell, who vied with Helen Hayes for the title of "First Lady of the American Theatre." Cornell learned that Selznick had purchased the rights to Margaret Buell Wilder's *Since You Went Away* and offered to play the lead, a mother of two whose husband was away at war. Selznick knew she was unsuited to the part, but proceeded cautiously, telling her that he wanted to be "very sure that it was the right thing for her to do."

Although Cornell's presence would have lent a theatrical aura to the film, few moviegoers would have known who she was, except perhaps those who saw her in a cameo role in *Stage Door Canteen* (1943). Many stage stars with larger-than-life personas did not fare well in Hollywood, particularly Ethel Merman and Mary Martin and, to some extent, Tallulah Bankhead and Helen Hayes, who both preferred the theatre and regarded film as a more lucrative but less satisfying medium. Cornell was one of them.

Selznick then turned to gossip columnist Hedda Hopper; four months after the film was released, Hopper decided to take some credit for its phenomenal success. In her syndicated column in the *Los Angeles Times* (29 October 1944), she reminisced about the time Selznick sought her advice about casting the leading role of Ann Hilton. When Hopper urged him to contact Claudette, Selznick hesitated, convinced Claudette would never consent to play a mother, especially one whose daughters would be sixteen-year-old Shirley Temple and twenty-four-year-old Jennifer Jones (who looked much younger and at the time was Selznick's lover and in 1949 became his wife). Selznick and Hopper seemed to have forgotten that

Claudette had played a mother brilliantly ten years earlier in *Imitation of Life*.

For Claudette, the chief problem was not playing a mother but the script, which did not yet exist. Claudette supposedly phoned Hopper, wondering if she should sign on without a script—something she had never done. Hopper then reminded her that Selznick did not produce flops, as if Claudette did not know about *A Star Is Born*, *Nothing Sacred*, and his greatest triumph, *Gone with the Wind*.

Claudette hardly needed a reminder. In addition to working for one of Hollywood's premier producers, she would have top billing over Jennifer Jones, who had just won an Oscar for *The Song of Bernadette*, and former child star Shirley Temple. In June 1943, David O. Selznick confirmed reports, which had circulated earlier, that Claudette was set for the lead. It was an excellent choice; in fact, the entire film was perfectly cast. The problem was its length: close to three hours with drama alternating with homespun sentiment, a running visual gag with a bull dog, the inevitable transformation of a misanthrope into a mensch, intimations of tragedy from looks of uncertainty and somber music as a young corporal leaves for war, and the hoped-for arrival of good news at the end.

Since You Went Away was Selznick's companion film to *Gone with the Wind*; it was a domestic epic about home front America. He believed so strongly in the film that he wrote the screenplay himself, as the credits attest: "Screen Play by the Producer." The opening title announced the theme: "This is the story of the unconquerable fortress—the American home, 1943." And the home of the Hiltons and their children was Selznick's paradigm of that home, a mythic construct and a soundstage creation that nonetheless gave hope to a war-weary America that took the film to its heart.

Ann Hilton was a perfect role for Claudette. She did not have the luxury of a glamorous wardrobe and looked perfectly at ease in clothes that a wife and mother would wear while her husband is in the service. And because Ann has to adjust to a captain's salary, she learns to economize and even takes in a boarder. Claudette made everything look so easy, as if esprit de corps would alleviate the anxiety wives felt when their husbands were in that no man's land called "destination unknown."

Selznick did not skimp on budget or schedule. "The final cost reached $3.25 million," including Claudette's salary, the highest she had ever received: $265,000. It was a long shoot: 19 September 1943 to 9 February 1944. The cast was huge: over two hundred speaking parts. Despite Selznick's enthusiasm for the subject matter, *Since You Went Away* was not in the same league as *Gone with the Wind*. So many narrative strands intersected that at times one wished that the producer-screenwriter had woven his tapestry less prodigiously. But audiences did not seem to mind. Moviegoers could not wait to get into New York's Capitol Theatre when the film opened on 20 July: "Crowds were lined up completely around the block. A week later, there was still a two-hour wait . . . and New York police finally gave orders that the theater doors were to open at 8:30 a.m. because crowds outside were obstructing traffic." The Academy of Motion Picture Arts and Sciences felt similarly, nominating the film for best picture, actress (Claudette), supporting actor (Monty Woolley), supporting actress (Jones), score (Max Steiner), interior decoration, special effects, editing, and cinematography (the extraordinary Stanley Cortez and Lee Garmes). Steiner won, and Claudette lost to Ingrid Bergman in *Gaslight*.

Since You Went Away still has great audience appeal and is often shown on cable television during the Christmas holidays. There are two scenes in particular whose poignancy has not diminished over the years. The first is the departure of Corporal William Smollett (Robert Walker) for active duty. He and Jane Hilton (Jennifer Jones) have fallen in love; there is an aching poignancy about the scene in which Jane bids farewell to him at the train station. They are the pure of heart—guileless lovers brimming with such innocence, or perhaps with too much of it, that one has the inescapable feeling that theirs is a doomed romance. Those who knew that in real life Jones and Walker were married (but whose marriage was steadily deteriorating because of Selznick's growing obsession with Jones) would find even greater poignancy in Smollett's departure, as Jane runs the length of the platform, waving goodbye. Her look of desperation, Max Steiner's soaring music that tries to rise to a triumphant crescendo but cannot, and the enveloping darkness from the low-key lighting portend Smollett's death.

The other is the finale. It is Christmas Eve, and Ann has received a present from her husband, a music box that plays their favorite song, "Together." The nostalgic melody and Ann's uncertainty of his whereabouts cause her to lose her composure for the first time. When the phone suddenly rings, Ann's tears and her despairing mood suggest the worst. It is a cablegram, which she asks to be read. When it is, Claudette's face, a mask of apprehension, slowly takes on a glow as she shouts the good news to her daughters. Cromwell frames the final shot of the three of them looking out of the upstairs window—the keepers of the hearth and the embodiment of that "unconquerable fortress, the American home."

Joseph Cotten, who played a naval lieutenant discreetly courting Ann in her husband's absence, adored Claudette, who was "one of the most complete, humorous, hard-working and delightfully, almost shockingly, honest creatures I have ever worked with." Shirley Temple felt differently. She had heard about Claudette's fixation with the left side of her face. However, Temple had been in the business long enough to know what it means to be upstaged. Claudette was not intimidated by Temple, who, once she became a teenager, was no longer America's curly-haired darling. In her autobiography, Temple recalls what happened when Claudette suspected she might be photographed on her right side: "Suddenly she reached out and grabbed my chin. Firmly holding my head faced away from the camera, she rotated herself to a left exposure, a not-so-gentle hint from mother to daughter that she would not tolerate any tricks." Temple soon learned who was the star of the film.

World War II beckoned again at the end of the 1940s, when Darryl F. Zanuck bought the rights to *Three Came Home*, Agnes Newton Keith's journalistic memoir of her internment in a Japanese concentration camp from 1942 to 1945. Agnes was the wife of a British colonial officer stationed in British North Borneo, which surrendered to the Japanese in January 1942. A few months later, the men and their wives were ordered to pack one suitcase each and report for relocation, with the women and children interned in one camp, and the men in another.

February 1950 was an odd time to release *Three Came Home*. The war had ended five years earlier, and while it would always be a plot point, it seemed somewhat irrelevant. What audiences may not have realized at the time was that it was one of the finest—and still unacknowledged—films about the war.

Although *Three Came Home* was a "Darryl F. Zanuck Presents" film, it was not one of his favorites. He assigned Nunnally Johnson to adapt the memoir as well as produce the film version. While vacationing in Sun Valley, Zanuck read the first draft and composed a nineteen-page memo to Johnson on 22 December 1948, insisting on the eventual reunion of Agnes and her husband and requesting more detail about their marriage—Agnes being American, and her husband British—which Johnson added through voiceover. Because Zanuck expected *Three Came Home* to be atypical of the usual World War II movie that reduced the Japanese to racial stereotypes, he also asked for the elimination of the scene in which Japanese pillaged the Keiths' house. But to be faithful to the memoir, Johnson could not minimize the inhumanity that the women experienced during their internment. With Keith herself as technical advisor, the details would not be fabricated.

Zanuck seemed more concerned about political correctness, even though that term was not yet in vogue. And if it were, Zanuck would have denied that it was an issue. Yet he did not request any changes in the scenes depicting the "attempted criminal assault" on Agnes (in the memoir, it was rape) or her torture when she refused to drop the charge.

In his 22 December memo, Zanuck suggested several possibilities for the part of Agnes Keith without ranking them: Ingrid Bergman, Claudette, Joan Fontaine, and Ida Lupino. One could envision Bergman or Lupino in the part, but not Fontaine. Bergman was occupied with Hitchcock's *Under Capricorn*, and Lupino was about to become an actress-director; as the latter, she would fill in the void that Dorothy Arzner left in 1943 when she turned her back on Hollywood and began teaching film at UCLA.

When Claudette was offered the role, she signed on, even though she knew it would be a grueling shoot and that she would be the object of violence, which, to be effective, had to be done realistically. However, she did not think she would end up with a broken back. In World War II movies, women were assaulted, but not on camera. Usually, the act was left to the imagination. In *So Proudly We Hail,* one of the nurses voiced her fear of being captured by the Japanese: "I was in Nanking. I saw what happened to the women there. When the Red Cross protested, the Japanese called it the privilege of serving his Imperial Majesty's troops. It's an honor you die from." In *Dragon Seed* (1944), the Japanese surround a helpless Chinese woman cowering on the ground. The fadeout says it all. In *Edge of Darkness* (1943), a woman is abducted while leaving a church and presumably gang raped.

In *Three Came Home,* Agnes is trying to take her clothes off the line during a rainstorm when a guard attacks her. Rather than portray it as the rape it was, Johnson made it clear that it was an abortive rape, and director Jean Negulesco shot the scene accordingly. Agnes, who earlier had to crawl under barbed wire to enjoy a few fleeting moments with her husband, is now subjected to more roughhouse than she had ever experienced before, including being thrown on the ground and then against the steps of the women's quarters. When Agnes makes the mistake of lodging a complaint, she is expected to sign a confession stating, in effect, that she fabricated the charge (which could mean death). When she refuses, one of the soldiers turns his back and looks out the window, as if he does not want to see what will happen. As Agnes is seated on a chair, another guard comes behind her and twists her arm behind her back. When she still refuses, she is thrown on the floor, on her back, and kicked in the ribs. At the time, Claudette did not know that she had broken her back, although anyone looking closely at the sequence would not have been surprised.

It is impossible to talk about *Three Came Home* without paying tribute to the superb Japanese actor Sessue Hayakawa, who played the educated Colonel Suga. When Suga discovers Agnes's presence, he summons her to his office to express his admiration for her book about Borneo and asks her to autograph it personally for him. In a later scene, he tells her that his entire family died in the bombing of Hiroshima. Agnes is sympathetic, even though she knows that he was aware of her brutalization. While Johnson's script only occasionally balanced acts of barbarism with humanitarian gestures, there were at least a few Japanese soldiers who were sympathetic to the women's hardships—not a bad record for a 1950 World War II movie.

Three Came Home wound up production in spring 1949. Zanuck could have released it that December, so that it could have been eligible for an Oscar nomination. However, in 1949 Zanuck was promoting *Twelve O'Clock High*, which he vastly preferred. Releasing *Three Came Home* in early 1950 meant that by the end of the year it would be forgotten, as indeed was the case. *Three Came Home* did not receive a single nomination; *Twelve O'Clock High* won for best supporting actor (Dean Jagger) and sound recording. Ironically, in 1950 Zanuck was given the Irving Thalberg award. At least *Three Came Home* was voted best film, and Claudette, best actor, at the Vichy Film Festival.

Regardless, Claudette sensed that she had given a performance that ranked among her best, even though it left her with chronic back pain. She expressed her feeling of accomplishment to Jean Negulesco, with whom she had never worked before (and would never again): "You know I'm not given to exaggeration so I hope you believe me when I say that working with you has been the most stimulating and happiest experience of my entire career. Wished the schedule was longer."

Fox's big film of 1950 was *All about Eve*, which won six Oscars, including best picture, director (Joseph L. Mankiewicz), and supporting actor (George Sanders). Claudette could have played Margo Channing in *Eve*, except that she was recovering from injuries sustained from the two graphically violent scenes in *Three Came Home*. Although Zanuck wanted Marlene Dietrich for Margo, Mankiewicz held out for Claudette, who could not commit to a three-month shoot that, ironically, began in April 1950 when *Three Came Home* was winding up production. Zanuck then contacted Bette Davis, who gave a performance that revived her waning career.

Anyone learning that Claudette was Mankiewicz's first choice for Margo Channing (an aging Broadway star who takes pity on Eve Harrington, an aspiring actress, only to find herself the victim of Eve's treachery) usually responds with a quizzical look: Claudette in one of Davis's signature roles? Mankiewicz wrote the script as high comedy in the Philip Barry–S. N. Behrman mode. Claudette could have given the film an airiness, a buoyancy that would have masked the darker implications of youth supplanting age. Davis looked like an aging actress; Claudette looked ageless. And the self-pity to which Margo succumbs would have just been ruefulness with Claudette. But there would have been no edge, bitterness, or voracious ego—the qualities that Davis brought to the part, along with memories of a career that had been in a downspin since 1946.

At the Museum of Modern Art's tribute to Mankiewicz on 3 February 1990, Claudette spoke briefly, admitting how sad she was to have missed out on *All about Eve*. She was actually fortunate, as was Mankiewicz. Davis imposed the stamp of her personality so forcefully on *Eve* that it became a story not about Broadway, with which neither Mankiewicz nor Davis was familiar, but about Hollywood, with a subtext about a movie star whose career had derailed and who needed a vehicle that would put her back on course. With Claudette, one would have had no problem accepting *Eve* as a tale of Broadway; with Davis, it would always be about Hollywood—and its *prima donna assoluta*.

CHAPTER 11

Slow Fade to Legend

When Claudette left Paramount in 1944, she did not have a set agenda. She knew only that she wanted to go on making movies on a freelance basis, with script and, of course, salary as the determining factors. For the rest of her film career she alternated between romantic comedies and serious dramas (film noir, war film, western, family melodrama), none of which were especially memorable except the previously discussed *Three Came Home*, which became her last film of any consequence. To remind audiences of her versatility, Claudette generally chose to follow a comedy with a drama, or a few comedies with a few dramas. For example, the romantic comedy *Guest Wife* (1945) was followed by the melodrama *Tomorrow Is Forever* (1946); another comedy, *Without Reservations*, by another melodrama, *The Secret Heart* (both 1946).

Guest Wife marked Claudette's first film as a freelancer. It was also the first of three films for Jack Skirball, who in 1944 founded Skirball-Manning Productions with writer Bruce Manning. Skirball is one of Old Hollywood's most intriguing figures. A devout Jew and committed humanitarian, he was even a rabbi for a while. While a student at Cincinnati's Hebrew Union

College and later the University of Chicago, he sold one- and two-reelers for Metro, hoping eventually to become a film producer. When he realized his goal was incompatible with the rabbinate, he ceased functioning as a rabbi and founded Education Films, which released the controversial *Birth of a Baby* (1938). In 1942, he formed Jack H. Skirball Productions, whose best-known films were Hitchcock's *Saboteur* (1942) and *Shadow of a Doubt* (1943), both released by Universal.

Skirball-Manning Productions was looking for stars from Hollywood's Golden Age who were no longer in demand but still had box office appeal. Thus, Skirball was able to recruit Claudette, Don Ameche, Myrna Loy, Ginger Rogers, Robert Young, George Brent, and Bette Davis. While they would have all agreed that the movies they made for Skirball would not eclipse those of their glory days, they also knew that they were in good hands, particularly with the directors that Skirball hired: e.g., Sam Wood for *Guest Wife*; Frank Borzage for *Magnificent Doll*, with Ginger Rogers, Burgess Meredith, and David Niven; Curtis Bernhardt for *Payment on Demand*, with Bette Davis and Barry Sullivan.

Even a fine director like Sam Wood could do little with *Guest Wife*, which was as disappointing as *Practically Yours*, but in different way. Claudette had to draw on every comedic device in her repertoire to keep audiences from remembering that they had seen it all before, and better, in *The Awful Truth* (1937), *His Girl Friday* (1940), and *My Favorite Wife* (1940). Claudette was Mary Price, the wife of a small-town banker, Chris (Dick Foran), which in itself requires a suspension of disbelief. Chris is the archetypal guileless fool, still in awe of his old college buddy Joe Jefferson (Don Ameche), now a famous foreign correspondent. Chris may love Mary, but he worships Joe.

When Joe arrives at the Prices' home as they are about to leave for New York, Chris is willing to defer the trip so the two can relive old times. But Joe has a reason for dropping in: He has convinced his boss, who believes married men are more responsible than bachelors, that he is married to Mary; and he has presented her picture as proof. He has also penned a series of fictitious letters attesting to Mary's love for him. Thus, when Joe asks

Mary to go along with the ruse, Chris not only answers for her but insists that his friend accompany them to New York. Chris even gives Joe his ticket and takes a later train.

Wood moved the action along at a clip to keep the audience from wondering what kind of a husband would allow his wife to masquerade as his best friend's spouse without considering the consequences, which could have spelled the end of his career (as it almost did), let alone his marriage.

In *Midnight*, Ameche was absent during most of the film's highlights. In *Guest Wife*, his almost ubiquitous presence and self-absorption force Claudette to do some real acting: To punish Joe for exploiting his friendship with Chris, Mary feigns affection for him and is so convincing that Joe, terrified of commitment, will do anything to extricate himself from a situation that has spun out of control. Here the writers, Bruce Manning and John Klorer, come to the rescue. Assuming nobody would question how such a transparent ruse went undetected, they manage to have everyone get what he or she wants. Joe's boss, who still believes that Joe and Mary are married, despite evidence to the contrary, consoles Joe, who has convinced him that Mary has run off with Chris. Instead of getting his comeuppance, Joe emerges from the charade with his career intact and a new assignment. And Chris and Mary head back to small-town America, which savvy moviegoers know is just a sop to optimists. Dick Foran looked as if he belonged there, if not on a farm; but if Claudette had to live in the boondocks, she would have turned it into a fashion center, illuminated by her high-voltage smile.

Guest Wife might have been better if Claudette had been paired with different actors. The role of Joe needed someone who could play a likeable con man, able to mute his narcissism and regulate the charm meter, someone like Robert Cummings, who could exhibit a reasonable degree of sophistication without behaving as if he had stepped out of a drawing-room comedy. The ideal Chris Price would have been Fred MacMurray, who could look befuddled as opposed to "clueless," which, if it existed in the 1940s vernacular, would have been the appropriate character description.

The average moviegoer probably ignored the "deception does pay" conclusion, but not those in the newspaper business. The *New York Times* publisher, Arthur Hays Sulzberger, caught the film in Toronto and immediately fired off an angry letter to Will Hays, branding it "the most immoral picture I have ever seen . . . because [Jefferson] tells his boss he is married, gets a $1,000 bonus and a house, which he accepts." Hays referred Sulzberger's complaint to Joseph Breen, who a week later replied that he had not read the script, which contradicts his earlier response to Skirball: "We have read the screenplay . . . for your proposed picture GUEST WIFE, and are happy to report that the basic story seems to meet the requirements of the Production Code." In one sense, Breen was right; the Production Code did not address journalistic ethics, except to state that "the sympathy of the audience should never be thrown to the side of crime, wrongdoing, evil or sin." Jefferson duped his boss with impunity. If that was not "wrongdoing," one would have to resort to euphemism and call it "violation of a policy that discriminated against the unmarried," making Jefferson a champion of civil liberties. Perhaps Hitchcock was right: "It's only a movie."

Stars do not go gently into the black hole. As the 1940s faded out, and the '50s came in, the stars of a certain age, male and female, girded themselves for the last hurrah, making movies that combined a '30s and '40s spirit with a postwar sensibility by turning back the clock to a time when they and Hollywood were in sync.

In April 1948, Skirball-Manning Productions was renamed Crest Productions, with Claudette's brother, Charles Wendling, as secretary-treasurer. Jeanne Chauchoin, determined to enhance her son's reputation in Hollywood, insisted that he become his sister's personal agent and business representative. Claudette played the dutiful daughter and may have even been eager to advance her brother's career.

Until 1946, Claudette was represented by Charles Feldman, one of the most powerful agents in Hollywood. Feldman, who allegedly "reads the novels of Henry James before breakfast," was educated at the University of Michigan, UCLA, and USC. After receiving a law degree, he became independent producer Edward Small's lawyer, which provided him with an education in the Hollywood school of economics, where he learned enough about percentages, package deals, and gross versus net profits to start his own agency, Famous Artists Corporation. By the mid 1940s, he could boast of three hundred clients, including such stars as Claudette, Charles Boyer, Marlene Dietrich, George Raft, Lauren Bacall, Tyrone Power, John Wayne, Randolph Scott, and Ingrid Bergman; directors Frank Borzage, John Stahl, Michael Curtiz, and Mitch Leisen; and writers Viña Delmar, Elmer Rice, and Sidney Buchman.

In 1945 Wendling, who had been working for Feldman, left to start his own agency at 8923 Sunset Boulevard. After Claudette, Maureen O'Hara was his most famous client, although he also represented Freddie Steele, Barton MacLane, Thurston Hall, and Peggy Stewart. Although Wendling was never a high-powered agent, his personal contacts and Claudette's influence made him eligible for the society pages, which took note of his second marriage in 1949 and the birth of his daughter two years later.

It may have been Wendling's idea that Manning fashion a script for his sister out of shards from her best-known films, banking on the charm of recognition that audiences experience when the past is recycled into something both new and old. And if Claudette sensed that some of her characters were spin-offs of earlier ones, there was little she could do to prevent her persona from becoming a cliché, except become a director and eventually a producer. In October 1949, Claudette was ready for a new addition to her resume: director. When she revealed her intentions to Hedda Hopper, the columnist was baffled. Claudette explained: "I've been acting in pictures 20 years. Secretly I've always longed to be a director. I have a passion for helping people do things that I know they can do if only shown how." A week later, she offered a different and more compelling reason: "Few women have had the courage to tackle directing, but this is no reason I can't make a success of it. Ida Lupino is doing a fine job. She hasn't given up her acting career either."

There was a difference between Claudette and Lupino. Lupino was one of Warner's tough dames; she sounded as if her vocal cords were coated with nicotine and looked as if she had insulated her body with steel to deflect life's slings and arrows. One could no more imagine Claudette in some of Lupino's films, such as *High Sierra* (1941), *The Sea Wolf* (1941), and *The Hard Way* (1942), than one could Lupino in *It Happened One Night*, *Midnight*, and *The Palm Beach Story*. While Claudette was primarily interested in camera angles and lighting that favored the left side of her face, Lupino was keenly interested in every aspect of moviemaking and revealed it in her first feature, *Not Wanted* (1949), which she had never intended to direct but took over when director Elmer Clifton had a heart attack.

It would have been understandable if Claudette told the press she was forming her own production company, as Rita Hayworth, Humphrey Bogart, and Rosalind Russell and her husband, producer Fred Brisson, did. However, Hayworth's Beckworth, Bogart's Santana, and Russell and Brisson's Independent Artists were short-lived. It wasn't until the corporatization of Hollywood in the late 1960s that the independents rose to challenge the studios' hegemony and vie with them for the public's favor. Claudette was meant for *acting*, the medium—stage, screen, or television—was irrelevant.

Still, one can understand her frustration with the scripts she was given, although it is hard to believe that, as a fledgling producer, she could have commissioned better ones. The wit that brightened *It Happened One Night*, *Midnight*, *Bluebeard's Eighth Wife*, and *The Palm Beach Story* was dimmed by writers who could not replicate Claudette Colbert dialogue and instead produced a facsimile. Lacking the genius of Robert Riskin, Billy Wilder and Charles Brackett, and Preston Sturges, they could only reach the middle of the comic pyramid, but not the apex.

Crest's *Bride for Sale* (1949), her second film for Skirball, was also coauthored by Manning and even more formulaic than *Guest Wife*; it was a pastiche of retreads from boss lady, screwball, and romantic comedies.

Mistaken Identity: Paul Martin (George Brent), head of a tax-returns firm, is so desperate for someone to appease his disgruntled employees that he hires a "Major Shelley," who turns out to be a former WAC, first name

Nora (Claudette). Compare Rosalind Russell as A. M. McGregor in *Take a Letter Darling* or Joan Crawford as M. J. in *They All Kissed the Bride* (both 1942).

Romantic Complications: Nora is only interested in the job because she wants access to the clients' financial assets in order to land a rich husband. Compare *The Palm Beach Story*.

Deception: Martin, fearing he might lose Nora, persuades his old college buddy, field archaeologist Steve Adams (Robert Young), to masquerade as a millionaire to keep Nora from defecting. Compare *Midnight, My Man Godfrey, The Major and the Minor*.

Getting Down and Dirty: In an attempt to add some slapstick to a comedy that is not especially funny, Manning has Nora and Adams attend a wrestling match, after which Nora demonstrates her mastery of jujitsu (a skill she picked up in the Far East) in a fish market, where she gets a bucket of sardines dumped on her. Compare the destruction of the club car in *The Palm Beach Story* or Claudette sloshing through the mud in *No Time for Love*.

Choosing Mr. Right: Soon Nora forgets her original reason for joining the firm and begins falling in love with Adams. Will Nora marry George Brent or Robert Young? Forget the characters' names; the audience did. Since the script was flexible enough to allow her to choose either, audiences might have thought that the man least likely to appeal to her was the archaeologist. But Claudette was such a pro, throwing her head back in the same rapturous way whenever one of them kissed her, that it seemed she could be content with either. When Brent starts getting serious about Nora, there is every indication that she will choose him. After all, Brent managed to shake Barbara Stanwyck out of the doldrums of widowhood in *My Reputation* (1946). Compare *It Happened One Night*, and a host of others including *The Awful Truth, The Philadelphia Story, Lady in the Dark*, and the Rosalind Russell comedies *What a Woman!* and *Tell it to the Judge*.

Retribution: When Nora comes upon a college yearbook and discovers that Young and Brent were classmates, she decides it is payback time. Although she leads Brent on, anyone who remembers *Guest Wife* will know that it is only a form of retaliation. Nora chooses Young and then announces ecstatically that they will be spending their honeymoon under a tent in a North African desert, even though it means leaving a job at which she excels to join him on an archaeological dig. Even in 1949, Hollywood was preaching the "Wherever thou goest, I go" doctrine. Compare *Tell it to the Judge* (1949), in which Rosalind Russell prefers to play housewife to Robert Cummings than become a federal judge in Washington. Postwar America was still a men's club, and Hollywood was no different.

Claudette's non-Skirball comedies of the late 1940s were more popular, but not much better. Although the pairing of Claudette with John Wayne in *Without Reservations* (RKO, 1946) might have seemed like the punch line in a Hollywood joke, it worked surprisingly well, even if Andrew Solt's script was a mingled yarn: a few threads from the Rosalind Russell movie *What a Woman!* combined with some from *It Happened One Night* and *The Palm Beach Story*. When Claudette played opposite a man who basked in his masculinity (which was rare, given her costars, all virile but unable to size up a woman with Gable's or Wayne's once-over), she would respond with a knowing slyness that made physical attraction deliciously erotic.

In 1946, John Wayne had not yet become a national icon. His was a persona in progress: westerns, war movies, a rare foray into romantic comedy, none of which then added up to "John Wayne, American." As early as 1939, Wayne proved that he could play a lover. When it was a pure love, even for a woman that had been run out of town for being a prostitute (Claire Trevor as Dallas in *Stagecoach*, 1939), Wayne gazed on her with compassion tinged with desire. In *Without Reservations*, Wayne took one look at Claudette and it was obvious that whatever problems they would encounter, sex, brains, and a happy ending would solve them. Claudette luxuriated in Wayne's masculinity, and he responded to her feline charm.

One only wished their one movie together had a better script. Claudette played the author of a bestseller, *Here Is Tomorrow*, which one of the studios

purchases as a vehicle for Cary Grant and Lana Turner. En route to Hollywood she learns that Grant is unavailable, and that the studio plans to con-
duct a nationwide search for the male lead. A similar crisis occurred three
years earlier in *What a Woman!* with Rosalind Russell as a literary agent
who sold the movie rights to a best-seller. When the studio finds it impossible to cast the male lead, Russell tracks down the author and discovers he
is not only an academic but a hunk as well and starts grooming him for the
role. The similarities end there, but the quest for an unknown is part of
Hollywood lore and as good a plot point as any.

Two marines, Wayne and his buddy (Don DeFore), are also on the west-
bound train with Claudette, who takes one look at Wayne, sheds another
ten years (she was forty-three, looked thirty, and behaved as if she were
twenty), and goes into flirtation mode. She has found her leading man.
Wayne seems to enjoy picking up on Claudette's body language, as she fab-
ricates a story about herself, not daring to reveal that she is the author of a
book that he thoroughly dislikes.

The real problem occurs when Claudette must change trains in
Chicago, where a drawing room has been reserved for her. Rather than lose
sight of Wayne, she boards his train; when the conductor comes around to
collect tickets, she feigns helplessness à la *The Palm Beach Story*, but not as
effectively. Like the Ale and Quail Club members, the marines help her out
of her predicament. Having invoked Sturges, Solt moves Claudette into the
club car—this time without the carnage, but with enough mayhem to get
her put off the train. The marines live up to their *semper fidelis* tradition and
also disembark; then it is time for a bit of *It Happened One Night*, with the
trio hitchhiking and ending up with a car. If anyone remembers the hay farm
sequence in *Night*, when Gable and Claudette came dangerously close to
making love, they would know where Solt got the idea of stranding Wayne
and Claudette in a similar location. As in Capra's film, nothing happens.

When Wayne discovers that Claudette is the author *Here Is Tomorrow*,
he assumes that she feigned interest in him because she wanted him for
the lead. After telling her what he thinks, he leaves, but can't put her out of

his mind. Time to resurrect the *It Happened One Night* denouement. It is as pointless to wonder whether or not Claudette will marry Wayne as it was to ask whether Ellie would go through with the wedding ceremony in *It Happened One Night*. We know that Claudette will be reunited with Wayne. But how? Solt did not come up with anything as ingenious as Riskin's ending in *It Happened One Night*. Instead, Wayne stops sulking and heads over to Claudette's house. In the final shot, Claudette looks out of her bedroom window and sees Wayne's car pulling up. She rushes down the stairs; the camera remains in the bedroom, with the bed dominating the frame. The walls of Jericho may not have fallen, but the best place for a reconciliation was very much in view.

Wayne was at first intimidated by the thought of working with Claudette, but he soon learned to appreciate her professionalism and especially her wit. But the director, Mervyn LeRoy, did not. Claudette was constantly offering LeRoy suggestions, but, as Wayne observed, "Mervyn wasn't letting any woman tell him what to do." LeRoy wrote that Claudette was "an interesting lady to work with" but "had a strange habit of never looking where she was going [and] kept bumping into things." LeRoy also had to comply with her left-side-only manifesto. However, he believed—and he was not alone—that "she looked very good on both sides."

It must have been the money that brought her back to Universal, then Universal-International (UI) for *The Egg and I*, the movie version of Betty McDonald's 1945 best-seller about the way the author's life changed when her husband decided to become a chicken farmer. As "outside talent," Claudette was paid a flat $200,000; her costar, Fred MacMurray, received $175,000. Although *The Egg and I* delighted audiences and turned a profit, it was not a happy experience for Claudette. She was ill periodically throughout the shoot, causing the set to be closed down for six days. *The Egg and I* was also not the kind of film that required an elaborate wardrobe (most of the time Claudette wore jeans or nondescript clothes, except for a tailored suit and a wedding gown); still, she rejected some of her costumes, causing UI to spend $3,901 for special purchases and $5,650 for studio creations.

The film begins and ends with Claudette speaking to the audience as Betty McDonald, ensconced in a train compartment as a porter is about to serve breakfast. When he accidentally drops a soft-boiled egg on the floor and starts cleaning up the spill, Claudette attempts to make him more egg-conscious. Then, looking straight into the lens, she says: "I'll bet you think an egg is something you order for breakfast when you can't think of any-thing else. So did I. But that was before " 'The Egg and I.' "

The credits, punctuated by sounds from the henhouse, should have prepared us for the McDonalds's journey into Hicksville. But this is the kind of film in which you cannot think of Betty and Bob McDonald (Betty and Robert Heskett in real life), but of Claudette Colbert and Fred MacMurray. Claudette is forced to play the subservient spouse, whose husband, back from World War II, buys a chicken farm without consulting her, assuming that she will feel similarly about his desire to return to the earth.

The Egg and I is also one of those movies in which the urban heroine is tested to the limit to see if she is one of the people. Thus, Claudette falls off a roof into a rain barrel and muddies herself while trying to drag a reluctant pig into the pen. To complicate matters, Harriet Parson (Louise Albritton), the owner of a thriving farm, sets her sights on MacMurray, who is too obtuse to recognize her tactics. Disillusioned and pregnant, Claudette goes home to mother and has her baby; but to please women everywhere who have stood by their men, she returns and finds that he has bought Parson's farm. When another emergency arises, MacMurray rushes off, and Claudette looks into the lens again and delivers the fadeout line: "See what I mean? I could write a book"—as Betty McDonald did, the only difference being that the Hesketts did not remain married. In 1942, Betty married Donald C. McDonald, becoming Betty McDonald, author and five years later a character in a Hollywood movie. But 1947 it hardly mattered, and *The Egg and I* became one of the year's most popular movies.

The Egg and I may have made UI, Claudette, and MacMurray richer, but it is best known for introducing Ma and Pa Kettle (Marjorie Main and Percy Kilbride) as the MacDonalds' neighbors. The Kettles so endeared themselves to the public that Universal-International rewarded them with a nine-film series of their own.

UI's *Family Honeymoon* (1948), the last pairing of Claudette and MacMurray, was the companion piece to *The Egg and I*, without the Kettles but with similar backwoods types that the couple encounter en route to the Grand Canyon on their honeymoon, which, as the title implies, is atypical. Claudette played a widow with three obnoxious children, who marries a botany professor (MacMurray), expecting to leave her brood with her sister during their honeymoon. When the sister breaks a leg, they have no other choice but to bring along the kids, who, true to form, behave abominably. To complicate matters, the professor's ex-flame (Rita Johnson), cloned from another potential home wrecker, Harriet Parson from *The Egg and I*, shows up at the Grand Canyon in an attempt to win back MacMurray. Throughout it all, Claudette retains her composure, even though her husband is unaware of the web that is being spun around him. In fact, it is Claudette who undermines Johnson's attempt to sabotage their marriage: she simply lets Johnson think they are separating, only to reclaim MacMurray at the end.

Claudette and MacMurray were an endearing team. Playing opposite MacMurray was a challenge; he was not especially amorous, and when he was supposed to be, he looked uncomfortable—until Claudette nestled against him, gazing up at him in adoration and working overtime to get him to respond. She had the gift—better, the talent—to make men feel better about themselves, particularly if they were prone to self-doubt and feelings of inadequacy. Claudette was the panacea for socially awkward and sexually backward males. When she had a costar like Gable, who was neither, she could give a relaxed performance, as she did so memorably in *It Happened One Night*. But most of the time she was teamed with actors competent in their own right, but not in her league when it came to sophistication. And when a role did not require sophistication, such as the widow in *Family Honeymoon*, she imbued the character with an intelligence that the script vaguely suggested, as she relied on her wits to keep her husband from falling into another woman's trap. Claudette behaves with such civility that her rival is convinced she is oblivious to her machinations.

If all the films that Claudette made in which she dealt with children—bathing them, tucking them into bed, reading to them, consoling them—were arranged in order of age, from infants to toddlers, pre-adolescents, teenagers, and adults, the image of a perfect mother would emerge. Perhaps Claudette was just a screen mother, but one would like to think that her films revealed the kind of mother Claudette might have been if she had children of her own. Even when she bathed her young son in *Family Honeymoon*, she did it with such naturalness that it seemed not only unrehearsed but also unfeigned. It was the same in *The Egg and I*, when she cupped the chicks in her hands as tenderly as she would hold an infant in her arms. Somehow one feels that changing diapers would have come as easily to Claudette as breezing down a staircase in a Travis Banton gown.

Claudette's postwar dramas were actually better than the comedies, especially the two that she made for Douglas Sirk, *Sleep My Love* (1948) and *Thunder on the Hill* (1951). In 1946, she appeared in two films, each at a different studio: *Tomorrow Is Forever*, produced by International Pictures for release by RKO, and *The Secret Heart* (MGM). The former, beautifully underplayed by Claudette and Orson Welles, was dismissed as a weepie; the latter was MGM's contribution to Hollywood's discovery of neurosis, a subject weighty enough to replace antifascism and flag-waving, which had now run their course.

In *The Secret Heart*, Claudette was the stepmother of June Allyson, whose pianist-father, unbeknownst to his daughter, committed suicide by throwing himself off a cliff. While courting Claudette, Walter Pidgeon tries to befriend the introverted June, who misinterprets his gesture of friendship as a sign of attraction. Who could blame her after Pidgeon sends her a charm bracelet that spells L-O-V-E? Once June realizes Pidgeon's real interest is Claudette, she heads for the cliff, from which she is ready to jump until Pidgeon arrives and talks some sense into her, resulting in a happy ending for a psychologically dubious film that maintained audience interest through the professionalism of the stars, notably, June Allyson, who had to create a character out of a case study.

The Secret Heart's significance has more to do with the script than with Claudette's typically professional but undemanding performance. One of the authors was Anne Morrison, now Anne Morrison Chapin, who two decades earlier was responsible for Claudette's Broadway debut in *The Wild Westcotts*. One would like to think that they met on the set, embraced, and reminisced, but there is no evidence that ever happened. There is, however, evidence of the close relationship that developed between Claudette and June Allyson, then one of MGM's newest stars. In her autobiography, Allyson recalled how Claudette taught her to dress with style and to recite the prayer that she always said before going on stage or before the camera: "Mon Dieu, aide moi." Claudette was the godmother to the daughter that Allyson and her husband, Dick Powell, adopted, and she even bought the child a christening gown in Paris.

Much better than *The Secret Heart* was another 1946 release, *Tomorrow Is Forever*. The critics, however, found them both mediocre. Yet *Tomorrow Is Forever* deserves a reappraisal as the emotionally restrained film that it was even in 1946. The problem then was that, with the end of World War II, the film seemed like a rehash of the isolationism-versus-intervention debate that dominated the late 1930s and formed the crux of another equally underrated film, *The Searching Wind* (1946). There was also the subject matter: a man, presumed dead, returns to find that his wife has remarried. Despite the *Enoch Arden* overtones and a slight resemblance to Claudette's earlier film *The Man from Yesterday*, by 1946 this was the stuff of screwball comedy, notably *My Favorite Wife* (1940), in which the sexes are reversed: a wife, who had been shipwrecked, comes back after seven years to discover that she has been supplanted and that her children do not recognize her.

In *Tomorrow Is Forever*, veteran screenwriter Leonore Coffee turned the missing spouse into a husband who went off to World War I and ended up with his face blown off and in need of plastic surgery. When his wife receives the usual telegram, she assumes he's dead, unaware that he had been brought to a German hospital, where his condition and lack of identification require both a new face and a new name. And so the former John Andrew MacDonald (Orson Welles) becomes Eric Kessler. John's wife, Elizabeth (Claudette), believing he is dead, marries Larry Hamilton (George Brent). With Claudette and Welles in the leads, there is bound to be a reunion of some sort. But how?

Even though Welles's name followed Claudette's in the credits, his character would not end up like Enoch Arden, peering into his wife's window. Since *Citizen Kane*, Welles's standing in Hollywood had diminished, but he was still a name and tended to dominate any film he was in, even one that he was not directing. *Tomorrow Is Forever*, decently directed by Irving Pichel, was one of them. Claudette held her own with Welles, whose theatrical makeup, especially the penciled age lines and exaggerated eyebrows, gave him the look of a haunted visionary. But Welles had the climactic speech, in which he tells Elizabeth, who is now convinced that he is her former husband, that she must stop reliving the past and face the future because "tomorrow is forever," a line that sounds pretentious when quoted, but not in context, where it is the only advice the dying Kessler can offer Elizabeth.

Coffee structured the script as a chain of events, each linked inexorably to the other. Kessler assumes the responsibility of bringing Margaret Ludwig (the eight-year-old Natalie Wood)—the daughter of the surgeon who gave him a new face and was later killed by the Nazis—to America. What better way for John MacDonald/Eric Kessler and the former Elizabeth MacDonald, now Mrs. Larry Hamilton, to meet than by his working as a chemist in Hamilton's company?

The scene in which Kessler is invited to the Hamiltons' home and sees Elizabeth descending the staircase is stunning. Despite the poorly applied makeup, Welles's disquieting gaze expresses something that Claudette cannot—but only because her character is not yet aware of who he is. It is far more painful for Kessler to meet his son, Drew, who was raised to think of Hamilton as his birth father.

Coffee may have considered whether at some point, ideally, at the end, Drew should learn that Kessler is his father. But Kessler is a tragic figure, obviously not long for this world. Instead, Kessler becomes Drew's confidante; when Drew, sensing that World War II is imminent, announces his intention to travel to Canada and join the Royal Air Force (RAF), Kessler is sympathetic. Elizabeth, fearing that Drew will suffer the same fate as her first husband, advocates isolationism, while Kessler remains non-committal, but clearly favors intervention. Elizabeth only accepts Drew's decision after Kessler braves torrential rain, thus shortening his life, to bring back Drew, who was planning to leave for Canada without telling her.

Virtually certain that Kessler is John MacDonald, Elizabeth confronts him with some of her memorabilia, demanding that he divulge his real identity. The scene needed a special kind of tension to keep the audience wondering if or when a revelation would occur. Welles and Claudette were up to the challenge. Kessler kept equivocating, even after Elizabeth knelt beside him, hoping he would admit the truth. Claudette played the scene as if Elizabeth were a woman who would rather live with her memories than face an uncertain present. At that moment, it was possible to forget Welles's stage makeup and Claudette's totally inappropriate but stunning gown and concentrate on two people, one of whom was thinking of the future and a better world; the other, of a past that haunts the present. Kessler refuses to tell Elizabeth that he is John MacDonald. If he did, everyone's life would have been irrevocably changed, and not for the better. What matters is not the past, where the truth resides, but the present, where hope does. Thus, Elizabeth relents and allows Drew to join the RAF, and she and Larry adopt the orphaned Margaret.

Claudette's scenes with Natalie Wood were especially warm, particularly the one in which Elizabeth teaches Margaret how to pitch horseshoes. To Natalie, Claudette was not just a mother figure, but a woman who should have been a mother: "I always felt it sad somehow that in real life, Claudette never became a mother, for she had so much to give that way." Claudette certainly did, but she channeled her love of children into art and enjoyed painting their pictures.

"Mary Pickford Presents *Sleep, My Love*" first appears on the screen accompanied by the image of a train speeding through the darkness. On board is Claudette as Allison Courtland, asleep in a compartment. When she awakens, she has no idea how she ended up on a Boston-bound train, much less why she has a revolver in her purse. It was a gripping start to a film that occasionally loses momentum but ultimately delivers a literally shattering climax. Pickford, who was once known as "America's Sweetheart," had not made a film since 1933 and had not produced one since 1936. What drew her to *Sleep, My Love* is unknown; perhaps Leo Rosten's story, which Rosten and St. Clair McKelway converted into a screenplay, reminded her of *Gaslight* (1944), the touchstone of the terrorized-wife film.

Claudette was paired for the third time with Don Ameche, as the demonic husband who drugs her bedtime cocoa to induce a trance that, he hopes, will result in her falling off the balcony of their Sutton Place home. He hires the owl-eyed George Coulouris, who ekes out his living as a photographer, to frighten her out of her wits and then disappear, not counting on his wife's chance meeting with Robert Cummings, with whom she experiences instant rapport. It is a delight to watch Claudette respond to Cummings's easy charm, as they both become playfully amorous— she as the married woman who is not averse to flirting and he as the respectful bachelor whose growing concern for her welfare suggests he is more than just a good Samaritan. By contrast, Ameche's anguished look and painfully low voice when he describes his wife's rapidly developing dementia is so blatantly insincere that, under ordinary circumstances, he would have been the prime suspect. Admittedly, the part did not allow Ameche to flesh out the character. Ray Milland faced a similar problem in *Dial M for Murder* (1954), but he at least made the husband fascinating by being alternately suave and insidious. Ameche simply lowered his voice and went on autopilot, as if he realized that, given third billing, his role was only a catalyst in the Claudette-Cummings reaction.

Claudette blooms in her scenes with Cummings, particularly when he invites her to a Chinese wedding, at which Claudette becomes tipsy and toasts everyone at the reception. Claudette did the scene brilliantly, retaining her famous wit, slightly slurring her syllables (but never sacrificing clarity in the process), and behaving as if she had been denied a first date and was making up for lost time. Cummings, five years younger than Claudette, responded to her rejuvenation by sloughing off some years himself. Together, they seemed like a couple in their mid thirties, instead of being forty-five and forty, respectively.

Cummings saves Claudette, to whom Ameche has administered a hypnotic drug, hoping that she will murder Coulouris so that he can have her committed and be free to marry his mistress. Claudette, however, shoots Coulouris, but not fatally; Coulouris kills Ameche and, attempting to escape, dies the same kind of death that had been intended for Claudette: falling from the balcony.

Douglas Sirk had little to say about the film: "The only thing I was interested in was the Claudette Colbert part . . . because of the way the plot was constructed. There was nothing else I could do." Actually, Sirk created a stylish film noir, where the winding staircase was not just part of the setting but an important component of the plot, and where the Sutton Place townhouse seemed too tastefully furnished to be the scene of a murder. But creating a discrepancy between the surface and the symbol has always been part of Sirk's visual style: strip away the veneer of a showcase home or a model community and you will find various levels of prejudice, racism, discrimination, and ageism. If there are so many substrata of evil, why not a husband's systematic attempt to drive his wife insane? If the husband succeeds, he gets the townhouse, which will still be impressive after he and his mistress occupy it.

The Secret Fury, her last Jack Skirball–Bruce Manning production, was a film that Claudette genuinely wanted to make because she was a coproducer, although uncredited. She was probably attracted to the script because it allowed her to go one step beyond the imperiled wife of *Sleep, My Love*, this time as a concert pianist who, on the day of her wedding, receives the same news that Jane Eyre did when an uninvited guest stormed down the aisle, insisting that the wedding not take place because one of the parties was still married. In *Jane Eyre*, it is Rochester; in *The Secret Fury*, it is Ellen (Claudette), who then finds herself caught in an ever-widening spiral of fabrication to the point that she doubts her own sanity. The evidence seems conclusive: a marriage license, a justice of the peace who performed the ceremony, witnesses, a maid who recognizes her, and a "husband" whom Ellen seems to have murdered.

The script had its share of possible suspects: Ellen's architect fiancé (Robert Ryan); her aunt (theatre stalwart, Jane Cowl, who was seriously ill when the film was being shot and died shortly after its release); and the district attorney (Paul Kelly), whom she rejected in favor of Ryan. The villain is not even a suspect, since he appears above reproach. The entire scheme has been concocted by Ellen's lawyer (Philip Ober), whom Ellen's father had committed to a mental institution for four years. Unable to avenge himself on the father, who has died, the lawyer makes Ellen the victim of his maniacal scenario, which is so convincing that it leads to Ellen's being institutionalized. After Ellen escapes from the asylum, she assumes the lawyer is her friend. Instead, she hears him disclose the details of his diabolical plot designed to culminate with Ellen's murdering him (apparently, he is tired of life), thus proving that she is criminally insane. The lawyer pursues Ellen up to the attic, where she is saved when a towering full-length mirror comes crashing down on him.

As implausible as *The Secret Fury* is, it is never boring. Whenever the action flagged, director Mel Ferrer added some noirish touches: sidewalks that looked as if they had been tarred, flashing neon signs, sleazy furnished rooms, and low-key lighting that streaked hair with silver, blanched faces, and left a trail of shadows. Claudette's wardrobe suited her character; except for her wedding gown, which was not all that elaborate, she was totally devoid of glamour. The matronly "new look," with its long skirts, did little for most stars, Claudette included. In the early part of the film, she was unflatteringly made up and coiffured. The close-ups accentuated her penciled eyebrows, and her hair looked has if it had been lacquered. The metallic hairdo continued until the plot got underway, after which her hairstyle was more in keeping with her signature bangs.

After *The Secret Fury*, Claudette had one more opportunity to work with Douglas Sirk, who would leave Hollywood at the end of the decade. The film was *Thunder on the Hill* (1951), based on a Charlotte Hastings play, *Bonaventure*, as it was known in London, where it premiered in 1949; it was called *High Ground* when it reached Broadway two years later, eliciting the kind of reviews that were not exactly pans but not strong enough to extend the run beyond twenty-three performances.

As Sister Mary Bonaventure, Claudette was thoroughly believable as the head of the Convent of Our Lady of Rheims, a nursing order in a Norwich village that has become a refuge for stranded travelers and residents driven from their homes by widespread flooding. Valerie (Sarat in the play) Carns (Ann Blyth) is being transported to Norwich prison to be hanged for her brother's murder when the storm forces the guards to bring her to the convent. Despite Valerie's smoldering hostility that has made her unapproachable, Sister Mary is convinced she is innocent and sets out to prove it. The plotting is ingenious; all the suspects are present in the convent, giving the film not just a unity of place but a quasi unity of time, since the action covers a twenty-four-hour period. As the climax approaches, Sirk brings the villain into the frame at the moment the conversation turns to a crucial piece of information that would prove Valerie's innocence.

When Sister Mary presents evidence that links Dr. Jeffreys, a staff physician, with the murder of Valerie's brother, he tries to throw her from the convent tower. Once Claudette realized that Sirk wanted a realistic climax, she prepared herself. Having no intention of sustaining another back injury, she wore a brace, which did not protect her from hitting her head during one of the takes.

The ending is similar to another and more famous one in Hitchcock's *Vertigo* (1958). There is no proof that Hitchcock had seen *Thunder,* or Val Lewton's production of *Cat People* (1942). Yet Hitchcock seems to be quoting *Cat People* in *The Birds* (1962), when Tippi Hedren's arrival in a pet store sets off a cacophony from the birds, just as Simone Simon's did in *Cat People*. Furthermore, the endings of *Thunder* and *Vertigo* have similar settings: the bell tower of a Catholic convent in *Thunder* and the bell tower of a mission church in *Vertigo*. An echo? An inspiration? A coincidence?

High Ground is a single-set play taking place entirely in the convent's Great Hall. The bell tower was the inspiration of the adapters, Oscar Saul and Andrew Solt, who obviously knew Hastings's drama, in which the bells toll frequently and the unseen tower is described as affording a "very desolate . . . yet beautiful view." After Sister Mary has unmasked Dr. Jeffreys (who until the third act was an unlikely suspect), he rushes up the stairs to the tower, from which he presumably leaps.

High Ground has a magnificently theatrical ending. The curtain slowly falls as Sister Mary embraces Sarat and begins reciting the *Magnificat* in Latin: "Magnificat anima mea Dominum, et exaltavit spiritus meus in Deo salutari meo" (My soul magnifies the Lord and my spirit rejoices in God my savior). The *Magnificat* provided a peaceful coda, with good triumphing over evil; and Sister Mary, whose search for a sign from heaven that would validate her vocation, receives an answer in the exoneration of Sarat, with whose fate she had linked her own. Since Saul and Solt downplayed the religious aspects of the play, they, and probably Sirk, must have thought that the *Magnificat* would be a pious intrusion into what was essentially a whodunit. Sirk captured the audience's attention from the outset with the relentless sound of the rain, the rising of the waters, the tensions within the community, and a camera that remains impartial until it is time to identify the killer; under these circumstances, a prayer, however eloquent, would have been out of place.

Claudette hardly knew anything about nuns, except for the ones who taught her catechism at the Church of St. Vincent Ferrer when she was in grade school. Still, she adopted the right posture, often folding her arms together at the waist as she walked. On 27 October 1959, she played one again, not in the movies, but on CBS television, in which she had Ingrid Bergman's role, Sister Benedict, in *The Bells of St. Mary's*. Unfortunately, the television version is unavailable, although one suspects Claudette brought a sly sense of humor to the scene in which she teaches a shy boy "the manly art of self defense" so he will not be cowed by the schoolyard bullies.

Claudette only received seventy-five thousand dollars for *Thunder*, a far cry from her last Universal picture, *Family Honeymoon*, for which she was paid a flat two hundred thousand dollars. But the 1950s were lean times in Hollywood. The 1948 Paramount decision forced the studios with theater chains to move out of exhibition, making them production and distribution companies. More to the point, Claudette was not the box-office attraction she had been a decade earlier, when she made fifteen films; in the 1950s, she made eight. In 1961, she made one—her last.

CHAPTER 12

The Last Picture Shows

By the early 1950s, Claudette had reached that stage in her career when she was expected to weave that old black magic and turn dross into silk; or as Ezra Pound put it, acorns into lilies. The magic was intact, but the scripts that came her way only allowed her to play a version of what she once had been. There was still the signature hairdo, the vitality, and the age-defying appearance. Even if you knew her birth date, you would ignore chronology and marvel at a face that never seemed to have undergone cosmetic surgery, although she did admit to "a tiny face lift" to make it less obvious that she had a short neck. Whatever the surgeon accomplished was not enough for Claudette, who continued to fret about her neck, which, like the right side of her face, was more apparent to herself than to the public.

It was one thing if financial security were Claudette's main reason for continuing in a business that bore little resemblance to the one in which she had started; but it wasn't. There was television, on which she began appearing in the early 1950s, and the stage, to which she returned around the same time. But she was still a movie star and had every intention of remaining one until she was no longer in demand, or until she felt that what she was being offered was unworthy of her. She was scheduled to appear in RKO's *One Minute to Zero* (1952), but a bout of pneumonia resulted in her being replaced by Ann Blyth, which meant that the part had to be rewritten for an actress twenty-five years younger than Claudette.

Actresses from Hollywood's golden age, which has been variously dated (the mid 1920s to the early 1960s being the least arguable), arrived at a point (somewhere in their early or mid forties) where one role would always be available to them: the imperiled heroine. Age did not matter. Ethel Barrymore played one in *Kind Lady* (1951) when she was in her early seventies. It was also an attention-getting kind of role. At forty, Barbara Stanwyck received an Oscar nomination for her performance in *Sorry, Wrong Number* (1948) as a bedridden psychosomatic who overhears a conversation about a planned murder and gradually figures out that she is the victim. That same year, Claudette appeared in *Sleep, My Love*, playing a wife systematically driven mad by a husband who hopes to inherit her fortune so he can marry his mistress. Later, Loretta Young encountered her share of peril in *Cause for Alarm* (1951); Joan Crawford was terrorized by a vindictive playwright in *Sudden Fear* (1952); Ida Lupino, who could intimidate as well as be intimidated, traveled the panic route in *Woman in Hiding* (1949) and *Beware, My Lovely* (1952). Stanwyck reprised her terrorized heroine in *Jeopardy* (1953) and *Witness to Murder* (1954). Bette Davis had too formidable a persona for such roles; instead, she terrorized her rival, Joan Crawford, in *Whatever Happened to Baby Jane?* (1962).

Fortunately, Claudette never had to play a grotesque, as Davis did in *Baby Jane*, yet she made two victimized women films, *Sleep, My Love* and *The Secret Fury*. Both provided her with excellent parts and generated their share of suspense; however, like most movies of this sort, they are best enjoyed for the moment, since they cannot withstand analysis—*The Secret Fury*, especially.

It was inevitable that Claudette, now pushing fifty (but still looking in her early thirties), would bid adieu to romantic comedy. Irene Dunne and Loretta Young had already done so in *It Grows on Trees* (1952) and *It Happens*

Every Thursday (1953), respectively. With Carole Lombard's death in 1942 and Jean Arthur's retirement from the screen until she came back one last time in a beautifully acted but totally uncharacteristic role in *Shane* (1953), Claudette was the surviving queen of romantic comedy, provided it was a comedy in which she could play a character close to her age—not just a mother but a recent, and gorgeous, grandmother.

Since there were still moviegoers who remembered when Claudette started in pictures, there was no point in her appearing as either a career woman or a compliant wife. In *Let's Make It Legal* (Fox, 1951), a comedy of remarriage, she was cast as a divorced grandmother whose daughter, son-in-law, and infant granddaughter are living with her. So that "grandmother" would not evoke the image of a woman in a gingham dress and rimless glasses knitting in a rocking chair, Claudette made her first appearance in shorts that proved her legs had not lost their fine curves since she flashed one of them fifteen years earlier in *It Happened One Night*.

The problem with *Let's Make It Legal* was the same that Rosalind Russell faced in another 1951 release, *Never Wave at a Wac*, also a comedy of remarriage, in which Russell ended up being reunited with Paul Douglas, whom she had previously divorced. Douglas was no more suited to Russell than MacDonald Carey, looking jowly and out of condition, was to Claudette. Trouper that she was, Claudette went along with the script, another generic "two men vying for the same woman" retread—the other man being the suave Zachary Scott, a millionaire with political aspirations, who was in love with her when he, Carey, and Claudette were in high school together. This should have made them around the same age, except that Carey looked, moved, and acted like a man in his late fifties. Scott used the same caddish charm on Claudette that he lavished on Joan Crawford in *Mildred Pierce* (1945); when Scott reenters Claudette's life, it is only to acquire a trophy wife.

The invariable complications include (a) Scott's disclosure that he and Carey shot craps for Claudette when they were in high school, with Carey the winner; and (b) embarrassing headlines when a drunken Carey is hauled off to jail, along with Claudette's son-in-law (Robert Wagner), causing her to rush down to the police station with her granddaughter in tow, only to be photographed standing next to her ex-husband holding a baby. Since Scott cannot afford such negative publicity, he dumps Claudette, who returns to Carey once he shows her the dice, explaining how he cheated to win her for himself.

The younger members of the cast—Barbara Bates and Robert Wagner as daughter and son-in-law, and Marilyn Monroe as a wannabe model (or whatever)—were initially nervous about appearing in a film with a screen legend. But Claudette radiated her usual bonhomie, even though she must have known that *Let's Make It Legal* was only a footnote in their careers. Tragically, Bates, who made the cover of *Life* in 1945 and seemed poised for a promising future, committed suicide at the age of forty-three in 1969.

Let's Make It Legal was Claudette's adieu to romantic comedy, at least on the screen. It was also an odd choice for Twentieth Century-Fox, especially since production chief Darryl F. Zanuck was ambivalent about it from the very beginning. Even though *Let's Make It Legal* was not a "Darryl F. Zanuck production" (Robert Bassler is credited as producer), Zanuck took a keen interest in it, as he did in other films that did not bear his imprint. What Zanuck originally envisioned was a movie with the working title "Don't Call Me Mother," about a close mother-daughter relationship on the order of *Claudia* (1943). Writer F. Hugh Herbert felt differently and submitted a script that Zanuck hated. The story conference memos in the Fox Collection at the University of Southern California show that the plot kept deviating from Zanuck's original concept and evolved into one about a young couple trying to marry off the wife's mother. Zanuck was finally satisfied when the plot took a turn of which he approved: daughter and husband living with mother, whom daughter wants to reunite with mother's ex-husband. Zanuck preferred the title "Grandma Was a Gold Digger," perhaps hoping it would revive memories of Claudette's gold digger movies, *Midnight* and *The Palm Beach Story*. In the early 1950s, Fox was going through its sentence-title phase (*Mother Was a Freshman, Mr. Belvedere Goes to College, Mother Didn't Tell Me, People Will Talk, Follow the Sun*, etc.). Once Zanuck brought in

Billy Wilder's new collaborator, I.A.L. "Izzie" Diamond, who ended up sharing screenplay credit with Herbert, "Grandma Was a Gold Digger" became *Let's Make It Legal*, which at least sounded more sophisticated, although the film was not.

Hollywood in the 1950s could accommodate actresses able to play women to whom age was irrelevant, offering them character roles raised to star status. Thus, actresses able to divest themselves of personas forged a decade or two earlier, or attempt roles that pointed to new directions along old paths, had a chance to continue working, even if the films themselves were not up to those they made in their heyday. There were exceptions, of course. Olivia de Havilland emerged triumphant at the end of the 1940s with *To Each His Own* (1946), which saw her age over twenty years; *The Snake Pit* (1948), in which she was a mental patient in the asylum from hell; and *The Heiress* (1949), in which she affected the plainness of a singularly unattractive woman who turns wondrously feminine from the attentions of a fortune hunter. That she won Oscars for both *To Each His Own* and *The Heiress* was not necessarily the acid test of her art. But the point is that de Havilland received scripts that Claudette did not. While de Havilland was working with Oscar material in *To Each His Own*, Claudette was filming *Tomorrow Is Forever*, an excellent film in its own right but not an award winner, and *The Secret Heart*, which was neither. When de Havilland was starring in *The Snake Pit*; Ingrid Bergman, in *Joan of Arc* (1948); and Jane Wyman, cast against type, in *Johnny Belinda* (1948), for which she deservedly won an Oscar; Claudette was being victimized in *Sleep, My Love*. And in *Three Came Home*, in which she gave a frighteningly realistic performance as a woman interned in a Japanese concentration camp, she did not even get a nomination.

Becoming a freelancer should have brought her better roles, at least Oscar-nominated ones. But the films she could easily have done went to others: Loretta Young (*The Farmer's Daughter, The Accused*), Barbara Stanwyck (*Sorry, Wrong Number*), Irene Dunne (*I Remember Mama*). The reason had nothing to with age, particularly for someone who looked as youthful as she.

It may well have been a combination of her agent-brother's inability to find her better parts and her off-the-set-at-five-o'clock-sharp and left-side-of-face manifestos. At any rate, Claudette had become a second-tier film actress.

The five o'clock law lost her the chance to star opposite Spencer Tracy in Frank Capra's *State of the Union* (1948) for the soon-to-be-extinct Liberty Films. Wendling told the press that "the five o clock clause is standard in [Claudette's] contract." However, it would not be standard in her *State of the Union* contract, which was not drawn up until production began on 28 September 1947. When Wendling presented Capra and Liberty's vice president, Samuel Briskin, with a contract that included the five o'clock clause, they refused to accept it. Wendling argued vainly that Claudette had to arise at 5:00 a.m. and needed her rest, which, if she were sixty-four instead of forty-four, might be understandable. Claudette would not relax her rule, and the role went to Katharine Hepburn. Hollywood correspondent Thomas F. Brady was not in the least sympathetic: "Miss Hepburn stepped into the breach on two days' notice with a notable lack of temperament and a 6 o'clock quitting time. According to Wendling, Miss Colbert would have made approximately $200,000 by appearing in the picture."

What Wendling could not tell the reporters was that Claudette was so desperate to have a successful marriage that she made it a rule to be home in time for Pressman and herself to have a 7:00 p.m. dinner when she was making a film. Although there are few traditional marriages between actresses and surgeons, Claudette at least wanted to go through the motions, knowing full well the price she would pay in the press. And how could she explain what was by now the traditional Friday night dinner with her mother and brother without sounding like a subservient daughter, which was completely at odds with her movie star image? *State of the Union* was not a milestone in anyone's career—Hepburn's or Capra's. Claudette resigned herself to appearing in films that at least offered her decent parts, even though the films themselves were not of the quality to which she had been accustomed. Fortunately, she had not put the theatre behind her. Stage trained from the beginning, Claudette had not lost the ability to learn her lines in toto, instead of mastering them a few pages at a time, which was standard in Hollywood. Thus, it was inevitable that Claudette would return to the theatre, where her name could still attract audiences. Even television would be more rewarding than making movies that brought out her diehard fans but left the critics struggling to find adjectives to describe professionalism in a vacuum.

In the meantime, Claudette took a brief hiatus from Hollywood and flew to Britain for a movie in which she had to shed her glamorous image and become the wife of a rubber plantation owner. The movie was *Outpost in Malaya* (1952), released as *The Planter's Wife* in Britain, filmed on location in what was then Ceylon and now Sri Lanka. The British title is more accurate since a planter's wife is exactly what Liz Fraser (Claudette) is. Although born in British Malaya (now the Malayan Peninsula) and interned in a Japanese concentration camp during World War II, Liz is determined to return to England with her son, despite her husband's (Jack Hawkins) reluctance to leave their plantation. The domestic drama becomes the background for an unusually violent (at least for a Claudette Colbert movie) confrontation between the planters and the "bandits" terrorizing them. The high points of the film are a real battle between a cobra that has slithered into the Fraser home and a mongoose that succeeds in killing it on camera, and the sight of Claudette behind a machine gun, firing away at the bandits.

Outpost in Malaya carefully avoids labeling the terrorists as anything other than bandits, on the assumption that when it was released in November 1952, Americans would have been too preoccupied with the Korean War to concern themselves with what was going on in Malaya. The terrorists, Communist insurgents belonging to the Malayan Races Liberation Army (MRLA), were really waging guerrilla warfare against the British. In the film, the Frasers successfully defend themselves against the attack and decide to remain in Malaya, after sending their son back to England.

It is odd that "communist," one of the most commonly heard words in the early 1950s, was not used to identify the terrorists, "bandits" being more of a euphemism than a synonym. The reason may have been that while Americans still believed that the communist threat was real, they did not support movies about it, such as *I Married a Communist* (1949), a title that was so off-putting that RKO changed it to *The Woman on Pier 13*, and Leo McCarey's *My Son John* (1952), despite the presence of Helen Hayes, Dean Jagger, and Robert Walker.

The writers were taking no chances with *Outpost in Malaya*. British audiences might make the connection between the bandits and the MRLA, but Americans considered *Outpost* another action flick, well directed by Ken Annakin. Although any actress could have played Liz Fraser, Claudette looked very much at home driving along a jungle road, firing a machine gun, and picking off a guerrilla before he got her.

Claudette was in England at a time when other American actors—for example, Dana Andrews, John Agar, Shelley Winters, Robert Hutton, Paul Douglas, Marguerite Chapman, Alan Ladd—also went abroad when nothing was forthcoming in Hollywood. Taxwise, working in Europe proved beneficial, especially to someone like Claudette, who equated making movies with making money. As she told the *Chicago Sunday Tribune* in 1947, "I couldn't be happy without working, and the aim of working is to make money." Four years earlier, when President Roosevelt asked for a $25,000 salary limit for 1943, Claudette tried to explain why she was then making $150,000. She claimed that she and her husband were planning to move into an apartment until they discovered that maintaining an empty house would cost as much: "The trouble with people like me is that we live like millionaires and we're not millionaires." The lady protested too much. Claudette enjoyed the good life, and deservedly so. But in the1950s, she was not making what she did earlier. Working in Europe, at least in a film or two, would mean less of a financial burden when it came time to file an income tax return.

When Claudette had the opportunity to make two pictures in France, she was thrilled. She even took an apartment in Paris, which she believed had the best shoe repair shops of any city in the world. Since Pressman was on the fast track and would eventually become professor and chief of head and neck surgery at the University of California at Los Angeles medical school, he regarded her absence as more of a location shoot than a change of residence. Actually, she was away for less than a year. Her desire to work in France, where she could use her native language, was understandable. But the films that came her way were nothing more than footnotes in a career that had been mostly text.

Both *Destineés* and *Si Versailles m'etait conté* (known as *Daughters of Destiny* and *Royal Affairs of Versailles*, respectively, in the United States) were made in 1954; the former was released in America in July 1954; the latter, not until 1957. *Daughters of Destiny*, a Franco-Italian production in which the Italian actors were badly dubbed in French, opens with a man in silhouette explaining that the tripartite film that follows is about three women whose destinies were forged by war: Elizabeth (Claudette Colbert) by World War II, Jeanne (Joan of Arc, portrayed by Michelle Morgan) by the Hundred Years War, and Aristophanes' heroine, Lysistrata (played by fellow Saint-Mandéenne, Martine Carol), by the Peloponnesian War.

Claudette's segment, *Elizabeth*, opens with the title character stepping off a jet that has just landed in Rome. She takes a cab to the United States military cemetery to visit the grave of her husband, Anthony Whitefield, who had been killed in the Second World War, with the intention of returning his body to America. Destiny intervenes when she meets a young farm woman, Angela (Eleanora Rossi-Drago), who sheltered Anthony from the Germans. Thrown together in such close proximity, the two became lovers, and Angela bore Whitefield a son, whom she named after him and is now raising as her own. Elizabeth, sadder and perhaps somewhat wiser, returns to America, presumably abandoning her plan to transport her husband's remains to the States.

Elizabeth is a visual hybrid of Italian neorealism and Hollywood gloss, the latter provided by Claudette, who throughout the brief film wears a Pierre Balmain suit, high heels, and a mink coat, in sharp (and ironic) contrast to the drab clothes of the peasants, who barely manage to eke out a living. But that may well have been director Marcello Pagliero's intention: the juxtaposition of affluence and poverty or, cinematically, of the artificial and the real. Rossi-Drago looks like an earth mother, vaunting her sensuality, which makes Elizabeth seem more of a mannequin than a woman. But the tension between them and Angela's unapologetic and almost defiant attitude toward her guest result in a character study, with Claudette and Rossi-Drago as the bright and dark sides of the anima, caught in an unresolvable conflict.

Claudette had even less to do in *Royal Affairs of Versailles*, which Sacha Guitry both wrote and directed as a historical extravaganza celebrating the history of Versailles, which originated as a simple chateau for Louis XIII, was turned into a palace by Louis XIV, and became a symbol of aristocratic excess to the masses, whose march on Versailles is one of the few exciting moments in the film, particularly when Edith Piaf climbs up the gate, fervently belting out a revolutionary anthem. The history lesson ends with the conversion of Versailles into a museum under Louis Philippe, the "citizen king," in the nineteenth century.

The English version is narrated by Orson Welles, who later appears as Benjamin Franklin trying to win French support for the colonies' struggle for independence. Welles was not the only star. Guitry raided the French firmament and recruited Jean-Pierre Aumont, Jean-Louis Barrault, Jean Marais, Micheline Presle, Gérard Philipe, Martine Carol, and the future sex symbol Brigitte Bardot, among others. Characters would appear and then be identified, often clumsily with a tag line, so that one gets to meet, however fleetingly, Molière, Fragonard, Lavoisier, Marivaux, La Fontaine, and so many others that one would need a cast list to reel them off.

The film ends with a *coup de cinéma* that alone justifies sitting through 152 minutes of sumptuous tedium. Descending a seemingly endless staircase to the accompaniment of the "Marseillaise" are all the historical and fictitious figures from the film, and perhaps even others. Since there are no close-ups, it is impossible to tell if Claudette was part of the grand finale. Claudette need not even have been part of the film. She only had a few scenes as Madame de Montespan, Louis XIV's mistress. Although she looked exquisite in period costumes, she was wasted in a film that was an overview of almost two hundred years of French history that meant little to Americans, to whom Versailles was a tourist attraction.

Claudette returned to Hollywood at a time when some of her golden age colleagues did not consider it beneath them to appear in westerns, even at Republic Studios, the home of Roy Rogers and Gene Autry, and, briefly, Joan Crawford in *Johnny Guitar* (1954), a fascinating cold war western with a persecuted heroine (Crawford) and her arch persecutor (Mercedes McCambridge), who took as cavalier a view of civil rights as did the House Committee on Un-American Activities (HUAC). By appearing in *Cattle Queen of Montana* (1954) and *Forty Guns* (1957), Barbara Stanwyck was gaining experience that would stand her in good stead for her television series, *Big Valley*, which ran for four seasons (1965–69). Even grand dame Greer Garson made a western, although an undistinguished one, *Strange Lady in Town* (1955). Marlene Dietrich had already spent time in the Old West in *Destry Rides Again* (1939), so *Rancho Notorious* (1952), now regarded as one of Dietrich's best, was not much of a stretch. Bette Davis wisely stayed off the range, for which she was ill suited.

Thus, moviegoers should not have been surprised to see Claudette in *Texas Lady* (1955) or discover that she was at home on horseback, able to mount and dismount with ease. She enjoyed riding the range at the cattle ranch she and Pressman owned in northeastern California's Lassen County. The script looked promising; it was the work of Horace McCoy, the pulp writer best known for *They Shoot Horses, Don't They?* But the difference between *Texas Lady* and *Johnny Guitar, Forty Guns, Rancho Notorious*, and even *Cattle Queen of Montana* is that *Texas Lady* was directed by Tim Whelan, a competent director but not in the same league with Nicholas Ray (*Johnny Guitar*), Samuel Fuller (*Forty Guns*), Fritz Lang (*Rancho Notorious*), and Allan Dwan (*Cattle Queen of Montana*).

In terms of plot, a woman traveling from New Orleans to a small Texas town to claim ownership of a newspaper deeded to her by her late father, McCoy's script would have made more sense with a younger actress in the lead. Traditionally, in movies about women inheriting property—for example, the "old dark house" mystery, *The Ghost Breakers* (1940); the psychological melodrama, *The Children's Hour* (1961); or one of Hollywood's earliest depictions of racism, *Pinky* (1949) —the roles were played by younger actresses: Paulette Goddard, Audrey Hepburn (and Merle Oberon in the earlier version, *Three Three* [1936]), and Jeanne Crain, respectively.

Then, too, there was the photography. *Texas Lady* was shot in color, which was not Claudette's ideal medium. She was best photographed in black and white; color tended to rob her features of suppleness. The makeup and heavily penciled eyebrows may not have made her look her age, then fifty-one; but she certainly looked middle-aged, and not the right match for her leading man, the trim forty-two-year-old Barry Sullivan.

The best scene in the film is the opening, in which Claudette and Sullivan are engaged in playing serious poker. Sullivan, a riverboat gambler, doesn't stand a chance against Claudette, decked out in a fancy black gown and acting as if she had grown up at the gaming table. Soon we learn why she is so eager to win: Sullivan was indirectly responsible for the suicide of her father, whom he had beaten at cards. Her father resorted to embezzlement and, in disgrace, killed himself. Claudette prepared herself for her inevitable match with Sullivan, so she could repay her father's debts. Since all her father left her was the deed to the newspaper, she is determined to give up the life of a card sharp and become a publisher. But once she has taken over the paper, which had become the mouthpiece of the cattle barons, she not only spearheads a "power to the people" movement but gets Barry Sullivan as well.

Texas Lady is the conservative's answer to *High Noon* (1952), in which the community refuses to come to the aid of its marshal (Gary Cooper) when he must face a showdown with the man determined to kill him. Saved by his Quaker wife (Grace Kelly), who puts her faith on hold and shoots the villain, the marshal throws his tin star on the ground, and he and his wife shake the dust of cowardice from their heels and move on to any place where integrity is respected. In *Texas Lady* the people throw off the yoke of tyranny and embrace democracy so enthusiastically that even the cattle barons must admit defeat and acknowledge the birth of a new era. *High Noon* offered a far more incisive and accurate portrait of human nature.

After *Texas Lady*, Claudette was absent from the screen for six years. But she was far from idle. She alternated between television and the stage, both of which will be discussed in the next chapters. The only possible reason for her comeback was not the film, the movie version of Mildred Savage's novel, *Parrish* (Warner Bros., 1961); it was the salary: one hundred thousand dollars for ten weeks, with four weeks free and then prorated at ten thousand dollars per week, netting her somewhere in the vicinity of two hundred thousand dollars. This was the highest she had been offered since *Family Honeymoon*.

Parrish told moviegoers more than they wanted to know about growing tobacco in the Connecticut River Valley, where the action takes place. Claudette played Ellen McLean—a widow and mother of Hollywood's latest hunk, Troy Donahue in the title role—whom tobacco grower Sala Post (Dean Jagger) hires to prepare his daughter for her entrance into Connecticut society, while Parrish becomes the object of every female's gaze, both the field workers' and the debutante daughter's. Meanwhile, Ellen attracts the attention of Post's rival, Judd Raike (Karl Malden), who alienates her when he implies that he prefers a mistress to a wife. Disillusioned, Ellen walks off Raike's houseboat, but not out of his life, at least not then. Raike reconsiders, proposes marriage, but is so abusive to Parrish, as well as to everyone else, that Ellen leaves him. Parrish, earlier just a lightweight in the tobacco business, undergoes the traditional novice-to-professional transformation and, by the end of the film, has become a tobacco czar himself.

In a world striving to be smoke-free, *Parrish*, which turned out to be Claudette's last Hollywood movie (there would be one more for television), seems not only irrelevant but also subversive, particularly in the scene in which one of the workers lovingly describes the planting of tobacco, as if she were speaking of giving birth. At least Claudette looked better than she did in *Texas Lady*; the color and lighting were more flattering, and the wardrobe, which included a tweed suit, a beaded gown, and a chiffon dress, brought back memories of her halcyon days when she was dressed by Adrian and Travis Banton.

Troy Donahue received star billing, with Claudette's name beneath his—not bad for a woman a few years shy of sixty in a relatively unimportant role. Claudette's best scene occurs when Raike discreetly propositions Ellen. Like Claudette, always the lady, Ellen declines his invitation more honestly than he phrased it, stating that she is not a woman of affairs. Claudette spoke her lines with such conviction that it seemed as if she were dismissing rumors of her own past, which gossip mongers colored more gaudily than it actually was.

At the time, Claudette had no idea that *Parrish* would be a turning point in her life. In 1961, Helen O'Hagan was vice president of public relations at Saks and an accomplished photographer as well. O'Hagan visited the set of *Parrish* when the company was on location in Old Saybrook, Connecticut, to photograph Claudette in her ten-thousand-dollar Saks wardrobe, created by Sophie Gimbel, one of Claudette's close friends. The rapport between O'Hagan and Claudette was immediate, and O'Hagan became her companion for the last two decades of her life after Pressman died in 1968. When Claudette had a stroke in 1992, O'Hagan took early retirement the following year so she could take care of Claudette, even preparing her for death by guiding her back to the Catholicism that she had practiced intermittently.

For Claudette, *Parrish* was not just a movie; it was an act of providence.

CHAPTER 13

The Long Voyage Home

"COLBERT PONDERS RETURN TO STAGE." So claimed the *New York Times* (10 March 1949), strongly implying that Claudette "may be lured back next fall to the Broadway stage which she deserted in 1928 for a career in motion pictures." Claudette had found a play, *Lily Henry*, that intrigued her, although it is difficult to understand why, since it seemed more like experimental theatre than conventional drama. The play's premise, or rather gimmick, was the separation of a woman's body and mind, portrayed as individual characters that do not interact with each other.

On 10 March 1949, two of Claudette's former costars were appearing on Broadway: Charles Boyer in Jean-Paul Sartre's *Red Gloves* and Melvyn Douglas in *Two Blind Mice*. Hollywood, in fact, was well represented on the New York stage that day. In addition to Boyer and Douglas, there were John Garfield in *The Big Knife*, Paul Muni in a revival of *They Knew What They Wanted*, Ralph Bellamy in *Detective Story*, and Madeleine Carroll in *Goodbye, My Fancy*. It seemed the right time for a return. *Lily Henry*, however, was never produced, and Claudette waited a few more years, starting on the "straw-hat circuit" before taking on New York.

In a sense, Claudette never left the stage. While she was in Hollywood, she continued to perform before a live audience, but on radio. She made twenty-five appearances on *Lux Radio Theatre*, which for the first two years (1934–36) emanated from New York and featured hour-long versions of Broadway plays. For example, in the first season, *The Barker*, which turned Claudette into a star, was broadcast on 23 October 1934 with Walter Huston in the lead, but without Claudette, who was toiling away in Hollywood. On 10 March 1935, however, Claudette, now an Oscar winner vacationing in New York, took advantage of the occasion to star in *Lux*'s adaptation of Philip Barry's *Holiday* in the same role that Katharine Hepburn played three years later in George Cukor's film.

In 1936, the program's emphasis shifted from stage to screen; and the broadcast center moved from New York to Los Angeles, with "Lux Presents Hollywood" as the dramatic opening of one of radio's best-loved series that delighted listeners for two decades. On 20 July 1936, Walter Huston, Claudette, and Norman Foster recreated their original roles in *The Barker*, which did double duty, ringing out the old and welcoming the new. That evening, *Lux* was celebrating the play, not the 1928 film version that was basically a silent movie with sound sequences, with Milton Sills, Dorothy Mackail in an unappreciated performance, and the dashing Douglas Fairbanks Jr. in the parts originated by Huston, Claudette, and Foster, respectively. At least audiences had a chance to *hear* how the trio sounded on stage.

From 1936 to 1954, Claudette either recreated her movie roles or appeared in those originated by others. In 1937, she and Fred MacMurray were reunited in *The Gilded Lily*; that same year Claudette assumed Carole Lombard's role in *Hands across the Table*. A year later she played the title character in *Alice Adams*, which will always be associated with its originator, Katharine Hepburn. Similarly, Ginger Rogers took over Claudette's part in *She Married Her Boss* (25 September 1939), while Claudette performed Rogers's in *Once upon a Honeymoon* (12 April 1943).

Casting on *Lux Radio Theatre* depended largely on availability. Sometimes the original cast could be reassembled, but more often the parts were spelled by other actors. Fortunately, Claudette and Gable were available for *It Happened One Night* in 1939; but that same year another classic screwball comedy, *The Awful Truth*, underwent a major change with Claudette in Irene Dunne's role, opposite Cary Grant, a holdover from the film. Although Claudette and Don Ameche were reunited for *Midnight* (20 May 1940), the magic was lost in the transmission, partly because Rosemary DeCamp and Gale Gordon had been cast in the roles created by Mary Astor and John Barrymore. While it is difficult, if not impossible, to envision anyone other than Rosalind Russell and Cary Grant as Hildy Johnson and Walter Burns in *His Girl Friday*, the *Lux* version substituted Claudette and Fred MacMurray, with Jack Carson in Ralph Bellamy's role. The men were miscast; MacMurray was charmless, and Carson was stolid instead of naive. Claudette, however, was a game Hildy but could not duplicate Russell's rapid-fire delivery.

Another problem with *Lux Radio Theatre* was the limited rehearsal time. Lines were often flubbed, but in the taped broadcasts available at the Margaret Herrick Library, Claudette was always letter-perfect. Her costars, however, sometimes were not. When she and MacMurray reenacted two of their vehicles, *The Egg and I* (5 May 1947) and *Family Honeymoon* (23 April 1951), MacMurray went up on several lines in each. In *Tomorrow Is Forever* (6 May 1946), Van Heflin had no problem with his lines, but his tentative German accent could not compare with that of Orson Welles, which, in addition to being authentic, also suggested a man on the last leg of life's journey.

Margaret Sullavan and James Stewart were so ideally cast in Ernst Lubitsch's *The Shop around the Corner* (1940) that their performance became the standard against which the radio version with Claudette and Don Ameche was measured. With either pair of actors, it was hard to believe that the setting was pre–World War II Vienna, but rather in an antipodal Vienna somewhere in Hollywood, where all that mattered was the pairing off of the right people. Lubitsch's sympathy with the lonely hearts who correspond with code names and post office boxes transcended time and place. Since Sullavan was a highly versatile actress, she was completely believable as a young woman looking for a job. Stewart could look worldly and wear expensive suits, as he did in *Bell, Book, and Candle* (1958); but his Everyman image was eminently suited to romantic comedy, as long as it did not unfold in a drawing room. (Imagine Stewart and Cary Grant exchanging roles in *The Philadelphia Story*.)

With *It Happened One Night*, Claudette arrived at the plateau of sophistication that rose incrementally until it reached its zenith in *Midnight* and *The Palm Beach Story*, after which the high style dropped down to a more comfortable ledge, where it remained for the rest of her career. While Claudette mustered up the requisite poignancy in the *Lux* version of *Shop*, her Klara sounded too worldly, as if she belonged in a boutique, not a novelty shop. She also lacked Sullavan's aching vulnerability, particularly at the end when Klara discovers the identity of her pen pal. With a slight tremolo in her voice, as if she were on the verge of sobbing but refrained for propriety's sake, Sullavan played the last scene with heartbreaking restraint, after realizing that the man who wrote her such poetically heartfelt letters was the same one to whom she had been so uncivil. Claudette brought sincerity to the scene but not poignancy. Ameche, while not exactly an Everyman, lent a quiet dignity to the final moments, although neither he nor Claudette could replicate the charm of the original.

Sometimes a generic comedy profited from a cast change on *Lux*. Robert Cummings assumed John Wayne's role in *Without Reservations* (26 August 1946), treating the dialogue cavalierly—throwing some lines away and using others for comedic effect—a far cry from Wayne, who played it straight, as if he found working with Claudette a liberating, although short-lived, experience that let him take off his gun belt and relax without John Ford hovering over him.

Claudette's best radio performance was in the *Lux* broadcast of *Magnificent Obsession* (13 November 1944), in which she and Ameche enacted the roles of Helen Phillips and Bob Merrick that were originally played by Irene Dunne and Robert Taylor in the 1935 film. After Merrick, a wealthy playboy, learns he was indirectly responsible for the death of Helen's husband, an eminent surgeon, when the only available respirator was used to revive him rather than Dr. Phillips, he tries to make amends by becoming a doctor himself. Eventually, he is able to perform a delicate eye operation on Helen that restores her sight. After the bandages were removed, Claudette adopted a totally different voice. First, it was a half whisper: "I think I see light." Then it became slightly tremulous until faith rushed in to fill the void that doubt had left: "Bob! My eyes—I think I see light." "Promise me you'll go to sleep now," Bob says. "Tomorrow," Helen replies softly, as if she were ending one chapter in her life and starting another with the man who gave her back her vision.

Claudette adapted well to radio. It gave her another medium to conquer, so that now she could be billed as star of stage, screen, and radio. The public could not get enough of Claudette Colbert, and Claudette obliged them. It was A. H. Woods who instilled in her the need to be constantly working by sending her on the road when there was nothing in New York or placing her in one play after another when there was.

Although *Lux* represented Claudette's best radio work, she appeared on other programs, even on the *Chase and Sanborn Hour*, an immensely popular show that premiered in 1928. When the ventriloquist Edgar Bergen and his wise-cracking wooden sidekick, Charlie McCarthy, came on board in 1937, the *Chase and Sanborn Hour* became known as *The Edgar Bergen and Charlie McCarthy Show* and continued for twelve more years. Don Ameche was a frequent guest and occasional announcer. At least on three occasions, he and Claudette appeared in comedy sketches: first, in "French Leave" (19 June 1938), in which a husband (Ameche), believing women should be irrational, grows so tired of his wife's (Claudette) unerring sense of logic that he decides to leave her. Her unemotional reaction, however, is so frustrating that he not only ends up staying but also joins her on a South American cruise.

When they teamed up again on 22 January 1939, the vehicle was Noël Coward's "Shadow Play," in which they were a couple on the verge of separating, suddenly finding themselves pulled into a time tunnel (or at least the wife was) and deposited in Venice, where they spent their honeymoon. The memory of a blissfully happy time was all that was necessary to end further talk of separation.

"Wedding Bells Ring," which Claudette and Ameche did a few months later on 9 April, anticipated *His Girl Friday* (1940), with its newspaper setting and story line about an ace reporter (Claudette) deciding to leave the business, much to the shock of her editor (Ameche), until a fire revives the news hound in her. The author, Edward James, assumed there were listeners who remembered the ending of *It Happened One Night*. It finally dawns on the editor that the reporter was throwing a subtle hint that marriage would be the best way to keep her on his staff. At the altar, the editor willingly says, "I do," but the reporter hesitates for a whole page, until she relents.

She did not consider low comedy beneath her; it brought her to the attention of a different kind of audience. Any actress appearing on the show was expected to perform in a skit with Charlie, and Claudette was no exception. It meant feeding punch lines to Charlie, who, naturally, got the laughs, except when Mae West came on the show. West threw in so many double entendres, to which Charlie replied in kind, that, as far as *The Chase and Sanborn Hour* was concerned, Mae West was persona non grata. In Claudette's case, the dialogue was not risqué; it was simply witless. When Charlie announces that he is going to make movies, Claudette asks if he plans to become an independent producer, to which Charlie replies, "Oh, I'm as sociable as the rest of them." The nadir occurred when Claudette had to admit her infatuation with Charlie:

COLBERT: Charlie, all my life I've been saving my love for you.

CHARLIE: Here go the savings of a lifetime. Ah, Claudette, let me take you away from all this.

COLBERT: Oh, darling, do you mean it? Let's take a boat trip to France and visit the Riviera.

CHARLIE: What I had in mind was a bus trip to Eagle Rock and have a malted milk.

COLBERT: But in France your money is worth double.

CHARLIE: Good! Then we can get a double malted.

Claudette was a good sport and may even have enjoyed playing straight woman to a dummy. She always maintained that laughter was the great panacea, and if the audience laughed, which they did, what did it matter if her dialogue was not the sort that she would ever have spoken on the screen?

With America's entry into World War II, Claudette, like so many other stars, hopped on the American bandwagon. When Claudette appeared on the show in May 1943, it was to address the subject of inflation, after which it was comedy time with Charlie. First, Claudette explained how inflation could be minimized: "We the people must ask ourselves and each other to limit our salaries, our earnings and our prices; to put excess spending money into bonds and savings." That year, Claudette made two films, *So Proudly We Hail* and *No Time for Love*, receiving $150,000 for each. One would like to assume that Claudette bought her share of bonds.

On 17 May 1954, Claudette made her final appearance on *Lux Radio Theatre* in the role of Miss Moffat in *The Corn Is Green*, which Bette Davis played so memorably in the 1944 film. A year later, on 7 June 1955, the curtain came down on *Lux Radio Theatre*. By that time, Claudette had already endeared herself to television viewers. She took a circuitous route back to Broadway; first it was television, then summer stock, and finally New York.

On 1 April 1951, Claudette did the unthinkable: she appeared on television, which, at the time, the Hollywood community did not consider a threat (although it would soon replace movies as a mass medium) as much as an arriviste whose only purpose was to extend the careers of actors whose moviemaking days were either over or numbered. Claudette was not the first movie star to try her hand at a medium that many of her colleagues held in contempt. The year before, her former film and radio costar Don Ameche replaced Edward Everett Horton as the host of CBS's *Holiday Hotel*, which in July 1951 was retitled *Don Ameche's Musical Playhouse*. Melvyn Douglas, Laraine Day, Ronald Colman, Margaret Sullavan, Louise Albritton, Jane Wyatt, Lynn Bari, Gale Storm, Don DeFore, and Zachary Scott, among others, had also preceded her by a year. There was, however, a difference: Claudette was STAR writ large; the others, at least in the early 1950s, were not ALL CAPS. Furthermore, Claudette had nothing to lose. She was in her late forties and must have sensed that her reign as doyenne of sophisticated comedy was over, at least on the big screen, although there was no reason why she could not enjoy a second life on the small screen, which Claudette did for a while. But it was the stage that gave her an open-ended run, on which she lowered the curtain herself at the age of eighty-two.

Claudette, who surprised Hollywood in 1934 when she graced Poverty Row by agreeing to make *It Happened One Night* for Columbia, did the same on 1 April 1951, when she made her television debut, but not in a live dramatic show such as *Studio One* or *Robert Montgomery Presents*. She did her share of live television, but not immediately. Instead, she chose *The Jack Benny Show*, which was filmed. It was not an arbitrary choice; Claudette had appeared several times on Benny's radio show and was also a good friend of Benny and his wife, Mary Livingstone. The material was not as mindless as the kind she was handed on the *Chase and Sanborn Hour*; at least she did not have to come on to a dummy. In a skit involving Benny, Basil Rathbone, and Claudette, Benny aspires to become a dramatic actor, hoping to replace Rathbone as Claudette's leading man. When Benny is reduced to playing a butler, he tries to upstage the stars by cracking walnuts and making a wrong entrance. As usual, Claudette seemed to be enjoying herself; Benny was Benny, and Rathbone looked as if he would rather be elsewhere.

On 22 July 1951, three months after making her television debut on *The Jack Benny Show*, Claudette made her first stage appearance in two decades, not on Broadway, but at Westport (Connecticut) Country Playhouse, the most prestigious of summer theaters, in Noël Coward's *Island Fling*, known in Britain as *South Sea Bubble*. The play, witty but unsubstantial, was never produced on Broadway, although it enjoyed a run of 276 performances at London's Lyric Theatre in 1956. However, as *Island Fling*, the comedy was so popular with Westport audiences that, after a week at the Cape Playhouse in Massachusetts, the company returned to Westport for another eight performances.

Best described as a political drawing-room comedy, *Island Fling* was set on the mythical Pacific island of Samolo (probably intended to evoke Fiji) during the twilight of British colonialism. Claudette played the wife of the island's liberal governor, whose Socialist sympathies and belief in self-determination have not endeared him to the People's Imperial Party. At her husband's request, she uses her wiles to persuade Hali Alani, the party's head, to think progressively. In a scene that must have unsettled some 1950s audiences, the two of them drink too much; when Hali becomes amorous, Coward has the wife hit him over her head with a bottle and take off. Coming upon a diamond clip that the wife has left behind, Hali's father threatens to inform the press about the affair unless the governor abandons his Socialist agenda and supports the People's Imperial Party, whose main goal is to keep Samolo a British colony. Naturally, the governor has no other choice but to concede.

Whether the play is called *Island Fling* or *South Sea Bubble*, it is the least revivable of Coward's works. It was politically incorrect even by 1950s' standards; in the twenty-first century, the second-act scene in the beach house with its racist overtones would occasion an uproar from people of color, who would be appalled at the wife's behavior. But the ultimate anachronism in a postcolonial world is the idea that a British possession would still want to remain part of the empire at a time when self-determination had become the equivalent of an inalienable right. The glowing notice that the Westport production received from drama critic and historian George Freedley in the *New York Telegraph* (20 August 1951) convinced Claudette that she had not lost the art of enthralling theatregoers. But until she found another vehicle, it was off to Sri Lanka for *Outpost in Malaya*.

Between 1952 and 1955, Claudette was bi-continental and bi-coastal, making movies abroad and in Hollywood. But, at the same time, she also straddled two other media, television (live and filmed) and theatre, thus escaping the oubliette reserved for those unable to make their mark in either. For Claudette, television was an epiphany. She had discovered a world where she could still be a star at a time when the screen was getting wider, décolletage more revealing, the soundtrack louder, and sophisticated comedy less frequent. Then, too, there was another generation of actors and filmmakers who did not feel bound by tradition and strove to leave their own mark on a Hollywood that was gradually assuming a corporate identity. If Hollywood was not sending out feelers to the over-forty contingent, there was always the tube. And as many of Claudette's contemporaries discovered, there was summer stock. There were even movies—not the sort that she made in her salad days, but respectable enough to forestall the inevitable "Whatever became of" question.

Claudette's experience with *Island Fling* made her ready for live television. On 16 September 1954, *The Best of Broadway* premiered on CBS, featuring hour-long versions of Broadway plays, the first of which was *The Royal Family*, by George S. Kaufman and Edna Ferber, loosely based on the Barrymore clan. The critics quibbled about the truncated version of a classic, but few could resist the stellar cast: Claudette along with Helen Hayes, Fredric March, Charles Coburn, Nancy Olson, and Kent Smith. Claudette came off well as the daughter, better, in fact, than Hayes as the matriarch, despite her "first lady of the American theatre" honorific. In her first live television appearance, Claudette did not seem at all uncomfortable. She was a natural actress who prided herself on never having studied acting. When Claudette left the stage for the screen, she adopted a naturalistic style that was moderately theatrical, just enough to herald the arrival of a star. When she returned to the stage, it was as if she had never left. Claudette could adapt to the various media—theater, film, radio, and television—because she instinctively understood how to approach each of them. No one had to teach her that in radio the voice does the acting, or that on television it is a matter of actor plus persona formatted to fit the confines of a screen that, in 1954, could have been a grand twelve inches.

Claudette readily embraced television, which revived the careers of Loretta Young, Jane Wyman, June Allyson, and, very briefly, Jean Arthur. Unlike the others, Claudette did not need a jump start: "Claudette Colbert is joining the march to television. She signed a contract in Palm Springs at the home of Jack Benny to do a series of half-hour situation comedy films for Rockhill Productions, a New York group," reported the *Los Angeles Times* in August 1954. The "series" was limited to two filmed half-hour shows for *Ford Theatre.*

The first was "Magic Formula," broadcast on NBC (6 January 1955). The script was studded with details of Claudette's personal life known to insiders, but not the general public. Claudette played an actress, Lorna Gilbert, with a surgeon-husband and an agent, whose name was exactly the same as her brother's, Charles Wendling. Lorna and her husband, Dr. Thomas Grant, met when he was called to the studio after she collapsed on the set. Claudette met Pressman when he removed her appendix. Believing her husband is attending a medical convention (he is actually leaving her and is en route to Manila), Lorna, a licensed pilot (like Joel Pressman, for whom Claudette bought a plane) embarks on a short vacation from the pressures of show business. Since Lorna is inexperienced, she crash lands on a beach. Prior to taking off, Lorna destroyed a letter that she thought contained her husband's phone number at the convention, not knowing that it was a farewell note that explained he was leaving her because he could no longer endure her determination to make him as successful as herself. Waiting for help, she recalls the past, realizing that the independence on which she prided herself had failed her. It is only when a dog leads a truck driver to the crash site that Lorna discovers how dependent people are on each other. The ending is tentative; the authorities manage to locate Grant, whose discovery that the letter was never read makes it possible for "Magic Formula" to end on a note of guarded optimism.

Many half-hour dramatic programs in the mid 1950s were able to pack a good deal of narrative into a constricting format. Apart from being engrossing, "Magic Formula" avoided the kind of closure that audiences expected, although optimists would assume that Lorna's marriage was no longer imperiled. The second *Ford Theatre* show, "While We're Young" (28 April 1955), was a comedy with some clever plot twists. Claudette is a widow with a teenage daughter, of whom she is overly protective. When the high school basketball coach (Tab Hunter) asks permission to take her daughter to a dance, Claudette at first refuses. Since the coach desperately needs a date that evening, he asks Claudette, after seeing what a good dancer she is. At first, "While We're Young" looked like a May-December (or at least May-September) romance. It seems headed in that direction after Claudette purchases a gown for the occasion and asks her daughter to model it for her. Then she tells her daughter that the gown is for her and that she and a doctor who has been courting her (Patric Knowles, who also played the husband in "Magic Formula") will attend as chaperones.

NBC had planned "While We're Young" as a pilot for a series starring Claudette. But the network did not think that the premise (widow and teenage daughter) could justify a series, which it probably could not. Besides, during the commercials, Claudette was expected to advertise the sponsor's product. "I am no saleswoman," Claudette emphatically told a sponsor.

Claudette preferred live to filmed television, although she did both. She was delighted to return to the *Best of Broadway* on 2 March 1955 in an adaptation of Ferenc Molnár's *The Guardsman*, opposite Franchot Tone, who was sadly miscast as a jealous actor who tests his actress-wife's fidelity by disguising himself as guardsman, who (supposedly) seduces her, leaving the audience to wonder whether or not she knew her seducer was her husband. Claudette was in great form in a role that would have been a natural for her on the stage, but with a costar like Charles Boyer or Claude Dauphin, who could give the text the sophistication it needed to stay on course and not crash on the reefs of farce.

A month later on 7 April, Claudette was back in Hollywood to star in the television version of her 1935 film, *Private Worlds*, on *Climax!* which originated live (although later some shows were filmed or taped) from CBS-TV's studio on Sunset Boulevard. A month later (5 May) she appeared again on *Climax!* in "The Deliverance of Sister Cecilia."

A live television version of Noël Coward's *Blithe Spirit* should have been a natural for her. The problem was the casting. Coward played the male lead, Charles Condomine, who is visited by the ghost of his first wife, Elvira, whom he alone can see and hear and whose entrance is always heralded by a few bars of Irving Berlin's "Always." Once his second wife, Ruth, dies because of Elvira's machinations, Charles finds himself visited by the ghosts of both women, leaving them the house which they proceed to trash.

Except for the "r"-trilling Coward and the scene-stealing Mildred Natwick as the medium Madame Arcati, the casting was not especially felicitous. Claudette played Ruth, the less flamboyant of the wives, while Lauren Bacall, top billed, was a rather brassy Elvira. Imagine Claudette dressed in shimmering silk, looking translucent and spectrally lit, and you have the perfect Elvira, which was not only the bigger role, but also the one better suited to her. She would have brought an air of sexy mischief to a play that is not just a drawing-room comedy but also one that takes place entirely in a drawing room. Bacall looked appropriately otherworldly but seemed to be back at Warner Bros. To her credit, Bacall, who was then unaccustomed to the stage (but would go on to become a two-time Tony winner), much less live television, did surprisingly well for someone who seemed to be in the wrong play. Ruth is essentially a character part as well as a thankless one. If, say, Claudette played Elvira with a Ruth who was attractive but not glamorous (e.g., Arlene Francis, Leora Dana, Kim Hunter, Nancy Kelly), the triangular structure apparent in the 1946 film version (with Rex Harrison, Constance Cummings, and Kay Hammond) would have remained intact. Instead, the triangle collapsed, with each side moving in its own direction.

Claudette had been less-than-ideally cast before in *Maid of Salem*, *Drums along the Mohawk*, and *Practically Yours*. Although she and Coward later became great friends, the *Blithe Spirit* experience was the sort that would have sabotaged all but the strongest of friendships. According to Ken Starrett, North American director of the Noël Coward Society, Coward reportedly said of Claudette, with whom he was having difficulty, "If she had a neck, I'd wring it." Claudette did have a short neck, of which she was acutely aware (and of which she made designers equally aware). Then, of course, the sets and blocking had to favor the left side of her face. Memorizing the text also posed a problem for Claudette, who usually had no difficulty learning lines. When Coward corrected her during a rehearsal, Claudette was almost despondent: "I don't understand. I knew these lines backwards this morning." Coward, never at a loss for a riposte, replied, "And that's just the way you're saying them now." When it came time for the telecast on 14 January 1956, Claudette had her lines down, but she too seemed to be in another play—one in which she was playing *to* her leading man, not *with* him. Only Coward and Natwick were doing *Blithe Spirit*. Although 1950s television had yet to become liberated, the more conservative viewers were probably shocked when Lauren Bacall spoke the first-act curtain line: "To hell with Ruth." The stage directions called for Elvira to speak the line "gently and sweetly." Not Bacall, who was not known, on or off screen, to speak gently and sweetly.

One of Claudette's best roles was as a widow (a character type more suited to her image than housewife) on *Playhouse 90*'s "One Coat of White" (21 February 1957). The script was written by Leonard Spiegelgass, who, two years later, scored a hit with his play *A Majority of One*. In the teleplay, Claudette is a Seattle widow with two self-absorbed daughters and their financially strapped husbands who think of her only in terms of the money they expect to inherit. Ignoring their advice to forego a European vacation, she sets off for Paris, where she encounters a famous artist with whom she embarks on the discreetest of affairs, at least by 1950s standards. The artist (Paul Henreid) follows her back to Seattle, where he paints her fence in the abstract expressionist style. The fence's uniqueness sets off a bidding war among museums, turns her culture maven friends into art historians, and solves her children's financial worries. But once the widow discovers how mercenary her family is, she returns to Paris to resume her relationship with the artist.

There was a delightful moment at the beginning of "One Coat of White" when the widow is practicing her French with a distinctly American accent, which Claudette reproduces perfectly, sounding exactly like someone who could never be mistaken for a native speaker. One suspects she enjoyed reproducing the sounds of tourist French.

By 1956, Loretta Young and Jane Wyman had their own television shows; and so, Charles Wendling reasoned, should his sister. There was a major difference. Neither *The Loretta Young Show* nor *Fireside Theatre* (later known as *The Jane Wyman Show*) was built around a recurring character; *The Claudette Colbert Show*, however, was to have starred Claudette as a newly elected congresswoman in the labyrinthine world of Washington politics. (The series originally bore the redundant title "Lady Congresswoman.") Wendling intended to function as associate producer, with considerable help, financial and creative, from Claudette. If NBC was not interested in a series about a widow and her daughter, it would hardly be attracted to one about a congresswoman and her family forced to relocate in Washington, particularly after screening the pilot, which dealt mainly with the family's search for an apartment. The response was tepid, and the pilot ended up, as most unsuccessful pilots did then, on *Colgate Theatre* in October 1957.

If a series was out of the question, there was still ample work on the tube for an actress who had no trouble with live television and did not balk at a three-day shoot for a thirty-minute dramatic show. What mattered is that, as more television sets were being purchased, more Americans were seeing Claudette Colbert, who, with each appearance, undermined the frequently used idiom, "retired from the screen" —the big one, perhaps, but not the small one. In early December 1957, "Novel Appeal," filmed between 5 and 7 September, was aired on *Telephone Time*, starring Claudette as mystery writer Mary Roberts Rinehart. The ingenious premise involved the author's fascination with an actual fifteen-year-old murder that she believes resulted in a wrongful conviction. Rather than present her evidence in a work of nonfiction, she chooses the form with which she is identified: the novel, in which she successfully unmasks the real murderer, who, it turns out, was the same as in real life. The reviews were excellent, with *Daily Variety* especially commending Claudette on her emotionally shaded performance in a part that could easily have been overplayed.

Even after she returned to the theatre, Claudette continued to appear on television until the early 1960s. She and Robert Preston stepped into the roles of Sister Benedict and Father O'Malley, created by Ingrid Bergman and Bing Crosby, in a ninety-minute television film of the 1945 classic, *The Bells of St. Mary's*, aired on 27 October 1959. *New York Times* critic Richard Shepard noted that that while they did not erase memories of the original performances, they did not copy them, either. They "performed ably," Shepard concluded.

Although Claudette never received a series of her own, she did become the host of CBS's hour-long daytime program, *Woman!* which premiered on 19 May 1959 and was devoted to issues of interest to women, such as the connection between teenage marriage and divorce. *Woman!* which involved parents, educators, and both high school and college students, was more of a round-table discussion than a series.

Because she never had a series, Claudette will never be known as a television star in the same way that Lucille Ball, Ann Sothern, and Barbara Bel Geddes are. Although Ball, Sothern, and Bel Geddes appeared in a number of films (and Bel Geddes, in plays as well), they are known primarily as Lucy Ricardo, Susie McNamara (*Private Secretary*), and Miss Ellie (*Dallas*). They also had the advantage of being in series now available on DVD. To sample Claudette's television work, one would have to visit the Paley Center for Media, formerly the Museum of Television and Radio, in either New York or Los Angeles, whose holdings include a representative selection that at least illustrates her ability to adapt to a new medium.

Claudette will always be regarded as a movie star; to theatre historians, she will also be known as a former stage actress turned movie star, who, after achieving fame in Hollywood, made a successful transition to live television and astonished Broadway, where she returned in 1956 with her stage technique intact and perhaps even burnished by the demands of live television.

CHAPTER 14

She's Back on Broadway

In February 1955, when Claudette was in New York rehearsing for *The Guardsman*, she told the *New York Times* that she would like to return to Broadway: "But I never shall. I don't want to be away from home on account of Joel Pressman." A year later, Claudette felt differently; live television prepared her to return to the medium in which she made her reputation. As for Pressman, he had become accustomed to their frequent separations. He also had his own career, which was completely independent of his wife's. In 1955 he was on the staff of St. John's Hospital in Santa Monica. Dr. Joel Pressman never had to worry about being called "Mr. Colbert."

On 2 April 1956, Claudette took over Margaret Sullavan's role in Carolyn Green's *Janus*, which she played until 9 June, followed by Imogene Coca, who finished the run.

Janus opened at Broadway's Plymouth Theatre on 24 November 1955, with Margaret Sullavan, Claude Dauphin, and Robert Preston in the leading roles. As one who saw Margaret Sullavan, but not Claudette, I can say that Sullavan approached comedy with an ingenuousness that kept a play, no matter how sophisticated it was (e.g., Samuel Taylor's *Sabrina Fair*), from sounding arch or condescending, the way drawing-room comedy can if improperly played. Yet there was a sense of joy missing in her performance— the joy that Shirley Booth radiated in *The Desk Set*, and Tallulah Bankhead in *Dear Charles*, two other plays of the mid 1950s, in which both actresses behaved as if they were having a good time even in flimsy vehicles and wanted audiences to feel the same. Sullavan was a superb technician who substituted intelligent line readings for spontaneity, assuming that would suffice until a more serious project came along. On the other hand, Sullavan had never done a play or even a movie like *Janus*, which took a decidedly emancipated view of a wife's extra-marital relationship with her writing partner, so that adultery seemed like a natural by-product of marriage.

Claudette approached comedy differently, as if the comic muse were within her, animating her and the audience as well. Claudette, who had done both screwball and romantic comedy, knew that *Janus* straddled both forms and that her character was, in part, the screwball who could mount a defense of adultery while at the same time bail her husband and lover out of a sticky financial mess. When drama critic John McClain reviewed Claudette's performance, he found *Janus* "a more skillful bit of work than original estimates indicated," noting that Claudette gave "a less flamboyant performance" than Sullavan but was still "enormously amusing." "Flamboyant" is the key. Claudette never descended upon a scene as if she were the centerpiece, with the rest of the cast surrounding her like favors at a banquet. But she couldn't help being the life of the party, even though she never behaved as if she were the guest of honor.

Janus is a witty, well-constructed boudoir comedy (as opposed to farce), a genre that has all but disappeared and resurfaces in occasional revivals of Georges Feydeau's works. Except for a few modern plays such as George Axelrod's *The Seven Year Itch*, Michael Frayn's *Noises Off*, and Neil Simon's *Rumors*, it is not a genre that has had much appeal since the 1950s. Gone are the days of *Up in Mabel's Room* and *Getting Gertie's Garter*. "Janus" is the nom de plume of two writers of romantic fiction (in contemporary terms, bodice-rippers): Jessica is a homemaker from Seattle who comes to New York each summer on the pretext of taking courses (or so Gil, her husband, thinks) but is actually staying in a Greenwich Village apartment, where she and Denny, a French teacher from Andover, create their best-sellers. The playwright never conceals the nature of their relationship; it is obviously adultery, which the first act makes abundantly clear. Construction is the playwright's main concern. What will happen when Jessica's husband drops in unexpectedly? And how will they all explain their income tax returns to an IRS investigator? But not, "Are they committing adultery?" That is a given.

Janus is the kind of play that would have been considered "adult" in the 1950s; "let's be adult about this" (sometimes "let's be civilized") was one of those lines beloved in the movies of the era when two characters, married or otherwise, skirted the boundaries of infidelity or fornication, preferring to consider it an "affair." When Gil is shocked by their arrangement, Jessica is quite rational, explaining that there is no comparison between a woman's infidelity and a man's: "A woman's infidelity is more serious than a man's. She's inclined to be *faithfully* unfaithful." Near the end, she is even more eloquent: "Gil, darling, I have loved you more *because* I have loved Denny, too." Since *Janus* is a comedy, there will be no divorce, especially after Jessica (for its time, the play was wickedly feminist) extricates her husband and lover from an IRS audit by discovering that the IRS representative harassing them has a mistress, whom he passes off as his wife.

Bedroom comedies suited Claudette, having made her share of them in Hollywood. When she returned to Broadway in 1959, it was in a play tailored to her comedic gifts: Leslie Stevens's *The Marriage Go-Round*, in which she played Content Lowell, PhD, a college dean married to an anthropology professor, who finds her marriage threatened by the arrival of a former student.

The Marriage-Go-Round, which opened on 29 October 1958 in the same theater in which Claudette had starred in *Janus*, was a huge hit, playing to standing room only at most performances during its thirteen-month run, the longest Claudette ever had. This time, Claudette was costarring with Charles Boyer, whose name came after hers in the playbill and ads.

The two of them spread charm like Peter Pan's fairy dust as they occasionally assumed their academic personas, standing at lecterns and discoursing on marriage and the family with considerably more wit than is found in a typical university classroom.

Julie Newmar played Katrin Sveg, a voluptuous blonde who sunbathes nude and has definite ideas about the man she has chosen to breed the perfect child—her former anthropology professor (Boyer), Content's husband. As she informs Content, "I am younger, prettier, slimmer, stronger, bigger, and more intelligent than you. Don't fight it." Newmar was entranced by Claudette, expressing admiration for her "style, energy, and the way she functioned in life." She even referred to the "extraordinary" effect Claudette had on her. Although Newmar and Claudette never socialized, they always conversed before the performance since they occupied the only two offstage dressing rooms, Boyer's being on the next level. Once Claudette even confided to Newmar about the kind of bra she wore, prompting Newmar to purchase the same model.

Claudette exuded the kind of warmth that a Hollywood icon does not often accord a relative newcomer like Newmar, whose other Broadway appearance had been in *Li'l Abner* the previous season. But Claudette respected a disciplined performer, and Newmar was that. Trained as a ballet dancer and singer, she appeared as one of the brides in MGM's *Seven Brides for Seven Brothers* (1954), in which she stood out because of her height, beauty, grace, and particularly her ability to execute Michael Kidd's intricate choreography, even in the bedroom, where the brides-to-be wistfully contemplate marriage and sway dreamily within the cramped confines of the room. Newmar ignored the constricting set and through a combination of facial expression and movement effortlessly communicated the longing the character felt.

Without knowing in what month Claudette was born, Newmar assumed she must have been a Virgo because of her great attention to detail. "There you go!" she exclaimed when she learned that Claudette was born on 13 September. As one who trained to be an artist and painted throughout her life, Claudette understood such concepts as order and harmony, the latter in the sense of the blending of all the elements of a piece into an organic whole. She even patted the lower part of her legs with pancake makeup before putting on her stockings, believing that when she sat, even her shins should look attractive.

During the run of the show Newmar tried to assimilate everything she could about Claudette's approach to life, which was quite different from her own. In the stage and screen versions of *Auntie Mame*, the title character's credo, "Life is a banquet, and most poor ['sons-of-bitches' in the play, 'suckers' in the movie] are starving to death," is now inscribed in the film buff's lexicon of memorable dialogue. Claudette would have agreed with the first part of the sentiment; as for the rest, she would have felt that the starving class required simple sustenance, not haute cuisine. To Claudette, life's banquet did not revolve only around food; it was more of a soirée with fashionably dressed and witty guests, or even a luncheon on a patio with gleaming silverware, cloth napkins, and freshly cut flowers on the table.

When speaking with Julie Newmar, one is immediately struck by her musically trained voice with its lyrical cadences. Perhaps she always sounded that way; but after spending thirteen months with Claudette, one suspects that her speech had even more of a lilt. And yet there was every reason for her to resent Claudette, even though it was Newmar who won the Tony award for Best Supporting Actress of the 1958–59 season. Claudette was nominated for Best Actress, but lost to Gertrude Berg for *A Majority of One*. Boyer, however, was not even nominated.

In act 2, Katrin is supposed to make her entrance clad only in a bath towel and then sit on a large ottoman, center stage front. But at each rehearsal the ottoman was moved further and further downstage, until Newmar had no other choice but to sit practically with her back to the audience, so that Claudette could dominate the scene. "Of course, she was upstaging me by having the ottoman moved," Newmar recalled. But Claudette did it so slyly that Newmar never held it against her, even though she had to play the rest of the scene standing, while trying to keep the towel from slipping.

A particularly smarmy PR agent like Sidney Falco (Tony Curtis) in *Sweet Smell of Success* (1957) approached Newmar about an ad campaign to showcase her natural endowments, not realizing that she had more to offer than the body beautiful. His idea was to plant a man in the audience who, at some point, would rush up on stage and pull off the towel. Newmar's immediate reaction was not the notoriety it would cause, but Claudette's reaction.

"Julie saw only one side of her," producer Paul Gregory insisted. "I was part of the show from the beginning—rehearsals and everything— and witnessed things that no one else saw. I argued with [Claudette] and desperately tried to keep order." To Gregory, Claudette was an "absolute bitch." When it came to costumes, Claudette was always particular. Displeased with the sketches of the costumes for *Cleopatra*, she called Joel Pressman, whom she would soon marry, and said, " 'Dear, they want me to use these sketches, and I want Travis Banton, and I'm going to have Travis Banton.' And Claudette Colbert got Travis Banton." For *The Marriage-Go-Round*, Claudette insisted her costumes be made in Paris by Lanvin-Castillo and then handed Gregory the bill for four thousand dollars. "What Julie may not have known is that Claudette was jealous of her figure," Gregory continued. Newmar's body was both sensuous and statuesque, as was apparent the previous season when she played the aptly named Stupyfin' Jones in *Li'l Abner*. Claudette requested, but to no avail, that Newmar's breasts be made less prominent even if they had to be taped. Next, she claimed that Boyer was "downstaging" her, which is quite unusual; it is upstaging that is generally the problem. Since the two must periodically speak at lecterns, Claudette demanded that his be on stage right and hers on stage left where her best side would be shown to advantage.

Boyer and Claudette drew on their vast reserves of professionalism to seduce the audience into believing that they relished each other's onstage company. On stage, Boyer and Claudette were Hollywood's gift to Broadway: the great lover and the doyenne of romantic comedy. At other times, Gregory, who had great respect for Boyer (and, in fact, produced *Lord Pengo*, Boyer's final Broadway show in 1962), honored the actor's plea: "Keep that woman away from me." As for the relocation of the ottoman, director Joseph Anthony was furious at Claudette's usurping his power. But what could he do? And what could Boyer do, with a star with whom his name was once linked and whose name appeared before his?

Claudette's insecurities were exacerbated by the celebrities who gathered backstage after the performance, many of whom came to see Boyer. Claudette may have been a star, or even an icon, but she never did to men what Boyer did to women. Boyer could seduce with his silken voice, worldly and soothing, and mesmeric eyes, which seemed like reflecting pools, throwing back whatever image was cast upon them. Look too deeply into them and you might drown. Claudette resented the attention he received and, rather than exit through the stage door, she left the Plymouth through the fire door when he had visitors, so that she would not be seen.

Yet despite his litany of grievances, Gregory called Claudette an "amazing but tormented woman." Whatever demons Claudette unleashed during the performance could be attributed to several factors. First was Boyer, who, although a compatriot, inspired a real cult ever since he appeared with the ethereally beautiful Hedy Lamarr in *Algiers* (1938). Claudette, on the other hand, had a following. In terms of Hollywood royalty, he was king; she, the eternally youthful crown princess. When she took over the lead in *Janus*, she was appearing with Claude Dauphin and Robert Preston, excellent actors but hardly household names. With Boyer, it was a different matter entirely.

"Great stars have great pride," Norma Desmond intoned oracularly in *Sunset Boulevard* (1950) when Joe Gillis (William Holden) reminded her that her era was over and that she should face up to being fifty. Claudette was fifty-five and faced with many more lines than she had in *Janus*, in addition to some lengthy monologues that required finely calibrated timing and the art of being witty without sounding it. It was the first time in thirty years that she was back on Broadway in a new play, not in one like *Janus*, in which she was a replacement. The production had to be perfect, even if it meant incurring the anger of producer, director, and costar.

She was also tormented in another way. Her screen career was almost over, leaving only television and the stage. Even though she looked forty, her type of comedy would become exceeding rare in the next two decades. Claudette needed some kind of assurance that she was not passé. Thus, when Verna Hull, a painter who became enamored of her, entered her life, taking on the role of chauffeur-companion, Claudette reveled in it, as Margo Channing did in *All about Eve*, when she allowed Eve Harrington to become her social secretary, personal maid, and confidante; and all the while Eve was becoming Margo's shadow, waiting for the day that she could eclipse her. If Claudette had played Margo, as Joseph L. Mankiewicz had intended, she might have sensed the similarity between Hull and Eve and kept their relationship on a purely social level. But once they met, which was shortly after the opening of *The Marriage Go-Round*, and discovered they had art in common, Claudette felt that she had at last found a kindred spirit. Hull's relationship with Claudette provoked much speculation, chiefly from those who see in any close friendship between two men or two women—however short-lived it was or how acrimonious it became—something between the homoerotic and the homosexual and, in the absence of definite proof, then the latter. There was never definite proof about Hull and Claudette; however, since Hull was a known lesbian, Claudette was the victim of guilt by association. Still, if Hull made the run of *The Marriage Go-Round* easier for Claudette, one shudders to imagine what the atmosphere backstage would have been like if Hull had not entered her life.

Claudette was supposed to have appeared next in *A Mighty Man Is He*, by George Oppenheimer and Arthur Kober, neither of whom was a novice. Oppenheimer had written *Here Today*, which became a summer stock perennial; a number of MGM screenplays including *Rendezvous* (1935), *Man-Proof* (1935), and *Broadway Melody of 1940*; and over twenty episodes of television's *Topper* series. Kober, Lillian Hellman's ex-husband, was the author of the long-running comedy *Having Wonderful Time* (1937), which became a film a year later and returned to Broadway in 1953 as a musical, *Wish You Were Here*. In the summer of 1955, Claudette appeared in a tryout of *A Mighty*

Man Is He at Maine's Ogunquit Playhouse, followed by a week at the Theatre by the Sea in Manunuck, Rhode Island.

Ken Starrett, who played a minor role in the Ogunquit production, found Claudette extremely gracious. He recalled a scene in the play in which he had to deliver a package containing a dress that Claudette had to open (but never wear), which elicited sighs from the audience. When Starrett mustered up the courage to speak with Claudette, he confessed his ambition to become a costume designer. Claudette was more than sympathetic: "I wanted to be a clothes designer before I became an actress." In appreciation, Starrett gave her a pair of golden earrings after the closing performance. The following year, he went to see her in *Janus*, only to discover that she was wearing the same earrings on stage. "She was a lady in every sense of the word," he said nostalgically, echoing the sentiments of most of the actors, male and female, who worked with her. But then, actors see their colleagues from a different perspective than do producers.

A Mighty Man Is He seemed more suited to Claudette than *Island Fling*. The play had the air of a French boulevard comedy, in which marital infidelity is airbrushed until it becomes an *affaire d'amour* conducted in accordance with the cardinal rule of the genre, in which adultery is relegated to the unseen bedroom; and the affair, or what is left of it, is reduced to civilized talk. Claudette played a theatrical producer's wife, who conspires with her husband's mistress to rid their ménage of a younger rival. Since the play, with its alliance of wife and mistress against an intruder, had the kind of amoral insouciance peculiar to bedroom comedy, it seemed like a perfect vehicle for her. But it was the kind of comedy that, if played too broadly, could turn shrill. That was not the case during the tryout. However, five years later, when it was finally ready for a Broadway production, Claudette bowed out, perhaps because by then she had done *Janus* and *The Marriage-Go-Round*, which were similar in theme, and felt that her next stage appearance should not be in another boudoir comedy. Nancy Kelly, a fine dramatic actress but without Claudette's comedic skill, took over the lead. The reviews were uniformly negative, and *A Mighty Man Is He* closed on 9 January 1960 after five performances.

Actually, *A Mighty Man Is He* did better than Claudette's next play, *Julia, Jake and Uncle Joe*, which opened and closed on the same night: Saturday, 28 January 1961. "I don't know why she was doing this play," said Marjorie Fox, the wife of the esteemed set designer Frederick Fox, whose impressive credits include both opera (Metropolitan Opera productions of *Tosca* and *Andrea Chenier*) and Broadway shows such as *Junior Miss, Anna Lucasta, John Loves Mary, Darkness at Noon, Light Up the Sky,* and *The Seven Year Itch.* Fox also designed the set as well as the costumes for *Julia, Jake and Uncle Joe.* As usual, Claudette was dissatisfied with what he had in mind for her and supplied her own wardrobe. An atmosphere of tension hung over the rehearsals. The set had to be constructed in such a way that Claudette's entrances would favor her best side; director Richard Whorf had to observe the same rule when blocking the scenes.

If tempers flared, it was because Claudette and perhaps others in the cast sensed disaster. Claudette was more imperious than usual because she was so convinced the play was not ready for New York that she tried, but to no avail, to get out of her contract during an out-of-town tryout in Wilmington, Delaware. And yet, *Julia, Jake and Uncle Joe* was adapted by playwright Howard Teichmann (best known for *The Solid Gold Cadillac*) from Oriana Atkinson's *Over at Uncle Joe*'s, which chronicled the year she and her husband, drama critic Brooks Atkinson, spent in Russia when he was the Moscow correspondent.

The producers, Roger L. Stevens and John Shubert, were important figures in the theatre. Stevens was a major producer (e.g., *A View from the Bridge, West Side Story, A Touch of the Poet*); Shubert was the son of J. J. Shubert, who, along with his brother, was a director of the Shubert Theatre Corporation. Yet they were determined to adhere to the premiere date, 28 January, probably believing that with the play's inevitable failure, it could become a write-off if it opened and closed on the same night, which is precisely what they decided to do without even waiting for the reviews. Howard Taubman's review in the *New York Times* two days later commended the cast, particularly Claudette, but objected to the stereotypical characters, the limp satire, and the strained humor. His conclusion—that there must be something seriously wrong with a play that only came to life when the Russians broke into an ethnic dance—should also have been evident to theatre veterans like Stevens and Shubert, who should have closed *Julia, Jake, and Uncle Joe* out of town, sparing the cast, especially the star, the embarrassment of a one-night stand.

Professionally, it was Claudette's worst experience in a career that was going into its fourth decade. But she had a resilience that left no room for self-pity, and three years later she was back on Broadway in a show that at least enjoyed a three-month run. Meanwhile, her life changed dramatically; she had found the earthly paradise.

In 1960, Claudette knew that her Hollywood career was about to end; television was always a possibility, but the chances of starring in a series were slim. Barbara Stanwyck was fortunate to be able to extend her career by playing the matriarch in *Big Valley* (1965–69), and Donna Reed enjoyed a last hurrah when she briefly replaced Barbara Bel Geddes in *Dallas* (1984–85) before dying a year later. Jane Wyman found a new following as well as a new persona when she played Angela Channing in *Falcon Crest* (1981–90). But the movie star who really triumphed against the odds in the last decades of the twentieth century was Angela Lansbury in *Murder, She Wrote* (1984–96). The role of mystery novelist Jessica Fletcher would have been ideal for Claudette, who did her share of sleuthing in *It's a Wonderful World* and solved a murder in *Thunder on the Hill*. In fact, in *A Talent for Murder*, her penultimate Broadway appearance, Claudette played such a novelist, whose powers of deduction were worthy of Sherlock Holmes.

A TV series would never materialize. Filmed television was all that remained; the era of live TV drama, which was part of television's golden age, had ended. Gone were *Studio One, Robert Montgomery Presents, Kraft Television Theatre*, and *Playhouse 90*.

Claudette was too chic to become a character actress like Bette Davis, who gallantly undertook the role of a Bronx housewife in *The Catered Affair*

(1956), looking appropriately frumpy but sounding like her old self, pronouncing *d*'s as *t*'s and delivering uninflected line readings as if such women had lost their sense of cadence, as she had herself. Davis's determination to work, despite the roles that were offered her, was blatantly apparent in *Whatever Happened to Baby Jane?* in which she was not afraid to play a grotesque as well as look like one with her face slathered with white makeup and ghoulishly adorned with a beauty mark.

Human gargoyles, grandmothers with rimless glasses, and boozy harridans were not for Claudette. Now there was only the theatre, to which she would return periodically. She would keep an apartment in New York, always on the East Side, which would become her pied-à-terre when she was in a play. But she was thinking more about her husband's approaching the mandatory retirement age of sixty-seven and a place with the serenity and grace of their Holmby Hills home. Their retirement home would not be in California; that chapter of their lives would be over even before Pressman turned sixty-seven. It was over even earlier.

Around 1960 set designer Oliver Messel introduced Claudette to Barbados, where he had a home. She had frequently been a house guest of Noël Coward, whose home in Jamaica inspired her to look outside of the United States for a place to retire, at least for her husband. For Claudette there was no mandatory retirement age; she had two more decades of performing ahead of her. Where she lived would not matter. Coward continued to perform both in New York and London after moving to Jamaica, which was far from an outpost. That Coward appeared in *Nude with Violin* in New York in 1957 and *A Tale of Twilight* in London in 1965 proved that a stage actor did not have to live in either Gotham or West End, or near either, to continue in his or her profession. Claudette felt similarly.

When Claudette first saw Barbados, it was not the island that attracted her, but the ocean. An expert swimmer, she realized that she would no longer have to swim in indoor pools but in nature's own waters—and on her back—until a stroke incapacitated her. Claudette had the same response to a nineteenth-century plantation home that she saw on the west coast of

Barbados as she did when she came upon the house on Fairing Drive in Holmby Hills. She knew it was the right place for herself and Pressman, but only after it had been thoroughly remodeled: "I saw the bones of a lovely house and I saw the beach." She had never had a beachfront home, and once she saw the estate that she would call "Bellerive," she envisioned exactly how it would look when the bones took on flesh and Bellerive became a reflection of the elegance and grace that permeated every aspect of her life.

When walls had been broken through, rooms widened, and baths added, Claudette followed Voltaire's mandate at the end of *Candide* and cultivated her garden, which had pretty much gone to seed. But Claudette restored it to a kind of Edenic splendor, with trees framing a pagoda where guests could have breakfast and lunch in a natural setting. Claudette's guests were so numerous that she had a cottage built on the grounds, so her frequent visitors could have privacy as well as their own kitchen.

The foyer looked like a stage setting, with a chandelier and an archway framed by plants on either side. It was not an awesome sight; rather, it was strikingly tasteful but not intimidating. After passing through it, the visitor was exposed to the equivalent of a gallery. In the living room, there was a beige armchair sprinkled with sprigs of green, alongside of which was an album with pictures from the round-the-world honeymoon trip that Claudette and Norman Foster took in 1927. Foster was, as she always admitted, her first love, and it was only right that their honeymoon album should be opposite a Lucite table decorously arranged with framed photos. The master bedroom looked like a stage set, everything in its proper place: draped windows, upholstered red chairs with pillows, a writing desk, a bed covered with a beige spread flecked with the same traces of greenery on the armchair in the living room, and an end table with mementos. Claudette was a work of art in her own way; so was Bellerive.

In a highly descriptive text that accompanied Dan Forer's pictures in *Architectural Digest*, Gerald Clark wrote that Claudette "took the name of her Barbadian refuge . . . from Blanche du Bois's Mississippi plantation, her lost Eden in Tennessee Williams's *A Streetcar Named Desire*." Claudette, who had actually been approached to play Blanche in the 1947 premiere of *A Streetcar Named Desire* (colossal miscasting, which fortunately never occurred), knew her French. The name of Blanche's plantation was "Belle Rêve," literally, "beautiful dream," which in context has a distinctly symbolic meaning: a dream turned nightmare that put Blanche on a streetcar named Desire to her sister's New Orleans apartment, where she met her fate. "Bellerive" is, literally, "beautiful stream," referring to the Atlantic outside Claudette's door.

Although Claudette had found her earthly paradise, she still brooded over the *Julia, Jake and Uncle Joe* fiasco, which was enough to sour her permanently on the theatre. Claudette, however, was determined to return in a play that would at least enjoy a respectable run. Until Bellerive was habitable, Claudette went back to New York, where she still had an apartment on East Sixty-fourth Street.

The Irregular Verb to Love enjoyed a moderately successful engagement at London's Criterion Theatre, where it opened on 11 April 1961 and starred Joan Greenwood and Hugh Williams, who also coauthored the play with his wife, Margaret. It was a combination of screwball and drawing-room comedy in which Greenwood, whose unique voice had a creamy throatiness, played Hedda Rankin, an animal activist who once drove around Algiers, bathing stray dogs. However, she also firebombed a London fur store, for which she was sentenced to a year in prison (eight months in the Broadway production). The play begins on the day of Hedda's release and her discovery that her daughter, Lucy, is pregnant and refuses to marry her lover, Michael; her beatnik son, Andrew, has returned from Sardinia with Fedra, a young Greek woman who cannot speak English; and Hedda's husband, Felix, has confessed to a short-lived affair during her incarceration, which he describes as "more a companionship than a relationship."

The Irregular Verb to Love seemed the right vehicle for Claudette. While Greenwood could turn her voice into a deep purr without losing cadence, Claudette could accomplish the same with hers, giving a lyrical tinkle to what Greenwood would have rendered as a chime on a grandfather clock. With some conniving on the part of Hedda and Felix, Michael proposes to Lucy; Andrew, to Fedra; and Hedda forgives Felix, who tries to win her sympathy by feigning a limp, only to have Hedda tell him, "Felix, you're limping with the wrong leg," an appropriate curtain line for a comedy with semi-serious overtones. At sixty, but looking forty, Claudette could still play screwball—mature screwball—while gradually shedding the "dizzy dame" image to become a mother who has to be told that her ministrations and meddling are no longer welcome: "Let go of us," Andrew cries, after Hedda whisks Fedra off to a beauty parlor and subjects her to a complete makeover.

As one who saw the New York production, I can vouch for Claudette's ability to steer a conventional but well-crafted narrative into darker waters and then turn it around, as if the play went off course, took a detour, and then returned to its true genre: a drawing-room comedy with overtones of generational tension. Claudette knew she could play screwball until it was time to turn Hedda from a fire-bombing activist to a sophisticated lady with a wardrobe that the average prison inmate could never afford. The writing forced her to return to the screwball mode when Hedda admits that bomb-making is still such an obsession that she is working on one in the bedroom. Will it go off? Of course. The play needs a climax, but one that will not send Hedda back to prison.

Claudette was fortunate to costar with Cyril Ritchard, who played Felix and whose mastery of the high style matched hers. Interestingly, Helen O'Hagan recalled that Claudette never spoke about working with Ritchard, whom the *Time* magazine critic (27 September 1963) thought was the best reason for seeing *The Irregular Verb to Love*. After the New York engagement, Celeste Holm went on tour with the play, with the then-unknown Christopher Reeve in the supporting cast. *The Irregular Verb to Love* also became a community theater favorite, both in Britain and America; for a while, it proved popular on the straw-hat circuit. Part of its appeal was logistical: a single-set play with a nine-member cast. But *The Irregular Verb to Love* also belonged to an age when a fire-bombing activist seemed more of an eccentric (or "kook," to use the 1960s idiom) than a menace. Since 11 September 2001, a fire-bomber is no longer an eccentric but a threat to national security, even if the timer has been set for the bomb to go off when no one is in the store. Understandably, *The Irregular Verb to Love* goes unrevived.

CHAPTER 15

The Stigma

When Claudette married Norman Foster in 1927, she was quite open about their marriage; it was a "modern marriage," a phrase that led to a great deal of speculation. Once Claudette told the fan magazines that she and Norman had separate residences, both in New York and later, briefly, in Los Angeles, the rumors began to fly. The press was relatively discreet, although when columnist Louis Sobol learned that the couple was having marital problems, he observed snidely that "the Claudette (Norman Foster) Colberts are pouting." Elsewhere, Norman was depicted as an acquiescent husband; Claudette, as a liberated woman, so liberated that the entertainment world wondered if theirs was an open marriage or *marriage blanc*, in which she and Foster pursued not so much their own interests as their own sexual preferences. According to one of Clark Gable's biographers, Gable met Claudette when he was appearing in Sophie Treadwell's *Machinal* on Broadway in 1928: "[Gable] knew that she was a lesbian in a sham marriage with gay actor-director Norman Foster." First, Foster had yet to turn director; second, Gable was notoriously homophobic. Although George Cukor, who was known to be gay as well as a good friend of Claudette, was set to direct *Gone with the*

Wind, Gable could not endure Cukor's presence on the set: "I won't be directed by a fairy. I have to work with a *real man*!" Consequently, macho Victor Fleming, who had directed Gable in *Red Dust,* took over, receiving sole directorial credit for the film. However, as Cukor's biographer Patrick McGilligan points out, Gable's homophobia may have originated in a one-night stand with actor Billy Haines, who later became designer to the stars; supposedly, in a "drunken moment," Gable and Haines had sex. However, McGilligan, an eminently responsible biographer, notes that despite Cukor's insistence that the incident took place, "only Gable and Haines know the precise circumstances." And the same is true of Claudette and her amours, if indeed there were any.

If Gable had any reservations about working with Claudette, it was never apparent in *It Happened One Night*; to watch that film is to see two artists at their peak, responding to each other as only a man can to a woman, not faking the chemistry but letting the reaction take place, as indeed it did, without a catalyst. Significantly, Gable, humbled on Oscar night 1935, thanked Capra and "Miss Claudette Colbert, who was gracious enough to costar with me in the same picture." Gable must have known the film would never have won the awards it did, and that he never would have received a Best Actor Oscar, if he had played opposite any of the other actresses who passed on the role of Ellie Andrews.

Gable—or no one, for what matter—knew that Claudette and Norman's "modern marriage" was a necessity, not an arrangement. Jeanne Chauchoin would not allow Norman in her home. Claudette, never able to extricate herself from her mother's shackles, played the obedient daughter, even though she was passionately in love with Norman in a way that she never was with Joel Pressman, who was a true friend and a husband, but not the love of her life. Until Jeanne died, Claudette remained in the shadow of her mother, preferring to acquiesce rather than endure her wrath.

Claudette's personal life should occupy a separate chapter in her biography, which is precisely what has been provided here. Under ordinary circumstances, it should merit a paragraph or two or, better, an extended footnote. But with the current trend of dredging up liaisons from the sub-cellars of celebrity lives, a biographer has two choices: go with the flow, to use the 1960s idiom, or go against it and offer an alternative version. I have chosen the latter because it requires more research than hearsay.

Claudette came of age in the 1920s; that was her era, and New York was her town. She looked like a flapper and undoubtedly was one. She was also a Broadway star and behaved like one. One could imagine her at one of Jay Gatsby's parties, leaving at dawn and looking bedewed, as if she had just arrived. She was part of the Jazz Age, and from what we know of her, she enjoyed every minute of it. It was a time when, to quote the title song from Cole Porter's *Anything Goes*, "If driving cars you like / If old hymns you like / If bare limbs you like / If Mae West you like / Or me undressed you like / Why, nobody will oppose."

Claudette's marriage to Norman might not have remained modern had it not been for her mother's interference in her daughter's pregnancy. Around 1979, Claudette told the eminent designer Arnold Scaasi, who was visiting Bellerive with his companion Parker Ladd, that she had an abortion at the instigation of her mother, who believed that "a child would spoil her career and screen image as a 'love goddess.' " Only Jeanne thought of her daughter as a "love goddess"; a Jean Harlow or a Greta Garbo, Claudette was not. The real reason is probably that Claudette provided her mother with the kind of life that might be jeopardized by the arrival of a child. "Claudette as mother" simply did not go with Hollywood's or the public's image of the star. Norman was crushed by her decision, which, one sus-pects, was not all that difficult because Claudette may well have agreed with her mother. Claudette could, and did, play mothers—and always con-vincingly. But Claudette Colbert and real motherhood were incompatible. Norman did not have to just play fathers; he became one after his marriage to Sally Blane.

To Claudette, talking about sex was preferable to having it. There was a playful sexiness about Claudette that kept her out of the "love goddess" category and placed her among the sensuous women at the lower end of the erotic spectrum, like Carole Lombard, Jean Arthur, and Barbara Stanwyck, whose wit and way with a wisecrack made them more like chums than lovers. That sexiness was alternately earthy and sophisticated, home-spun and imperious. Claudette, on the other hand, was not a creature of extremes but a reconciler of them. As an actress she found a face for each character, which was always hers, but over which another's was superim-posed. In her private life, Claudette still had a face, or a mask, for each occasion. What seemed like extremes was a harmony of contrasts that a sensitive male would detect. A derrière-pincher like Fredric March would have just thought Claudette was hot and sexy, not saucy and coy, which she really was.

Claudette could toss off a witticism worthy of Wilde or Coward. She also had a salty tongue and was not above saying "Who the fuck are you?" to featured actress Patricia Medina on the set of *The Secret Heart*. That was Claudette. She could be earthy and urbane, a self-sufficient woman and a star with a retinue. She always did her own makeup, applying it before breakfast and even wearing it when she went swimming. She also had her makeup on when she died. She would make her own breakfast (generally oatmeal) and wash the dishes.

Lunch was different. Vegetables were accompanied by the appropriate dressing, and wine was served in crystal goblets. Tea in the Bellerive pagoda was a ritual unto itself; guests sat on red lacquered mahogany chairs that matched the table and were served watercress sandwiches and pastries by two young women in gingham dresses. Claudette staged the tea as if it were a scene from a movie that she was directing: "When the young ladies were through serving, they retreated and sat on chairs behind the trellised panels . . . until their mistress summoned them by ringing a small silver bell."

Propriety prevailed on social occasions, but never to the extent of depriving Claudette of the gossip she longed to hear or the myths that she could deflate. When the question of Clark Gable's sexual prowess came up, as well as his anatomy, Claudette offered a firsthand account. Not only did she admit to going "all the way with him," but she also challenged agent

Minna Wallis's description of her former client's physical endowments, implying that Gable was far better equipped than Wallis claimed. Apparently, not all of Gable's erections on the *It Happened One Night* set were simulated. So much for Gable's avoiding Claudette because he suspected she was a lesbian. Look at their scenes in *Boom Town*, and you will see that they would still produce a chemical reaction—again, without a catalyst.

The allegations of lesbianism originated in New York when she was working in the theatre; once she announced her "modern marriage" to Norman Foster, he became the object of similar and unproven gossip. The "stigma," as Claudette referred to it, resurfaced in Hollywood because of an innocuous photo that appeared in various newspapers showing Claudette between Marlene Dietrich's raised legs, as the two of them slid down a chute at the Venice Pier Fun House. The occasion was a party given by Carole Lombard in mid June 1935, attended by Hollywood's royalty, including Errol Flynn, Cary Grant, Henry Fonda, Ruth Chatterton, Clifton Webb, and Cesar Romero; directors George Cukor, Raoul Walsh, Frank Capra, Joseph L. Mankiewicz, and Mitchell Leisen; and Joel Pressman, whom Claudette would marry six months later.

Although Claudette and Dietrich were both Paramount stars, Claudette had little use for Dietrich, whose somnambulist persona was at odds with her own unaffected vitality; Dietrich felt similarly about " 'that ugly Claudette Colbert, so shopgirl French.' " Claudette always claimed that a photographer pushed her against Dietrich and sent the two of them down the slide. That would have been in keeping with the tenor of the evening, in which director Mitchell Leisen "took [Dietrich] to the top of the highest and longest slide . . . [and] tied her arms to her sides with a burlap sack and then placed another sack over her head before sending her sliding on her way." In his biography of gay actor-turned-designer William Haines, William J. Mann makes much of the photo, claiming that Claudette and Dietrich wore pants, "a code for lesbianism or at least sexual rebellion." Actually, Dietrich wore shorts; Claudette wore slacks with elasticized ruffled cuffs at the ankles. Any woman planning to attend the affair should have thought twice about wearing a dress or a skirt, particularly in a fun house where "air shafts sent skirts soaring." Lombard herself wore pants, as did Toby Wing. As for slacks as code for lesbianism and liberation, 1935 newspaper ads featured women's lounging pajamas for entertaining, corduroy trousers and two-piece halter-pants combinations suitable for the outdoors, not to mention riding togs and ski suits. What Claudette wore for the occasion was actually quite feminine. The allegation that Paramount told Claudette to "straighten out," resulting in her divorcing Foster and marrying Pressman in December 1935, is also untrue. Claudette told the press on 2 March 1935, three months before Lombard's party, that she was divorcing Foster; she and Pressman planned to marry in early 1936 but changed the date after Pressman turned violent when a reporter tried to take his picture after he and Claudette deplaned at the San Francisco airport on 29 November 1935. The negative publicity, which has already been described, portrayed Pressman as a humorless bully and Claudette as something more than his fiancée. They had no other choice but to settle on an earlier marriage date, which turned out to be Christmas Eve—a sentimental ending to a stormy scenario.

In Maria Riva's biography of her mother, Marlene Dietrich, the author includes only a few casual references to Claudette, but not in connection with Dietrich. She recalls sneaking onto the *Cleopatra* set and attending a party where Claudette and Maurice Chevalier were engaged in "a charming tête à tête." Riva describes a new governess as "not a spinster version of Claudette Colbert—if there ever was such a thing as a Colbert with overtones of spinsterhood." She also enumerates her mother's lovers, more male (John Gilbert, Brian Aherne, Ronald Colman, Richard Barthelmess, Erich Maria Remarque, Yul Brynner, Edward R. Murrow) than female (Mercedes deAcosta and, perhaps, Colette, whom Dietrich found " 'wonderful!' "). Although it is true that Claudette was still living at the time of the book's publication, and the lovers Riva enumerated had died, Riva does not even suggest that Dietrich and Claudette socialized. Riva understood her mother better than any of Dietrich's other biographers. Dietrich was a thorough romantic, obsessed with the same gauzy idea of *grand amour* that the movies of her era immortalized with their luminously white bedrooms and phones, satin peignoirs, inviting chaises lounges, and ethereal lighting: "But all Dietrich ever wanted, needed, desired, was Romance with every capital R available . . . and accepted the accompanying sex as the inescapable burden women had to endure." While Claudette was also a romantic, she had no intention of being encumbered by the burden of sex and preferred to hear about the liaisons of others, as if they were plot points in a film that she would shoot in her imagination, freeing her from having to consummate what others had done for her.

Another cause of the stigma, which was more like a spreading stain, was her relationship with artist Verna Hull, whom she met in the late 1950s. Hull, who was ten years younger than Claudette, began exhibiting in New York, in the mid 1950s; her first show was at the Circulating Library of Painting on East Seventy-second Street on Friday, 28 October 1955. The *New York Times* review remarked on the "evanescent charm" of Hull's work, with its "pretty and feminine" colors, but found most of it unsubstantial. By 1962, her paintings were on display at the Monede Gallery on Madison Avenue. Later, she turned to abstract expressionism, at which she excelled, according to Arnold Scaasi, who saw some of her paintings when he visited her in Barbados, much to Claudette's chagrin. The proverbial best-friend relationship between Claudette and Hull, so intense that the financially independent Hull took a house next door to Claudette and Pressman's in Barbados, deteriorated to the point that Claudette had a fence erected between their properties.

But in the late 1950s and early '60s, Claudette and Hull became, in the gossip column idiom, an item. The stigma resurfaced, and the stain began to spread. Verna Hull was another Eve Harrington—the sycophant who ingratiated herself into Margo Channing's graces in *All About Eve*—becoming a combination social secretary and confidante, then Margo's understudy, and finally the lead in the play that was to have been Margo's next vehicle.

There are subtle lesbianic overtones in Anne Baxter's performance as Eve, who weaves a web of seduction, figuratively, around Margo, whose shadow she becomes, and, literally, around the playwright, Lloyd Richards, whose marriage she intends to break up, even though it was his wife who introduced her to Margo. There is a rather explicit scene, at least by 1950s standards, in which Eve asks a young woman in her rooming house to phone Richards, claiming that Eve is in a state of acute depression brought on by the imminent out-of-town tryout of his new play, in which she is starring. When Richards promises to come over, the young woman hangs up. Eve is seen standing near the phone, and triumphantly the two of them walk up the stairs with their arms around each other's waist.

Claudette obviously saw *All about Eve*, but she would not have been so naive about Hull if she had played Margo. If Hull had courted Bette Davis as she did Claudette, Davis would have sensed another Eve Harrington, and that would have been the end of a relationship that was destined for the ash heap of misbegotten friendships.

Claudette's closest relationships were with women. She was raised in a matriarchal household, where she enjoyed the affection of her grandmother and Tantine, who compensated for her mother's indifference to her talent, but not her paycheck. She went to Washington Irving when it was an all-girls high school; although we know nothing about her circle of friends there, she was active in student government and appeared in at least two of the stage productions. It was also a woman, playwright Anne Morrison, who was responsible for her Broadway debut.

To Claudette, women were non-threatening. With women, she did not have to worry about getting her bottom pinched, being propositioned, groped after a take, or subjected to simulated erections during a shoot. Her best friends were women: Edith Goetz, the wife of producer William Goetz; singer-actor Kitty Carlisle Hart, with whom she frequently went swimming; and designer Sophie Gimbel, the wife of Saks cofounder Adam Gimbel. Fashion designers, whether they were men (Travis Banton, Bill Blass, Arnold Scaasi) or women (such as Sophie Gimbel, but not Edith Head, who disliked her), became part of her circle.

Sophie had been dubbed "Sophie of Saks," who ordered clothes from the leading Paris designers, which she featured, along with her own creations, at her Salon Moderne at Saks Fifth Avenue. When World War II prevented her from buying Paris originals, Sophie marketed her own line and did so even after the war ended. If Claudette looked especially chic in her last film, *Parrish*, it was because Sophie had designed her wardrobe.

Although Helen O'Hagan was vice president of Public Relations at Saks, she also had a keen sense of fashion and was a lifelong friend of Bill Blass. Rosalind Russell, who also reveled in designer clothes (although her favorite was James Galanos), was the one actress to whom Claudette remained close during her Hollywood years. Russell, taller than Claudette, was the screen's definitive career woman, in pin-striped or tailored suits that broadened her shoulders and defined the contours of her body and, for evening wear, a shimmering creation that fell in folds or a strapless gown with a hint of décolletage. Claudette's wardrobe was more feminine; Russell's, more professional and often, as in *Auntie Mame* and *Gypsy*, more flamboyant.

Claudette and Russell met while they were both on loan at Fox, shooting their one and only movie together, *Under Two Flags* (1936). Russell and her husband, producer Fred Brisson, and Claudette and Pressman often socialized and were frequent guests on Frank Sinatra's yacht at a time when Sinatra was trying to refurbish his image by consorting with respectable Hollywood couples. Had Sinatra believed any of the rumors about Claudette—which during her Hollywood years circulated only among closet gays who enjoyed embellishing myths until they took on the gaudy palette of Technicolor—he certainly would have chosen another couple. But he enjoyed Claudette for her vivacity and Russell for her wit. The three of them also had Catholicism in common, but in varying degrees. Russell was a practicing Catholic, while Claudette was a meditative one, dropping by at St. Vincent Ferrer and attending an occasional Sunday Mass when she was in New York; Sinatra was a lapsed Catholic until he wanted to marry Barbara Marx. Then he managed to get an annulment from his first wife and shortly thereafter was seen taking communion at

St. Patrick's Cathedral. When Sinatra staged a twenty-fifth anniversary celebration in Las Vegas for Russell and Brisson, Claudette and Pressman were invited, and Claudette and Russell reminisced about making *Under Two Flags.*

In one way, it was amazing that Claudette sustained a friendship with Russell, since she was always wary of other actresses. It was not that she feared competition, which did not exist, since no other actress in Hollywood had the effervescence of champagne and looked as if she should never drink it except in a fluted glass. It was that she preferred the company of women, who, like Russell, were not part of Hollywood, but just worked there. Her other close Hollywood friend was Edith Goetz, the daughter of MGM tycoon Louis Mayer. Although Edith married producer William Goetz, she never coveted the high profile of her sister, theatrical agent Irene Selznick. Women such as Gimbel, Russell, Goetz, and O'Hagan gave her security. Men like Fredric March and Ray Milland, both of whom found her desirable, were unable to separate the woman from the actress. The actress could muster the sensuality a love scene needed and looked as if she enjoyed the kiss, the embrace, or the mere physical proximity to a man. No doubt Claudette did; but she did not carry the scene over into a real-life relationship with the actor who had just made love to her. Gable may have been the exception, but even there one strongly suspects that Claudette was alternately coy and aloof on the set, as the crew of *It Happened One Night* admitted, and that Gable's inability to decode the ambivalent signals she was transmitting so frustrated him that Claudette, probably out of sheer glee at having gotten the best of the sexiest actor on the screen, finally yielded. Playwright Leonard Gershe was probably correct when he claimed that "Claudette liked to flirt with men, but she liked women for companionship. . . . [She] was always curious about everyone else's sex life. But for her it was like listening to fairy tales. I wondered whether it wasn't to compensate for the fact that there was really nothing going on in her own life." Her true love was Norman Foster; Pressman was the male companion of her dreams, unthreatening, undemanding, and unwilling to interfere with her career even when it took her to New York for extended periods of time. Having his own career, he had no need to bask in the reflected glory of hers.

It is true that Claudette was comfortable among gay males in the arts because she enjoyed being around witty men and could exchange barbs and trade gossip with the best of them. With Claudette, the parlor was a salon at which she presided, where guests such as Noël Coward, William Haines, Robert Shaw, Arnold Scaasi, Bill Blass, and George Cukor turned into conversationalists; and their conversations, into dialogue. For Claudette, artifice was all, especially when she was holding court.

It was her sense of beauty, both in life and in art, that drew men and women to her. She may not have understood what an aesthetic sense is, but she possessed it, revealing it whenever she decorated an apartment and especially when she looked at the blueprints of the old Bellerive and immediately saw how it could be restored to its former glory. Of course, Claudette knew Haines was gay. But he was creative, and she wanted him to design her bedroom in her Fairing Road home. Even Bellerive has a Haines touch: a lamp with a curved Lucite stand opposite a table designed by Oliver Messel, which faced an upholstered chair with one of Claudette's needlepoint pillows. Haines remained a close friend. But there were others who wanted to make her part of their circle and turn her into a gay icon; in the process, they sullied her reputation—although they would have argued otherwise—by declaring her a Hollywood lesbian, whose relationships, covert and otherwise, were with women.

"If Claudette were a lesbian, don't you think I would have known it?" Helen O'Hagan exclaimed, noting that the rumor was double-edged and cut into her life as well. Helen O'Hagan presents a no-nonsense image; she does not suffer fools and is willing to talk with writers who can establish their credibility by providing samples of their work. She is the self-designated keeper of the flame, maintaining a personal archive consisting of memories, photos, and an exchange of letters between Claudette and Pressman that will be available only after her death. The past meant little to Claudette. She discarded her scripts, except, for some reason, the bound one of *The Egg and I*. When she tired of clothes, they went to the thrift shop, as if she knew that fashion, like fame, is ever changing; and should the same styles return, they will never be exactly what they were. It was that subtle change of pattern or blend of color that made the difference between the old and the new. And why keep the old if you could afford the new?

Claudette considered television writer Robert Shaw a friend; Shaw wrote "After All These Years," in which she appeared on *Robert Montgomery Presents* (24 September 1954). Claudette enjoyed the experience, even though the plot, which centered around a woman whose husband had disappeared, made no demands on her. However, Shaw seems to have been the one who originated the rumor that with Pressman's death, Claudette instructed her staff and friends to think of O'Hagan as her "spouse." And so the same writer who made much of Claudette's slacks at Carole Lombard's 1935 party claims that Claudette "came out . . . as a lesbian upon her husband's death in 1968."

O'Hagan scoffs at the idea that Claudette would have told anyone to regard her as a "husband," just on the basis of Claudette's frequent Bellerive guests: Rex Harrison, former New York governor Averell Harriman and his wife, Pamela, William F. Buckley Jr., Anthony Eden, Lillian Hellman, Frank Sinatra, Kitty Carlisle Hart, Brooke Astor, Joan Collins, and Dominick Dunne.

If Ronald Reagan thought that there was any stigma attached to Claudette, he would never have remained such a close friend, particularly during his presidency. Claudette merits seven entries in Reagan's *Diaries*. After a performance of *Sugar Babies* in March 1981 with Mickey Rooney and Ann Miller, the Reagans and several of their friends, including Claudette, went on to dinner. Reagan made it a point to see her when she was appearing in *The Kingfisher* and *Aren't We All?* Except for one occasion, the Reagans stayed at Bellerive when they visited Barbados. However, in April 1982, Reagan had become so outspoken about Cuba's attempt to spread Communism throughout the Caribbean that, for security purposes, the Reagans were housed elsewhere on the island. Since the Reagans had no intention of missing one of Claudette's legendary dinners, they were transported by helicopter to Bellerive. "Miss Colbert's got a good cook," a spokesperson explained.

Claudette was also a frequent guest at the White House. In fact, she was a "special guest" at a 1985 Christmas Day celebration, which Reagan described as "a fun time & Claudette was wonderful as always." The guest list for a 1987 state dinner for Soviet leader Mikhail Gorbachev included Billy Graham, James Stewart, Pearl Bailey, and Claudette. Claudette was an asset at a dinner party. Whoever sat next to or across from her never had to worry about making conversation. Claudette knew how to get the reticent to talk.

Until Claudette's stroke, O'Hagan was just another guest at Bellerive. In New York, O'Hagan and Claudette did not live together; they lived in the same Fifth Avenue apartment house, right opposite Central Park: Claudette on the tenth floor and O'Hagan on the eighth. In fact, it was O'Hagan who alerted her to a vacancy in the building when Claudette was looking for an apartment after she decided to give up the one she had taken next to Hull's.

The only possible explanation for the "husband" myth is that Claudette explained to one of her Barbadian servants, who never met O'Hagan, that she was to be treated with the same respect that they had accorded Pressman. It is impossible that O'Hagan would have been introduced to the Reagans and the Harrimans as Claudette's husband! Unfortunately, the wrong kind of person was given information that lent itself not just to rumor, but rumor converted to fact, with only hearsay and conjecture as evidence. And so Claudette became the lover of two of Hollywood's superstars, Greta Garbo and Marlene Dietrich, who were, reportedly, Verna Hull's lovers; thus, Hull's old flames became Claudette's. It was not so much guilt, as sex, by association.

Claudette hardly knew Garbo. They were at two different studios: Garbo was at MGM. Although Garbo may have been attracted to Claudette's sensuousness, she could never have understood that what she considered sensuous—a body language suggesting an eagerness to partake of every pleasure the flesh has to offer—was, to Claudette, merely an expression of an unquenchable joy of living, which circulated throughout her body, much to the puzzlement of those who assumed she was "on the town," the euphemism for "available." All Claudette really wanted was to enjoy herself and then retire for the evening.

Three months before Claudette's death, *Vanity Fair* published a list of the answers she gave to its Proust Questionnaire: To the question, "What is your greatest fear?" she answered, "Being alone."

The fulfillment—or, to put it bluntly, sex—was not what Claudette was seeking in either women or men. Verna Hull brought out the girl that Claudette once was, who envisioned a career as an artist or designer. She had never met someone with whom she could paint; it was art, in addition to Hull's adulation, which Claudette could not resist (what actress could?), that brought them together. Painting with Hull brought back her girlhood and at the same time made her feel like the star she was, as Hull ran errands for her, doted on her, and became her chauffeur, even though Claudette was an excellent driver. Claudette was also an outstanding painter. Displayed prominently on the wall of O'Hagan's apartment is Claudette's portrait of Deborah Kerr's daughter that was once exhibited at the Country Art Gallery in Westbury, Long Island. The girl has a pensive, but not vacant, look; her unfocused eyes are those of a dreamer, oblivious to what she sees around her because she is caught up in her own reverie. Claudette has exquisitely captured the look of a child in her own world, perhaps because she had the same look at that age.

Rumors meant nothing to Claudette; she delighted in Hull's company, and when they were together, Claudette behaved as if she were a teenager back at the Art Students League who discovered her first artist-friend. If she rushed headlong into a relationship with Hull, it was part of her greatest fear: being alone. And in the mid 1950s, she would have been in New York without her husband. But more important, Claudette had returned to a profession that she had abandoned in 1929: stage acting. If Hull assuaged her anxieties and dispelled the loneliness, she more than served her purpose. But it was for the short term. Whether Hull considered Claudette a future conquest or a fellow artist is unimportant. Claudette was reliving her girlhood: she had a girl friend.

They found two penthouse apartments on the same floor in a building on East Sixty-fourth Street, not that far from the one in which Claudette first lived when she came to the States. Claudette never believed there would even be a breath of scandal. In 1960, she told Lyn Tornabene of *Cosmopolitan* that she had taken a five-year lease on apartment across the hall from that of "her closest friend, painter Verna Hull, [whose] apartment is the first one Claudette ever helped to decorate." At the time, Claudette only knew that she had a kindred spirit, a woman, who shared her love of art. Throughout her life, Claudette looked for women to fill the void left by Tantine and her grandmother, who had given her the affection that her own mother did not. And once Claudette became a star, it was not just affection; it was also respect, an awareness that she was an artist who mastered her craft and expected recognition for it, from her friends as well as peers.

When Claudette moved to Barbados, so did Hull, taking a house next to hers. Pressman hated Hull, and so did Marie Corbin, Claudette's Barbadian housekeeper. Claudette hoped to limit their painting sessions, until Pressman demanded that she rid herself of the "monster," a term that Claudette soon adopted. It is difficult to know if Claudette was following her husband's mandate or if she, too, had sensed an unhealthy possessiveness. At any rate, a fence, and later a wall, went up between their properties, but that did not stop Hull from spying on her lost friend. Hull told everyone she knew about the end of what should have been a perfect friendship, including Britain's first transsexual, April Ashley, when Ashley visited Barbados.

What Hull did not tell Ashley was the reason for the dissolution of their friendship. O'Hagan informed Amy Fine Collins, when Collins was researching her 1998 *Vanity Fair* article on Claudette, that when Hull learned that Pressman was dying, she sent word to Claudette that he "might . . . kill her and possibly himself too, in order to take her with him when he died." If this was Hull's attempt to restore a friendship that had become so frayed that it was unraveling, Claudette pulled that string that reduced it to a spool of yarn.

"Claudette never had a sexual relationship with a woman," O'Hagan insists. She was the victim of misinterpretation, wishful thinking, and guilt by association.

CHAPTER 16

Slow Fade to Black

The Irregular Verb to Love closed in December 1963 after 115 performances. Claudette hoped it would have a longer run, but the play paid the price for opening early in a season that, while not particularly distinguished (the main attractions were Carol Channing in *Hello, Dolly!* and Barbra Streisand in *Funny Girl*), included two comedies that proved hugely popular: *Barefoot in the Park* and *Any Wednesday*. Still, it lasted longer than *Julia, Jake and Uncle Joe*, and even though none of her other plays would equal the run of *The Marriage-Go-Round*, she at least knew she could attract an audience—admittedly, smaller than it was in her glory days—on the basis of her name, even if the vehicles were slight.

Since there were no further prospects in New York, Claudette returned to Barbados. Bellerive had been restored to her satisfaction, and she looked forward to semi-retirement, never total, because she knew she would be an actress to the very end. In the *Vanity Fair* questionnaire (April 1996), Claudette—then a stroke victim a few months away from death—answered the question, "What is your greatest regret?" with "At the moment, not to be working."

Joel Pressman, on the other hand, looked forward to *complete* retirement. He could not wait to plant a vegetable garden and simply enjoy the good life. In late 1967, he returned to Los Angeles to wind up his affairs at UCLA Medical Center, where he had been chief of the division of head and neck surgery. He experienced a sharp pain in his side that grew steadily worse. The diagnosis was grim: liver cancer. Knowing that it was inoperable, Pressman flew back to Barbados to spend his remaining time with Claudette. When it became evident that the cancer had metastasized, Claudette phoned Frank Sinatra, who agreed to fly Pressman back to UCLA Medical Center on his private jet. Although Sinatra may have seemed a strange choice, he genuinely enjoyed Claudette's company, and she felt similarly about his. But it was also important for Sinatra to refurbish his "rat pack" image by socializing with respectable couples, so theirs was a relationship based as much on mutual affection (and in Sinatra's case, admiration) and expediency (on Sinatra's part). But Claudette, who did not want to be indebted to anyone, insisted on paying for the trip, and Helen O'Hagan has the cancelled check to prove it. The end came quickly; Pressman, then only sixty-seven, died on 26 February 1968 at UCLA Medical Center. A memorial service was conducted two days later at the Pierce Bros. Beverly Hills Chapel; and the body was flown back to Barbados for burial. Knowing of her husband's aversion to inhumation, Claudette arranged for his body to be entombed in the Parish of St. Peter Cemetery in Barbados, within walking distance of Bellerive. The same mausoleum also contains the remains of Claudette's mother and herself.

Two years later Jeanne Chauchoin died, and on 31 March 1971, her brother Charles suffered a fatal heart attack while vacationing in Florida. Claudette was now completely alone. To assuage her loneliness, she became the hostess of Bellerive, which at times was more of a salon with guest rooms. She would fret if a day went by without guests, and it was not uncommon for some of them to look upon Bellerive as a resort. Claudette would continue to entertain until her death, but she also knew that when the guests left and she had to face an empty house, there was still the void that no amount of socializing could fill.

Although they made only one film together, Claudette and George Cukor were longtime friends. Cukor knew how shattered he was by his mother's death of stomach cancer in 1936. He did not so much love Helena Cukor as adore her. And yet he knew the only anodyne for grief was work, which at least can consume the days, thereby making the nights more bearable. Although Cukor made no films in 1937, he had two in release in 1938: *Holiday* and *Zaza*.

On 6 May, three months after Pressman's death, Cukor wrote to Claudette about his progress in securing the rights from Columbia for a television remake of *Ladies in Retirement,* which he conceived as a starring vehicle for her. Claudette was excited about the prospect of teaming up with her friend, especially in the role in which Ida Lupino gave such a powerful performance in 1941. Although Claudette was now sixty-five, as opposed to Lupino, who was twenty-seven (but looked older) when she made the film, she could still pass for a middle-aged woman. In *Ladies in Retirement,* the main character (a housekeeper who kills her employer to make room for her two retarded sisters) is of indeterminate age.

In June, Cukor was optimistic: "DEAREST CLAUDETTE BASIC AGREEMENT REACHED ACQUISITION LADIES FINAL DETAILS TO BE WORKED OUT IN FEW DAYS LOVE GEORGE." By August 12, the scenario had changed. Columbia was unwilling to part with the rights, claiming that if the *Ladies* remake proved successful, the stockholders would wonder why the studio relinquished the rights when it had a television unit, Screen Gems, which would have been a logical choice—except that Cukor was thinking of a major network like ABC or NBC, not Screen Gems, where he could not be assured of the same quality.

Claudette was disappointed, and in an undated letter on blue stationery she unburdened herself to Cukor:

> I get offers for guest spots (another one to-day) but they make me shudder—the same old crap—and, also, now even older!!
>
> My dearest Jack is finally at rest in the prettiest spot (only a short walk from our house) and I pray he would like it. I realize more and more

how blessed I was to have had all my friends around me these last months. I've had some bad bad moments since my return here—but it was inevitable—all his clothes and all the gadgets he loved to tinker with—and unfinished lists we'd saved for him to do when he retired in June—but I'm keeping busy.

Claudette may not have been hurting financially, but she was not generating anything near the income that came in during her period of stardom. She had expensive but not extravagant taste; while she thought nothing of preparing her own breakfast and washing the breakfast dishes, she had definite ideas about the luncheon and dinner menus, especially when there were guests. The upkeep on Bellerive was not as high as it was on Fairing Road, but she now had a larger staff: her housekeeper, Marie; her cook, Beulah; and servants. Perhaps out of a combination of aimlessness and nostalgia, she found a pied-à-terre in Paris but did not make frequent use of it.

Since she had become a non-resident of the United States, she could only spend six months there: "It's an idiotic law as I see it—because I pay full Federal Income Tax anyway—and avoid State Tax—and probably if I shoot a film in California, I'll have to pay California tax." In 1974 she told a journalist: " 'I pay full federal taxes. I consider myself a Barbadian. . . . You know you have a permanent residence and a legal residence. My legal residence is the Chase Manhattan Bank.' "

In 1970, Claudette was hoping to return to Broadway, even as a replacement. In 1967, the *Hollywood Reporter* and the *New York Times* ran stories about Rosalind Russell's return to Broadway in the musical *Coco*, produced by her husband, Fred Brisson. Although Claudette would have been perfect in the role of the legendary French couturière, Gabrielle "Coco" Chanel, Russell, despite a mastectomy, was still hoping to appear in another musical, thus proving that her success in Leonard Bernstein's *Wonderful Town* was not a fluke. Brisson expected composer André Previn and lyricist Alan Jay Lerner to come up with the same kind of score that Bernstein, Betty Comden, and Adolph Green created in *Wonderful Town*: one that played to Russell's musical strengths, which consisted of a few good notes, so that at least some numbers were singable, with the others rendered as speech-song, with Russell speaking the lyrics rhythmically and singing an occasional phrase.

When Lerner realized the score that Previn had composed, and the book and lyrics that he had written, were unsuited to Russell's performance style, he informed Brisson, who was profoundly disappointed. Russell probably was, too, although she gave no inkling of it. Claudette was not mentioned among Brisson's other choices, which included Julie Christie and Melina Mercouri, neither of whom remotely resembled Chanel. Claudette's name could attract audiences for a non-musical, but not a big-budget production like *Coco*. But Katharine Hepburn—who by the time *Coco* opened in December 1969 had won her third Oscar for *A Lion in Winter* (1968)—could. Hepburn was even less of a singer than Russell, but she made it possible for a musical that received mixed reviews to turn a profit. Hepburn did not so much resort to speak-song as declamation. If she were delivering the lyrics in French, it would sound like an exaggerated version of Racine at the Comédie-Française. However, when Claudette read in the *New York Times* (18 March 1970) that Brisson and Lerner were seeking a replacement for Hepburn, who was leaving the show at the end of July 1970, and were considering Danielle Darrieux, Jeanmarie, Lilli Palmer, Margaret Leighton, and herself, Claudette believed she had a chance. At least she could sing what Hepburn declaimed in a hybrid form of *Sprechgesang* and patter. Claudette contacted her close friend Kitty Carlisle Hart and began taking voice lessons with her. Hart recalled that she had "a beautiful mezzo voice," which should come as no surprise to anyone who remembered her singing in *Torch Singer* and *Zaza*.

Hepburn's replacement, however, turned out to be French actress Danielle Darrieux, who had studied voice at the Paris Conservatory and gave Previn and Lerner's score the musicality that Hepburn could not: "For the first time, one hears the entire score impeccably sung," critic Mel Gussow noted. Darrieux was also an authentic Chanel, unlike Hepburn, who played the part as if the character were a transplanted Yankee. Claudette could also have given a distinctly French coloring to the songs. Besides, Claudette looked like Chanel. But despite her fine reviews, Darrieux was not a big enough draw, and *Coco* ended its run on 3 October 1970. Later Hepburn toured with it, and the grosses increased.

It was not until 1974 that Claudette returned to the stage, from which she had been absent for ten years. The reason was not so much money as her desire to refurbish her star persona for those who thought that she had fallen into a black hole. *Coco* would have been perfect; it would have done for Claudette what *Wonderful Town* did for Rosalind Russell: reveal an entirely new dimension of her talent, so that for the first time audiences would see Claudette Colbert not as a movie star but as a singing actress. The comeback vehicle had to be right; if not a musical, then a comedy of manners, so audiences could see the Claudette of the silver screen, with her sunrise smile, lyrical voice, and a wardrobe that Claudette and her character could wear, since by then the person, the persona, and the character were identical.

Claudette thought that she had found the right property in Jerome Chodorov's *A Community of Two*, as the divorced mother of a Harvard undergraduate who accidentally locks herself out of her apartment on the night of a major winter storm and turns for help to the occupant of the apartment next door, a distinguished middle-aged man. If nothing else, the plot had an unusual "meet cute." Chodorov and Joseph Fields wrote the play *My Sister Eileen* (1940), which became a profitable Columbia film two years later, bringing Rosalind Russell her first Oscar nomination; the team was recruited again to create the book for the Broadway musical version of *My Sister Eileen*, *Wonderful Town* (1953), in which Russell's leading man was George Gaynes, a baritone with matinee idol looks.

Twenty years later, Gaynes still cut a handsome figure and would be a perfect costar for Claudette in *A Community of Two*. Born in Finland, fluent in French, and thoroughly continental, Gaynes could match Claudette in sophistication and wit, which is exactly what the play required. It seemed perfect casting and was; the play, however, was far from perfect. The producers believed that *A Community of Two* should tour before coming to Broadway.

After opening in Wilmington, Delaware, in March 1974, the company moved on to St. Louis, Missouri, and then Los Angeles. The opening night curtain went up a half hour late because of an accident that occurred when Claudette was brewing tea in her dressing room:

> As she was trying to relax in her dressing room . . . half hour to curtain, the stage manager made a mistake in time. . . . Claudette sprang up from that deep chair on the thick wide top of which she had balanced the hot water kettle for her tea. The kettle tipped down the chair and poured boiling water down her derrière. . . . Doctor was called, curtain delayed, Claudette managed to get dressed and was ready to go on with only a half hour's delay on the curtain. Now in the middle of the first act she is compelled by the script to accomplish a complete change of clothes in a sleeping bag, in the middle of the stage. Undeterred, she did it. That for me goes into the annals of courage and endurance on stage. She healed well, and she never missed a show.

Rarely did a cast member speak ill of Claudette. If the *Julia, Jake, and Uncle Joe* company found her obsession with her face and wardrobe irksome, it was because she realized she was in a preordained flop, although she never expected it to be so short-lived. Gaynes, like most of the others, held her in the greatest respect: "Another example of her gallantry was when in St. Louis, Missouri, the management announced that we were henceforth on half pay . . . and that included our star. Claudette promptly invited all to a party on a riverboat, where we all had a great time, and got some consolation for our restricted incomes."

A Community of Two never reached New York. Claudette, however, was not discouraged. At least it was not a disaster like *Julia, Jake, and Uncle Joe*. There would be other plays, she reasoned. Besides, she was only seventy-one.

" 'It's difficult to find roles at my age,' Miss Colbert says. She is lowering her voice and widening her eyes, and it is hard to know what she means." Claudette, then seventy-five, knew exactly what she meant, even though her interviewer thought she looked no different than she did in *It Happened One Night*. Claudette's problem was not age, but audience. In 1978, she had been absent from the New York stage since the 1963–64 season and had made her last film in 1961. When she returned in *The Kingfisher* in 1978, it was to a radically different Broadway. *Hair* had ushered in the rock musical and literally made nudity *au naturel*. "Fuck," once the ultimate taboo word uttered only off Broadway, and then selectively, went mainstream in Lillian Hellman's *My Mother, My Father, and Me*. And soon it became part of the theatre's standard vocabulary, used by Edward Albee, Paul Zindel, Peter Shaffer, and Howard Davies, among others. "Shit," on the other hand, was a mild expletive. Even Katharine Hepburn said it in *Coco*, but only once; later, so did Claudette in *A Talent for Murder*.

In the late 1960s and throughout the 1970s, former movie stars were good for at least limited runs, attracting primarily those eager to see their old icons in person. Katharine Hepburn followed her success in *Coco* with Enid Bagnold's enigmatic *A Matter of Gravity* and the far better *West Side Waltz*. When Julie Harris left *Forty Carats*, June Allyson, who, like Claudette, seemed ageless, stepped into the role and miraculously transformed the Morosco theater into a soundstage with her twinkling eyes, girl-next-door smile, and deliciously husky, cream-coated voice that evoked memories of her MGM days.

In June 1978, when Rex Harrison and Claudette were announced as the stars of William Douglas Home's *The Kingfisher* in the roles created by Ralph Richardson and Celia Johnson, his name preceded hers in the ads and in the program. Apart from Harrison's being the bigger part, to theatregoers he was the bigger draw. Like Henry Fonda, Harrison enjoyed a bicoastal career, alternating between Hollywood and Broadway. Two years after making his American film debut in Fox's *Anna and the King of Siam* (1946), he was starring on Broadway in Maxwell Anderson's *Anne of the Thousand Days* (1948), followed by *Bell, Book, and Candle* (1950) with his then wife, Lilli Palmer, who also costarred with him in *Venice Observed* (1952) and *The Love of Four Colonels* (1953). While Harrison and Palmer were not quite

Alfred Lunt and Lynn Fontanne, they specialized in the same kind of civilized comedy and had mastered the art of turning dialogue into aphorisms.

If there is one Broadway show for which Harrison will always be remembered, it is *My Fair Lady* (1956), which netted him his second Tony award (his first was for *Anne of the Thousand Days*); the 1964 film version brought him his only Oscar. Claudette's Oscar was by then thirty years old. When *The Kingfisher* opened, Harrison deserved first billing if, for no other reason, the phenomenal success of *My Fair Lady* (the play and the film), in which his Henry Higgins became the standard against which subsequent interpretations would be judged. Harrison's was a familiar name to theatergoers. After *My Fair Lady*, he appeared regularly in New York, if not always in smash hits, then in enough respectable productions (*The Fighting Cock* [1959], Pirandello's *Henry IV* [1973], Terence Rattigan's *In Praise of Love* [1974], and Shaw's *Caesar and Cleopatra* [1977]) to legitimize his credentials as a stage actor. Harrison had also not abandoned film; after the movie version of *My Fair Lady* (1964), he appeared in *The Agony and the Ecstasy* (1965), *Doctor Doolittle* (1967), and *The Yellow Rolls-Royce* (1967) and continued to make movies until 1986, four years before his death. He ended his career in his favorite medium, theatre. Harrison's final New York appearance was in a revival of W. Somerset Maugham's *The Circle* in 1989. Within two weeks of its closing on 20 May 1990, Harrison died. Rex Harrison was truly a creature of the stage. Even in 1978, there was no doubt that Harrison was the star of *The Kingfisher*; and Claudette, the ex-movie star making one of her infrequent returns to Broadway, where she began at a time so enshrouded in mist that few even remembered that she was a stage star before she entered the movies.

Neither Harrison nor Claudette was originally slated for the New York production, which was scheduled to open on 6 December 1978. The producers, Elliot Martin and Hank Shimberg, had hoped that Richardson and Johnson would reprise their roles. Johnson, however, was reluctant to come to New York; she had not been on Broadway since 1931 when she played Ophelia to Raymond Massey's Hamlet. Richardson refused to play opposite anyone else, even though he continued to cross the Atlantic after his Broadway debut as Mercutio opposite Katharine Cornell's Juliet and Maurice Evans's Romeo in 1935. World War II prevented his returning until 1946 in the Old Vic's productions of *Henry IV* (both parts) as Falstaff, *Uncle Vanya*, *Oedipus Rex*, and *The Critic*. He returned to New York three more times in Jean Anouilh's *The Waltz of the Toreadors* (1957), David Storey's *Home* (1970), and Harold Pinter's *No Man's Land* (1976). But *The Kingfisher* was a special play, and Richardson knew he achieved a rapport with Johnson that could never be repeated with another actress. So the roles went to Harrison and Claudette by default.

Even if Richardson agreed to perform without Johnson and with Claudette, their styles would never have meshed. Richardson was a superb character actor, overshadowed by Laurence Olivier and John Gielgud, both of whom lacked his range but possessed either a stunning technique that passed for acting (Olivier) or a liquid voice (Gielgud) that made music out of words. Richardson was not a matinee idol type like Harrison, nor did Celia Johnson possess Claudette's sparkle and wit. Johnson is best remembered as Laura Jesson, the plain British homemaker in David Lean's *Brief Encounter* (1946), yearning for an extramarital romance to make her drab existence bearable. Thus, when Johnson performed *The Kingfisher* in London, she brought an air of ruefulness to the play, even though it is nominally a comedy about a man and a woman who were once in love with each other (or at least the woman was in love with the man) and are about to meet for the first time in fifty years.

Harrison and Claudette approached the roles quite differently. At first, it seemed odd casting—at least Harrison thought so. In his autobiography, *A Damned Serious Business*, Harrison claimed that he "had the idea of asking the famous Hollywood star Claudette Colbert" to appear opposite him. It is hard to believe that was the case; it would have made more sense for Harrison to choose a British actress such as Joan Greenwood, Margaret Lockwood, Glynis Johns, or Coral Browne as his costar. Harrison was the quintessentially British actor. When Claudette played comedy, it was with a Gallic worldliness that masqueraded as deliberate coyness conveyed by a knowing glance, an inflection, or a look of amused skepticism. One could imagine how Claudette would have played Ellie in a French *It Happened One Night* opposite Jean Gabin's Peter Warne.

Although Harrison claimed he was delighted to be working with Claudette, his biographer, Alexander Walker, believed otherwise after speaking with the play's director, Lindsay Anderson: "But when Claudette Colbert was proposed as his co-star, he looked wary. . . . She was likely to play Rex for every point in the game." Harrison knew that while he had the superior reputation as a stage actor, she was a Hollywood legend. Would audiences be coming to see Henry Higgins or Ellie Andrews? Claudette was equally wary of Harrison, a stage icon and Tony award winner, while she was only a Tony nominee.

The rehearsals were not easy. At one point, Harrison turned on her, shouting, "You're not going to talk like that when we do the play, are you?" "She's going to ruin it," he railed at Anderson. Claudette said nothing, letting Harrison fume until his anger subsided and the rehearsal resumed. But after the play opened, and Claudette missed a few performances because of illness, Harrison was frantic; he had grown accustomed to her face, her timing, and her line readings. " 'Get Claudette back at once,' he snapped." The producer Elliot Martin had flowers sent to her and even cajoled Harrison into writing a personal note: "Hope you'll get back soon."

The Kingfisher is a slight three-character, two-act comedy, even less substantial than *The Irregular Verb to Love*, which at least was sufficiently complicated to sustain interest over three acts. Written in clipped, pithy dialogue, *The Kingfisher* is a typical British comedy of manners, a cross between Noël Coward and Somerset Maugham but not as clever as either *Private Lives* or *The Constant Wife*. The opening scene is pure exposition, in which we learn that the eminent author Sir Cecil Warburton (Harrison) is expecting a visit from his first love, Lady Evelyn Townsend (Claudette). The occasion has more potential than Home extracts from it: Evelyn is returning from her husband's funeral, and Cecil's estate is on the way. Since the text makes it clear that Cecil and Evelyn almost became lovers fifty years earlier when he stole a kiss under a beech tree, Harrison and Claudette could play their own age, even though Harrison was younger by five years. While Harrison did not have Claudette's brand of agelessness, he had the same kind of masculine urbanity that Cary Grant, David Niven, and Brian Aherne did—the kind that did not diminish with time because theirs emanated from within before it was enhanced by the usual accoutrements of costume, makeup, and hairstyle.

With Evelyn's arrival, the play turns into a "will they or won't they?" But will they or won't they do *what*? Have an affair or marry? So much depends upon the direction. At the end of act 2, scene 1, Evelyn decides to spend the night at Cecil's home, but in the guest room. After retiring, she calls down for a hot water bottle, to which Cecil obligingly replies, "I'll bring one up, old girl." CURTAIN.

One will never know what transpired between the first and second scenes, except that Cecil's butler, Hawkins (George Rose), admits to having already placed a hot water bottle in Evelyn's bed. So much also depends upon the director's conception of the piece and the actors' ability to explore the play's subtext rather than adhere to a literal interpretation, which only teases without providing a payoff. The ending is similarly unresolved, unless the final scene is played with an air of hopefulness. The title refers to an elusive bird that symbolizes the evanescence of love— something to be caught before it flies away. But since the kingfisher artfully avoids capture, it remains a symbol of the unattainable, something to be pursued but never caged, like love that resists the confinements of convention. In the play's final moments, Evelyn and Cecil both admit to having spotted the kingfisher. Evelyn asks Cecil for his binoculars:

CECIL: Why?
EVELYN: We might find the kingfisher again. (*She goes—he follows.*)
THE CURTAIN FALLS.

Having seen the London production (but not the Broadway one), I can brush the dust from my memory and report that Richardson and Johnson gave the *The Kingfisher* far greater depth than the text implied. Their acting styles were compatible; Richardson and Johnson had worked together in two films: *This Happy Breed* (1944) and *The Holly and the Ivy* (1954). In London, the eroticism, implicit in the text, remained muted. Evelyn and Cecil were two people going through the motions of a late-life courtship, with Evelyn playing coy and Cecil playing inquisitive, mainly because the playwright has saddled both of them with so much exposition. Even so, Richardson and Johnson kept their relationship on a platonic plane. One suspects that when Cecil brought Evelyn the hot water bottle, she never let on that she had one but instead engaged him in conversation, as they recalled the past.

And when Cecil and Evelyn went off looking for the kingfisher, one sensed it would fly away before they had a chance to see it. But at least they had something to which to look forward: a sighting that would afford a glimmer of hope for two people in the late autumn, or early winter, of their lives.

The reviews of the New York production suggested that Harrison and Claudette played *The Kingfisher* as high comedy, as if Henry Higgins had been paired with Nicole de Loiselle from *Bluebeard's Eighth Wife*. Despite mixed notices, their star power resulted in a run of 181 performances. One reason is that *The Kingfisher* had little competition in a season when comedy was at a premium. The only other comedy of note was Alan Ayckbourn's *Bedroom Farce*, which was far more literate, a mix of the absurd and the whimsical.

There has always been room on Broadway for a good melodrama, even a thriller, although from the 1940s to the present the genre declined in popularity as the plot conventions were appropriated by film and television; what is especially striking is that during the past fifty years detective fiction has increased in popularity with its variety of authors, exotic settings, series detectives, and methods of murder, some of which are so bizarre that they sustain interest by their sheer ingenuity. However, the best stage melodramas (e.g., *Night Must Fall, Rope, Angel Street, Dial M for Murder, Sleuth,*

Deathtrap) avoid the novelistic practice of a character's detailed explanation of a crime. Either one knows how it was done (*Rope, Dial M for Murder*) and waits for a sleuth, either professional (*Angel Street, Dial M for Murder*) or amateur (*Rope*), to solve the crime; watches as suspicion mounts until the perpetrator is identified (*Night Must Fall*); or becomes a spectator at a diabolical game that leaves at least one, or perhaps both, of the players dead (*Sleuth, Deathtrap*).

Since only one murder mystery had been announced for the 1980–81 Broadway season (the hugely successful *Agnes of God* was more of a psychological, or theological, melodrama), it would at least have a certain distinction; on the other hand, it could be an anachronism. Such a play was Claudette's next vehicle, Jerome Chodorov and Norman Panama's *A Talent for Murder*, which opened at her favorite theater, the Biltmore, on 1 October 1981. So that audiences did not think that Claudette was returning in a mere thriller, the play was billed as "a mystery comedy." It was certainly a mystery; in fact, the *New York Times* Sunday drama critic, Walter Kerr, entitled his 11 October essay: "The Only Mystery Is Why."

The play qualified as a mystery, quite a convoluted one, with some high-tech gimmicks including a bugged brooch and a device, referred to as the "electronic genie," that, when activated, could bring a garage door down on an unsuspecting driver, preventing him or her from turning off the ignition and resulting in death by asphyxiation. Anne Royce McClain, a best-selling mystery writer with an estate in the Berkshires, planned to use the electronic-eye method of murder in her latest novel. One can understand why Claudette was attracted to the part of Anne. For one thing, she would be the star. Anne was also a preposterously multifaceted character, so much so that she seemed thoroughly unreal. Perhaps Claudette thought that she could add a third dimension to the cardboard figure that had been assembled from a Mary Roberts Rinehart–Agatha Christie cutout. Apart from being a best-selling author, Anne has a $20 million art collection; spent the 1920s in Paris, where she met Hemingway, Fitzgerald, Stein, and Toklas; had affairs with Matisse and Picasso; is a functional alcoholic; seems confined to a wheelchair, which, like Sheridan Whiteside in *The Man Who Came to Dinner*, she can leave at will; and causes fires from her careless cigar smoking. Regardless, Anne is not addled, only eccentric, and has worked out ingenious methods of murder and detection, including spreading snail poison on carpets, which turns the soles of the suspect's shoes purple.

When Anne discovers that her scheming daughter-in-law, Sheila, plans to have her shipped off to a retirement community in Florida, Anne gives her a brooch that happens to be bugged and records a conversation between Sheila and Mark, the husband of Anne's late daughter, with whom Sheila is having an affair. Anne is not above blackmail, but Sheila still has the upper hand because of Anne's erratic behavior, particularly her history of starting fires. Naturally, Sheila has to die by asphyxiation; naturally, Anne is a suspect.

Claudette's leading man, the suave Jean-Pierre Aumont, played Anne's personal physician and ex-lover. The character was originally conceived as a British Francophile, Anthony Wainwright, but the name was changed to Paul Marchand when Aumont was cast in the part. Aumont was one of the most colorful actors with whom Claudette ever worked. He was a stage and screen star in Paris before coming to Hollywood shortly after Pearl Harbor to play a French resistance fighter in MGM's *Assignment in Brittany* (1943). He identified with the role so strongly that he began to feel guilty about leading the good life while thousands of French men and women were not: "I couldn't keep raking in money for smiling in front of a camera while so many of my friends and countrymen were either dead, hunted, departed, or without food." After another MGM resistance film, the powerful *Cross of Lorraine* (1943), he joined the Free French for the duration of the war. Aumont served his country well, receiving the Croix de Guerre for his heroism.

However, on his return to Hollywood, it was typecasting time. Aumont was perceived as a "ladies' man," as other French actors had been (e.g., Maurice Chevalier, Charles Boyer, Claude Dauphin). And so he usually played the continental lover romancing Ginger Rogers in *Heartbeat* (1946) and Yvonne De Carlo in *Song of Scheherazade* (1947), befriending Leslie Caron in *Lili* (1953), driving Jean Simmons to the brink of suicide in *Hilda Crane* (1956), and committing adultery with Eleanor Parker in *The Seventh Sin* (1957).

Aumont's great love was the stage. But of the six Broadway shows in which he appeared between 1949 and 1971, only one, the musical version of *Tovarich* (1963), in which he and a singing and dancing Vivien Leigh recreated the roles that Charles Boyer and Claudette had played in the 1937 film, had a respectable run of 264 performances. The straw-hat circuit and live television were the only alternatives to Broadway, and Aumont embraced both. He appeared on all the dramatic television shows (*Studio One*, *Omnibus*, *Philco Television Playhouse*, *Robert Montgomery Presents*, *United States Steel Hour*, *Lux Video Theatre*, *Playhouse 90*, and *Climax*!). He did not consider it beneath him to appear as a mystery guest on *What's My Line?* or on *The Merv Griffin Show*, *Here's Hollywood*, and *Hollywood Palace*. Television never made Aumont into a household name, but it gave him far greater exposure than either film or theatre could.

When Aumont was offered the role of Marchand in *A Talent for Murder*, he was seventy-two. Although he realized the character was an old roué, in keeping with his Hollywood image, he accepted the part. At least it meant costarring with a compatriot, who had also reached a stage in her career when she, too, was playing versions of her cinematic self, recycling her screwball/romantic comedy heroine through a time machine from which she would emerge looking as fresh as she did during her heyday.

Aumont and Claudette had appeared in one film together, *Royal Affairs of Versailles*, but neither had a significant role in what was really a historical pageant. Because Aumont respected Claudette, who became a close friend, he was able to inject a personal element into his characterization. He played Marchand as someone who cared deeply about Anne and was aware of Sheila's plan to ship her off to Florida. He also knows the combination to Anne's safe, which even she cannot remember, and is familiar with Anne's novels and methods of murder, including the way the electronic genie is activated. In the very last moments of the play, Marchand asks Anne, "Who dunnit?" Anne answers in detail and concludes by saying, "That's exactly how you did it, isn't it, Doc?"

She arrived at her conclusion by piecing seemingly trivial evidence together, such as a bicycle and a grease-stained right trouser cuff. At the intermission of an operetta they were attending, Marchand commandeered a bicycle and rode back to the estate in time to activate the electronic genie and trap Sheila in the garage. Suspecting Marchand and knowing he was a meticulous dresser, Anne wondered why, after the intermission, his right cuff was turned up. But what really aroused Anne's suspicions was a remark Marchand made after Anne discovered that a tape was missing; if it fell into the hands of the police, it would make Anne the chief suspect in Sheila's murder. The tape not only included the damning conversation between Sheila and Mark, but also the description of the entrapment method that Anne planned to use in her next novel. "I didn't put *my* murder on tape," Marchand said, in a slip of the tongue to which even the shrewdest criminals are prone. Anne's final deduction, then, is that Marchand took the tape from the safe before Sheila had a chance to steal it. After such a display of devotion, Anne could not possibly turn Marchand over to the authorities. And so, crime does pay—and well. Marchand will continue to be Anne's physician and perhaps even resume his amorous duties. Besides, Anne cannot play chess by herself.

A Talent for Murder found no favor with the critics and closed after seventy-seven performances. Claudette could do no harm, they concluded, but her writers could. Chodorov and Panama were out of their element, since neither was an experienced mystery writer. Anne's deductive summary, reminiscent of Agatha Christie and Mary Robert Rinehart, belonged in a novel, where, at the end, the sleuth often reconstructs the crime so elaborately that a day or two later, the reader has forgotten who killed whom as well as how it was done.

A Talent for Murder would have also worked better as a film, in which Anne's reconstruction could have been intercut with flashbacks of

Marchand's bicycle ride and his return to the estate, where he committed the murder. Even more important, Sheila's asphyxiation could have been dramatized. Had the play truly been a "mystery comedy," wit would have filled in the void left by overplotting. But there is little wit, just some one-liners that may have elicited a chuckle, depending on how humorous one finds Anne's Indian servant, Rashi, an ex-convict who dispenses aphoristic wisdom: "If music soothes the savage beast, why has not the tiger a victrola?"

Audiences came primarily to see Claudette, secondly, to watch a dapper Frenchman and the screen's original sophisticated lady play off each other. They did, and quite engagingly; even in his early seventies, Aumont looked trim and debonair. He may not have been given much in the way of sparkling dialogue, but he could play a murderer with such silken charm that Sheila's death seemed more like the elimination of a nuisance than the taking of a life. And Claudette, looking wickedly elegant in Bill Blass's creations, had a great entrance line. When Marchand informed Rashi that Anne's drinking had to be curtailed, Claudette's offstage voice boomed, "Who says so?" as she wheeled herself onto the stage in what must have been her most theatrical entrance. Those expecting to see Claudette as an arthritic invalid soon discovered that, to Anne Royce McClain, the wheelchair was the equivalent of a throne, from which she could easily descend. Anne had been a mystery novelist so long that she found deception in real life as exhilarating as it is in fiction. She could even playact as being dotty, only to reveal that she did not wear the motley on her brain.

According to Claudette, Rex Harrison phoned her in 1983 and said, "Wouldn't you like to do a play in London?" Apparently Harrison's animus toward her had abated; however, Harrison was shrewd when it came to a costar. He knew that Claudette's role was not the lead; in fact, it was much smaller than her part in *The Kingfisher*. But he also needed a name, which Claudette could provide. Claudette knew she could hold her own with Harrison. She rarely went up on her lines; besides, her memory was superior to his. Naturally, she agreed. The part made few demands on her; it required sheer technique, which she possessed in abundance. She hadn't played

London since 1928 when she appeared in *The Barker* and knew that no matter what the critics thought of the play, they would be captivated by her.

The play was a revival of Frederick Lonsdale's *Aren't We All?* (1923), a well-crafted comedy as airy as a soufflé and as unsubstantial. Its charm was evanescent; a week after seeing it, one might recall it dreamily, remembering it as a pleasant diversion and perhaps even admiring the playwright's wisdom in matters of the heart. If love conquers all, it also makes fools of all, both the professionals and the novices.

The play revolves around two couples: Lord Greenham (Rex Harrison), a widower and philanderer, and Lady Frinton (Claudette), a widow determined to marry him to put an end to his dalliances with younger women; and Greenham's son, Willie, and his wife, Margot, who accidentally sees her husband kissing an actress. To Margot the kiss is grounds for divorce, and it is at this point that the elders come to the aid of the befuddled Willie, who does not know that while Margot was vacationing alone in Egypt she met an Australian who wooed her and may have given her more than a kiss. When Greenham learns that the Australian's name is John Willocks, who also happens to be in London looking for his mysterious inamorata, Greenham invites him to his home for the weekend.

Frantic, Margot seeks out Lady Frinton, who delivers a note to Willocks, explaining the situation and asking that he show no sign of ever having met Margot. In return, Margot plants a notice in the London *Times* announcing Lord Greenham's forthcoming marriage to Lady Frinton. As in classic comedy, people behave foolishly, deceiving and being deceived, until amends are made and order is restored. With the curtain about to fall, Greenham delivers the curtain line. When the vicar, his brother-in-law, remarks how hurt he was by one of Greenham's remarks, Greenham asks him to cite it. "Greenham, you called me a bloody old fool!" he cries, almost in tears. Consolingly, Greenham replies, "But aren't we all, old friend!"

Harrison may have had the lead and the curtain line, but Claudette had a great entrance line. When Willie exclaims how young she looks, Lady Frinton replies, "I'm glad of that because it takes most of the day to become it." Claudette was generally letter perfect, except that on one occasion during the New York run she went up on a line. According to Lynn Redgrave, who played Margot in the New York production, "After weeks of flawless performances Claudette slightly flubbed a line. She was nervous. Kate [Hepburn] was in front. The flub was minor but after the show Claudette . . . was in tears. She still cared about her work so much that she was mortified to have been anything less than perfect."

Harrison, however, was going up on lines frequently, in London, New York, and on tour. As one who saw the London production, I can vouch for the fact that Harrison did not have total command of the text. Since he has always been a charmer, he compensated for his less-than-perfect delivery by conveying the essence of the script, if not always in Lonsdale's language. At the beginning of the London run, when Harrison had a memory lapse, Claudette would feed him the lines, which enraged him. At one performance, he turned to the audience and said, " 'She's given me my lines, but . . . how *could* she be so stupid!—they're the wrong lines.' " They probably weren't, but one can well understand how an actor who has mastered his craft finds that the memory is not what it was back in his salad days. Christopher Plummer played *King Lear* in his mid seventies; Alvin Epstein, in his eighties. They are the exceptions. At sixty-seven, Helen Hayes, once dubbed the "first lady of the American theatre," appeared in a revival of George Kelly's *The Show Off*, in which she gave a superb performance but not always in Kelly's words. But Hayes was wise enough to know that there was always an occasional film and television role, especially after winning a supporting actress Oscar for *Airplane* (1970).

For a while, Harrison improved. The play was a success in London, and then moved on to New York in 1985, where it ran for ninety-three performances, after which it went on tour: first to Los Angeles, and then to Melbourne, which Claudette found utterly uncosmopolitan, and, finally, Sydney, which delighted her; so did media tycoon Rupert Murdoch, who was then on the verge of adding Twentieth Century-Fox to his ever expanding empire, News Corp. Claudette and Harrison had now grown accustomed to each other. Harrison was a delightful conversationalist, which, to Claudette, covered a multitude of sins. She had made peace with his memory, knowing that he could usually get the lines out in some way, even if they were an approximation of the original dialogue. He was also experienced enough to know how to get a laugh out of a memory lapse. "In Sydney, while waiting in the wings for her entrance, Claudette heard an eruption of laugher. She was puzzled; the scene had never gotten laughs before. When she asked the stage manager about it, he replied that Harrison had missed his cue and said, 'What?' He then turned toward the prompter, who gave him the line, after which Harrison said, 'Thank you.'"

When the tour ended, so did Claudette's stage—but not her acting—career.

CHAPTER 17

Envoi

By 1984, Claudette had become more than a star; she had become venerable, which meant tributes and accolades. In April 1984, shortly before she left for London to start rehearsals for *Aren't We All?* she attended the dedication of the Claudette Colbert Building at Kaufman Astoria Studios, where her film career began fifty-five years earlier. The facilities were a vast improvement over the ones that she and Edward G. Robinson encountered when they made *The Hole in the Wall*, but at least someone knew that Claudette Colbert had made twelve films there between 1929 and 1932.

Two weeks after the dedication, Claudette was feted by the Film Society of Lincoln Center on 23 April. What should have been a celebratory occasion turned into a montage of clips from some of her best-known films (*It Happened One Night*, *The Palm Beach Story*, *The Sign of the Cross*), along with some lesser ones such as *I Cover the Waterfront*, *Torch Song*, and *The Gilded Lily*. The evening was a major disappointment. Although Claudette looked her usual soigné self in a red organdy gown, she had little to say. She expressed her gratitude and admitted that she had some great-looking male costars, few of whom, except for Ray Milland, were in attendance, although they were still living.

The *Los Angeles Times* was especially critical of the event, wondering why Claudette had placed such restrictions on the clips that could be shown, particularly since they "provided no strong feeling for [her] film career." *Variety* agreed, having found the delivery of the tributes "languidly paced and the content poorly conceived." Another reason for Claudette's perfunctory expression of gratitude may have had something to do with her leaving two days later for London to begin rehearsals for *Aren't We All?* Claudette knew that her film career was over, but she still had a life on the stage. The Film Society of Lincoln Center, however, was not interested in her stage work. The society had envisioned a fund-raiser, which obviously did not live up to its expectations. In 1984, Claudette had not made a movie for two decades. She was being honored for her work during her Hollywood years, which deserved recognition for its own sake. If Claudette played censor, allowing only clips that favored her left side (even if it meant scenes from unmemorable films such as *Bride for Sale* and *Parrish*), then she underestimated the audience. The fans that packed Avery Fisher Hall that evening wanted a movie star who reminisced about her films, her co-stars, and directors, interspersing memories with humorous anecdotes and gossip temptingly rendered. What they received were a few platitudes, after which Claudette took off for London.

When the *Aren't We All?* tour ended in 1986, Claudette sensed that her stage career had also ended. She may not have looked eighty-three, but there were times when she felt it. Still, there was one final role in the offing, and it was on television.

In 1985, Dominick Dunne's *The Two Mrs. Grenvilles* was published and became an instant best-seller; two years later, it was an NBC two-part miniseries, aired on Sunday and Monday evenings, 8 and 9 February 1987. When Claudette learned about the miniseries, she knew there was one role in it for her: not the lead, the second Mrs. Grenville, but the first. Claudette campaigned for the part of Alice Grenville; Dunne, a close friend, did some behind-the-scenes maneuvering himself when producer Preston Fischer was unable to persuade his first choice, Loretta Young, to take on what was essentially a supporting role. The part went to Claudette, perhaps because she could play a steel-willed matriarch by expressing condescension and contempt as civilly as she would show concern and compassion.

The Two Mrs. Grenvilles is a *roman à clef* inspired by the notorious 1955 Woodward case, in which William Woodward II, wealthy banker and playboy, was shot by his wife, Ann, as he stepped out of the shower. Because a prowler had been spotted on the grounds of their Long Island estate, Ann insisted that she thought the man who approached the bed was the prowler. Ann was acquitted because the Woodwards had contacts powerful enough to ward off any scandal. Before Ann became Mrs. William Woodward II, she was or, rather, went by the name of Ann Eden. After a brief fling with William Woodward Sr., she learned what the privileged class was like and wanted to be part of it. Applying the same tactics to the son that she had used on the father, Ann easily became the second Mrs. Grenville, the first being her mother-in-law, called Alice in the novel.

Dunne made the inevitable name changes. William Woodward II became William "Billy" Grenville, called "Junior" by his mother; his mother, Alice Grenville; Ann Eden, Ann Arden. Ann is now a chorus girl, but Billy is no different than Junior. The novel is a flashback, beginning with the discovery of Ann Grenville's body on the bedroom floor. Alice Grenville, a believer in euphemism and decorum, would not have the Grenville name sullied by anything as ugly as a suicide from a combination of vodka and Seconal. Heart failure is more genteel, and heart failure it was—in the novel, only. The historical Ann Woodward used cyanide, and there was no cover-up. The novel also has a narrator: Basil Plant, a stand in for Truman Capote; if anyone is the villain in the piece, it is Capote, whose 1975 *Esquire* story about the case drove Ann Woodward to suicide, even though one could argue that it was merely a piece of fiction. The problem was that the fiction may have been fact.

In the novel, after Ann accepted Grenville's proposal, she wanted, and got, the entire package even in wartime: church wedding, white gown, and gifts. She also inherited a mother-in-law, whom she called *"mère,"* as Alice

Grenville's children had been trained to do. Ann knows that Alice not only dislikes her but also finds her common. But Ann is determined to be accepted, in her own way: "I want to talk like them, dress like them, handwrite like them, think like them. Then I'll add my special thing on top of that." Her "special thing" was a trashy glamour that conjured up a world of costume jewelry and feather boas even when she was wearing real pearls and a Mainbocher dress.

She became a first nighter, world traveler, and one of the idle rich, who even managed to get an audience with the pope. She also became an alcoholic, as did Junior. Their marriage, like that of the Woodwards, deteriorated to the point that no amount of liquor or sex could save it. Grenville wanted the voluptuary from the chorus, and Ann wanted social acceptance. When Grenville broached the subject of divorce, Ann demanded such an exorbitant settlement that he confronted her with information he acquired during a trip to Kansas: her marriage to a high school beau. Since there was no divorce, Ann is guilty of bigamy, which would invalidate her marriage to Grenville. Thus, Dunne provides the perfect motive for Ann's using the prowler as a pretext for murder.

Alice suspects Ann of killing her son, but the governor insists that the Grenvilles close rank and that Alice stand by her daughter-in-law. Alice pulls enough strings so that a prowler is even produced who admits to being on the roof of the Grenville mansion the night of the shooting. Although Ann is exonerated, she becomes a social pariah, and finally a suicide, after Plant's story, "Annie Get Your Gun," is published in *Monsieur*, just as Capote's "La Cote Basque" was in *Esquire*. According to Katherine Restaino, "After reading the fictional account of her husband's death, Woodward ingested cyanide on 9 October 1975. Dunne believed that the story led to Woodward's suicide, although Capote denied the connection."

The miniseries opens like a Douglas Sirk film of the 1950s. The picture frame credits appear against pink satin, accompanied by Marvin Hamlisch's throbbingly melodramatic score, which periodically gives way to Kurt Weill's "Speak Low," occasionally played on a solo violin. There is no doubt that

Ann-Margret (Ann Arden) is the star; she delivers a bravura performance, which must have proved a revelation to those who thought of her only as Elvis Presley's costar in *Viva Las Vegas* (1964) but never saw her in Mike Nichols's *Carnal Knowledge* (1971), for which she received an Oscar nomination, or in the television version of *A Streetcar Named Desire* (1984), in which she gave a shattering performance as Blanche DuBois.

Claudette, who does not appear until after the first half hour, has a total of twelve scenes, beginning with Ann's first visit to Alice Grenville's mansion for tea. While Ann-Margret's costumes are haute couture, Claudette's are those befitting a matriarch, not a matron, but rather a woman who dresses in accord with her age and station. Wearing a light gray dress that flowed down her frame in pleated folds, Alice welcomed her son's fiancée as one would an interloper without conveying the obvious signs of dismay over his choice of wife. Alice's clothes are always in unerring taste—a red suit and hat, a mink jacket and a black gown—elegant without being ostentatious, as opposed to Ann's, which were both.

Claudette was now eighty-three. She spoke in measured tones, as Alice would. But they were also her own. Although she articulated each word, which is more than can be said of some of the other cast members, the lilt had disappeared from the voice. It was darker, deeper, still throaty but without the effervescence that marked her romantic comedy days. Still, she had a sense of rhythm, which, combined with her aristocratic delivery, seemed thoroughly in character. Lines that might have sounded sarcastic became veiled reprimands. When Ann informs Alice that she is breaking with tradition and christening her son Christopher instead of William Grenville III, Claudette replies, "I'm sure we'll all learn to accept that," as she leaves, turning it into an exit line. At a cocktail party, Alice expresses her disapproval of Ann's openness: "Understatement is a virtue that can hide almost everything."

Claudette's best scene, brief as it was, was at grave site service for Christopher, who committed suicide by jumping out of a window. Swathed in black, with her face the mask of tragedy, Alice, somberly but not vindictively, remarks that now Ann knows what it is like for a mother to lose a son, suggesting that the two Mrs. Grenvilles at last have something in common. And as the final but always ladylike thrust of the knife, Alice reminds Ann that Christopher jumped from the window on Mother's Day.

Banished from New York society, Ann becomes the equivalent of a stateless person, constantly traveling and changing lovers as often as she changes countries. Ann-Margret plays the two scenes on board the cruise ship that frame the narrative as if Ann is tired of a life that has become meaningless. In the television version, Ann knows who and what Plant is and still agrees to talk to him. In both scenes, Ann-Margret has the spectral, desensitized look of someone who is spiritually dead and ready to move on to the next and final stage: physical death. Plant may get the last word ("I sensed I just wasn't writing an article for the society pages. I was writing her obituary"). Ann, however, gets the last image. Returning to her stateroom, she takes a white tablet with vodka and lies down on the bed. *The Two Mrs. Grenvilles* fades out with Ann-Margret's face in repose, her eyes open.

Both Ann-Margret and Claudette gave outstanding performances, and each was nominated for a Golden Globe award: Ann-Margret for best actress in a miniseries category and Claudette for best supporting actress. Claudette won, but Ann-Margret lost to Gena Rowlands for *The Betty Ford Story*.

Two years later, Claudette received her final tribute, the Kennedy Center Honors. In 1978, George Stevens Jr.'s dream of an annual celebration of performing artists who have enriched America's cultural life was realized. The setting was the John F. Kennedy Center of the Performing Arts in Washington, D.C. The gala was televised; the recipients were seated in a box, where the television cameras could capture their reactions when colleagues delivered accolades, and career milestones were recreated. The board of trustees of the Kennedy Center did not distinguish between high and popular culture. Throughout the years, the recipients included film stars such as Henry Fonda, Lillian Gish, James Stewart, Gregory Peck, Bette Davis, Lauren Bacall, Julie Andrews, Kirk Douglas, Robert Redford; singers

(Ella Fitzgerald, Lena Horne, Harry Belafonte, Perry Como, Tony Martin, Aretha Franklin, Dolly Parton); opera stars (Rïse Stevens, Marilyn Horne, Joan Sutherland, Placido Domingo, Luciano Pavarotti, Beverly Sills, Leontyne Price); film and stage directors (Elia Kazan, Mike Nichols, Billy Wilder, George Abbott, Steven Spielberg); choreographers (George Balanchine, Alvin Ailey, Paul Taylor, Agnes deMille, Merce Cunningham, Jerome Robbins, Arthur Mitchell, Judith Jamison); Broadway composers and lyricists (Richard Rodgers, Betty Comden and Adolph Green, Stephen Sondheim, Jule Styne, Alan Jay Lerner and Frederick Loewe, Fred Ebb and John Kander, Andrew Lloyd Webber); television personalities (Lucille Ball, Carol Burnett, Johnny Carson, Bill Cosby), concert artists (Arthur Rubinstein, Rudolph Serkin, Isaac Stern, Nathan Milstein, Van Cliburn, Itzak Perlman, Mstislav Rostopovich), playwrights (Arthur Miller, Tennessee Williams, Edward Albee, Neil Simon); classical composers (Aaron Copland, Gian Carlo Menotti, Leonard Bernstein, Morton Gould); and ballet dancers (Maria Tallchief, Suzanne Farrell, Martha Graham, Jacques d'Amboise).

Like the films selected each year for their cultural and historical significance by the Library of Congress's National Film Registry, the Kennedy Center recipients continue to grow in number, attesting to the country's commitment to the arts even at times when the arts seem irrelevant. Whatever else the Kennedy Center Honors accomplished, they made audiences aware that the arts in America are not elitist but as democratic as the country itself.

On 3 December 1989, it was Claudette's turn. She had already been preceded by Fred Astaire (1978), Henry Fonda (1979), James Cagney (1980), Cary Grant (1981), Gene Kelly (1982), Frank Sinatra (1983), Danny Kaye (1984), Irene Dunne (1985), Ray Charles (1986), Sammy Davis Jr. (1987), and Myrna Loy (1988). That evening, she would be sharing the spotlight with folk singer, actor, and activist Harry Belafonte; the ballerina Alexandra Danilova; Broadway veteran Mary Martin; and composer William Schuman. Given the occasion, she wanted a gown that had a courtly elegance about it, nothing décolleté with hand-sewn beads but the kind that a Washington grande dame might wear at a Christmas party she was hosting in her Georgetown home.

Claudette had never before worn an Arnold Scaasi gown. Scaasi's friend Peter Rogers, who created the Blackglama ad campaign, "What Becomes a Legend Most?" in which legends such as Claudette, Rosalind Russell, and even Lillian Hellman were photographed luxuriating in Blackglama mink, saw one of Scaasi's creations and felt it would be ideal for the occasion: "It had a black velvet top with sharp white camellias around the neck and wrists. The long skirt of many layers of black silk tulle was quite full and moved beautifully." That is what Claudette wore.

The evening began, appropriately, with *The Star-Spangled Banner*. Then Walter Cronkite, one of the most recognizable (and least formidable) figures in broadcast journalism, delivered the traditional welcome, in which he quoted Tolstoy on the ennobling nature of art. He was brief, realizing that the audience had come to be entertained. And there was no dearth of entertainment that evening.

Mary Martin was the first honoree. Bernadette Peters in a black strapless gown came on stage and recalled the time she saw Martin on television in the role with which she will always be associated: Peter Pan in the musical version that Martin first did on Broadway in 1954. The following year, *Peter Pan* with the original stars, Martin and Cyril Ritchard as Captain Hook, was telecast live on NBC's *Producers Showcase*, where it proved so popular that it was repeated within less than a year and eventually filmed in color for a new generation. Charlotte d'Amboise as Peter and some game children recreated the scene in which Peter teaches Wendy, Michael, and John Darling how to fly ("I'm Flying"). The audience was enthralled by the sight of the classically trained d'Amboise doing a space ballet, while the children thrashed about in mid air and then flew through the window. For a moment, one forgot that they were all suspended on wires that looked invisible and sat in awe of the magic of stagecraft.

A montage of musical excerpts ("My Heart Belongs to Daddy," "I'm in Love with a Wonderful Guy," "I'm Gonna Wash That Man Right out of

My Hair," "The Sound of Music," "My Favorite Things") was followed by a surprise appearance from Martin's son, Larry Hagman, known to audiences as J. R. from the first hour-long evening soap, *Dallas*, which was still on the air. Hagman reminisced, Martin was touched, and her segment came to a rousing close with the U.S. Naval Academy Glee Club honoring Martin in their own way with "There Is Nothing like a Dame" from *South Pacific*, after which the men filed from the stage down the aisles, tossing their hats into the air as they exited. Martin caught one of the hats, placed it on her head, and for a moment the years dissolved, and she was *South Pacific*'s Nellie Forbush singing "Honey Bun" in an oversized sailor suit.

The Mary Martin portion was the evening's highlight. Next came Danilova, who, with William Schuman, was the least familiar name, although she was undeniably an extraordinary dancer. Claudette, in the Scaasi gown and tinted glasses, and seated between Danilova and Schuman, was third. The pace picked up a bit. Humor, film clips, and song certainly helped. Gregory Peck recreated the evening of Oscar night 1935 when Claudette was about to depart for New York, believing that either Norma Shearer or Grace Moore would receive the Best Actress award. When she was told that the Oscar was the Hollywood's equivalent of the Nobel prize, she returned to the banquet, thanked Capra, and returned to the station in time to catch the train to New York. Then came the obligatory montage of film clips (*Cleopatra, The Sign of the Cross, It Happened One Night, Bluebeard's Eighth Wife, Arise, My Love, The Palm Beach Story*). And the segment closed with Don Ameche and Lynn Redgrave singing special lyrics to "You Brought a New Kind of Love to Me," which Maurice Chevalier sang to Claudette in *The Big Pond*: "On this special night / We raise a glass / To someone who has so much class / You brought a new kind of love / You taught me a new kind of love / Cherie."

The Harry Belafonte tribute combined history (footage of Belafonte with Dr. Martin Luther King, an in-person appearance by Archbishop Desmond Tutu) with song, but William Schuman suffered the fate of being last and, to the show biz audience, least, despite the fact that he was much honored (e.g., recipient of the first Pulitzer prize for music in 1943 and an American Academy of Arts and Letters gold medalist). Pianist Van Cliburn spoke from personal experience about his years at Julliard when Schuman was president, but his presence brought an air of gravitas to an evening pulsating with the kind of nostalgia that comes from shared memories, which did not include the music of William Schuman.

Once the gala came to an end, it was time for Claudette to return to Bellerive and play hostess to what she hoped would be a steady stream of visitors. There was no dearth of visitors. Claudette was in reasonably good health for an eighty-nine-year-old woman with arthritis and hypertension, until 3 March 1993. Around 10:00 p.m., she placed a call to O'Hagan in New York. "I'm having a stroke," Claudette moaned. O'Hagan had already retired for the night, and when she received the call, she thought she was dreaming and fell asleep for fifteen minutes. She then called Claudette, who, fortunately, had a phone by her night table and was able to speak with O'Hagan, who realized it was not a dream. O'Hagan drew on her contacts at American Airlines to get the next flight to Miami, with a connecting one to Barbados. Meanwhile, Claudette managed to crawl out of bed and over to Marie's room. For some reason, which even O'Hagan has never understood, Claudette was not brought to the hospital for several hours. Probably, she preferred to wait for O'Hagan's arrival, although O'Hagan still believes that if she had been treated within the first three or four hours, the stroke would have been less severe. As it was, Claudette was paralyzed on her left side. Fortunately, her speech and mind were not affected. Claudette was as glamorous a stroke victim as she was a star. She continued to entertain, take her vitamins, drink her vodka, and draw with her right hand. She still applied her makeup each day, although Marie now had to hold the mirror for her.

At the time of Claudette's stroke, O'Hagan had not yet retired from Saks; that would not be until 1994, after which she stayed on as a consultant. Meanwhile, she went back to New York, returning periodically to Bellerive to make certain that the staff she had hired was taking proper care of Claudette. She was in New York on 28 July 1996 when she received a frantic call from Marie, who told her that Claudette was not speaking. O'Hagan told Marie to call Father James Grear, a diocesan priest stationed in Barbados, to administer the last rites, which he did on 29 July.

Shortly after Claudette's stroke, O'Hagan, a devout Catholic, felt that Claudette should return to the faith into which she was born. Although not a regular churchgoer, Claudette was especially fond of the Church of St. Vincent Ferrer on Lexington Avenue between Sixty-fifth and Sixty-sixth streets, where she was confirmed and where she would often drop in to meditate when she was in New York, occasionally even attending Sunday mass. It is understandable that someone with a strong aesthetic sense like Claudette would be attracted to St. Vincent Ferrer. It was built by Dominicans, members of a religious order founded by St. Dominic in the thirteenth century. The church, an outstanding example of French Gothic architecture, dates back to 1918 and is a work of art in itself. The stations of the cross are oil paintings. The high altar exerts a centripetal force, drawing the spectator to it as the church's focal point. Its tomb-like shape was designed to recall the Roman catacombs, where the early Christians held mass during the time of persecution. When the sunlight streams through the stained glass windows, the result is a luminous display of color: "The windows with dominant blues interact with the windows with dominant reds, and with the help of the sun they create an exquisite mix of light in the front of the church."

O'Hagan arranged a meeting between Claudette and Father Grear. At first Claudette was reluctant to see him, but soon relented because of O'Hagan's insistence. Father Grear was invited to lunch; Claudette looked every inch the movie star, with every hair in place, except that her condition was at odds with her image: Marie had to feed her. The luncheon was short-lived. Father Grear was so captivated by her sheer presence that he could not help sounding like a fan: "I only know of one word to describe you." Claudette was intrigued: "What is it?" "Exquisite," Father Grear replied. Beaming, Claudette acknowledged the compliment. The audience was over.

Father Grear did not see Claudette again until he was summoned to her bedside on 29 July to administer the sacrament of Extreme Unction. "Your priest is here," Marie whispered to Claudette, who, with her left hand, pulled him down to her with a grip stronger than any to which he had been accustomed. At first, he wondered if he could extricate himself from her grasp to perform the last anointing. After he freed himself, Father Grear and the household staff said an Our Father, Hail Mary, and Gloria. Then he made the sign of the cross on her forehead with holy oil.

The end came on 30 July. Claudette, barely breathing, said, "I want to go home," pointing upwards. O'Hagan stayed with her until the end. Father Grear and the Bellerive staff remained outside her hospital room. Then O'Hagan noticed something unusual: a double rainbow arched across the sky. Since cremation was forbidden in Barbados, O'Hagan had Claudette's body shipped back to New York, so that her remains could be placed in an urn in the family crypt at the Parish of St. Peter Cemetery in Barbados, where the ashes of her husband and mother had already been placed.

Claudette was fortunate to have a friend in Helen O'Hagan, a celebrity in her own right. Widely known as the voice of Saks, she numbered the leading designers among her circle. In 2000, she hosted a retirement party for Bill Blass at the Waldorf, where she presented a slide show of his career, followed by a luncheon consisting of his favorite foods: meat loaf and oatmeal cookies. She was also the one who informed the *New York Times* of Blass's death of cancer two years later. Helen O'Hagan was always good for a quote about fashion, a designer's legacy, the latest trendy restaurant, or the advantages of being an early riser. Naturally, it was she who arranged Claudette's memorial service.

After Claudette had her stroke, O'Hagan knew her place was at her friend's side. Although only sixty-three, she took early retirement in April 1994, informing the *New York Times* (29 March 1994) that she planned to return to Barbados. Her retirement was even noted by *Women's Wear Daily*. It was a difficult time for both women. O'Hagan had to arrange for help and have a ramp built for the wheelchair-bound Claudette, so that she could maneuver her way out of Bellerive to look at the sea. O'Hagan would have been financially comfortable without the generous provisions that Claudette made in her will: Claudette bequeathed her $3.5 million estate to her.

Claudette's cremation did not mark the end of Helen O'Hagan's work. She wanted a memorial service at the church that meant more to Claudette than any other: the Church of St. Vincent Ferrer, where O'Hagan was also a parishioner. On Wednesday, 4 September 1996, a requiem mass was offered there in Claudette's memory. Among the seven hundred who attended were Claudette's niece, Claudette "Coco" Lewis, Douglas Fairbanks Jr., Bobby Short, Betty Comden, Dominick Dunne, Bill Blass, and Arnold Scaasi. The celebrants were Father Boniface Ramsay and Father Frederick D. Hoesli. Father Grear read the gospel, and Father Jerome Vereb, a representative from the Vatican, delivered the homily. O'Hagan chose the music: "I Know That My Redeemer Liveth," from Handel's *Messiah*, for the processional; "O, God of Loveliness" as the offertory hymn; "Pie Jesu," from Gabriel Fauré's *Requiem*, as the communion solo; and "Amazing Grace" for the post communion.

In the "Reflections" part of the service, O'Hagan read excerpts from the letters of friends unable to attend. Father Grear extolled Claudette's refusal to succumb to self-pity even though the stroke had left her immobile. When a visiting friend wondered if Claudette ever asked herself, or God, "Why me?" Claudette replied, "Hey, why not me?" Playwright Leonard Gershe recalled an encounter Claudette had in Venice with a paparazzo, who told her he could put her in the prestigious *Oggi*. Claudette smiled at him and said, "Baby, I don't need you any more." Kitty Carlisle Hart remembered her as a friend and talented singer with a voice that was infrequently heard on the screen and never on the musical stage. Her physician, Dr. Robert Ascheim, told of the time Claudette tactfully informed his son that he needed braces. Robert Bernstein, former chairman of Random House, described a cocktail party at which a guest was behaving boorishly, prompting Claudette to whisper to a friend, "When you're born dumb, it's for a long time."

The service lasted a little more than an hour and a half. Although the occasion had its share of levity, sobriety returned at the recessional with the last musical selection, "For All the Saints," with its final chorus uniting both the living and the dead: "We, feeble, struggle, / they in glory shine. / Yet all are one in Thee / for all are Thine." The memorial was a reflection of both Claudette and her career. Although she was known primarily as an actress with impeccable timing, whose forte was romantic comedy, she made her share of serious films, one of which, *Three Came Home*, revealed an emotional depth totally at odds with her image. Unquestionably, it was one of her finest moments on the screen, although it went unacknowledged by the Academy of Motion Picture Arts and Sciences.

But there was another side of Claudette that was inconsistent with her public image of sophisticated lady, screwball comedienne, and arbiter of elegance. Although not a practicing Catholic like Rosalind Russell, Loretta Young, Jane Wyman, and Ricardo Montalban, she had never abandoned her faith, nor did she lose her affection for St. Vincent Ferrer. Just as Ethel Merman would frequently stop in at St. Bartholomew's Church on Park Avenue to meditate, Claudette would do the same at St. Vincent Ferrer. Occasionally, she would attend Sunday Mass. Father Hoesli even remembered where she would sit. Claudette practiced her faith in her own way, unostentatiously and privately, which was quite the reverse of her screen persona. There was party time and there was prayer time; Claudette knew the difference, even though the world knew her only from the former.

She may have run afoul of a director like John Ford, a producer like Paul Gregory, or a set designer like Frederick Fox, but most actors, both men and women, were drawn to her. Her leading men were attracted to her sensuality, which was really a zest for life that manifested itself in a teasing playfulness. Gays responded to her wit as much as she did to theirs. Young actresses appreciated her way of putting them at ease, and established ones envied the bonhomie that she radiated.

Between 1986 and 1987, John Mainieri, presently maitre d' at Mario Batali's upscale Babbo in Greenwich Village, was working as a waiter at a French bistro, Sel et Poivre, on Lexington and Sixty-fifth, where Claudette would often dine alone. Whenever he served her, he found her, as did so many others, gracious and unaffected. In 1990, Mainieri was at another French restaurant, Aureole, on an evening when Claudette was again having dinner. None of the other patrons paid attention to her, not knowing who she was. Then the actresses Sally Field, Kate Capshaw, Darryl Hannah, and Goldie Hahn arrived: "The dining room was abuzz over the presence of those four, and I started to get pissed off that nobody recognized Miss Colbert, until the four ladies quietly wrote a note and had it passed to the great lady. In it, they told her they would never have had the chance to succeed had it not been for her. . . . I watched Miss Colbert read the note, fold it up and smile graciously at the younger actresses. They never spoke that night, but her smile spoke volumes."

At the reception at Mortimer's after the memorial service, Marie Corbin, who faithfully served Claudette for thirty-one years, recalled a dream she had after Claudette's death: "I dreamt that she's happy; I saw her laughing." And that is the way Claudette Colbert should always be remembered—happy and laughing.

BROADWAY PLAYS

The Wild Westcotts (1923)
A Kiss in a Taxi (1925)
The Ghost Train (1926)
The Pearl of Great Price (1926)
The Barker (1927)
The Mulberry Bush (1927)
La Gringa (1928)
Within the Law (1928)
Fast Life (1928)
Tin Pan Alley (1928)
Dynamo (1929)
See Naples and Die (1929)
Janus (replacement for Margaret Sullavan, 1956)
The Marriage-Go-Round (1958)
Julia, Jake and Uncle Joe (1961)
The Irregular Verb to Love (1963)
The Kingfisher (1978)
A Talent for Murder (1981)
Aren't We All? (1985)

MAJOR RADIO APPEARANCES

**Hands across the Table	(Lux, 3 May 1937)
**The Ex-Mrs. Bradford	(Lux, 19 June 1939)
**Private Worlds	(Gulf Screen Guild Theater, 26 January 1940)
*Midnight	(20 May 1940)
*His Girl Friday	(30 September 1940)
* ** The Shop around the Corner	(23 June 1941)
* ** Skylark	(2 February 1942)
* ** Once Upon a Honeymoon	(12 April 1943)
* Magnificent Obsession	(13 November 1944)
* Practically Yours	(27 August 1945)
* Tomorrow Is Forever	(6 May 1946)
* ** Without Reservations	(26 August 1946)
* The Egg and I	(5 May 1947)
** The Secret Heart	(Screen Guild Players, 17 November 1947)
* Family Honeymoon	(4 April 1949)
* Thunder on the Hill	(9 November 1953)

* LRTC/FCMPS (Lux Radio Theatre Collection, Margaret Herrick Library at the Fairbanks Center for Motion Picture Study)
** *Original Old Time Radio* (http://www.originaloldradio.com/claudette_colbert_collection_html)

The following radio programs are at the Paley Center for Media, formerly the Museum of Television and Radio, in New York and Beverly Hills:

Hollywood Hotel (CBS, 5 October 1934)
I'm an American (NBC, 3 November 1940)
Chase and Sanborn Hour (NBC, 16 May 1943)

Democratic National Committee: The Roosevelt Special (CBS, 6 November 1944)

Command Performance: Victory Edition (Armed Forces Radio System [AFRS], 14 August 1945)

This Is Hollywood (CBS, 4 January 1947)

The Bing Crosby Show (ABC, 30 April 1948)

Meet Ethel Barrymore (NBC, 20 March 1955)

MAJOR TELEVISION APPEARANCES

All of the following are at the Paley Center for Media, formerly the Museum of Television and Radio, in New York and Beverly Hills:

The Jack Benny Program   (CBS, 4 January 1951)
Magic Formula   (Ford Theatre–NBC, 6 January 1955)
The Guardsman   (Best of Broadway–CBS, 2 March 1955)
Blithe Spirit   (Ford Star Jubilee–CBS, 14 January 1956)
One Coat of White   (Playhouse 90–CBS, 21 February 1957)
The Galaxy Being   (The Outer Limits–ABC, 16 September 1963)
The Two Mrs. Grenvilles   (NBC, 8 and 9 February 1987)

FILMOGRAPHY

Film	Studio/ Distributor	Director
For the Love of Mike (1927)	First National	Frank Capra
The Hole in the Wall (1929)	Paramount/Astoria	Robert Florey
The Lady Lies (1929)	Paramount/Astoria	Hobart Henley
The Big Pond (1930) and *La Grande Mare* (French version)	Paramount/Astoria	Hobart Henley
Young Man of Manhattan (1930)	Paramount/Astoria	Monta Bell
Manslaughter (1930)	Paramount/Astoria	George Abbott
L'enigmatique Monsieur Parkes (French version of *Slightly Scarlet* [1930])	Paramount/Astoria	Louis Gasnier
Honor among Lovers (1931)	Paramount/Astoria	Dorothy Arzner
The Smiling Lieutenant (1931)	Paramount/Astoria	Ernst Lubitsch
Secrets of a Secretary (1931)	Paramount/Astoria	George Abbott
His Woman (1931)	Paramount/Astoria	Edward Sloman
The Wiser Sex (1932)	Paramount/Astoria	Berthold Viertel
The Misleading Lady (1932)	Paramount/Astoria	Stuart Walker
The Man from Yesterday (1932)	Paramount	Berthold Viertel
Make Me a Star (1932)	Paramount	William Beaudine
The Phantom President (1932)	Paramount	Norman Taurog
The Sign of the Cross (1932)	Paramount	Cecil B. DeMille
Tonight Is Ours (1933)	Paramount	Stuart Walker/Mitchell Leisen
I Cover the Waterfront (1933)	United Artists	James Cruze
Three Cornered Moon (1933)	Paramount	Elliott Nugent
Torch Singer (1933)	Paramount	Alexander Hall
Four Frightened People (1934)	Paramount	Cecil B. DeMille
It Happened One Night (1934)	Columbia	Frank Capra
Cleopatra (1934)	Paramount	Cecil B. DeMille
Imitation of Life (1934)	Universal	John M. Stahl

The Gilded Lily (1935)	Paramount	Wesley Ruggles
Private Worlds (1935)	Paramount	Gregory La Cava
She Married Her Boss (1935)	Columbia	Gregory La Cava
The Bride Comes Home (1935)	Paramount	Wesley Ruggles
Under Two Flags (1936)	Fox	Frank Lloyd/Otto Brower
Maid of Salem (1937)	Paramount	Frank Lloyd
I Met Him in Paris (1937)	Paramount	Wesley Ruggles
Tovarich (1937)	Warner Bros.	Anatole Litvak
Bluebeard's Eighth Wife (1938)	Paramount	Ernst Lubitsch
Zaza (1939)	Paramount	George Cukor
Midnight (1939)	Paramount	Mitchell Leisen
It's a Wonderful World (1940)	MGM	W. S. Van Dyke II
Drums along the Mohawk (1939)	Fox	John Ford
Boom Town (1940)	MGM	Jack Conway
Arise, My Love (1940)	Paramount	Mitchell Leisen
Skylark (1941)	Paramount	Mark Sandrich
Remember the Day (1941)	Fox	Henry King
The Palm Beach Story (1942)	Paramount	Preston Sturges
So Proudly We Hail (1943)	Paramount	Mark Sandrich
No Time for Love (1943)	Paramount	Mitchell Leisen
Since You Went Away (1944)	Selznick International (United Artists)	John Cromwell
Practically Yours (1944)	Paramount	Mitchell Leisen
Guest Wife (1945)	United Artists	Sam Wood
Tomorrow Is Forever (1946)	International (RKO)	Irving Pichel
Without Reservations (1946)	RKO	Mervyn LeRoy
The Secret Heart (1946)	MGM	Robert Z. Leonard
The Egg and I (1947)	Universal-International	Chester Erskine
Sleep, My Love (1948)	United Artists	Douglas Sirk
Family Honeymoon (1948)	Universal-International	Claude Binyon
Bride for Sale (1949)	RKO	William D. Russell
Three Came Home (1950)	Fox	Jean Negulesco
The Secret Fury (1950)	RKO	Mel Ferrer
Thunder on the Hill (1951)	Universal-International	Douglas Sirk
Let's Make It Legal (1951)	Fox	Richard Sale
Outpost in Malaya (1952)	United Artists	Ken Annakin
Elizabeth, in *Daughters of Destiny* (1954)	Arlan and Cinédis	Marcello Pagliaro
Royal Affairs of Versailles (1954)	Cocinar and Times	Sacha Guitry
Texas Lady (1955)	RKO	Tim Whelan
Parrish (1961)	Warner Bros.	Delmer Daves

SOURCE NOTES

The following archives, files, and collections were used in researching this book (the abbreviations are used in the notes). Unless otherwise indicated, quoted dialogue and information appearing in the opening credits are taken directly from the films.

Cinema/TV Collection, University of Southern California, Los Angeles
Edgar Bergen Collection	EBC-USC
Hal Humphrey Collection	HHC-USC
Hal Roach Collection	HRC-USC
Jack Warner Collection	JWC-USC
Twentieth Century-Fox Collection	TCFC-USC
Universal Collection	UC-USC

Margaret Herrick Library at the Fairbanks Center for Motion Picture Study, Beverly Hills, California
Claudette Colbert Clippings File	CCCF-FCMPS
George Cukor Collection	GCC-FCMPS
Jean Negulesco Collection	JNC-FCMPS
Lux Radio Theatre Collection	LRTC-FCMPS
Mark Sandrich Collection	MSC-FCMPS
Motion Picture Association of America, Production Code Administration	MPAA/PCA-FCMPS
Norman Foster Clippings File	NFCF-FCMPS
Paramount Collection	PC-FCMPS

New York Public Library for the Performing Arts, New York, New York
Claudette Colbert Clippings File	CCCF-NYPLPA

Washington Irving High School Archives, New York, New York
Washington Irving High School Archives	WIHSA

Chapter 1: Lily of Saint-Mandé

To document the Chauchoin family's trips to the United States, I have used ship manifests (*List or Manifest of Alien Passengers for the U.S. Immigration Officer at Point of Arrival*, 24 November 1905; *List or Manifest of Alien Passengers for the Commissioner of Immigration*, 18 September 1906; and *List of Alien Passengers for the United States*, 30 September 1911); passenger arrival records obtained from the National Archives in April 2006; and passenger records from the Ellis Island Foundation (http://www.ellisisland.org, accessed 5 January and 4 April 2006). Information taken from the 1910, 1920, and 1930 U.S. Federal Census Reports was obtained from http://www.ancestry.com, accessed 22 and 24 June 2006.

Information about Claudette Colbert's early life derives from CCCF-FCMPS and CCCF-NYPLPA; obituaries in the *New York Times, Los Angeles Times, Variety,* and *Hollywood Reporter;* conversations with Helen O'Hagan; Claudette's reminiscence, "I Remember Grandma," *Saturday Evening Post,* 25 March 1950, 30+; Gerald Clark, "It Happened One Lifetime," *Fame,* December 1989, 135–141; Amy Fine Collins, "A Perfect Star," *Vanity Fair,* January 1998, 112–127; Ville de Saint-Mandé Service Archives, which identified the street where Claudette's family lived and where her father had his pastry shop; and WIHSA.

4   "A sort of *esprit de famille*" and "her mission . . . accomplished": Colbert, "I Remember Grandma," *Saturday Evening Post,* 25 March 1950, 30, 130.

4   "baker," "lost one eye," and "blind in right eye": *List or Manifest of Alien Passengers for the U.S. Immigration Office at Port of Arrival,* 18 September 1906.

5   "dressmaker": *List or Manifest of Alien Passengers for the U.S. Immigration Officer at Port of Arrival,* 24 November 1906.

5   "The enumerator wrote down": http://www.ask census@custhelp.com, accessed 6 July 2006.

6   "Third Avenue," "cook," "dressmaker," and "English": 1910 Federal Census Records, http://www.ancestry.com, accessed 24 June 2006.

6   "A gentleman, a saint": Colbert, "I Remember Grandma," 127.

7   "friend": *List of Alien Passengers for the United States,* 30 September 1911.

7   "manager" and "secretary": 1920 U.S. Census Report, http://www.ancestry.com, accessed 24 June 2006.

9   "Your friend from Pilgrim Hill": Emmanual Levy, *George Cukor: Master of Elegance* (New York: Morrow, 1994), 24.

12   "A girl in the class play": Amy Fine Collins, "A Perfect Star," *Vanity Fair,* January 1998, 115.

12   "my first play": Colbert, "I Remember Grandma," 129.

12, 14 "Claudette chose the Art Course," "I know you think," and "Miss Colbert": *Washington Irving Sketch Book,* n.d., p. 40, WIHSA.

Chapter 2: Becoming Claudette Colbert

On the significance of Alice Rostetter, see Judith E. Barlow, "Influence, Echo and Coincidence: O'Neill and Provincetown's Women Writers," *Eugene O'Neill Review*, 2005, http://www.eoneill.com/library/review/27/27c.htm. The text of *The Widow's Veil* can be found in *The Flying Flag Stage Plays*, no. 9 (New York: Egmond Arens, 1920) in the Billy Rose Collection, NYPLPA. On A. H. Woods, see Julian M. Kaufman, "A. H. Woods, Producer: A Thrill a Minute," in *Art, Glitter, and Glitz: Playwrights and Popular Theatre in 1920s America*, ed. Arthur Gewirtz and James J. Kolb (Westport, CT: Praeger, 2004), 209–216.

16 "We ran a couple of weeks": Leonard Maltin, "Claudette Colbert," *Film Fan Monthly*, April 1970, 3.

16 "During the four months" and "Later on, I even dramatized": Sonia Lee, "The Calamity in Colbert's Life," *Hollywood*, December 1935, 24, 49.

17 "one of the most beautiful": *New York Times*, 14 December 1919, sec. 8, 2.

22 "I am not ashamed": Kaufman, "A. H. Woods," 215.

25 "[Lonsdale] didn't like": Michael Buckley, "Remembering Claudette Colbert, 1903–1996," *Theatre Week*, 19-25 August 1996, 41. (Buckley is incorrect in saying that *The Fake* closed in Washington, D.C. It ran for eighty-eight performances on Broadway.)

25 "Claudette Colbert, that little": CCCF-NYPLPA.

26 "I think those folks": *Daily Telegraph*, 23 January 1927, CCCF-NYPLPA.

26 "brings a good deal of feeling": *New York Times*, 2 November 1926, 34.

27 "a very promising young actress": *New York Times*, 2 February 1926.

27 "Miss Colbert gave": *New York Times*, 6 March 1928, 20.

27 "one of our very best": *Daily Mirror*, 6 March 1928, CCCF-NYPLPA.

28 "Mr. Foster gives": *New York Times*, 19 January 1927, 20.

28 "Mr. Foster does not": *New York Times*, 13 September 1928, 31.

28 "calefacient," "self-consciously," "delightfully," and "ingratiating": *New York Times*, 2 November 1928, 29.

29 "Mr. Foster played": *New York Times*, 10 October 1929, 34.

29 "not practical for everyone": Adele Whitely Fletcher, "Marriage à la Colbert," *Modern Screen*, July 1931, 114.

30 "Between a husband and a career": Laura Benham, "Part-Time Wife," *New Movie Magazine*, March 1932, 43.

30 "bachelor husband": Nina Wilcox Putnam, "The Bachelor Husband Speaks His Mind," *Modern Screen*, September 1932, 40.

30 "It was Norman's idea": "Our Modern Marriage: It's Okay," *Modern Screen*, February 1934, 31.

30   "it's better": Putnam, "The Bachelor Husband," 40.

31   "strange dark interlude": Eugene O'Neill, *Strange Interlude* in *Three Plays* (New York: Vintage, 1959), 221.

32   "a great, dark mother" and "Never let me go," Eugene O'Neill, *Dynamo*, in *Complete Plays 1920–1931* (New York: Library of America, 1988), 871, 884.

32   "lurid dialogue" and "best performance in her career": *New York Times*, 12 February 1929, 22.

33–34   "Well, I do think" and "We are the enemies": Elmer Rice, *See Naples and Die* (New York: Samuel French, 1930), 77, 171–72.

34   "self-conscious": *New York Times*, 27 September 1929, 22.

34–35   "From every point of view": *New York Times*, 30 October 1929, 1.

Chapter 3: Commuting to Work

For the history of Paramount's Astoria studio, see Richard Koszarski, *The Astoria Studio and Its Fabulous Films* (New York: Dover, 1983). The source of Edward G. Robinson's salary for *The Hole in the Wall* is Alan Gansberg, *Little Caesar: A Biography of Edward G. Robinson* (Lanham, MD: Scarecrow, 2006), 36. Salaries for *Manslaughter* come from PC-FCMPS, "Paramount Productions–General."

37   "Claudette Colbert . . . lends": *New York Times*, 24 August 1927, 27.

38   "See and hear": Leslie Halliwell, *Mountain of Dreams: The Golden Years of Paramount Pictures* (New York: Stonehill, 1976), 145.

38   "It was a nightmare": Lawrence J. Quirk, *Claudette Colbert: An Illustrated Biography* (New York: Crown, 1985), 20.

40   "We weren't too bad": Edward G. Robinson, with Leonard Spiegelgass, *All My Yesterdays: An Autobiography by Edward G. Robinson* (New York: Hawthorn, 1973), 101.

41   "in what has lately": *New York Times*, 19 February 1929, 22.

44   "Decor in a Paramount production": John Baxter, *Hollywood in the Thirties* (New York: Paperback Library, 1970), 46–47.

44   "one of the greatest" and "a tie of men": Adolph Zukor, with Dale Kramer, *The Public Is Never Wrong: My Fifty Years in Motion Pictures* (New York: Putnam's, 1953), 256, 257.

46   "rewriting most of the dialogue": James Ursini, *Preston Sturges, An American Dreamer* (New York: Paperback Library, 1973), 37.

49   "the best picture": George Abbott, *Mister Abbott* (New York: Random House, 1963), 134.

49   "woman picture director": Judith Mayne, *Directed by Dorothy Arzner* (Bloomington: Indiana University Press, 1994), 164.

Chapter 4: "Ready When You Are, C. B."

Biographical information about Norman Foster comes from NFCF-FCMPS. For Cecil B. DeMille's life, I have used the director's autobiography, Cecil B. DeMille, *The Autobiography of Cecil B. DeMille*, ed. Donald Hayne (Englewood Cliffs, NJ: Prentice-Hall, 1959). On Claudette's salary and billing for *The Sign of the Cross*, see *The Sign of the Cross* (Reissue) file, #9049, PC-FCMPS.

60   "Norman Foster emerges": *New York Times*, 19 April 1930, 15.

62   "There was a tremendous": Lawrence J. Quirk, *Claudette Colbert: An Illustrated Biography* (New York: Crown, 1985), 131.

62   "[Gable] put a hammer": Lyn Tornabe, *Long Live the King: A Biography of Clark Gable* (New York: Putnam's, 1976), 174.

64   "My profession": Cecil B. DeMille, *The Autobiography of Cecil B. DeMille*, ed. Donald Hayne (Englewood Cliffs, NJ: Prentice-Hall, 1959), 213.

66   "Claudette, how would you": DeMille, *The Autobiography*, 322.

66   "no other feminine player": Robert S. Birchard, *Cecil B. DeMille's Hollywood* (Lexington: University Press of Kentucky, 2004), 254.

67   "Cecil B. DeMille's": *The Sign of the Cross* file, PC-FCMPS.

67   "cheap and disgusting": Rev. Christian F. Reisner to A. L. Selig (advertising and exploitation manager), 5 October 1932, *The Sign of the Cross* file, PC-FCMPS.

68   "really believed" and "circumspectly attired": *New York Times*, 16 November 1979, 31.

69   "Miss Colbert is capital": *New York Times*, 1 December 1932, 25.

70   "somnambules," "ladies with sleep": Parker Tyler, *The Hollywood Hallucination* (New York: Simon and Schuster, 1970), 74.

70   "creature of myth": Molly Haskell, *From Reverence to Rape: The Treatment of Women in the Movies*, 2nd ed. (Chicago: University of Chicago Press, 1987), 109.

71   "I saw it once by accident": "Introduction," in *The Collected Plays of Noël Coward*, *Play Parade*, vol. 3 (London: Heinemann, 1959), viii.

74   "as a torch singer": Jeanine Basinger, *A Woman's View: How Hollywood Spoke to Women, 1930–1960* (Hanover, NH: Wesleyan University Press/University Press of New England, 1993), 399.

Chapter 5: That Wonderful Year

On Universal under Carl Laemmle Jr. and for production information about *Imitation of Life*, see Bernard F. Dick, *City of Dreams: The Making and Remaking of Universal Pictures*

(Lexington: University Press of Kentucky, 1997), 73–82. The career of the extraordinary Fredi Washington has been well documented by Cheryl Black, "Looking White, Acting Black: Cast(e)ing Fredi Washington," *Theatre Survey* 45, no. 1 (May 2004): 19–40.

77   "Through the resonant cave" and "his physiognomy was blunt": Samuel Hopkins Adams, *Night Bus* (New York: Dell, 1934), 3, 6.

79   "a duo": Ian Scott, *In Capra's Shadow: The Life and Career of Robert Riskin* (Lexington: University Press of Kentucky, 2006), 72.

80   "by no stretch of charity": Adams, *Night Bus*, 6.

80   "Casting Colbert": Joseph McBride, *Frank Capra: The Catastrophe of Success* (New York: Simon & Schuster, 1992), 304.

81   "It was about King Westley": Adams, *Night Bus*, 13.

82–83   "Bitchy," "snooty," "standoffish," and "Awww! . . . *You guys!*": McBride, *Frank Capra*, 307.

85   "the end of the extravagant": Elizabeth Kendall, *The Runaway Bride: Hollywood Romantic Comedy of the 1930s* (New York: Doubleday/Anchor, 1990), 49.

86   "Claudette Colbert has been engaged": *New York Times*, 24 May 1934, 28.

91   "I sho does" and "the purfectest": Fannie Hurst, *Imitation of Life*, edited with an introduction by Daniel Itzkovitz (Durham, NC: Duke University Press, 2004), 11, 75–76.

91   "a tame-cat word," "Let me go," and "They were so young": Hurst, *Imitation of Life*, 148, 251, 292.

95   "not only violates": Joseph Breen to assistant general manager Harry Zehner, 9 March 1934, MPAA/PCA-FCMPS.

95   "This picture satisfactorily meets": Breen to Zehner, 14 November 1934, MPAA/PCA-FCMPS.

95   "Moving Picture Censor" and "negro mammy": Robert Gaylord to Breen, 8 January 1935, MPAA/PCA-FCMPS.

95   "regretted the scene," "an accurate reproduction," "I do not think," and "no negro masonery": Breen to Gaylord, 23 January 1935, MPPA/PCA-FCMPS.

96   "cheapen the Order" and "ape the attire": Gaylord to Carl Laemmle Jr., 25 January 1935, MPPA/PCA-FCMPS.

96, 98 "only if we are absolutely stuck" and "The blow was somewhat assuaged": Birchard, *Cecil B. DeMille's Hollywood*, 287, 307.

98, 99 "see every picture," "she has that priceless something," and "Counting both pictures and radio": LRTC-FCMPS.

Chapter 6: A Night to Remember

Oscar night, 27 February 1935, is vividly described by Mason Wiley and Damien Bona in *Inside Oscar: An Unofficial History of the Academy Awards* (New York: Ballantine, 1987), 53–56.

101 "most promising write-in candidate": *Los Angeles Times,* 28 February 1935, A1.

104 "in those days": McBride, *Frank Capra,* 325.

105 "outstanding contribution": Wiley and Bona, *Inside Oscar,* 688.

105 "'I could just hear the people'" and "a cute picture": *New York Times,* 24 March 1935, X4.

105 "who was gracious enough": McBride, *Frank Capra,* 325.

Chapter 7: The End of a Modern Marriage

Claudette's $150,000 per picture contract was reported in the *New York Sunday News,* 12 July 1936, CCCF-FCMPS. On Norman Foster's involvement in *Journey into Fear* and *It's All True,* see Charles Higham, *The Films of Orson Welles* (Berkeley: University of California Press, 1971), 72, 84–86.

110 "'I believe that one of the troubles'": Mary Stevens, "This Time It's No Modern Marriage," *Photoplay,* February 1936, 22.

111 "[Foster's] marriage to Claudette Colbert" and "You're never going": *Directed by Norman Foster, Mr. Moto Collection,* vol. 4, Twentieth Century Fox-Home Entertainment, 2006.

111 "ended up hauling Foster off": Amy Fine Collins, "A Perfect Star," *Vanity Fair,* January 1998, 122.

113 "With hair blackening": Stephen D. Youngkin, *The Lost One: A Life of Peter Lorre* (Lexington: University Press of Kentucky, 2005), 167.

116 "Waiting newspapermen and cameramen": *Los Angeles Herald Examiner,* 30 November 1935, CCCF-FCMPS.

117 "Pressman smashed the flashlight bulbs": *Hollywood Citizen-News,* 29 November 1935, CCCF-FCMPS.

117 "It is customary to accompany": *Los Angeles Herald Examiner,* 30 November 1935, CCCF-FCMPS.

117 "I do not mind being photographed": *Hollywood Citizen-News,* 30 November 1936, CCCF-FCMPS.

118 "She's my favorite actress": *New York Times,* 25 December 1935, 30.

119 "The entrance hall": Lyle Wheeler, "English with a French Accent," *Photoplay,* March 1952, 76.

Chapter 8: Life after Oscar

123 "she appeared one day": *New York Times,* 26 April 1936, X4.

127 "There was bohemian Paris": Leslie Halliwell, *Mountain of Dreams: The Golden Years of Paramount Pictures* (New York: Stonehill, 1976), 21.

127   "supervisor": Bernard F. Dick, *Hal Wallis, Producer to the Stars* (Lexington: University Press of Kentucky, 2004), 34, 35.

128   "a very stubborn director": Bette Davis, *The Lonely Life: An Autobiography* (New York: Lancer Books, 1966), 136.

128   "a sad, meek little man" and "completely off balance": Memo from Robert Lord to Hal Wallis, 29 January 1937, in *Inside Warner Bros., 1935–1951*, selected, edited, and annotated by Rudy Behlmer (New York: Simon & Schuster, 1985), 32–33.

130   "Ingrid, it's only a movie": Donald Spoto, *The Art of Alfred Hitchcock*, 2nd ed. (New York: Doubleday/Anchor, 1979), 176.

130   "After several pointed remarks": "Hollywood through the Mutoscope," *New York Times*, 5 September 1937, 121.

133   "adulterous affair": Joseph Breen to Luigi Luraschi (Paramount's head of censorship), 15 June 1938, MPPA/PCA-FCMPS.

133   "alley cat" and "only one lover at a time": Breen to Luraschi, 20 June 1938, MPPA/PCA-FCMPS.

134   "My botany teacher" and "Were you ever in love": *Zaza* production file, PC-FCMPS.

136   "adultery and illicit sex": Breen to Luraschi, 12 October 1938. MPAA/PCA-FCMPS.

139   "See Miss Colbert's bathtub": Gregory Mank, *"Drums along the Mohawk: A Retrospective,"* *Classic Images* (spring 2005): 50.

139   "But I'll never": Mank, *"Drums along the Mohawk,"* 51.

140   "miscast": Andrew Sinclair, *John Ford: A Biography* (New York: Ungar, 1984), 93.

Chapter 9: Blaze of Noon

Claudette's various contracts can be found in PC/Contracts-FCMPS. Zanuck's involvement, which seems to have been minimal, in the making of *Three Came Home* comes from the *Three Came Home* file, TCFC-USC.

147   "Putting aside their dialectical materialism": *New York Times*, 2 January 1938, 24.

148   "aggressively heterosexual": Charles Higham, *Louis B. Mayer, M.G.M., and the Secret Hollywood* (New York: Dell, 1993), 66.

153   "great—overwritten": *Remember the Day* file, first draft continuity, 20 March 1941, TCFC-USC.

161   "by five o'clock": Diane Jacobs, *Christmas in July: The Life and Art of Preston Sturges* (Berkeley: U of California Press, 1992), 275–76.

161   "'I adored Mitch'": David Chierichetti, *Hollywood Director: The Career of Mitchell Leisen* (New York: Curtis Books, 1973), 133.

165   "Claudette, the trouble with this picture": Chierichetti, *Hollywood Director*, 216.

Chapter 10: Claudette and the "Good War"

Production information about *So Proudly We Hail* and *Three Came Home* comes from PC-FCMPS and TCFC-USC, respectively. Claudette's participation in the 1941 army show and the 1942 bond tour can be verified in MSC/Scrapbook-FCMPS.

169 "a bit too full," "preachy," and "Isn't that pressing it a bit": Buddy DeSylva (Paramount production head) to Mark Sandrich, 5 November 1942, *So Proudly We Hail* file, PC-FCMPS.

170 "the battling bastards of Bataan": C. L. Sulzberger, *The American Heritage Picture History of World War II* (New York: Crown, 1966), 148.

171 "very sure that it was the right thing": David O. Selznick to Katharine Cornell, 6 May 1943, in *Memo from David O. Selznick*, selected and edited by Rudy Behlmer (New York: Avon, 1973), 381.

173 "The final cost reached $3.25 million": Thomas Schatz, *The Genius of the System: Hollywood Filmmaking in the Studio Era* (New York: Pantheon, 1988), 325.

173 "Crowds were lined up": *Hollywood Reporter*, 4 August 1944, 37.

174 "one of the most complete": Joseph Cotten, *Vanity Will Get You Somewhere* (San Francisco: Mercury House, 1987), 56.

174 "Suddenly she reached out": Shirley Temple Black, *Child Star: An Autobiography* (New York: McGraw-Hill, 1988), 356.

177 "You know I'm not given": Claudette to Jean Negulesco, 9 June 1949, JNC-FCMPS.

Chapter 11: Slow Fade to Legend

Production information about *The Egg and I, Family Honeymoon*, and *Thunder on the Hill* comes from UC-USC. June Allyson discusses her close friendship with Claudette in her autobiography, *June Allyson*, with Frances Spitz Leighton (New York: Putnam's, 1982).

182 "the most immoral picture": C. L. Sulzberger to Will Hays, 26 September 1945, MPAA/PCA-FCMPS.

182 "We have read the screenplay": Joseph Breen to Jack Skirball, 14 February 1945, MPAA/PCA-FCMPS.

182 "reads the novels of Henry James": Cameron Shipp, "Portrait of a Hollywood Agent," *Esquire*, March 1947, 81.

183 "'I've been acting in pictures'": *Los Angeles Times*, 19 October 1949, C1.

183 "'Few women have had the courage'": *Los Angeles Times*, 30 October 1949, D1.

188   "Mervyn wasn't letting any woman": Randy Roberts and James S. Olson, *John Wayne: American* (New York: Free Press, 1995), 278.

188   "an interesting lady to work with" and "she looked very good": Mervyn LeRoy, as told to Dick Kleiner, *Take One* (New York: Hawthorn Books, 1974), 164.

194   "I've always felt it sad": Suzanne Finstad, *Natasha: A Biography of Natalie Wood* (New York: Harmony Books, 2001), 37.

196   "'The only thing I was interested in'": Douglas Sirk quoted in Jon Halliday, *Sirk on Sirk* (New York: Viking, 1972), 75.

199   "very desolate" and "*Magnificat anima mea*": Charlotte Hastings, *High Ground* (New York: Samuel French, 1951), 72, 117.

Chapter 12: The Last Picture Shows

Production information about *Let's Make It Legal* and *Parrish* comes from TCFC-USC and Box 27, JWC-USC, respectively.

201   "a tiny face lift": Arnold Scaasi, *Women I Have Dressed (and Undressed)* (New York: Scribner, 2004), 153.

206   "the five o'clock clause": *New York Times*, 11 October 1947, 11.

206   "Miss Hepburn stepped into the breach": *New York Times*, 19 October 1947, X3.

208   "I couldn't be happy": *Chicago Sunday Tribune*, 19 October 1947, CCCF-FCMPS.

208   "The trouble with people like me": MSC/Scrapbook-FCMPS.

Chapter 13: The Long Voyage Home

On Claudette's *Lux Radio Theatre* appearances, see "Major Radio Appearances." Quotations from Claudette and Don Ameche's comedy sketches (1938–39) on the *Chase and Sanborn Hour (Edgar Bergen and Charlie McCarthy Show)* are taken from scripts in EBC-USC. The script of "Novel Appeal" can be found in HRC-USC. For a complete list of Claudette's television appearances, see James Robert Parish and Vincent Terrace, *The Complete Actors' Television Credits, 1948–1988*, 2nd ed., vol. 2 (Metuchen, NJ: Scarecrow Press, 1990).

215   "COLBERT PONDERS RETURN": *New York Times*, 10 March 1949, 35.

220   "Oh, I'm as sociable": "McCarthy-Colbert," 19 June 1938, EBC-USC, 27.

220   "Charlie, all my life": "Guest Spot," 21 December 1947, EBC-USC, 17.

221   "We the people": "Opening," 16 May 1943, EBC-USC, 15.

224   "Claudette Colbert is joining the march": *Los Angeles Times*, 6 August 1954, 24.

226   "I am no saleswoman": *Mirror*, 3 September 1954, HHC-USC.

227–28 "If she had a neck" and "I don't understand": Starrett to author, 3 June 2006.

230   "performed ably": *New York Times*, 28 October 1959, 75.

Chapter 14: She's Back on Broadway

Statements attributed to Julie Newmar and Paul Gregory come from phone interviews conducted by the author with both on 11 July 2006.

231   "But I never shall": *New York Times*, 27 February 1955, X17.

232   "a more skillful bit of work": *New York-Journal American*, 13 April 1956, 19.

233   "A woman's infidelity" and "Gil, darling": Carolyn Green, *Janus* (New York: Samuel French, 1956), 40 and 58.

234   "I am younger": Leslie Stevens, *The Marriage-Go-Round* (New York: Samuel French, 1959), 40.

236   "'Dear, they want me to use'": An oral history with sketch artist Adele Balkan, interviewed by Barbara Hall, 1999, from Oral History Program, FCMPS.

239   "I wanted to be a clothes designer" and "She was a lady": phone interview with Ken Starrett, 27 December 2006.

240   "I don't know why": phone interview with Marjorie Fox, 30 June 2006.

243   "took the name of her Barbadian refuge": Gerald Clark, *Architectural Digest*, April 1998, 309.

Chapter 15: The Stigma

247   "The Claudette . . . Colberts are pouting": *Journal*, 18 September 1931, CCCF-NYPLPA.

247   "[Gable] knew she was a lesbian": Warren G. Harris, *Clark Gable: A Biography* (New York: Harmony, 2002), 113.

248   "I won't be directed," "drunken moment," and "only Gable and Haines": Patrick McGilligan, *George Cukor: A Biography of a Gentleman Director* (New York: St. Martin's, 1991), 150.

248   "Miss Claudette Colbert": Joseph McBride, *Frank Capra: The Catastrophe of Success* (New York: Simon & Schuster, 1992), 325.

249   "If driving cars you like": *Cole Porter: Selected Lyrics*, ed. Robert Kimball (New York: American Poets Project/Library of America, 2006), 97.

249   "a child would spoil": Scaasi, *Women I Have Dressed*, 154.

250   "Who the fuck are you?" and "all the way with him": Amy Fine Collins, "A Perfect Star," *Vanity Fair*, January 1998, 124, 121.

250   "When the young ladies": Scaasi, *Women I Have Dressed*, 151–152.

251   "stigma": Phone conversation with Helen O'Hagan, 23 June 2006.

251   "'that ugly Claudette Colbert'": Marlene Dietrich quoted in Collins, "A Perfect Star," 123.

251   "took [Dietrich] to the top" and "air shafts sent skirts": Marchall Kester, "Dignity Flits as Notables Enjoy Evening on 'Kid' Toys," *Los Angeles Times*, 23 June 1935, B6.

251   "a code for lesbianism" and "straighten out": William J. Mann, *Wisecracker: The Life and Times of William Haines, Hollywood's First Openly Gay Star* (New York: Viking, 1998), 259.

252–53   "a charming tête à tête," "not a spinster version," "'wonderful,'" and "But all that Dietrich ever wanted": Maria Riva, *Marlene Dietrich* (New York: Ballantine, 1992), 350, 46, 423, and 165.

253   "evanescent charm" and "pretty and feminine": *New York Times*, 2 November 1955, 31.

256   "Claudette liked to flirt": Leonard Gershe quoted in Collins, *Vanity Fair*, 125.

257   "If Claudette were a lesbian": phone conversation with Helen O'Hagan, 23 June 2006.

258   "spouse" and "came out": William J. Mann, *Behind the Screen: How Gays and Lesbians Shaped Hollywood* (New York: Viking, 2001), 82.

259   "Miss Colbert's got a good cook": *Boston Globe*, 11 April 1982, 1.

259   "special guest" and "a fun time": *The Reagan Diaries*, ed. Douglas Brinkley (New York: HarperCollins, 2007), 379.

260   "What is your greatest fear?": "Social Study," *Vanity Fair*, April 1996, 318.

261   "her closest friend": Lynn Tornabee, "Lunch Date with Claudette," *Cosmopolitan*, July 1960, 24.

261   "might . . . kill her": Collins, "A Perfect Star," 126. (O'Hagan was the one who supplied this information.)

262   "Claudette never had": phone conversation with Helen O'Hagan, 25 March 2007.

Chapter 16: Slow Fade to Black

Details about Jean Pierre Aumont's life come from his autobiography, *Sun and Shadow*, translated by Bruce Benderson (New York: Norton, 1977).

265–66   "DEAREST CLAUDETTE," "I get offers," and "It's an idiotic law": GCC-FCMPS, Folder 19, 4 June 1968 night cable, undated letter, and 16 June 1968 letter to George Cukor.

266   "'I pay full federal taxes'": *Los Angeles Times*, 24 March 1974, 76.

267   "a beautiful mezzo voice": phone interview with Kitty Carlisle Hart, 27 September 2006.

267   "For the first time": *New York Times*, 7 August 1970, 28.

269   "As she was trying to relax" and "Another example of her gallantry": e-mail from George Gaynes to author, 30 September 2005.

269   "'It's difficult to find roles'": *New York Times*, 2 June 1978, C2.

272   "had the idea": Rex Harrison, *A Damned Serious Business* (New York: Bantam, 1991), 24.

273   "But when Claudette," "You're not going to talk," "'Get Claudette back,'" and "Hope you'll get back": Alexander Walker, *Fatal Charm: The Life of Rex Harrison* (New York: St. Martin's, 1992), 367–368.

274   "I'll bring one up" and "Why?": William Douglas Home, *The Kingfisher* (New York: Samuel French, 1981), 50, 62.

277   "I couldn't keep raking in money": Aumont, *Sun and Shadow*, 77.

279   "Who dunnit?" "I didn't put *my* murder," and "If music soothes": Jerome Chodorov and Norman Panama, *A Talent for Murder* (New York: Samuel French, 1982), 67, 48.

280   "Wouldn't you": *Los Angeles Times*, 13 October 1985, 32.

281   "Greenham, you called me" and "I'm glad of that": Frederick Lonsdale, *Aren't We All?* (New York: Samuel French, 1953), 97, 10.

282   "After weeks": e-mail from Lynn Redgrave to author, 15 August 2005.

282   "'She's given me my lines'": Rex Harrison quoted in Walker, *Fatal Charm*, 389.

283   "In Sydney": phone conversation with Helen O'Hagan, 23 June 2006.

Chapter 17: Envoi

Information about Claudette's last years come from personal interviews and phone conversations with Helen O'Hagan. Anthony Greco provided me with a tape of the 1989 Kennedy Center Honors. On the Woodward case, see Mark Gribbin, "Tragedy in High Society," http:www.crimelibrary.com/notorious_murders/celebrity/Woodwards, accessed 22 May 2007. Dialogue from *The Two Mrs. Grenvilles* is taken directly from the miniseries.

285   "provided no strong feeling": *Los Angeles Times*, 25 April 1984, VI, 3.

285   "languidly paced": *Variety*, 25 April 1984, 14.

287   "I want to talk like them": Dominick Dunne, *The Two Mrs. Grenvilles* (New York: Ballantine, 1985), 106.

287   "After reading the fictional account": Katherine Restaino, "Dominick Dunne," *Dictionary of Literary Biography*, vol. 306 (Framington Hills, MI: Thomson/Gale, 2005), 122.

291   "It had a black velvet top": Scaasi, *Women I Have Dressed*, 155.

294   "The windows with dominant blues": Tim McHale, "St. Vincent Ferrer," http://www.fordham.edu/halsall/medny/mchale.html, accessed 17 May 2007.

294–95   "I only know of one word" and "Your priest is here": phone interview with Father James Grear, 13 September 2005.

295   "I want to go home": O'Hagan interview, 20 April 2006.

296   "Hey, why not me?" *Hollywood Reporter*, 15 September 1996, CCCF-FCMPS.

296   "Baby, I don't need you": O'Hagan interview, 20 April 2006.

296   "When you're born dumb": Claudette quoted in *New York Times*, 5 September 1996, D21.

298   "The dining room was abuzz": e-mail from John Mainieri to author, 14 September 2006.

298   "I dreamt that she's happy": Marie Corbin quoted in *New York Times*, 5 September 1996, D21.

INDEX